TERESA M. BECK, ALICIA M. MENENDEZ,
AND SHAYNA M. STEINFELD
EDITORS

her story

BOOK 2

The Resilient Woman Lawyer's Guide to Conquering Obstacles

AMERICAN**BAR**ASSOCIATION

Litigation Section

Cover design by Elmarie Jara/ABA Design

The materials contained herein represent the opinions of the authors and/or the editors and should not be construed to be the views or opinions of the law firms or companies that such persons are in partnership with, associated with, or employed by, nor of the American Bar Association or the Litigation Section, unless adopted pursuant to the bylaws of the Association.

Nothing contained in this book is to be considered as the rendering of legal advice for specific cases, and readers are responsible for obtaining such advice from their own legal counsel. This book is intended for educational and informational purposes only.

© 2024 American Bar Association. All rights reserved.

No part of this publication may be reproduced, stored in a retrieval system, or transmitted in any form or by any means, electronic, mechanical, photocopying, recording, or otherwise, without the prior written permission of the publisher. For permission, complete the request form at www.americanbar.org/reprint or email ABA Publishing at copyright@americanbar.org.

Printed in the United States of America.

27 26 25 24   5 4 3 2

Library of Congress Cataloging-in-Publication Data

Names: Beck, Teresa, editor. | Menendez, Alicia M., editor. | Steinfeld, Shayna M., editor. | American Bar Association. Section of Litigation, sponsoring body.
Title: Her story 2 : the resilient woman lawyer's guide to conquering obstacles / editors, Teresa M. Beck, Alicia M. Menendez, Shayna M. Steinfeld.
Description: Chicago : American Bar Association, Section Litigation, 2023. | Summary: "This book is a collection of voices that persist in a profession that still lags behind in hearing them. We share these stories because the profession is enriched by the stories and the lawyers who tell them. This book is a form of virtual mentoring to build up the next generation of woman advocates so that they, too, may add their stories. In this book, we provide information about the status of women in the legal profession, and stories about identifying and overcoming bias and the hidden hazards in the practice of law, for men and women, while addressing the business of law. The stories in this book then go on to explain the value of being true to ourselves, establishing unique career paths, and finding guideposts and beacons to help enlighten us along the way to success"-- Provided by publisher.
Identifiers: LCCN 2023037804 (print) | LCCN 2023037805 (ebook) | ISBN 9781639054008 (paperback) | ISBN 9781639054015 (epub)
Subjects: LCSH: Women lawyers--United States--Biography.
Classification: LCC KF299.W6 H475 2023 (print) | LCC KF299.W6 (ebook) | DDC 340.092/520973--dc23/eng/20230927
LC record available at https://lccn.loc.gov/2023037804
LC ebook record available at https://lccn.loc.gov/2023037805

ISBN 978-1-63905-400-8

Discounts are available for books ordered in bulk. Special consideration is given to state bars, CLE programs, and other bar-related organizations. Inquire at Book Publishing, ABA Publishing, American Bar Association, 321 N. Clark Street, Chicago, Illinois 60654-7598.

www.shopABA.org

Contents

Foreword	ix
Preface	xi
About the Editors	xv
Acknowledgments	xvii

Chapter 1
Recognize the Obstacles Ahead: Get a Head Start	1
Women in the Law: Where to Go and How to Get There	3
By Stephanie A. Scharf	
The Status of Women in the Law: The NAWL Survey Data	15
By Karen M. Richardson	
Recognize the Obstacles Ahead: A Deeper Dive into the Statistics Affecting Women and Women of Color in the Legal Profession	24
By S. Claire Gibson	
Calling a Crisis a Crisis: The Lack of Women at the Top of the Legal Profession	34
By Sheryl L. Axelrod	
Getting Out of the Box (No Matter How We Got In)	44
By Tara N. Cho	
Mandatory Magic: Being Black and a Woman in Big Law	51
By Yendelela Neely Holston	
Defining Ourselves	58
By Abby R. Rubenfeld	
Inclusion of Women and Diverse Men at the Highest Levels Holds Incredible Potential for All of Us	66
By Bruce A. McMullen	

Chapter 2
Understanding and Conquering Bias: Bypassing Barriers — 71
How Bias Holds Us Back and What We Can Do about It — 72
By Andrea S. Kramer
Meeting and Overcoming Socioeconomic Barriers to Law Practice — 83
By Mary A. Prebula
Turning Obstacles into Opportunities — 91
By Hon. Abbe F. Fletman
Discovering Soft Discrimination: The Persistent Underestimation of Women in the Legal Profession and a Strategy to Contest It — 100
By Diana Flynn
The Systems Currently Addressing Sexual Harassment in the Workplace Are "Still Broken" and Need to Be Fixed — 107
By Cory M. Amron
Sexual Harassment: The Interplay of Bullying and Bias in the Profession — 116
By Francine Friedman Griesing
How We as Men Can Make a Meaningful Difference in the Fight for Gender Parity — 124
By Steven Velkei

Chapter 3
Hidden Hazards and How to Overcome Them — 135
Redefining Obstacles as Opportunities for Growth — 136
By Erika R. Bales
Learn How to Define Your Priorities and Use Them for Success: How to Get Unfrazzled — 143
By Kate Ahern
Drains on Personal Time — 152
By Chancellor Anne C. Martin
Overcoming Imposter Syndrome: Living for Yourself or for Others? — 159
By Shayna M. Steinfeld
From Fear to Trust: Lessons from My Recovery for the Legal Community — 166
By K. Brooke Welch
Grateful to Be a Sober Female Lawyer — 175
By Jessica R. Blaemire
Confronting and Defeating Anxiety on a Journey to Inner Peace — 183
By Janet E. Sobel
Suicide: Returning from the (Nearly) Dead — 190
By Eric C. Lang

Chapter 4
Going Places We've Never Been Before: Succeeding at the
Business of Law   199
   An Unanticipated Career Path to Greater Opportunities   200
   By Gwen Keyes Fleming
   Accessing Opportunities and Experiences to Succeed   210
   By Sharonda R. Williams
   My Blueprint to Success: Conquering Inexperience
   and Embracing Challenges   215
   By Tamara P. Nash
   Gamechanger! Redesigning How to Practice Law   220
   By Laura Hartnett
   Building a Personal Brand to Grow Your Career and Bring Personal
   Life Satisfaction   228
   By Katy Goshtasbi
   Time Management Challenges   235
   By Beth-Ann E. Krimsky
   Where to Work: Flexibility and Advancement
   in a New Day and Age   242
   By Heather Linn Rosing
   Demystifying Rainmaking: A Practical Guide
   to Building Your Book   249
   By Kristin Housh
   Building a Book of Business: Sometimes the Only Person
   in Your Way Is You   256
   By Jennifer Olmedo-Rodriguez
   How to Negotiate Your Compensation—Even When
   You Don't Want to   264
   By Lee Tarte Wallace
   How to Manage a Team Effectively: Advice from the Field   273
   By Tiffany J. deGruy

Chapter 5
Own Your Unique Career Path and Be True
to Your Genuine Self   283
   An Undeterred Dream: Five Tips from a Practical Dreamer on
   Managing Your Legal Career Paths   285
   By Deborah Enix-Ross
   Be Authentic: Navigating Complex and (Sometimes)
   Paradoxical Identities   291
   By Michal Rogson

Be Resilient: Lessons from Reviving My Family's Business	298
By Stephanie Stuckey	
Maintain Perspective When All Is Not Well	306
By Heather Torres	
The Best Advice I Didn't Take: Lessons in Getting Involved Outside of the Office	313
By Katie Larkin-Wong	
From Big Law Commercial Litigation Partner to Art Museum General Counsel: The Unexpected Path to a Second Act Dream Job	319
By M. Thérèse Vento	
Career Transitions: Interval Training for Life	327
By Amy Ragen	
Forging Your Own Way: Transitioning to Public Interest and In-House	335
By Christina Yang	
Finding Success in Public Health and as In-House Government Counsel	342
By Heather Anderson-Fintak	
Changing Career Paths: The Challenge to Have a Dream Career	350
By Mary Catherine Roper	

Chapter 6

Guideposts and Beacons: Getting More of Us on the Road	357
The Value of Effective Goal-Setting	359
By Patricia H. Thompson	
The Gift and Challenge of Longevity: Preparing for Long Careers Marked by Changes	369
By Ida O. Abbott	
Considerations on Retirement and Succession Planning for Lawyers	377
By Eileen M. Letts	
Pursuing the Path for Progress Toward Diversity in the Legal Profession	383
By Hon. Bernice B. Donald	
The Power of Women Leadership in the Legal Profession	390
By Ashley Coleman	
Mentoring and Supporting Each Other on the Road Ahead	396
By Hon. Ebony M. Scott	
The Mentor's Toolkit: Action Steps to Help Mentees	402
By Kristen Reeves Jones	
The Importance of Role Models	410
By Grace Speights	

Mentoring and Supporting Each Other: Supportive Male
Mentoring of Women Attorneys Yields Success 417
By R. William Ide III and Judy Perry Martinez
Male Leaders Hold Keys to Accelerated Advancement of Diversity,
Equity, and Inclusion 427
By Teresa M. Beck

Foreword

Her Story 2 is a collection of voices that persist in a profession that still lags behind in hearing them. We share these stories because the profession is enriched by the stories and the lawyers who tell them. This book is a form of virtual mentoring meant to build up the next generation of woman advocates so they, too, may add their stories.

Our first edition of this book included my essay on why it is so important to stop thinking of women as "balancing" "work" and "life." Channeling the advice of a dear Litigation Section mentor, I encouraged all women lawyers to start thinking about our role as "managers," who allocate resources among various tasks and responsibilities. The image of perilously balancing on a tightrope has proven stubborn, however. With that as our model, we continue to have women so exhausted by teetering on that imaginary highwire that our progress in the profession is still not where we want it to be. Yet when you look at what those women are accomplishing each day, the women lawyers I know are some of the most exceptional managers around. Sharing our stories of how we manage our responsibilities and how many different forms that management takes is an important piece to advancing women in the profession. The more we share our stories, the more we let go of an idealized image of a tightrope walker.

Sharing stories is what made the American Bar Association (ABA) Litigation Section Woman Advocate Committee such a welcoming home. Immediately upon walking alone into my very first dinner with the Woman Advocate Committee, I was greeted by someone wanting to know my story—who I was, where I was from, what my practice was like, how I defined my family. As that evening and many subsequent ones passed, I learned the stories of those around me. I credit a lot of my longevity in the profession to the women who took me under their wings and were about 15 years older than I was. They told stories of their love of trying cases to juries, stories of how they fit business development into their busy days, stories of how to advocate for compensation, and stories of how to manage a thriving practice with a thriving family. All of these women approached management of their lives in different ways, but each demonstrated that I could do so as well. I was not the only one who these woman advocates mentored, however. I had colleagues in the Litigation Section of my own age as well. We've served as each other's personal boards of directors, coached each other through career twists and turns, and been there for each other during life crises. Their stories, too, inspired and energized me. Upon my return from Litigation Section meetings, my family and colleagues would sense the energy generated from having shared stories and experiences with a diverse set of voices from across the country.

I encourage all of you to read the stories in this book and think about how they inform your management decisions. But don't let the investment in yourself stop there. Come join the Litigation Section at a meeting, get involved with the Woman Advocate Committee, and benefit from the community it will provide you. Feed off of that energy so that you can manage all that life throws at you. I promise you that you will be welcomed and your stories will be heard.

Anne Marie Seibel
Chair, ABA Litigation Section

Preface

Women lawyers have made great strides over the past few decades. We now have four women Supreme Court Justices, including a Black female Supreme Court Justice, and a Hispanic female Supreme Court Justice. Some women lawyers have reached high levels of success in the public and private sectors. Yet work remains to be done because women still lag behind men at the highest levels of the profession, even though for many decades women have graduated from law school in numbers equal to or greater than men.[1] Although women lawyers were only 3 percent of the profession from the 1960s and into the 1980s,[2] today women are still only 38 percent of the profession.[3] These statistics suggest that women lawyers face obstacles to success over the course of their careers, leading some women to leave the profession entirely.[4]

The legal profession, like many other professions, has not dismantled the obstacles that impact women. In Chapter 1, our readers will see the stark statistics regarding women in the profession in general and women of color in the profession in particular. These statistics are not just numbers.

---

1. *ABA Profile of the Legal Profession 2022: Women in the Legal Profession* (2022), AM. BAR ASS'N, www.abalegalprofile.com.
2. *Id.*
3. *Id.*
4. Roberta D. Liebenberg and Stephanie A. Scharf, *Walking Out the Door: The Facts, Figures, and Future of Experienced Women Lawyers in Private Practice*, AM. BAR ASS'N (2019), *available at* www.americanbar.org/groups/diversity/women/initiatives_awards/long-term-careers-for-women/walking-out-the-door.

Behind every study are real women and real stories. Many women entered the profession believing the workplace was fully open to us. But it can take years to realize that there are obstacles to our advancement and success, and then it can take many more years of trial and error to accept and understand that fact and determine how we can address the obstacles we encounter.

Some might say we should alter our mindset about obstacles—that we should be grateful for obstacles because they make us stronger and help us develop grit and a growth mindset. Some might say we just need to develop tougher skin. While many of us nurture a deep sense of gratitude daily to maintain our fortitude, the better argument may be that obstacles are meant to be overcome and that our sister lawyers (and a few brother lawyers) possess wisdom in their stories that we can use to transform ourselves.

In this book, we present a collection of essays with information about the status of women in the legal profession and stories about identifying and overcoming bias and the hidden hazards in the practice of law while addressing the *business* of law. The stories in this book then go on to explain the value of being true to ourselves, establishing unique career paths, and finding guideposts and beacons to help enlighten us along the way to success.

There is nothing more powerful than powerful women (and a few good guys) sharing their stories. These stories tell us that we are not alone, that there is a sisterhood in the profession that supports us, and that we can learn from one another and lift up others who share our experiences. We hope you find ideas and hope in these stories. We need each of you in the profession, and we intend for this book to provide a guidebook through tough times, a road map for eliminating the obstacles we can change, as well as ideas for tackling obstacles that seem more intractable.

This book is a product of a team effort from the members of The Woman Advocate Committee (WAC) of the ABA Litigation Section, which addresses many of the hurdles and obstacles still faced by women, people of color, and others in the practice of law. WAC seeks to provide positive tools, encouragement, and support to elevate the careers of women lawyers, and to move women lawyers forward in practice and life.

The book is designed to be read in its entirety. It may be read by individual essay or by isolated chapter. Each chapter has an introduction and concludes with discussion questions to be used for a book club or networking event, either within a firm or elsewhere.

And now, we have some incredible, deeply meaningful, inspiring, and hope-filled stories to tell you.

Teresa M. Beck
Alicia M. Menendez
Shayna M. Steinfeld
Editors

About the Editors

Teresa M. Beck is the Managing Shareholder of Arizona and Nevada for Klinedinst PC, and Co-chair of the firm's Diversity, Equity, Inclusion, and Belonging Committee. Ms. Beck is a longtime SuperLawyer and an AV Rated Civil Litigator. She handles litigation in California, Arizona, and Nevada. She is Immediate Past President of the National Conference of Women's Bar Association and a Board Member of California ChangeLawyers. Along with co-editors Jacqueline Mecchella Bushwack and Shayna Steinfeld, she is a co-editor of *Her Story: Lessons in Success from Lawyers Who Live It*, the prequel to this book, released by the ABA Litigation Section in 2017.

Alicia M. Menendez is a Senior Counsel at Shook, Hardy & Bacon, LLP, a law firm with 18 offices in the United States and in London. Ms. Menendez focuses her practice on complex product liability and commercial litigation, as well as international disputes and managing aspects of cases in mass litigation across multiple jurisdictions. Giving back to the community, Ms. Menendez actively participates in bar associations, having earned awards for her service. In addition to service for the ABA's Litigation Section, she previously served as Chair of the Florida Bar's Code & Rules of Evidence Committee, Chair of its Educational Subcommittee, Program Chair and Moderator of its annual evidence-related seminars, and as Vice Chair of the Florida Bar's Grievance Committee. She has also served on the Steering Committee for the Florida Bar's International Commercial Arbitration Vis Pre-Moot Competitions and has been a volunteer judge of mock trial, negotiation, and international arbitration competitions. She is fluent in Spanish. She can be reached at amenendez@shb.com.

Shayna M. Steinfeld is Board Certified by the American Board of Certification in both consumer and business bankruptcy law, a shareholder of Steinfeld & Steinfeld, PC, and practices with her husband, Bruce, a Fellow of the American Academy of Matrimonial Lawyers. She is a past-president of the Atlanta Bar Association, the Georgia Association for Women Lawyers, a co-founder and past-president of the Georgia International Women's Insolvency and Restructuring Confederation (IWRC) Network, a past-chair of the Sole Practitioner/Small Firm Section of the Atlanta Bar and the Bankruptcy Sections of both the Atlanta Bar and the State Bar of Georgia. She is past chair of the bankruptcy committee of the ABA Family Law Section and currently is a subcommittee co-chair for the ABA Litigation Section. She has received many accolades, including "Section of the Year" and "Outstanding Woman in the Profession," and is regularly named a "Georgia Super Lawyer," one of the top 50 women, and has been previously recognized as one of the top 100 Lawyers in the State. A graduate of Emory University (BA, JD, and MBA), Shayna frequently lectures and has authored many publications, including *The Family Lawyer's Guide to Bankruptcy*, which is published by the ABA Family Law Section and is in its fourth edition, and she is a co-editor of *Her Story: Lessons in Success from Lawyers Who Live It*, the prequel to this book, along with Teresa Beck, released by the ABA Litigation Section in 2017.

Acknowledgments

The Woman Advocate Book Committee co-editors wish to thank everyone who has given their time to *Her Story 2* over the past few years. *Her Story 2* has been a work of love, which has been in the works for several years under different Woman Advocate Committee chairs within the ABA Litigation Section, and without all of their support, the support of the Woman Advocate Committee as a whole, and the support of the Book Committee, *Her Story 2* could not have taken form and come together. We would also like to extend our thanks to the many essay writers, editors, associate editors, spouses, children, partners, associates, summer associates, secretaries, paralegals, and all others who provide daily support in the lives of working women who litigate, without which *Her Story 2* could not be told and published. Thank you very much to all of you for all you have done. Although we are unable to specifically name everyone who provided their helping hands, know that we appreciate everyone who has touched, guided, and assisted with *Her Story 2: The Resilient Woman Lawyer's Guide to Conquering Obstacles*. Thank you.

Special thanks to The Woman Advocate Committee co-chairs (2022–2023): Elizabeth Timkovich, Atlantic Union Bank; Michal Rogson, Skyward Specialty Insurance; Pilar Kraman, Young Conaway; and Tiffany Degruy, Bradley Arant Boult Cummings LLP; and to Roxana Morelli and Helen Valdes, of Shook, Hardy & Bacon, LLP, for their administrative assistance.

Editors

Teresa M. Beck, Klinedinst PC, San Diego, CA
Alicia M. Menendez, Shook, Hardy & Bacon, LLP, Miami, FL
Shayna M. Steinfeld, Steinfeld & Steinfeld, PC, Atlanta, GA

Associate Editors

Jacqueline M. Bushwack, Rivkin Radler, LLP, Uniondale, NY
Lauren R. Greenspoon, Shook, Hardy & Bacon, LLP, Hartford, CT
Liz Tipping, Neal & Harwell, PLC, Nashville, TN
Julia K. Whitelock, Hudson Cook LLP, Washington, DC
LaFonda Willis, Davis Wright Tremaine LLC, Washington, DC

Teresa M. Beck
Alicia M. Menendez
Shayna M. Steinfeld
Editors

CHAPTER 1

Recognize the Obstacles Ahead: Get a Head Start

This book is intended to be a guidebook to overcoming obstacles in the legal profession. In *Her Story 2*, women lawyers share practical tips about a number of obstacles faced by women (and sometimes men) in the profession. Before we can move forward in any circumstance, however, it is important to know where we are.

Many women enter the profession expecting to be on an equal footing with men in general. It is surprising to learn that even though men and women graduate from law school in roughly similar numbers, women do not advance at the same levels as men. We are all familiar with the old law school adage warning law students to look at the student to their right and the student to their left, and understand that after the first year of law school, one of these people will not succeed in law school. This can be a shocking realization. It is even more surprising to consider that if we were to gather all the women in a particular law school class, after 20 years, a significant number might no longer even be in the profession.

This chapter contains cutting-edge information from the former chair of the ABA Commission on Women in the Profession, Stephanie Scharf, about where women stand in the legal profession in terms of representation at the highest levels. It is critical to understand that women are not represented in the highest levels of the profession at the same levels as their male counterparts. Even more importantly, it is not the fault of individual women that they do not advance at the same rate as their male counterparts. Rather, the legal system, long dominated by male attorneys, still does not always recognize or promote female talent. Being aware of these obstacles is key to overcoming them.

In this chapter, authors probe statistics about the profession from various angles. They also present stories about women of color in the profession—observations that empower all of us. Finally, this chapter contains discussions about the benefits of recognizing female talent, including the great financial rewards that come to firms and companies that cultivate female talent.

Women in the Law: Where to Go and How to Get There[1,2]

By Stephanie A. Scharf

I graduated from law school in 1985, and I vividly recall my "call-back" interview with the prominent Big Law firm that I later joined as a first-year associate. I had already been introduced to multiple male partners and was asked to return to meet the women partners. There were only a few women in the partnership, and when I asked why, the explanation was consistently the same: women had not been graduating from law school in large enough numbers for any firm to have a robust cadre of female partners. I was assured that because women now made up a large number of law school graduates, many women would soon be advancing into the highest levels.

That explanation made perfect sense to me. It was simply a matter of numbers. Wait a few years until enough women graduate from law school, and then the gender gap will disappear.

That result—a legal profession without a gender gap—did not occur as predicted. Year after year, even as women became close to 50 percent of law school graduates, women left associate positions in greater numbers than men; and promotion into partnership and ultimately equity partnership continues to show a marked gender gap.

The explanation of why any given woman lawyer left a firm often varied depending on whom you asked. Senior leaders typically concluded, "she wanted to stay home with her kids," or "this firm was not a good fit," without any explanation as to what "fit" meant. When I would speak with individual women, it was usually a very different story: frustration, regret, sadness, anger, and a host of emotions around the feeling that they had

---

1. I thank my Scharf Banks Marmor colleagues for their outstanding practice of law and their collaborative and highly supportive approach to colleagues at all levels. I thank my colleagues at The Red Bee Group, LLC, for their innovation, good humor, commitment, and leadership around issues of DEIB (diversity, equity, inclusion, and belonging). I especially thank Roberta (Bobbi) Liebenberg, my research partner, who is an inspiration to all who know her.

2. Portions of this chapter contain content that was first presented in reports and articles copyrighted or licensed for use by the author; those publications are cited when referenced in this chapter.

been left behind and let down by their firms. Meaningful data were largely anecdotal, with no systematic approach to measuring the trajectories of male and female legal careers, and certainly little if any data on why the gender gap existed.

The lack of systematic data led me to create the National Association of Women Lawyers (NAWL) Annual Survey of Women in Law, which I had the privilege of conducting for 8 years, from 2006 through 2014.[3] At the time, there were no other national surveys of law firm employers focusing on the status of women in law that looked at promotion into equity partnership, compensation at all levels, and other indicators of how women were faring in private practice settings.

Today, of course, there are multiple sources of data on how women progress in private practice. The broadest base consists of annual data from the National Association of Law Placement, supplemented by data from the NAWL Survey, *American Lawyer*'s annual statistics on large firms, and data collated by the American Bar Association (ABA) Diversity Center.

As useful as such studies have been, they are largely based on the status of women in private practice. There continues to be a consistent gap in knowledge about women in settings other than large private firms. Census data do not have the specificity about practicing lawyers that makes the data useful for tracking change. There are some surveys of corporate law departments, although they are not as readily available as more public bar association data.

The Current Status of Women in the Legal Profession

Especially in private practice, the data continue to show entrenched differences in the trajectory of legal careers for women compared to men, even with the number of women law graduates consistently close to the 50 percent mark for decades. Women enter the legal profession at about the same rate as men, but they leave the law in higher numbers than most

---

3. The National Association of Women Lawyers Survey is now conducted by my Red Bee colleague Destiny Peery.

people realize.[4] Within the profession, there are gender differences by multiple objective measures. For example:

- Women are less likely to be promoted to partner and have even lower odds of being promoted to equity partner: 78 percent of equity partners are male and 22 percent are female.[5]
- Women receive lower compensation than men at the same level, and these differences begin at the early stages of associateship. Women equity partners, for example, earn 78 percent of what men earn.[6] To put another frame around that number, women equity partners have to work 14 and a half months in the same job to earn what male equity partners make in 12 months.
- Women occupy fewer leadership roles than men. In 2020, women represented 12 percent of managing partners, 28 percent of governance committee members, and 27 percent of practice group leaders.[7]

The essays in this chapter in which Karen Richardson, Sheryl Axelrod, and Claire Gibson probe statistics about the profession from various angles provide more detail. It is well established that people from diverse backgrounds, working together, produce more innovation and achieve better solutions and results. At the same time, clients are demanding strong teams of diverse lawyers. The organization that effectively promotes personnel from diverse backgrounds will be increasingly able to

---

4. Unpublished Data from Career Trajectories: A Study of Law School Alumni Graduating 15 Years Ago or Longer (collated by Stephane Scharf and Roberta Liebenberg).

5. *Report of the 2021 NAWL Survey on Promotion and Retention of Women in Law Firms*, NAT. ASS'N OF WOMEN LAWYERS (2021) (hereinafter *2021 NAWL Survey*), *available at* https://www.nawl.org/page/nawl-survey.

6. *Id.* As another example, a recent Major, Lindsey & Africa survey reported that male partners in major law firms saw an increase of 42 percent in their overall compensation over the past decade, as compared to 22 percent growth for female partners. *See also* Ronit Dinovitzer, Bryant Garth, Robert L. Nelson, Rebecca L. Sandefur, Gabriele Plickert, Joyce Sterling, and David B. Wilkins, *After the JD III: Third Results from a National Study of Legal Careers*, AM. BAR FOUND. AND NALP FOUND. FOR L. CAREER RES. AND EDUC. (2014), *available at* https://www.americanbarfoundation.org/wp-content/uploads/2022/12/after-the-jd-phase-3.pdf.

7. *2021 NAWL Survey, supra* note 5.

attract and retain a broad range of diverse talent, which is a huge competitive advantage.

The lack of talented female lawyers at all levels poses longer-term business risks. Without a robust pipeline of women all the way up the ranks into senior levels, it will be increasingly harder to attract women at junior levels or maintain the array of talent needed at senior levels. I can foresee a future where those firms skilled at retaining and promoting a diverse array of lawyers will be much more attractive for all hires and clients than firms late in understanding or doing something about diversity.

Why Do Women Leave?

The question about why women leave speaks to two levels of "leaving" law. One aspect is why do women lawyers leave one employer for another? Another equally important aspect is why do women leave the legal profession entirely?

Our *Walking Out the Door*[8] survey of the nation's 500 largest firms showed that women most frequently leave law firms because of caretaking commitments, followed closely by the level of stress at work, too great an emphasis on marketing or originating business, and the number of billable hours—a package of related factors. Concern about the work-life balance, personal or family health concerns, and the wish to discontinue practicing law were also reasons explaining why even experienced women left. Very notably, women lawyers had significantly more responsibility for childcare than men: they were responsible for everything from arranging for childcare, leaving work for childcare, overseeing children's extracurricular activities, and evening and daytime childcare. Any one of these childcare factors takes time and effort, and the combination is all the more stressful given the competing commitments expected for a successful law practice.

Another striking finding was the disconnect between how managing partners and senior men understood a firm's culture and its impact on women compared to what experienced women say about their firms.

---

8. Roberta D. Liebenberg & Stephanie A. Scharf, Walking Out the Door: The Facts, Figures, and Future of Experienced Women Lawyers in Private Practice (ABA 2019).

The large majority of managing partners and senior men believe that their firms are active advocates for gender diversity, that gender diversity is widely acknowledged as a firm priority, and that the firm has been successful in advancing women into top positions. Women, in contrast, are far less likely to share those positive views about their firms.

There is a good deal of anecdotal evidence showing that women with children are treated differently from men, leading to what has been termed a "motherhood penalty." After women have children, they are often implicitly put on the "mommy track": they are not offered work that requires travel, they have trouble getting assignments or staffing matters, they receive demeaning comments about being a parent, or their evaluation focuses on status as a mother. Women may not be offered the same level of stretch assignments as men or are passed over for the "tough" roles. As a result, by the time they are ready to be promoted to partner or equity partner, they are viewed as less able than their male peers. This is not to say that all women would necessarily accept all opportunities offered. The point is that the individual lawyer should decide, rather than have the firm foreclose opportunity by not even presenting it.

In this age when more and more lawyers are choosing to work remotely—some full-time and many at least part-time—employers face multiple challenges. The issues are not simply about how work will get done, how teams will function, and how to adapt training to remote or hybrid schedules. An equally important issue centers on how to ensure that there are policies and practices within the firm that do not penalize those who are working remotely, especially since many are expected to be women.

Employers may wish to address this question: what is the long-term cost versus the benefit of providing support such as backup childcare, stipends to help defray childcare costs, robust parental leave after childbirth, or strong vacation policies, to name a few possibilities? Not all firms need to implement a large set of changes. Even a few focused adjustments to policies or practices can have a large and positive impact on how people work and how they feel about their workplace.

There are enormous stakes for employers, as women lawyers raise these questions: Why am I working like this? Why stay at this firm? Maybe there is a better way, and a better place, to balance all the things that are important to me.

What Can Employers Do about It?

If employers could wave a magic wand and create the precise policies and practices needed to retain women lawyers, no doubt they would have done so years ago. From what we know, the problem is most acute in private practice firms, where typically there are greater pressures to work more hours, fluid boundaries between work time and time off, inattention to vacation or other breaks that give lawyers a chance to refresh, and less emphasis on fostering long-term careers in the workplace.

Certainly, not all workplace cultures are the same—and not all cultures have the same impact on the women who work there. But if an employer tracks its company's gender differences in hiring, retention, and promotion—which is certainly a simple set of metrics—and finds a continuing gender difference, then for the sake of the long-term health of the firm, it makes sense to consider what can be done differently.

Many creative and tailored approaches can be used to enlarge the retention and advancement of women lawyers. Below is a partial list of ideas that employers can adopt, with a focus on attaining the goal of enhanced gender diversity.

Ask Lawyers What They Need to Succeed at the Firm

For reasons that are somewhat opaque, often firms are reluctant to ask the people who work there: what can the firm do to help you succeed? Leaders and senior men in firms frequently have very different views than women about how the firm operates, even compared to women at the partner level.

As someone who believes in the power of data, it would be relatively easy for an employer to conduct a simple survey of the lawyers who work there, asking: What kinds of resources do you need? What can the firm do to help you have a stronger career? What policy or practice would help you with the practice of law? Such a survey can be supplemented with small group meetings or other ways of eliciting such information.

Getting views at all levels on factors that impact careers will pay multiple dividends: (1) the firm will actually know what helps and what hinders careers for women lawyers rather than assuming that the experience of (mostly male) senior level lawyers works for everyone; (2) lawyers at all levels will know that the firm cares about their perspective and is trying to help them build a career; (3) the firm will have a better reputation as a business that cares about gender diversity; and (4) the firm can pivot to policies and practices that resonate with women lawyers and are a foundation for enhanced retention and advancement.

Implement Flextime and Part-Time Policies That in Practice Allow Advancement

Women think long and hard about flextime or part-time work because, traditionally, those positions have put a halt to advancement. Women who work flextime or part-time may be tainted with the assumption that they lack dedication and commitment, may receive more negative evaluations, and may receive fewer opportunities to work on major matters for important clients—all of which are critical to success.

While the COVID-19 pandemic has destigmatized remote working, flextime and part-time policies may better enable female lawyers to accommodate work and family schedules. In fact, for many working mothers, having flexibility in their work schedules is of primary importance. It is also possible that men would welcome the opportunity for flextime and part-time work if they, too, were confident that there would be no penalty for taking advantage of those policies.

Set Goals and Use Metrics to Understand the Impact of Law Firm Dynamics on Female Lawyers

My experience is that change works well when it is based on a strategy with concrete goals and a timeline for reaching the goals. Examples of goals are: increase by 20 percent the number of women promoted from associate to junior partner in a 3-year period; increase by 15 percent the percentage of women assigned second chair trial/deal experience in a 1-year period; assess the impact of fully remote or partially remote working on promotion of women lawyers in a 2-year period; and of course many more. Goals, along with a timeline, are ideally set through discussion at all levels so that a meaningful strategy evolves about what can work best in a given workplace to achieve better retention and advancement of women lawyers.

Many companies routinely use metrics for deciding compensation, evaluating performance, and allocating credit for business. But metrics can also be key to understanding the day-to-day aspects of practice and advancing diversity, such as understanding how many women and women of color are being assigned to significant matters or are invited to participate in client pitches and other business development opportunities; or assessing who performs other types of nonbillable activities, such as recruiting or organizing continuing legal education programs, which typically have little if any impact on advancement within the firm.

Metrics, of course, are not the goal, but rather, the means to inform change and measure how effective changes have been. Even a small change can have a large impact. Imagine, for example, if a lawyer could have, without penalty, "down time" every day between 5 and 7 p.m.—no emails, no texts, no telephone calls, no demands for an immediate answer. An employer could measure whether that change was well received by lawyers at all levels and whether it actually enhanced good will and a feeling of belonging without jeopardizing client service.

What Can Women Lawyers Do?

Over the course of my career, I have spoken to thousands of women lawyers about the dilemma they face navigating their careers. All too often there is a disconnect between what an individual woman sees as the trajectory of her legal career and the actual course of her career, which meets up with employer policies, practices, and unspoken rules about what a "successful" lawyer needs to do. That said, a woman can control many aspects of her career so that it does not prohibit living a life that she enjoys and values. Here are some things to keep in mind.

What You Would Like to Do Is the Right Thing to Do

When you are in the midst of a job, it can be hard to step back and assess whether you and the job are a good fit for each other. Looking around at others who appear to have it all together can be demoralizing, and working with people who do not share your values or social circumstances can feel isolating. But you and your career are not glued to any given workplace. The legal profession offers many ways in which to practice law, and many lawyers also work in jobs where a law degree is useful even if the job does not entail the formal practice of law. If you are not happy with your job, or feel stressed on a daily basis, or have lost enjoyment at work, it's time to rethink whether you and the job are a good fit and to consider what to do next. Below are some tips about getting help to rethink your next steps.

Have a Vision and Be Ready to Pivot

A career can last many years—really a lifetime. Career trajectories are rarely straight lines. Instead, careers are much like labyrinths, where you may possibly take a long curving path forward, or reach a dead end and need to turn around to find another way, or take an elaborate path that goes sideways or even backwards before it moves forward.

In today's profession, it is extremely rare for a woman to end her career at the same company or firm where she started her career. Embrace that reality. Speak to people—all sorts of people—about how legal careers can develop. Other people's stories will often resonate with you and give you the grit or the inspiration to stay on your current path or explore other pathways.

Reach Out Beyond Your Workplace

Go outside your workplace on a regular basis so you can learn up front about where lawyers can practice and the array of jobs available for someone with your talents. Many activities do not take a lot of time and can be personally enjoyable. Joining a community group or bar association will give you a supportive network and introduce you to people you can learn from and who can provide help when needed. As another example, being on a nonprofit board will enhance your "soft" skills of leadership and teamwork and, at the same time, provide external recognition that will resonate at your workplace.

Have a Conversation about How You Would Like to Advance

Speak to people in your workplace about things that can make your work more productive and more enjoyable. That type of conversation may entail raising a subject, coming back to discuss possible changes, and figuring out jointly what can work for you, your family, and your employer. Be patient about the process and be brave—you are a lawyer!

Stephanie A. Scharf

Career

Partner, Scharf Banks Marmor LLC; Principal, The Red Bee Group LLC

Education
- JD, University of Chicago Law School (1985)
- PhD, Social Psychology, University of Chicago
- MA, Communications, Stanford University
- BA, Rutgers University
- Advanced Training in Clinical Trials Management, University of Chicago

Best Advice

Be brave. Everyone you meet has fears about how they are doing; they just don't tell you about it. You won't be perfect—and neither is anyone else. Keep going even when you are scared. You will end up feeling better about yourself and doing what you really would like to do.

Personal

Stephanie Scharf has been practicing law for more than 35 years. In 2011, she founded Scharf Banks Marmor LLC, a prominent women-owned law firm that represents corporations and businesses around the United States. Before forming her current firm, Stephanie was a partner for many years at two Big Law firms, Kirkland & Ellis and Jenner & Block. Along with an active practice, Stephanie has been president of the NAWL and chair of the ABA Commission on Women in the Profession; active in many bar groups and community organizations; and authored dozens of research reports and opinion pieces about the status of women in the law and best practices for achieving gender parity (many with her research partner, Roberta Liebenberg). Stephanie recently co-founded The Red Bee Group, LLC, a consulting firm that advises corporations, law firms, and not-for-profits about strategies for growth, leadership, and talent development with DEIB values and initiatives. Stephanie has been very fortunate over the years to have the support of her husband, Jeff Mandell, their two children, Meredith and Jonathan, and many other well-loved family members,

(Continued)

family pets, personal friends, and business partners—all of whom have made life both easier and a lot of fun!

For More Information

https://www.scharfbanks.com/who-we-are/attorneys/stephanie-scharf-0
https://www.linkedin.com/in/stephaniescharf

The Status of Women in the Law: The NAWL Survey Data

By Karen M. Richardson

In 2006, the National Association of Women Lawyers (NAWL) pioneered quantitatively studying the status of women in the legal profession through the *Report of the Survey on the Promotion and Retention of Women in Law Firms* (the Survey Report). This inaugural Survey Report provided statistical proof that women were underrepresented in leadership, ownership, and decision-making positions in law firms, and that the few women in the top echelon were still undercompensated.[9] While some advances have been made over the last 17 years, the trend of significant attrition of women from law firms as their careers advance persists despite some positive, but small, increases in the representation of women at partnership levels. These incremental changes continue to occur slowly, despite a substantial rise in both interest and investment in increasing and maintaining the representation of women and other attorneys from underrepresented backgrounds (including people of color, LGBTQIA+ people, and people with disabilities) in the legal profession. Data suggest that the legal profession has not fully committed to the actions necessary to address the persistent loss of talent and experience from the legal profession.

The Beginning

In 2006, the NAWL Survey Report found that women lawyers were well represented at the lowest level of the profession (constituting 45 percent of associates) but not at the top of the profession (making up only 16 percent of equity partners—the law firm owners). Even when women lawyers did achieve the status of equity partner, there was a gendered compensation gap, with women equity partners earning an average of $81,000 less than male equity partners. Moreover, women held on average only 16 percent of seats on their firm's highest governing committee, and only 5 percent of managing partners were women. The 2006 Survey Report found that law firm decision making on critical firm-wide issues, such as long-term

---

9. NAWL Survey Reports are available at www.nawl.org/research.

strategy and growth, business development, partner compensation and advancement, and policies and practices related to the retention and promotion of women lawyers, were decisions "still being made in a decidedly male environment."

Over Time

The now-classic headline statistic used to describe the state of women in large law firms is their representation among the ranks of equity partners. While there have been some advances, especially over the longer view of 15 years (women now make up around 21 percent of equity partners in contrast to 16 percent in 2006), the data show a modest, incremental increase in the representation of women as nonequity and equity partners. Unfortunately, the number of women among law firm partners continues to reflect significant attrition relative to their representation among law school graduates and law firm associates.

The Leadership Gap

In addition to achieving the rank of partner, women's participation in law firm governance is understood to be important for incorporating their perspectives in key decisions at the firm and reducing barriers for women that may arise in decisions made at the governance level. Over time, NAWL's data have shown that the number of women represented in these positions of influence in law firms has increased significantly (almost doubling in some cases) over the last 15 years. Further, their representation in these roles matches or exceeds their representation in the equity partner ranks, but there is still considerable room for growth in women's participation in firm leadership roles.

The Compensation Gap

Compensation data have long been considered a simple indicator for equity in the workplace, and NAWL's unique compensation data collected at the firm level offers a long-term view on compensation in large law firms. Over the last 15 years, NAWL data have captured the persistence of gender gaps in compensation at all stages of an attorney's career in the firm. Even at the entry level, women are paid less than men, and these gaps often grow as women and men advance to partnership, with the largest gaps occurring between equity partners. In addition, women continue to be largely shut out of the highest levels of compensation. Men remain the most highly compensated attorneys in law firms, with the highest paid attorney at a firm nearly always being a man and women rarely breaking into the top 10 at the firm.

The data highlight the slow or stalled progress of women in large firms over the last 17 years. *The short version of the story is that not a lot has changed*. This fact has frustrated and puzzled many in the profession, given the substantial increase in both interest and investment in these numbers. There is near-universal adoption of diversity initiatives, including diversity committees and dedicated diversity officers, and increased awareness of the challenges women attorneys face in their advancement through the law firm. To better understand this pattern and to provide more useful information to the profession, over the last several years, NAWL has looked more deeply into the mechanisms underlying these well-known statistics by asking additional questions about the inputs—policies, practices, and procedures—to better understand the outputs—how they affect women and other diverse attorneys in law firms. We asked firms to share their specific processes for purposes such as credit assignment/sharing, origination, and succession planning. Additionally, we asked firms if they were engaging in specific practices known to reduce biased decision making regarding recruitment and hiring, compensation, evaluation, and promotion.

In 2020, a new pattern emerged: law firms became reluctant to engage in processes most likely to reduce biased decision making, instead preferring activities that signal a commitment to diversity but that are not guaranteed to produce it. For example, firms were more likely to report engaging in bias-interruption earlier in the employment relationship (i.e., recruitment and hiring). Since disparities between men and women are much smaller at earlier career stages, the emphasis on bias interruption at earlier career stages may have reduced disparities. However, the stalled progress of women at subsequent levels may evidence that firms need to expand their bias-reduction efforts to include decisions made once a woman or diverse attorney is at the firm and advancing through that person's career.

Moving Beyond the Numbers

The 2021 Survey Report identifies three key areas to focus on, as these processes are central to the advancement of attorneys in the legal profession: compensation, performance evaluation and promotion, and succession. Notably, each of these areas is characterized by subjective and opaque decision-making processes. That is, these are the processes that are more prone to bias.

Compensation

The compensation gap between women and men is persistent inside and outside of the legal profession. Over the years, there have been several common explanations offered regarding the persistent compensation gaps between women and men; however, much pay equity research has concluded that, despite the possibility of variables other than bias, bias is often the only surviving explanation. In other words, gender discrimination in various forms, whether explicit or implicit, plays a role in the gendered compensation gaps in every profession, including the legal profession. After acknowledging the role of bias in compensation decisions, we can ask what law firms are doing to combat the potential for bias in their compensation decision-making processes. Unfortunately, recent NAWL data shows that firms are not engaging consistently in many known and recommended bias interrupters when determining compensation, and all firms could be doing more to reduce the potential for bias in their compensation decisions.[10]

Like all the processes highlighted here, compensation decisions are considered "black box" decisions. That is, decisions about compensation remain too opaque, with many across the legal profession feeling it is unclear exactly what factors into compensation decisions and how those factors are weighed in any given case and across multiple individuals within a law firm. The 2021 Survey Report enumerates key questions for

---

10. *See Report of the 2020 NAWL Survey on Promotion and Retention of Women in Law Firms*, NAT. ASS'N OF WOMEN LAWYERS (2020), https://irp.cdn-website.com/2df22e83/files/uploaded/2020%20Survey%20Report%20(16).pdf; *Report of the 2019 NAWL Survey on Promotion and Retention of Women in Law Firms*, NAT. ASS'N OF WOMEN LAWYERS (2019), https://irp.cdn-website.com/2df22e83/files/uploaded/2019%20NAWL%20Survey%20Report.pdf.

law firms to ask and answer and specific actions firms can take now to address bias in compensation. Chief among these are:

- Who is responsible for making compensation decisions? What are the demographics of this group?
- What are the criteria for compensation decisions?
- What data are made available to the group that makes compensation decisions? Who provides that data?
- Does your firm analyze compensation data for potential biases and disparities? What analyses does your firm conduct? How often?

Performance Evaluation and Promotion

Research has shown consistently that performance evaluations and promotion decisions are often biased against women, people of color, LGBTQIA+ people, and people with disabilities. Decades of research on professional women in many fields has shown consistently the myriad ways that gender stereotypes affect both performance evaluations and the likelihood of promotion.[11] These gendered biases are more likely to show up in subjective evaluation processes without well-defined criteria, and law firm evaluations, like those in many professional spaces, are rife with undefined criteria. A 2020 study highlighted that bigger biases show up, for example, when evaluations focus on personality, potential, and perceptions of exceptionalism rather than evidence-based work performance.[12]

NAWL data on how firms are addressing the biases in their performance evaluation and promotion processes show that law firms do not consistently report using practices known to interrupt the very types of biases noted above. While all firms claim to have formal processes, little is known about the evaluation and promotion processes at law firms, especially across the profession. Although most firms say they set clear and specific criteria, anecdotal data suggest that many continue to find the process of promotion to partner particularly opaque. The NAWL data show fewer firms reporting that they take actions such as separating

---

11. *See, e.g.*, Jessica Nordell, *This Is How Everyday Sexism Could Stop You from Getting That Promotion*, N.Y. Times (Oct. 14, 2021), www.nytimes.com/interactive/2021/10/14/opinion/gender-bias.html.
12. NAWL (2020), *supra* note 10.

potential from performance or considering personality independent of skill, which may suggest that the criteria firms continue to use remain more subjective than necessary to interrupt biases.

Much remains to be learned about how law firms structure and implement their evaluation and promotion processes, particularly if we want to understand where bias continues to contribute to persistent disparities for women, people of color, LGBTQIA+ people, and people with disabilities. The 2021 Survey Report enumerates key questions for law firms to ask and answer, as well as specific actions firms can take now to address bias in performance evaluation and promotion. These actions include:

- Who conducts and provides input into performance evaluations?
- Who makes decisions about promotion to partner? What are the demographics of these people? Who is informed of this process and when?
- Does your firm have a standardized process that everyone being evaluated or seeking promotion goes through? What is that standardized process?
- What criteria are the basis for performance evaluations and promotion decisions in your firm?

Succession

The NAWL has collected (or attempted to collect) information about succession planning and succession processes for client relationships in the last couple of years, but the information available to the legal profession at large about succession processes remains limited. In 2020, only 39 percent of firms reported having formal written succession plans.[13] These data are consistent with a 2018 survey of midsized law firms, which found that only 37 percent of firms reported they had a formal succession planning process already in place or were creating one.[14] Further, the 2018 study

---

13. *Id.*
14. *Thinking about a Succession Plan for Your Law Firm?*, THOMSON REUTERS (Oct. 23, 2019), legal.thomsonreuters.com/blog/thinking-about-a-succession-plan-for-your-law-firm.

found that 43 percent of firms said they had an informal process or did not have succession planning on their radar.[15]

Relationship partner transitions provide a significant opportunity for law firms to diversify the ranks of relationship partners, particularly for major clients, but this will occur only with thoughtful planning; leadership development of younger attorneys; and intentional efforts to take diversity, equity, and inclusion into account as these transitions approach. In addition, the NAWL data on firms' top 30 clients show a small but positive trend toward not only increasing who has access to those relationship partner roles, but also the demographics of the departing and new relationship partners, particularly for women. For example, in 2020, in examining relationship partner transitions for a firm's top clients, we found that women accounted for 23 percent of the departing partners and 32 percent of new relationship partners. However, we saw little to no increase in the representation of people of color, LGBTQIA+ people, or people with disabilities in these transitions.

Our data also suggest that these top clients are more likely to be shared after a relationship transition, with the overall number of relationship partners serving those clients increasing when we compare the number of departing relationship partners to the number of new relationship partners. While the sharing of credit has been regularly touted as an equity measure that will allow women, people of color, LGBTQIA+ people, and people with disabilities more access to critical building blocks for advancement in the firm, there is reason to worry that the splitting or sharing of credit may dilute the impact of these client relationships when it comes to compensation, evaluation, and promotion, especially for women, people of color, LGBTQIA+ people, and people with disabilities. Research has shown that women often receive less credit for work they do in teams, and this is particularly true when they are working with men.[16]

---

15. *Id.*

16. Nicole Torres, *Proof That Women Get Less Credit for Teamwork*, Harv. Bus. Rev. (Feb. 9, 2016), hbr.org/2016/02/proof-that-women-get-less-credit-for-teamwork. Full research paper available at scholar.harvard.edu/files/sarsons/files/gender_groupwork .pdf?m=1449178759.

These concerns over the potential unintended negative consequences of credit sharing also have implications for who is seen as a potential successor for a client. It has been recommended that one action firms can begin to take is to analyze and map out their client relationships, particularly for their top 30 to 50 clients, to see who works with those clients across the firm. This information allows identification of potential successors to the existing relationship partner(s) that reflects who actually knows and works with the client. If women's contributions are devalued within the context of who has been servicing the client, women are likely to be passed over as potential successors, for they will be perceived as having contributed less to maintaining the client relationship or working on the client's matters.

Where Do We Go from Here?

We have come a long way since 2006 when NAWL set out to study the status of women in the law. No, the numbers have not significantly changed—women are still underrepresented in leadership, ownership, and decision-making positions in law firms, and the few women in the top echelon are still undercompensated. However, the legal profession, and law firms specifically, are showing increased interest in and commitment to understanding the challenges women and other diverse attorneys face professionally. As the legal profession struggles with action and results, an important opportunity to understand the root cause of these challenges presents itself: it is time to move beyond the numbers toward promoting a better understanding of why and how meaningful and significant progress on diversity, equity, and inclusion remains elusive.

The data and research are clear: the effects of exclusion, biases, and underrepresentation build on themselves. The legal profession needs to be bold in considering how to address the exponential impact of even subtle biases or disparities that are built into the culture and systems of law firms and the profession. The disparities at any stage of attorneys' careers accumulate in ways that derail the career trajectories of too many, affecting some groups of attorneys more than others.

Karen M. Richardson

Career

Executive Director, National Association of Women Lawyers

Education

- JD, Loyola University Chicago School of Law (2012)
- BA Political Science, Loyola University Chicago (2007)

Best Advice

Embrace an abundance mindset.

Personal

Karen M. Richardson currently lives in northern Vermont and spends most of her free time skiing and hiking with her family.

For More Information

https://www.nawl.org/staff

Recognize the Obstacles Ahead: A Deeper Dive into the Statistics Affecting Women and Women of Color in the Legal Profession

By S. Claire Gibson

As I write this essay, the Supreme Court of the United States (SCOTUS) has been holding the confirmation hearing of Judge Ketanji Brown Jackson for multiple days. Judge Brown Jackson holds an AB *magna cum laude* from Harvard University in addition to a JD *cum laude* from Harvard Law School. She was the supervising editor of the *Harvard Law Review*, has

"Women belong in all places where decisions are being made. It shouldn't be that women are the exception."

—RUTH BADER GINSBURG, Former Associate Justice of the Supreme Court of the United States

clerked at every level of the federal judiciary, and is by many accounts an exemplary jurist. Later confirmed, Judge Brown Jackson became only the sixth woman and first ever Black woman to sit on SCOTUS. Witnessing the confirmation hearing became an emotional rollercoaster.[17] My heart swelled with utter pride at seeing another Black woman, ivy grad, and attorney be nominated for the highest court in the land, and my heart was also broken watching this highly accomplished woman endure a combination of sexism and racism unprecedented in SCOTUS hearings. Judge Brown Jackson's hearing has been a concise display of the obstacles that women, and in particular women of color, face in the legal profession.

The Status of Women in the Profession

Since 2016, reports indicate that women outnumber men at American Bar Association (ABA) accredited law schools.[18] In 2020, women comprised 54.09 percent of students at ABA accredited law schools, and there

---

17. Associate Justice of the Supreme Court of the United States Ketanji Onyika Brown Jackson was confirmed by the United States Senate on April 7, 2022, and sworn into office on June 30.

18. Stephanie Francis Ward, *Women Outnumber Men in Law Schools for First Time, Newly Updated Data Show*, ABA J. (Dec. 2016), https://www.abajournal.com/news/article/women_outnumber_men_in_law_schools_for_first_time_newly_updated_data_show.

were 9,610 more female than male students.[19] Yet despite these enrollment numbers, which would imply gender equality in the profession, the 2020 National Association of Women Lawyers (NAWL) Survey Report on the Promotion and Retention of Women in Law Firms (2020 NAWL Report) shows that 47 percent of all law firm associates are women, but only 31 percent of nonequity partners are women, and an even more dismal mere 21 percent of equity partners are women.[20] These numbers clearly indicate that the law school to partnership pipeline is littered with obstacles for women. Despite the progress women have made in law school admissions, matriculation, and passing the bar exam, this progress slows to a crawl once women enter the law firm environment. Further, these numbers show only marginal improvement over the last several years. According to the 2021 ABA Profile of the Legal Profession (2021 ABA Profile),

> About 21% of all equity partners were female in 2020, according to [NAWL]. That's unchanged from 2019, but up from 15% in 2012. Also, about 31% of all non-equity partners were female in 2020, also unchanged from 2019, but up from 25% in 2011.[21]

Further to these marginal improvements in the partnership numbers, a deep dive into law firm profiles shows that even in leadership roles within firms, women are drastically underrepresented. The 2020 NAWL Report shows that women comprise only 28 percent of Governance Committees, 29 percent of Compensation Committees, 19 percent of Firm-wide Managing Partners, 28 percent of Office Managing Partners, and 25 percent of Practice Group Leaders.[22] While these numbers are a far cry from the 54 percent of women law school students, the one positive is that they are trending in the right direction and even at a seemingly faster pace than partnership numbers. "In the last 10 years,

---

19. *American Bar Association Profile of the Legal Profession 2021*, AM. BAR ASS'N, 81 (July 21, 2021), https://www.americanbar.org/content/dam/aba/administrative/news/2021/0721/polp.pdf.
20. NAWL (2020), *supra* note 10, at 28–30.
21. *ABA Profile of the Legal Profession*, *supra* note 19, at 82.
22. NAWL (2020), *supra* note 10, at 9.

the participation of women on these committees has increased substantially, with the numbers from the last three years nearly double those from 2007 (15%)."[23]

For women who do manage to enter the law firm environment and climb the ladder, there are notable unfavorable compensation disparities. On average, male associates make a salary of $217,898, while female associates make $198,687, a difference of almost $20,000. That gender pay gap continues to grow into the ranks of law firm partnership, with women nonequity partners making on average $26,000 less than men. The gap becomes a chasm at the equity partner level, with women making on average $132,000 less than their male counterparts.[24] The earnings gap is even wider for women of color attorneys, as studies show that the earnings increase with a law degree over a bachelor's degree is significantly less for persons of color.[25]

Special Issues Facing Women of Color

Further examination of the law firm climate shows that Black, Indigenous, and women of color (BIWOC) fare even worse than their white women peers. The ABA 2021 Profile reports that in 2020 only 14 percent of law firm associates were women of color (including Black, Asian/Pacific Islander, Hispanic/Latinx, Native American/American Indian, Middle Eastern/North African, and multiracial women), while the NAWL 2021 Report reflecting 2019 fiscal and calendar year data shows that women of color accounted for only 22 percent of law firm associates.[26] Both reports show that only 4 percent of nonequity partners and only 3 percent of

---

23. *Id.* at 36.
24. *ABA Profile of the Legal Profession, supra* note 19, at 83.
25. Debra Cassens Weiss, *A Law Degree Provides a Larger Earnings Boost to Whites Than Minorities, Researchers Say*, ABA J. (Oct. 2, 2017), https://www.abajournal.com/news/article/a_law_degree_provides_a_larger_earnings_boost_to_whites_than_minorities_res; *see also* Lynette S. Hoag, *I'm an Attorney and Have $50,000 in My Retirement Account. My White Attorney Friend Has $1 Million in Hers — and It's Not Because She Went to a Better School,* Bus. Insider (June 26, 2020), https://www.businessinsider.com/personal-finance/racial-wealth-gap-black-attorney-2020-6.
26. *ABA Profile of the Legal Profession, supra* note 19 at 82; NAWL (2020), *supra* note 10 at 6.

equity partners are women of color.[27] By comparison, note that women of color comprise 37 percent of the U.S. population. What is even more disheartening about these numbers is that according to *Left Out and Left Behind: The Hurdles, Hassles, and Heartaches of Achieving Long-Term Legal Careers for Women of Color,* 70 percent of women of color attorneys report leaving or considering leaving the legal profession. Indeed, women of color have the highest rate of attrition from law firms.[28] This means that in addition to being underrepresented in entering the ranks of the profession, women of color are far less likely to enter the partnership ranks even if they do become associates. Dr. Tsedale Melaku, author of *You Don't Look Like a Lawyer: Black Women and Systematic Gendered Racism,* sheds some light on the obstacles faced by BIWOC attorneys:

> The terms of employment for women and professionals of color often include what I call an invisible labor clause. That is, they are required to perform added, unacknowledged, and uncompensated labor and to pay additional "taxes" for their inclusion in these social and professional spaces that would otherwise view these professionals' inherent differences as obstacles to their career advancement. One of these taxes is what I call an inclusion tax, which is levied in the form of time, money, and mental and emotional energy required to gain entry to and acceptance from traditionally white and male institutional spaces. That can include the hours at the hair salon needed to conform to European standards of beauty and the tailoring of clothing to fit within white norms of professional attire, both of which are costly to women of color. Adding to this cumbersome load is the emotional and mental burden inflicted upon those who are perpetually the only person of color, or woman, or person of a modest economic background in the room.[29]

---

27. *ABA Profile of the Legal Profession, supra* note 19 at 82; NAWL (2020), *supra* note 10 at 7–8.

28. Destiny Peery, Paulette Brown, and Eileen Letts, *Left Out and Left Behind: The Hurdles, Hassles and Heartaches of Achieving Long-Term Legal Careers for Women of Color,* Am. Bar Ass'n 13 (2020).

29. Tsedale Melaku, *Why Women and People of Color in Law Still Hear "You Don't Look Like a Lawyer,"* Harv. Bus. Rev. (Aug. 7, 2019), https://hbr.org/2019/08/why-women-and-people-of-color-in-law-still-hear-you-dont-look-like-a-lawyer.

What Dr. Melaku describes, and what is affirmed in *Left Out and Left Behind*, is that law firm culture is hostile to women of color attorneys and is simply not designed to facilitate their success. Further, the advancement of white women in the legal profession does not readily translate to advancement for women of color attorneys because, as discussed in *Left Out and Left Behind,* white women attorneys who manage to advance despite gender bias often replicate the status quo, engaging the racist gatekeeping that prevents women of color attorneys from similar advancement.[30]

Women Lawyers Have Not Achieved Equity

In *Walking Out the Door: The Facts, Figures, and Future of Experienced Women Lawyers in Private Practice*, authors Roberta Liebenberg and Stephanie Scharf put a magnifying glass on the career satisfaction of experienced women in the law firm environment. They surveyed managing partners and individual attorneys who had been in practice for at least 15 years. Consistent with what would be expected based on the findings in *Left Out and Left Behind*, there were not enough attorneys of color at the partner level for the *Walking Out the Door* survey to comment on issues of racism that lead to attrition among women of color attorneys. Nonetheless, the study's findings showed the drastic differences in career satisfaction between men and women attorneys, sufficient to conclude that the realities of the profession are a lot harsher for women attorneys than for men attorneys. On every point surveyed, including recognition, compensation determination, actual compensation, opportunities for advancement, gender diversity, and firm leadership, there was an average 20 percent difference in satisfaction between men and women participants in the study.[31]

The differences in perspective only widened when respondents were asked about whether their firms do well in advancing experienced women. There was an average of over 30 percent difference in the opinions of male

---

30. Peery et al., *supra* note 28 at 10–11.
31. Roberta D. Liebenberg & Stephanie A. Scharf, Walking Out the Door: The Facts, Figures, and Future of Experienced Women Lawyers in Private Practice 5–6 (ABA 2019).

Recognition received for their work

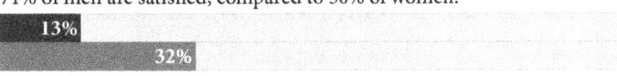

71% of men are satisfied, compared to 50% of women.

At the other end of the scale, almost a third of women–32%–are dissatisfied, compared to 13% of men.

Women are also more intensely dissatisfied: 14% are "extremely" dissatisfied compared to 2% of men.

Actual compensation

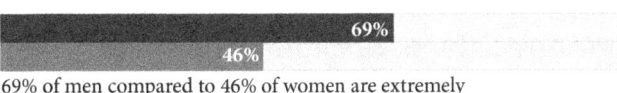

75% of men and 61% of women are extremely or somewhat satisfied.

At the other end of the scale, 12% of men and 28% of women are "extremely" or "somewhat" dissatisfied with their compensation.

The methods by which compensation is determined (including salary, benefits, and bonus)

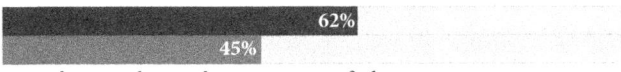

69% of men compared to 46% of women are extremely or somewhat satisfied.

At the other end of the scale, 17% of men are dissatisfied and 38% of women are dissatisfied.

Opportunities for advancement

62% of men and 45% of women are satisfied.

At the other end of the scale, 11% of men and 33% of women are dissatisfied.

Workplace gender diversity

Considerably more men (67%) are satisfied than women (43%)

At the other end of the scale, substantially more women expressed higher levels of dissatisfaction (32%) than men (7%).

Leadership of their firm

Substantially more men are satisfied (73%) than women (53%).

Source: ROBERTA D. LIEBENBERG & STEPHANIE A. SCHARF, *Walking Out the Door: The Facts, Figures, and Future of Experienced Women Lawyers in Private Practice* 5–6 (ABA 2019).

and female respondents on questions of whether firm leadership advocates for gender diversity, prioritizes gender diversity, and promotes and retains experienced women. Of particular note,

> 71% of managing partners believe that their firm "has been successful at advancing/promoting female attorneys into equity partnership." A similar level of agreement exists among experienced male lawyers (79%). Substantially fewer experienced women—48%—agree that their firm has been successful at advancing women into equity partnership, and 35% disagree with that statement. [32]

Keep in mind that only 21 percent of all equity partners were female in 2020 and only 3 percent of equity partners were women of color, yet 71 percent of managing partners and 79 percent of experienced male partners believe that firms are successfully promoting women to equity partnership.[33] If a rate of only 21 percent of equity partners being women is perceived as successful, it is safe to conclude that not only are we quite a way from women's achieving equity in the legal field, but also we need a drastic shift in perspective before equity can be achieved, because women attorneys are being gaslighted about the realities of what they are experiencing in this profession.

Inclusion of Women and Diverse Men at the Highest Levels Holds Incredible Potential for All of Us

Law firms are first and foremost businesses, and all businesses are driven by profitability. Advocacy for gender diversity in law firms is often rebutted with commentary that women attorneys lack qualifications or dedication, which would impact a firm's bottom line, but the numbers show that these counterarguments are baseless. According to McKinsey & Company's *Diversity Wins: How Inclusion Matters*, businesses with diverse

---

32. *Id.* at 15.
33. *ABA Profile of the Legal Profession, supra* note 19 at 82.

leadership consistently financially outperform those with more homogeneous leadership:

> [T]he relationship between diversity on executive teams and the likelihood of financial outperformance has strengthened over time. . . . Our latest analysis reaffirms the strong business case for both gender diversity and ethnic and cultural diversity in corporate leadership. . . . The most diverse companies are now more likely than ever to outperform less diverse peers on profitability. Our 2019 analysis finds that companies in the top quartile for gender diversity on executive teams were 25 percent more likely to have above-average profitability than companies in the fourth quartile.[34]

Simply put, gender and racial diversity in decision-making roles translates to a tangible increase in profits. Firms that continue to ignore or resist this fact may soon find that they can no longer compete in a market with increasing demands for diversity. Corporate clients such as Facebook, Hewlett-Packard, and Microsoft have all implemented gender and racial diversity requirements for the law firms they retain, and since persons of color are predicted to be the majority U.S. population in the next two decades, the demand for diversity can only be expected to increase.[35]

Beyond the financial benefit, law firms have an ethical responsibility to provide clients with the best advocacy and representation. There is no debating that creative and innovative solutions are born out of diverse perspectives and experiences. Law firms owe it to their clients, the legal profession, and society in general to provide representation and advice that has the advantage of being vetted by diverse perspectives.

---

34. Sundiatu Dixon-Fyle, Kevin Dolan, Vivian Hunt, and Sara Prince, *Diversity Wins: How Inclusion Matters*, McKinsey & Co. (May 19, 2020), *available at* https://www.mckinsey.com/featured-insights/diversity-and-inclusion/diversity-wins-how-inclusion-matters.

35. Colleen Cochran, *Demographics as Destiny: Making the Case for Law Firm Diversity and Inclusion*, ABA J. (June 22, 2021), https://www.americanbar.org/groups/journal/articles/2021/demographics-as-destiny-making-the-case-for-law-firm-diversity.

The Way Forward

The numbers in these various reports show a daunting reality, and individually our ability to effect change across the profession can be limited. All the same, there is still much that we as women attorneys can do to advance individually and collectively. Throughout this book, my co-authors will share their experiences and counsel for overcoming many of the obstacles faced by women lawyers. Hopefully, through these shared stories, we will all be further inspired to change the realities of this profession for all women.

S. Claire Gibson

Career
Intellectual Property Attorney, Partner at Dunlap, Bennett and Ludwig; President, Military Spouse JD Network

Education
- JD, Brooklyn Law School (2009)
- BA, Political Science, Sociology, Columbia University (2006)

Best Advice
Always show up authentically and be willing to move through fear.

Personal
Claire Gibson is an Intellectual Property attorney and a Partner at Dunlap, Bennett & Ludwig. Claire's practice is focused on providing domestic and international trademark and copyright prosecution, rights enforcement, licensing, and related IP advice. With almost two decades of experience in domestic and international IP matters, Claire works closely with emerging and established businesses to develop, protect, and monetize their IP portfolios. In addition to her work as an IP attorney, Claire serves as the President of the Military Spouse JD Network, a bar association for military spouses that is focused on removing barriers to career advancement for military spouse attorneys. The daughter of Barbadian immigrants, Claire was born in New York but spent her childhood in Barbados. Claire is the spouse of an active-duty Marine with 20 years of service and "hooman" to two toy poodles, Bajan and Toussaint.

For More Information
cgibson@dbllawyers.com
https://www.linkedin.com/in/clairegibsonesq

Calling a Crisis a Crisis: The Lack of Women at the Top of the Legal Profession

By Sheryl L. Axelrod

Across Our Courts, Among General Counsel, Law Firm Partners, and Our Law School Deans, Women Are Generally Outnumbered by Men by a Factor of More Than 1.5 to 1

On the Bench

As of 2019, women made up only about 34.5 percent of our active federal appellate judges, according to the Report Examining the Demographic Compositions of U.S. Circuit and District Courts.[36] This means women judges on our federal courts of appeals are outnumbered by men by a factor of nearly 2 to 1 (1.89 to 1).

That is much the same situation as that of women on our highest state courts. Women judges serving on the nation's highest state courts are outnumbered by men by a factor of almost 3 to 1 (2.79 to 1), according to the National Association of Women Judges.[37] On intermediate appellate courts, there are some more women judges, so they are outnumbered by the men by a lower factor of about 1.5 to 1 (1.56).

In Law Firms

In law firms, women do worse than they do on the bench. Women represent only a quarter, 25 percent, of law firm partners, according to Law360's

---

36. *See* The Democracy and Government Reform Team, *Examining the Demographic Compositions of U.S. Circuit and District Courts*, CTR. FOR AM. PROGRESS (Feb. 13, 2020), https://www.americanprogress.org/article/examining-demographic-compositions-u-s-circuit-district-courts.
37. *See 2022 US State Court Women Judges*, NAT. ASS'N OF WOMEN JUDGES, https://www.nawj.org/statistics/2022-us-state-court-women-judges.

seventh annual Glass Ceiling Report.[38] This means that for every woman partner, there are three male partners.

In Corporations

Women do slightly better in corporations than they do on the bench or in law firms. According to Zippia's General Counsel Demographics and Statistics in the U.S.,[39] women general counsel are outnumbered by men by a factor of over 1.5 to 1.

Law School Deans

There is nearly the same percentage of women law school deans as there are women serving as general counsel. According to the American Law School Dean Study[40] of law schools in 2020, for every woman law school dean, there are 1.5 men in the role.

These Numbers Are Appalling

Women should not be outnumbered by men by any factor, let alone by factors of 1.5 to 3. Assume it takes approximately 10 to 15 years to become a partner at a law firm. Take a look at how many women attended law school relative to men for the past 20 years.

Beginning over 20 years ago, men and women started attending law school in nearly equal numbers. The percentage of women attending law schools has gone up since that time. According to the ABA, by 2021, over half—55.3 percent—of students at ABA-accredited law schools were women.

---

38. *See* Jacqueline Bell, *Law360's Glass Ceiling Report: What You Need to Know*, Law360 (Sept. 13, 2021), https://www.law360.com/articles/1418221/law360-s-glass-ceiling-report-what-you-need-to-know.

39. *See General Counsel Demographics and Statistics in the US*, Zippia, https://www.zippia.com/general-counsel-jobs/demographics.

40. *See* Stephanie Francis Ward, *Diversity Increases with Law School Deans, According to New AALS Study*, ABA J. (Apr. 4, 2022), https://www.abajournal.com/web/article/diversity-increases-with-law-school-deans-according-to-aals-study.

That means that by now, we should be seeing equal numbers of male and female partners. So why don't we? Women face a host of added barriers to advancement, and they leave the profession in far greater numbers than men.

Women Make Up Only 37 Percent of Lawyers in Private Practice

Only 37 percent of lawyers are women, according to the U.S. Census.[41] So while for the past 20 years, roughly the same number of women have been attending law school as men—and in fact, *more* women attended law school than men between 2016 and 2022—women leave the profession in much higher numbers than men.

"Women are twice as likely to make early exits [from law firms] as men, and they continue to disappear even after making partner," as Joyce Sterling and Linda Chanow lay out in the ABA report, "In Their Own Words: Experienced Women Lawyers Explain Why They Are Leaving Their Law Firms and the Profession."[42]

There are many reasons why.

Women Lawyers Are Unfairly Treated in the Profession in a Myriad of Ways

Unfairly Not Promoted

As noted above, few women get promoted to partnership. Firms so unfairly disadvantage women seeking partnership that "[m]ale attorneys were *twice as likely* to be hired into equity partner roles as female attorneys,"

---

41. *See* Jennifer Cheeseman Day, *Number of Women Lawyers at Record High But Men Still Highest Earners*, U.S. CENSUS BUREAU (May 8, 2018), https://www.census.gov/library/stories/2018/05/women-lawyers.html.

42. *See* Joyce Sterling and Linda Chanow, *In Their Own Words: Experienced Women Lawyers Explain Why They Are Leaving their Law Firms and the Profession*, AM. BAR. ASS'N (2021), *available at* https://www.americanbar.org/content/dam/aba/administrative/women/intheirownwords-f-4-19-21-final.pdf.

according to the 2021 ABA Model Diversity Survey.[43] No data were found indicating that more men than women seek promotions.[44]

Unfairly Excluded from Inheriting Business

Heidi Gardner reported on how women are excluded from inheriting business in the Harvard study, "On Gender and Origination in the Legal Profession (Perspective)." She found that those departing law firms with books of business—mostly men—were unlikely to bequeath their books to women. Instead, they gave their books of business to other men, and law firms generally do not disrupt this repeating phenomenon, which may be the single biggest barrier to women rising in law firms.[45]

Unfairly Paid

According to 2020 data compiled by Joan C. Williams,[46] director of the Center for WorkLife Law at UC Hastings College of the Law, women partners get paid less than their male counterparts. Women partners are paid approximately 44 percent less, receiving $784,000 per year as compared to male partners, who are paid $1.13 million per year. This amounts to a $346,000 per year partner gender pay penalty. At 6 percent interest over 20 years, the partner gender pay penalty amounts to a loss of *nearly $4 million* ($3,915,098.93) to women partners.

---

43. *See 2021 ABA Model Diversity Survey*, Am. Bar Ass'n (2021), *available at* https://www.americanbar.org/content/dam/aba/administrative/diversity-inclusion-center/2021-md-survey-2nd-edition.pdf.

44. Indeed, it has been the author's experience that attorneys are generally considered for partnership along with those at their firm who graduated from law school in the same year they did.

45. This author could not find any data suggesting that more men seek to inherit business than women. Rather, the data show that those with the books of business are deciding to whom to pass on their books, and they are choosing to give their books primarily to men.

46. *See* Joan C. Williams, *Male Partners Get Paid More Than Female Partners—Lots More*, Bloomberg L. (June, 9, 2022), https://news.bloomberglaw.com/business-and-practice/male-partners-get-paid-more-than-female-partners-lots-more.

There is a general counsel gender pay penalty as well. In its 2021 study,[47] Zippia reported that women general counsel were paid 95 percent of what men were paid, as opposed to all they earned, which should have been the same dollar for dollar pay as men.

We cannot blame the women for the pay disparity. "In repeated studies, the social cost of negotiating for higher pay has been found to be greater for women than it is for men."[48] In other words, while people are willing to work with men who negotiate for higher pay, people don't want to work with women who do.[49]

Thus, while it is true that more men than women seek higher pay, the data are clear that when women seek higher pay, they are penalized for doing so, at times to the point of having their job offers revoked, whereas men are not penalized for seeking higher pay.[50]

Women Suffer a Motherhood Penalty, Whereas Men Get a Fatherhood Bonus

The argument that women choose to have families rather than advance in their professions is false. Men also choose to have families. However, studies show that only women are *penalized* for having children. Professor Joya Misra and doctoral student Eunjung Jee, in the University of Massachusetts Amherst School of Public Policy and Departments of Sociology and Economics, and Marta Murray-Close, a researcher with the U.S. Census Bureau, researched motherhood penalties in the United States from 1986 to 2014 and found that during that time period, the workforce changed from 47 percent women (meaning a nearly equal number of men and women) to 70 percent women (meaning women made up over two-thirds of the workforce). In addition, women also had

---

47. *See General Counsel Overview*, Zippia, https://www.zippia.com/general-counsel-jobs/demographics.

48. *See* Hannah Riley Bowles, *Why Women Don't Negotiate Their Job Offers*, Harv. Bus. Rev. (June 19, 2014).

49. *Id. See also* Maria Konnikova, *Lean Out: The Dangers for Women Who Negotiate*, The New Yorker (June 10, 2014), https://www.newyorker.com/science/maria-konnikova/lean-out-the-dangers-for-women-who-negotiate, which discusses this phenomenon, and the studies examining it, at length.

50. Konnikova, *supra* note 49.

higher levels of education, accounting for the majority of the college population. While one would think that the pay penalty women must accept for having children would have decreased during this time period, their study revealed just the *reverse*. Even among workers with the same level of education and work experience, the motherhood wage gap remained unchanged during this nearly 30-year period. On average, a mother with one child in the United States is now paid 14 percent less than a woman with no children, a gap that *increased 6 percent* during this time period (from 8 percent). Further, the motherhood penalty in pay only dips a percentage point as women have another child, and then it *increases* as they have more children. Mothers of two are paid on average 13 percent less than childless women, and, on average, mothers of three or more children are paid 18 percent less than childless women.[51]

While women face the motherhood penalty when they have children, men get fatherhood *bonuses* when they have children. Men with children are more likely to be hired than men without children, and men tend to be paid *more* after they have children. "These differences persist even after controlling for factors like the hours people work, the types of jobs they choose and the salaries of their spouses. So the disparity is not because mothers actually become less productive employees and fathers work harder when they become parents—but because employers expect them to."[52]

Michelle Budig, a sociology professor at the University of Massachusetts, Amherst, found from reviewing the data that high-income men (think male partners in law firms) get the biggest fatherhood bonuses. In fact, on average, men's earnings *increased more than 6 percent* when they had children (as long as they lived with them), even after controlling for factors such as experience, education, hours worked, and spousal incomes.[53]

---

51. *See* Maureen Turner, *Misra and Colleagues Find Workplace "Motherhood Penalty" Persists in New Study*, U. MASS. AMHERST (Mar. 26, 2018), https://www.umass.edu/spp/news/misra-and-colleagues-find-workplace-%E2%80%9Cmotherhood-penalty%E2%80%9D-persists-new-study.

52. *See* Claire Cain Miller, *The Motherhood Penalty vs. the Fatherhood Bonus*, N.Y. TIMES (Sept. 6, 2014), https://www.nytimes.com/2014/09/07/upshot/a-child-helps-your-career-if-youre-a-man.html.

53. *Id.*

Unfairly Billed at Lower Rates

Not only are women bequeathed less business from exiting lawyers, paid less, and promoted less, they also are billed at lower hourly rates than men, according to Sky Analytics' study of $3.4 billion in legal spending. So at the end of any given year, women lawyers are credited for bringing in fewer dollars than men, which may in turn result in a vicious cycle of their being paid less than men because, as a result of the factors above, they generated less revenue than their male counterparts did.

Unfairly Assigned Less Desirable Assignments and More Housework and Interrupted More

Men are given more plum assignments than women lawyers. According to a survey of lawyers cited by Kim Elsesser in her piece, "Female Lawyers Face Widespread Gender Bias, According to New Study,"[54] women are more likely than men to have to perform more office "housekeeping," to have less access to plum job assignments, and are more likely to be interrupted.

The unfair manner in which women are treated is so widespread that even women judges are mistreated. In fact, Tonja Jacobi and Dylan Schweers's empirical study,[55] reported in the *Harvard Business Review*, found that even on the United States Supreme Court, the female justices get interrupted more than the male justices.

Sexually Harassed and/or Assaulted

Additionally, some women lawyers are sexually harassed and/or assaulted. As set out in the Women Lawyers on Guard's survey, "Still Broken: Sexual

---

54. See Kim Elesser, *Female Lawyers Face Widespread Gender Bias, According to New Study*, FORBES (Oct. 1, 2018), https://www.forbes.com/sites/kimelsesser/2018/10/01/female-lawyers-face-widespread-gender-bias-according-to-new-study/?sh=796aaeac4b55.

55. See Tonja Jacobi and Dylan Schweers, *Female Supreme Court Justices Are Interrupted More by Male Justices and Advocates*, HARV. BUS. REV. (Apr. 11, 2017), https://hbr.org/2017/04/female-supreme-court-justices-are-interrupted-more-by-male-justices-and-advocates#:~:text=Our%20new%20empirical%20study%20shows,as%20often%20as%20vice%20versa.

Misconduct and Harassment in the Legal Profession"[56] (the Survey), a "broad spectrum of sexual misconduct and harassing behaviors—from criminal to civilly actionable to simply unconscionable—continue to plague all walks of the legal profession." However, most harassers "face few to no negative consequences (financial or otherwise)."

Conclusion: We Need to Change Our Ways to Retain Our Talent

In short, by the time women leave the profession, they have often suffered a career death by a thousand cuts,[57] and, finally, they choose to go. If all things were equal, we'd expect women to stay in the profession to the same degree men do. In short, the rate of attrition of women in the legal profession is a reflection of their lack of inclusion within it. More women would continue to practice law, including those who are mothers (like this author), if they were treated more fairly and equally in the profession.[58]

The data suggest that if women were more equally treated, we would have more women on our federal and state appellate benches, more female general counsel, more women law firm partners, and more women serving as deans in law schools. For instance, law firms should promote women equally and pay women equally. Law firms also should ensure that women equally share in business inheritance, are billed out at equal rates as their male counterparts, and are given an equal share of plum assignments. Law firms also should ensure that men are given an equal share of firm housekeeping duties and that women are not interrupted more than men are. Furthermore, systems need to be put in place to make sexual harassers and assaulters pay such a steep price for their behavior that they do not continue to commit these offenses.

---

56. *See Still Broken: Sexual Harassment and Misconduct in the Legal Profession*, WOMEN LAWYERS ON GUARD (2020), https://womenlawyersonguard.org/still-broken.

57. *See* Leopard Solutions, *Why Are Women Lawyers Leaving the Legal Industry?*, JD SUPRA (Mar. 9, 2022), https://www.jdsupra.com/legalnews/why-are-women-lawyers-leaving-the-legal-3000987/#:~:text=Lack%20of%20promotion%20opportunities%2C%20the,women%20are%20leaving%20the%20law, and Derald Wing Sue, *Microagressions: Death by a Thousand Cuts*, SCIENTIFIC AM. (Mar. 30, 2021), https://www.scientificamerican.com/article/microaggressions-death-by-a-thousand-cuts.

58. *Id.*

Women represent only 37 percent of the practicing lawyers in the United States, whereas we should represent at least 50 percent of practicing lawyers. This tells us that *we lose almost 13 percent of all women lawyers.* Having so few women at the top of the profession stifles our voices and results in women's further disenfranchisement in the profession.

The loss of 13 percent of women lawyers from the over 50 percent of lawyers in which we start—in other words, the loss of over one in every five women lawyers—represents a huge loss of talent. With the departing lawyers goes their institutional knowledge, the mentorship and sponsorship they have given, and all the wisdom and training they have gained throughout their practice.

The numbers are a sobering reflection of a profession to which we've dedicated our professional lives. At some point, we must start to get our arms around the enormous loss we are suffering and begin addressing the reasons women leave the legal profession, so that more women will stay in it.

Sheryl L. Axelrod

Career

President and CEO, The Axelrod Firm, PC

Education

- JD, Temple University Beasley School of Law
- BA, *cum laude*, Brandeis University
- Community College of Philadelphia, Certificate of Entrepreneurship, Goldman Sachs 10,000 Small Businesses Program

Best Advice

Carve out a path outside of the old boys' network.

Do everything they say—work hard, study the rules, and so on—but get out there and build relationships. You will become successful in proportion to the number of people who care about you, think highly of you, believe in you, and want to see you succeed; so take the time to sit down and talk with other people. Invest in building relationships. Also, be strategic. Think about business development from the beginning of your career and come up with a plan to attract clients that fit your personality.

Think about launching a firm. Many women found firms as a last resort. Instead, consider planning for it.

If you really want to go far, have a vision, clearly define it, and pursue it. Law firms generally do a terrible job of defining their vision. Being the best, most reputable, the brightest, and the like, isn't a vision. When have you achieved that vision? How far are your competitors from reaching it? Come up with a vision that distinguishes who you are (brand yourself) and make that vision concrete.

Personal

Sheryl L. Axelrod is passionate about diversity, equity, and inclusion. She has a 4-year-old daughter, is one of eight kids, speaks Spanish, is addicted to pickleball, and plays regularly (generally, around 3 hours at a time), and dances salsa and bachata.

For More Information

https://theaxelrodfirm.com/sheryl-l-axelrod

Getting Out of the Box
(No Matter How We Got In)

By Tara N. Cho

When asked to define what equality means to me and what strategies I employed to overcome obstacles to achieving it, I have to start with my past and my upbringing. Reflecting back, I recall that my childhood was full of contradictions in philosophy, creating tensions that pulled me in opposite directions. I was raised by my father, a first-generation Korean immigrant, and my mother, an American raised on a farm in rural Tennessee.

We were one of the only Asian families in the small Tennessee town where I grew up. At that time, my parents stressed the importance of assimilating into the community and culture as much as possible. But they also engrained in us not to be "followers" and to have the confidence to forge our own paths. Again, conflicting tensions. In college, I transferred schools midsemester, so integration was more challenging as cliques had already formed. In addition, I was older than many of my classmates, and as was typical for me, I felt like an outsider. I retreated within myself and again attempted to assimilate and go unnoticed.

Fast forward to law school and those tensions became stronger once again. This time, I was living in Boston, competing in the law school race to "win" the best summer clerkship, class rank, or prospect of a future. I knew I wouldn't be number one in the class, but I also knew I was miserable holding myself back throughout college. I was determined not to repeat that mistake: finally, I was no longer among a small number of Asian Americans, and the LGBTQIA+ community was the largest I had ever seen. By completely embracing myself, uninhibited, and without self-limitations, I not only enjoyed law school but succeeded there. Yet, I still felt out of place. In law school I experienced a different version of discrimination and classism than the more overt encounters I had learned to navigate as an Asian American lesbian in a small, southern town. No, not all Bostonians fit these labels; nor do all Southerners. I love my hometown and the people and community where I was raised; I also enjoyed living in Boston more than any other city I have lived in to date. The common denominator skewing my experiences across states, decades, jobs, and interactions is me.

It has taken years to realize that the constant inclination to fit the model minority role is a taxing way to go through life, particularly when one is working in a cutthroat profession. For example, fresh out of law school in the midst of the Great Recession, having just moved to a new state, I found myself staring across the desk of an older, male attorney. He had already given clear signals of my nonexistent prospects of being selected for the job, but he proceeded with the interview and asked me which of the North Carolina college teams I cheered for. After hearing my answer, he said, "Well little lady, that may be the best response you've given this whole interview." [insert awkward pause here . . .] Through the course of one interview, I felt more out of place than I had in most of my adult life: *no, I didn't attend a North Carolina law school; no, I am not from North Carolina; no, I do not have generations of family in North Carolina; and no, I do not feel comfortable that you would accept my explanation that my brilliant wife was accepted to the number one Physician Assistant master's program in the country, and that led me to relocate to this state.*

That was a tough year, as I saw top-ranked classmates and friends across top-tier law schools I perceived as much worthier than mine have clerkships and first-year associate jobs deferred or stripped away altogether due to the recession. I constantly asked myself: How will I possibly get a job if this is happening to the really smart and successful graduates? This interview and my interaction with this man stuck with me, and I can still recall his face and demeanor toward me to this day. It is the driving force I have used to motivate myself throughout my career and to strive to effect change in the legal profession.

I have spoken with many diverse attorneys who also tend to underestimate themselves, who are always deferential, and who fight the inner battle of imposter syndrome on a daily basis. Searching for that sense of belonging and acceptance, those constant issues of identity surface again and again for me and others as well. I want to be part of this amazing bar of Asian American and Pacific Islander attorneys, but that little voice questions whether being half-Korean is sufficient. I want to share aspects of my family life with those around me, but what about clients who may not accept me? I can do this work and do it well, but how can I win the work if I am terrible at golf, so I don't join the pitch team. I can't apply for that position; I probably don't qualify or won't have a shot. Thank goodness my hair is graying, so I won't be mistaken for a junior assistant.

It sounds cliché to say that you are your own worst enemy, but it is absolutely true that you will never win the race if you eliminate yourself.

Despite all that, I found a way to quiet those voices, at least for short periods of time, to work my way to being the chair of a specialty practice at an AmLaw 100, transatlantic law firm. My parents' teachings to never give up and to give your best to all you do quashed (at least periodically) my inclination to assimilate, fit in, find acceptance, and derive the value of my contributions only from those around me.

So, how can the voices of self-doubt be silenced? For me, it is one day at a time. I have also slowly learned to reprioritize my professional values and to recognize what I want and need in my career. As attorneys, we spend a tremendous amount of time solving problems and working, many of us spending time with colleagues as much or more than the hours we spend with our own families. I have learned that I am the most effective and successful attorney I can be when I do not try to assimilate. When I bring my "whole self" to work and confidently conduct myself, I thrive. This is also when I am the happiest; being a chameleon is quite exhausting and occupies time that could be better spent on delivering quality work and forming real and meaningful relationships. Posing as something you are not or inhibiting yourself can become mentally oppressive and cause you to lose your sense of self along the way—or it creates unhealthy levels of resentment. Instead, embodying and bringing your authentic self to the situation (for this audience, practicing law) can help ground you, avoiding those self-imposed barriers of reading other people's minds and adapting and molding yourself to something that isn't all of you.

Is it easy to find a professional setting where you feel comfortable to be fully yourself? For many people, the answer is no, it is not easy—particularly when you are "different" from the majority in some manner. Finding an organization that truly fosters diversity and inclusion and that rewards and values individual contributions in an equitable manner surely sounds like a fairytale, but it shouldn't be, nor should we feel we must take on the responsibility of diversity, equity, and inclusion in our companies and organizations. This is the burden of leadership and the pathway to fostering growth within the organization where you dedicate so much of your precious time. A toxic work environment spreads negativity like wildfire, but the opposite is also true. Caring and investing in those around you, your organization, and your community can be equally infectious.

Many of the tools I use to overcome prejudice, self-doubt, fear, and other obstacles are implements I didn't even know I had accumulated along my journey, but in retrospect, I would definitely recommend:

- *Know your value.* Hone your skills and think about what types of work you most enjoy. Plenty of research indicates that people do better at things they enjoy and that they enjoy the things they are good at. It takes time to understand what you bring to the table, but it is essential to be an expert in your own proficiencies. Similarly, understanding your weak spots eventually lends itself to good leadership and project management as you start to identify opportunities to leverage the expertise of others. Do not undersell your expertise or contributions, because if you do, those around you will certainly discount you in the same manner.
- *Find a mentor; be a mentor.* Seek out a mentor. Mentorship comes in many different guises and can mean finding inspiration in a role model or engaging in regular discussions within a more formalized mentorship relationship. Do not feel limited to just one either; many attorneys rely on a personal board of directors for mentorship. Mentors can be found within your profession or not, they can include family members and friends, and age is not a determinant. The critical factor is that you trust these individuals and value their wisdom and advice, and in turn, you know they will be upfront and honest with you—the good, the bad, and the ugly—as you need it all. On the flip side, make time to mentor others, which helps those around you but also helps you to continue to grow and learn, avoiding stagnation or apathy.
- *Get an advocate.* An advocate is different from a mentor or ally. An advocate has your best interests in mind but often has position, power, or pure will to help you on your path. I have been fortunate to have had several strong, female advocates (some of whom also serve as mentors) throughout my career. Advocacy can also come from persons who are not in positions of power, but who support you from other angles and stand up for what is right.

Identifying an advocate can be a daunting task. Look for good leadership and people management; this usually means strong advocates are around you. Like all of these recommendations, there are two sides to this coin; it can be quite telling when a leader or your own management is unwilling to advocate for you or, even worse, takes steps to limit or stifle your growth. Take stock of your role and responsibilities and the future you envision for yourself. Determine whether there are roadblocks or facilitators in your path, or worse, no succession plan at all. An advocate or good leader is usually as excited, if not more excited, as you are, for your shining moments.

- *Be the change.* These thoughts are not original, but it is important to lead by example, even if it means having to "fake it 'til you make it." Nothing debases an effort for equality faster than speaking without action, complaining without leadership, or remaining silent in the face of wrongdoing. Whether asserting yourself or advocating for others, finding the courage to do what is right is necessary to bring change. If no one raises a hand, there will never be diversity of thought or growth.
- *Never give up.* Life is not meant to be a battlefield, nor is your career meant to be one. By no means should anyone have to endure an endless struggle in a toxic situation. However, we must never give up on ourselves. We must not accept less than what we deserve. Not long after my father passed away, a grief counselor told me I should quit my job. With absolute certainty, she had determined that my work situation was an unhealthy one and that I should quit. For most of the attorneys I know, that would be a preposterous idea in any circumstance: who can just quit their job because it is making them unhappy? Never giving up does not always mean persisting and resisting the obstacles before us; it can also mean taking steps to change our circumstances, either by speaking up to assert ourselves or by believing in ourselves enough to take a big scary leap, to move away from the safety of known discontent to an unknown potential of something else.

Most of what I have described is not new information, and, unfortunately, my experiences and challenges are not unique. But this also means that no matter the differences among us, none of us is alone in challenges, desire, and willingness to overcome these obstacles. My father came to the United States when he was 18, spoke broken English, and worked his way to integrate into his new home country; to him, equality meant being treated the same as his American counterparts. He was excited the first time his Vanderbilt professor made him submit his exam within the same time period as the other English-speaking students, while the international students continued working. While I understand his viewpoint, particularly in the 1960s, my version of equality is different from his: a playing field that we must in part level ourselves. There are plenty of people to hold us back, to feed us negativity, people who remain in implicit and explicit bias. This is why it is so important to believe in ourselves, to have faith in our own abilities, and to never give up the fight against those internal voices of doubt. These things are easier said than done, and no, it is not our job to change the world or convince others that baseless discrimination is irrational and the purest form of oppression, which acts to the detriment of any organization. But we can and must lead by example and have the courage not to hold ourselves back. My equality means not letting others put me in a box, but also not enclosing myself in a box either. I must be able to be my true self and not defined or even qualified by my ethnicity, gender, sexuality, or, dare I say even the North Carolina collegiate team I cheer on—#goduke.

Tara N. Cho

Career
Partner, Chair of Privacy and Cybersecurity Team, Womble Bond Dickinson (U.S.) LLP

Education
- JD, Health Law, New England School of Law
- BA, English, Rhodes College

Best Advice
Be humble but not submissive, persistent but not blindly stubborn, sincere to others and true to yourself, and intentional but not passive.

Personal
Outside of work, Tara N. Cho treasures every moment with her family.

For More Information
https://www.womblebonddickinson.com/us/people/tara-n-cho
https://www.linkedin.com/in/tara-cho

Mandatory Magic: Being Black and a Woman in Big Law

By Yendelela Neely Holston

The hashtag "Black Girl Magic" has been around since the early 2010s, but it hit particular prominence in 2020. "Stacey Abrams turns Georgia Blue. #BlackGirlMagic." "Kamala Harris becomes Vice President. #BlackGirlMagic." While often used to celebrate accomplishments, the phrase "Black Girl Magic" also

"In the end anti-black, anti-female, and all forms of discrimination are equivalent to the same thing: anti-humanism."

—Shirley Chisholm

recognizes that Black women and girls do not have the luxury of simply being ordinary. This reality is a constant reminder of two aspects of our identity—Black and woman—that require us to make extraordinary efforts every day. We must be magical to be noticed, acknowledged, and occasionally appreciated.

My most vivid memory of the necessity of magic is from my senior year of high school. I have always been pretty good with numbers. Thus, I decided to take Advanced Placement Calculus AB as a senior, with little regard for how it might impact my grade point average. Unfortunately, I spent the first semester struggling. Something about calculus just did not click with me—until one night it did. The next morning, I woke up knowing how to do the problems to which I went to sleep not knowing the answers to. I was ecstatic. Two weeks later, I got a chance to show my growth on a test. And I scored 100! I was so excited that as soon as I got home from school, I ran to show my father. My father, the teacher of many hard life lessons, carefully reviewed my test without expression. Once he looked over the whole thing, he pointed out that I had missed two questions. Still happy with my grade, I said "Yeah I know, but I made 100." To which he replied, "But it looks like there were more than 100 points available." "Right. I got the extra credit questions so I made 100," I added. And that's when my father closed his eyes gently and told me "You are smart. But you don't get to just be smart. You have to be better than everyone around you or you won't get a shot. It is unfair, but it is your reality.

You can't be good. You must be great." It was in that conversation that I learned I must be magical; and I have spoken with enough other Black women to know that I am not the only one to have received a message like this: Black girl magic is mandatory for success.

Contrary to the popular myth and rhetoric surrounding affirmative action, Black women are rarely, if ever, "given" anything. We have to work harder and be smarter even to reach a point where we are being evaluated against white men, white women, Black men, and so on. The fact that there had never been a Black woman justice of the United States Supreme Court until 2022 was not due to a lack of qualified professionals. Indeed, the list of Black women who were under consideration to replace Justice Breyer included a federal appellate judge, a federal district court judge, a state supreme court justice with significant experience before the U.S. Supreme Court, and the former head of the NAACP Legal Defense and Education Fund, an organization founded by former Supreme Court Justice Thurgood Marshall. Nonetheless, President Biden's announcement in January 2022 that his Supreme Court nominee would be a Black woman was met with substantial backlash. For example, then-incoming Georgetown University Law Center executive director Iyla Shapiro, whom Georgetown University Law Center hired to shape the minds of future lawyers, tweeted that "we'll get [sic] lesser Black woman" and that the nominee "will always have an asterisk attached." While Shapiro may have been the person crass enough to tweet it, he was not the only person who thought it. While Justice Ketanji Brown Jackson has proven to be everything but a "lesser" jurist since she joined the High Court, the sentiment undergirding Shapiro's comments persists, infecting law firms and influencing the lives of Black women lawyers daily. Shapiro's tweets are just a verbal articulation of a silent sentiment that has long permeated, and continues to permeate, our profession: Black women are "lesser."

Black women in law firms are often noted as lacking "intellectual horsepower." This term has no real meaning because when pressed, people can rarely provide a definition for it, let alone give concrete examples of it. "Intellectual horsepower" has essentially become code for the supposition that there is no way this person (a Black woman) can meet our standards, so she must lack something. All of our hiring checks and balances must have failed. She must have lied. Obviously, she was hired because we need a Black woman attorney for our numbers. She cannot actually deserve to be here. In addition to shaping how Black women are perceived by the people with whom they work, this sentiment and its associated gaslighting can cause Black women attorneys to doubt themselves, which in turn leads to mistakes that fuel the prophecy. I, like many, encountered this phenomenon early in my career.

I graduated undergrad *magna cum laude*, I graduated *cum laude* from Duke University School of Law with a 3.6 GPA, and as a 1L summer associate for my firm, I authored a winning motion to dismiss, including developing the theory upon which the motion was based. Nonetheless, when I started my career as a first-year associate at the firm, many of the partners on my team treated me as though I lacked "intellectual horsepower." Approximately one month after I started working, a white male partner asked me to prepare a declaration for a witness in one of his cases. I had never prepared a declaration. As a result, I looked in the firm's document management system for several examples of declarations that had been prepared in that partner's cases in the past. I studied them all carefully and prepared a declaration consistent with his previous work. Once I finished the declaration, I took it to the partner, who glanced at it (without reading it) and asked, "Does it contain the necessary federal language?" I responded, "I do not know what 'federal language you are referring to,' but it contains the standard language that I saw in your other declarations." The partner stood up and marched me down the hall to the office of a third-year white woman associate. He handed her my declaration and asked if it contained the "federal language," and the woman said it did not. They both chuckled and sent me on my way to "fix" the declaration. Once I returned to my office, I googled "federal language for declarations" and discovered 28 U.S. § 1746, which provides that declarations must contain the following:

> "I declare (or certify, verify, or state) under penalty of perjury under the laws of the United States of America that the foregoing is true and correct. Executed on (date). (Signature)."

That was it. Just one sentence. One sentence that was in fact already included in the declaration that I had drafted and that had been publicly ridiculed. It was my time to march. I marched back into the partner's office. I handed him my declaration and a copy of 28 U.S. § 1746, and said,

"I am sorry. What 'federal language' am I missing?" As I left his office he grumbled, "Smartass." Internally, I beamed and thought, "Yes, I am smart, and you are not going to ever make me question that or my capacity."

This anecdote is one of many experiences I have had and stories I have been told showing the "intellectual horsepower" gaslighting that Black women confront daily. For example, 3 years ago, a junior Black woman associate came to me with tears of frustration after a similar incident. The associate had been tasked with assessing evidence for an upcoming hearing. In so doing, she located a local rule that would preclude the introduction of a particularly troublesome piece of evidence. She rushed to tell the white male partner who had given her the assignment. When she entered his office, he did not look up from his computer or make eye contact with her. She nonetheless explained her theory and provided him the procedural manual, which he read in silence. After reading, he called a first-year white male associate to his office to essentially ask that attorney's opinion on the fourth-year Black woman attorney's theory. Specifically, he handed the procedural manual to the white male associate and said, "You are smart. What do you make of this rule?" The white male associate articulated the same conclusion that the Black woman associate had provided, and the partner responded to the white man, "Awesome. So glad we have you on our team." The partner then turned to the Black woman, making eye contact with her for the first time, and told her to write up her analysis and send it to the first-year for his review. The Black woman told me that this experience made her feel like she was in the twilight zone. It also made her realize that she could not succeed at that firm; she began looking for a new job the next day. Unfortunately, her experience is not anomalous, remarkable, or particularly egregious in the grand scheme of the experiences that Black women face in Big Law daily.

While I refer to the experience in Big Law as "intellectual horsepower" gaslighting, there is a term for the combination of racism and sexism that Black women encounter broadly. "Misogynoir" refers to the unique discrimination that Black women face. Racism is the way that anti-Black animus appears in and impacts the lives of Black people. Sexism is the prejudice, discrimination, and stereotyping based on sex that generally works to the detriment of women. Misogynoir recognizes the frequently unacknowledged ways in which the hideous by-product of racism and sexism impacts Black women. Our experience is not entirely like that of Black men, although there is some overlap. And it is not entirely like that of white women, although again there is some overlap. The failure to appreciate misogynoir and the intersectionality of race and gender has led to our interests being largely overlooked by the Black rights and feminist movements, and therefore they have been left unaddressed.

There is a benefit of the doubt that I am routinely denied due to my race and my gender. I, along with other Black women, must continually be magic to remain in the room. The significant underrepresentation of Black women in law firms highlights this. Black women are approximately 13 percent of the U.S. population. The American Bar Association's data on U.S. law schools shows that Black women made up 5 percent of the individuals entering U.S. law schools in the years 2018–2021. According to the National Association for Law Placement's "2022 Report on Diversity in U.S. Law Firms," Black women have been only between 2 and 3 percent of law firm associates over the last decade, with a low of 2.31 percent in 2014 and a high of 3.45 percent in 2022. The numbers only get worse at the partner level. Black women have never reached even 1 percent of partners and currently represent a meager 0.94 percent of partners at U.S. law firms, a percentage less than that of their white, Asian, and Latinx counterparts. At less than 1 percent, a Black woman partner is truly a unicorn, the rarest of magical creatures.

However, our poor representation is not at all due to our ineptitude. The questions surrounding Black women's "intellectual horsepower" fuel doubt that exacerbates imposter syndrome, a phenomenon whereby people (often women) feel like frauds and question whether they are deserving of their accomplishments. This mindset causes some to self-destruct; others simply leave firms (or the legal profession as a whole), wrongly believing they lack what is necessary to succeed. Many other Black women drop out of the practice as a form of self-preservation. "Magical" is an unfair and draining standard to maintain. Constantly having to prove yourself through inordinate feats is emotionally, mentally, and physically taxing. It is also unstainable and unhealthy.

By January of my first year of practice, I was ready to tap-out. I was unwilling to commit to a career where my worth was questioned and where I would continually have to fight to be seen. It was around this time that a junior white woman partner came into my office and asked if I wanted to work with her on a case. When others saw me as "lacking intellectual horsepower," she saw me as a first-year associate with first-year associate knowledge. She staffed me on her case and provided the guidance and oversight that one would typically provide a first-year associate. And when the case went to trial 2 years later, I was her second chair examining, witnesses and arguing motions. She regularly told others that I was smart and capable, which led to my getting more work and more opportunities. More importantly, this partner treated my magic as magic, so she did not expect it or require it. My work with her was a turning point in my career; without it, I am positive I would not be a partner today. Her ability to see me as "Yendelela" the person, and not just as a Black woman, kept me in the profession.

I eventually reached a point at my firm where I finally felt that I had overcome my race and my gender. However, it took a lot of mentorship from other Black women, investment from white women and Black men, sponsorship from white men, and significant amounts of magic to get to that point. While I and the other Black women who make up 0.94 percent of law firm partners have chosen to endure the pressures of mandatory magic, that endurance should not be a requirement. Instead, we as a profession must recognize misogynoir, acknowledge its impact, and commit to creating a profession where Black women do not have to be magical and can just be human.

Yendelela Neely Holston

Career

Partner, Kilpatrick Townsend & Stockton LLP

Education

- JD, *cum laude*, Duke University School of Law (2006)
- BA, *magna cum laude*, Political Science and History, Furman University (2003)

Best Advice

Obstacles are invitations for creative thinking. I do not look at obstacles as roadblocks. Instead, I see them as an opportunity to engage my critical thinking skills to determine another (and often overlooked, better) way to reach my goals.

Personal

Yendelela Neely Holston is a partner with and the Chief Diversity and Inclusion Officer for Kilpatrick Townsend & Stockton, LLP. While Yendelela is a lawyer by trade, she is a cookie artist and social change agent by passion. Nonetheless, her favorite job by far is being a mother and role model to her son. She is proud to raise a man who understands that a woman's place is wherever she wants it to be and whose last Lego creation was an "office building with a mommy at her computer." Yendelela is committed to equity in the profession and equality of access to opportunity for all and continues to fight for both from Atlanta, Georgia.

For More Information

https://kilpatricktownsend.com/en/people/h/holstonyendelelaneely

Defining Ourselves

By Abby R. Rubenfeld

Too often each of us is automatically defined or labeled by other people, including colleagues in the legal system, based on how those people see us through their own eyes, no matter what our political persuasion or on which side of the table we are seated. In my case, for example, I am, among other things, female, Jewish, white, a lesbian, and short. While these characteristics were at times obstacles in some aspects of my life, they also shaped my journey as a civil rights lawyer, family law attorney, and person.

I am frequently reminded of those nuances of each characteristic in how I am treated by other people. Sometimes those people are subtle, often they are covert, and occasionally they seem intentional. I am also an empath, which serves me well most of the time. I cannot be any other way, but at times it makes my life more difficult. I put myself in the place of those who are hurting and who are not treated fairly. I feel their pain, their indignities, their anger, their despair. Even as a young person, I was acutely aware of the injustices and indignities suffered by people who happen not to fit perfectly into our society's "worthy" compartments, those who had been given "less than" labels, and I did not like it one bit.

My maternal grandfather and two of my uncles were lawyers, but that was not the primary factor in my decision to become a lawyer. I knew from a young age I wanted to be a lawyer, likely motivated in large part by knowing that my parents so valued justice and equity, combined with my apparently innate sense of fairness and justice.

My parents were always in agreement with my decision to be an attorney and supported me from the very beginning of my education and going forward. That made a huge difference in my options in terms of jobs. I was privileged in not being forced to take a high-paying corporate job right out of law school so I could pay off education loans. That still affects me today, based on how profoundly it influenced the start of my career. I could not have based my career on social justice, equality, and the issues important to me had my parents not been so supportive in every way.

While I was fortunate to grow up in a loving, supportive, progressive, and financially comfortable family, I learned at an early age that is not the case for many people. Again, I am grateful to my parents because they taught me about justice, equity, and empathy. They were very principled about race discrimination and antisemitism and helped me understand how those things affected me as a white person and as a Jew. They taught me to try to be sensitive to and recognize white privilege and injustice to people of color and those with fewer resources, and to invest the time and energy to challenge such longstanding inequities.

We moved to Florida from upstate New York in 1961 when I was 7 years old, right when integration was starting to be implemented but was far from the norm. Racial segregation and discrimination were still overt in many public establishments, with hateful signs cruelly displayed proudly and defiantly so that no one could miss their meaning. To my childlike amazement, there were still signs on drinking fountains and businesses designating "white only" or "colored." On our drive South, my family discussed how wrong segregation was and decided as a family not to stop or pay at places that were segregated. In addition to talking, we took a stand against it. We decided not to participate in or support discrimination by giving such businesses our money.

Some of my first personal acts of standing up to discrimination were based on the continued race discrimination we witnessed daily. These were small acts of civil disobedience, but they were meaningful to us and our personal sense of justice. When my brother and I went to the summer movies for kids, we learned that the Black kids were required to sit in the balcony, so we decided to sit with them. On public buses, we also learned that all Black people were supposed to sit in the back, where we, simply as kids, wanted to sit—so we sat in the back with the Black people. I became very conscious about those types of discrimination and was eager to help overcome them.

In Florida, schools were still segregated. I guess they still had not heard of that pesky *Brown* decision, which had been decided 7 years earlier. I was, of course, assigned to a white school. I went to segregated schools until high school in 1968—14 years after *Brown* was decided. Maybe they walked the decision to Florida.

My early encounters with discrimination did not stop at race though. In junior high, when privileged kids who lived on the water like me had boats they could use without a driver's license, my friends took me to a really nice tennis club that you could go to by boat and then go to the cool snack bar. I came home really, really excited and told my parents we should join the club – after which my mom gently sat me down and explained that our family could not join because we were Jewish. I was shocked and in disbelief. I did not understand why being Jewish would have anything whatsoever to do with joining a tennis club.

In addition, at that time, the Supreme Court decision prohibiting prayer in school was not observed in Florida, at least not in the school I attended. I remember being sent out of the classroom while the other (Christian) kids prayed. It was embarrassing, and I did not understand why I was being singled out. At that young age, I had already personally felt the sting and indignities of discrimination and have never forgotten it.

As an adult, I identify as Jewish and am proud of it, but I am Jewish in name only. I do not go to synagogue, am not observant, and do not know Hebrew. Nonetheless, I am treated in life and in the judicial system like anyone else who is Jewish. I know that if they again come for Jews as the Nazis did, I will be among those taken. That is another reason I have devoted my career to fighting injustice.

In my late teens and early twenties, I struggled with my sexual orientation as a lesbian, another label causing discrimination and persecution. Deep down, I think I knew who I was, but I was also aware of the stigma associated with the words that on some level I knew applied to me.

My family generally allowed me to be whomever I wanted to be, although when I was young, my mom tried to push me into traditionally girly things, like saving all her dolls for me. I did not like them and, to her great disappointment, rolled her life-size ones down a hill. She also made me take ballet. I wore overalls over the stupid outfit and then got myself kicked out. And she made me get my hair all done up for yearly pictures. Fortunately, however, I was never made to think that the goal in life was to get married (to a man) and have kids. Ironically, I am married now (to a woman) and have two wonderful children and a stepchild.

My parents knew I always wanted to be a lawyer and were supportive. I also had political aspirations, but I feared there was a hitch in my plan. I was aware, as was practically everyone, of the ridicule and vitriol aimed at gay people at the time. Gay people were "less than," objects of derision, and, according to some Christians, "an abomination." I ended up struggling intensely during college because I worried that I might be a lesbian, which, in my mind, did not fit in my blueprint for my future. That was so silly in retrospect, but hindsight is definitely 20/20. I did not start seriously thinking about my possibly being a lesbian until the early 1970s while I was still in college.

I figured there were at least three reasons I had to accept my sexual orientation. One was because someone close to me came out as gay and it made me think about myself, which I initially resisted. Was I or wasn't I? I needed to know one way or another for my own peace of mind.

The second reason was that being gay did not fit into my plans for a political future. I had it all planned out. I would run for Congress when I became 25, for the Senate when I reached 30, and for president when I became 35. However, being a lesbian in 1971 was considered a fatal flaw in a potential political candidate at even a local position, let alone POTUS. My being a lesbian would end all that, at least in my mind at the time. After years of grappling with my plan, however, I finally realized how miserable I was personally and that going into politics was probably not my thing anyway. What if I won and had to serve with the many bona fide jerks already in politics?

The third reason I had to figure out my sexual orientation was that I was being bombarded by people around me who had already assumed I was a lesbian. My best friend and I were both going through the same thing: our best friends from high school had come out as gay, and everyone around us assumed we were too. Reflexively and defensively, we both resisted, but finally we both happily accepted the truth. I have never looked back and have absolutely no regrets.

Not surprisingly, for me as a woman, a lesbian, and a Jew, the primary impetus for my work as an attorney is that I am either blessed, or cursed, with a strong loathing of injustice, especially injustice when my characteristics are the target. Equally motivating, as hokey as it sounds, I continue to feel the need to help people less fortunate than me, who did not grow up with all the privilege that I did. I feel compelled to try to correct wrongs I see around me—people losing their children just because they are gay; people being abused by police just because they are not white; people being denied rights others have because they are poor or disabled or a member of any other disfavored group. The way much of the world is accepting now in terms of allowing or ignoring or even promoting overt discrimination is disheartening, but it also makes me even more motivated to do something about it.

I have to admit that I try my best to be relentless in the face of challenges and obstacles, which has served me well in my personal life as well as in my career. For instance, I did not let being only five feet tall prevent me from lettering at Princeton in rowing and basketball, two tall-person sports. By sheer dint of will and hard work, and because there were not many women at Princeton in those early days of coeducation, I hold the title of being the shortest person ever to letter in basketball in Princeton history—a record that will likely never be broken! It was good practice for later facing legal challenges that were seemingly out of my reach.

The legacies and "good trouble" created by my heroes, John Lewis and Barbara Jordan, inspire me on many levels. They hit injustice and prejudice brick walls again and again and yet never took "no" for an answer. They stayed the course and made a positive difference in the lives of so many people who might otherwise have suffered because of discrimination and bigotry within the judicial system. I, too, try to follow their example and be relentless, staying the course when necessary, never giving up.

Working within our legal and judicial systems that are too frequently tainted by prejudices and reliance on inaccurate and damaging stereotypes remains a challenge for clients and me alike. Those obstacles are too often not covert or even subtle, even in this day and age. Such attitudes continue to be displayed openly in various courtrooms across America. Regrettably, there are still judges who treat women litigants and women attorneys differently from males. They are often sexist, dismissive, or condescending. Some are unaware of their disrespect; others are deliberate. We women know which ones are which.

One example from when I was a young attorney was a court of appeals judge calling me "little lady" when I asked to reserve time for rebuttal. Somehow, I knew to thank him rather than tell him how incredibly inappropriate and sexist his comment was. It was in my client's best interest as well as mine to let it slide, so I let it slide, but I did not forget it.

Another time, I had a summer job as a law clerk in Nashville after my second year in law school. It was at an entity with seven law clerks. The summer went great; I worked on a project with another clerk that resulted in the first publication on domestic violence in Davidson County history. The next year, the entity hired six of us seven law clerks for full-time attorney jobs. The only one left out was me. They hired the woman with whom I did the project. They hired other Jewish attorneys and other women. The only person they did not hire, without giving any reason, was the gay one. Again, the reason I was not chosen was obviously unfair and seemed to have nothing to do with my performance or abilities.

As an out lesbian who often represents LGBTQIA+ and other marginalized clients, I have seen that the legal system is frequently not fair and not applied impartially or equally to marginalized people. I have become accustomed to slights and indignities given for whatever reason and I usually ignore them, but as an empath and fighter for the underdog, working within systems that have arbitrary and sometimes incredibly unfair rules for my clients is heartbreaking and infuriating. Seeing people unjustly lose something of great importance in their life—sometimes including their freedom or custody of their children—simply because of their color, sex, sexual orientation, economic status, or religion makes me even more determined to fight the good fight, even if we lose. At least those on the wrong side of decency will know they were in for a fight.

Or at least most of the time they will know they were in for a fight. Again, when I was a young attorney in 1979 or the early 1980s, I was in chambers with the other attorney on a divorce case that had settled. We had explained the settlement to the judge, who was a prominent lawyer sitting as a special judge. My client, the father, was gay. I had lucked out, and the lawyer on the other side was an ACLU type and did not use the fact of my client's being gay against him. Once the judge approved the divorce agreement, the other lawyer and I decided to ask him if it would have mattered to him if he had known my client was gay. The judge sat back in his chair, put his hands behind his head, put his feet up on the desk, and said, "It would not have changed my ruling, but I hate those people. I think they all should be lined up against the wall and shot." That was terrifying to me as a young lawyer. I have never forgotten that an experienced, well-respected lawyer in Nashville, Tennessee, thought it was okay to say something like that in the late twentieth century.

The hard-fought victories, though invigorating and satisfying, are not the only things that keep me going in the face of such a steep mountain to climb. Of course, having had the opportunity to help achieve marriage equality nationally and overturning the Tennessee sodomy law were very gratifying. However, the one-on-one cases such as protecting custody for a lesbian mom or for someone who made a mistake but then made up for it, or winning and protecting a parent's rights to their children, are all hugely satisfying victories. My hope, my goal, is to make a positive difference in the lives of individual people. I go home every day knowing I helped lift the legal burden in someone's life—and doing that is why I became a lawyer.

As I embark on my 44th year of practicing law, the losses, the inexplicable injustices also compel me to keep fighting the good fight. Those losses gnaw at me still.

My clients are the reason I work almost all the time. When people ask about my work-life balance, I laugh. Not that it's healthy or that I advise others to be a workaholic, but I am driven by what I hope to achieve to help make my clients' lives better. I am disciplined about work, focused when I must be, and not satisfied until I have done everything I believe is within my power to do for them at that moment. Accordingly, I try to be attentive to details, compassionate, focused, sensitive, understanding, accurate, and forceful when necessary. And I don't accept "no" very often.

My legacy? I hope the victories I obtained or helped obtain remain as victories. It is frightening to see how our current Supreme Court overturns established and popular precedents. The slippery slope of *Dobbs* could potentially undo decades of our work and progress on LGBT rights, as well as reproductive and other women's rights. I hope not—but I am also committed to helping prevent that.

For what it's worth, my advice to young LGBT/women/Jewish attorneys to help them navigate the profession is to be yourself. Don't change because white, straight, older, Christian men think you should be something that you are not. Be yourself. And be diligent. Good things come to people who work for it. Pay attention to details, know the law, be open to other ideas and other ways to look at the world. And never accept that you are any less than anyone, including the white, straight, older Christian men who dominate our profession.

Abby R. Rubenfeld

Career

Senior Partner, Lawyer, Rubenfeld Law Office, PC

Education

- JD, Boston University School of Law (1979)
- AB, Princeton University

Best Advice

Be yourself and be persistent. We can be the change we need.

Personal

Abby R. Rubenfeld has been a lawyer for 44 years, married 14 years, has two daughters and one stepdaughter, is a Tennessee Titans fan, and is the shortest person in the history of Princeton University to letter in basketball—a record that will never be broken.

For More Information

https://cle.tba.org/faculty/profile/5798
http://www.rubenfeldlaw.com

Inclusion of Women and Diverse Men at the Highest Levels Holds Incredible Potential for All of Us

By Bruce A. McMullen

When we look at organizations, particularly law firms and corporations, regardless of how structured or formal they are, they are made up of humans. This means they operate through the prism of the exposures, emotions, and experiences of that firm's collective body. And, when you look at the highest level of these organizations, that prism through which the decision makers look is even more narrow.

Intentional or unintentional, opportunities are given to those whom the decision makers can relate to and understand. The decision makers recognize the potential and can look past minor flaws because the unconscious reality is that they see themselves in that person. Simply put, the decision makers can envision certain candidates doing well with the opportunity and sometimes unconsciously will exclude candidates whom they cannot relate to or envision in the role the opportunity is providing. To those decision makers, minorities and women are less relatable, and they do not see their potential and track to success in certain roles. This is precisely why it is so important to have women and diverse people take part in the decision-making process. The organization gets a view of the candidates through a less homogeneous prism. It expands the analysis of the talent pool and who can be envisioned in the role provided by the opportunity.

In almost every organization, there is a decision room. In that room is either the C-suite, a group of firm leaders, the Board of Directors, or a combination of all three. It is made up of the highest levels of leadership in the organization. Some call it the "sausage room," or it is referenced as "having a seat at the table." Regardless of what one calls it, it is where opportunities are given, salaries are adjusted, bonuses are determined, and terminations are decided.

Getting a seat at this table is not easy, and especially not for women or minorities. However, having women and other diverse people in these leadership positions not only positively impacts the women and other diverse employees, but also the entire organization.

Those who are at this table have tremendous influence in the subjective areas of the evaluation process. They also have the ability to put in perspective some of the perceived deficiencies of employees for the other members at the table. At this level, understanding can be given, missteps can be explained, perspective can be espoused, and outcomes can be changed.

Having a diverse leader who can relate to an employee who is a first-generation college graduate and does not have the context to navigate the firm's construct flawlessly is a tremendous asset. The employee may have made a few minor missteps, but recognizing the talent, a diverse leader will advocate for support such as professional coaching. This type of support may be the ticket to activate this employee's potential and give them the opportunity to grow and advance in the firm. When one can relate to a person, it helps one's ability to envision that person in a role and advocate for them.

I have seen the impact of diverse leadership in operation. My firm has some great female and minority advocates in the "sausage room" and on the Board of Directors. Watching them operate and the impact they have is amazing.

I have witnessed female advocates explain how a highly skilled female associate with two kids under three had dropped everything at the last second on the weekend and focused 18 hours on an important project. She burned the midnight oil to help deliver excellent service to a client, who subsequently added other engagements that did not show up in the associate's column. I simultaneously watched the shareholder whose column it did show up in perk up, realizing his good year had started with that original engagement. Once he realized how the engagements were linked to that associate, he joined in to support that associate's elevation to shareholder. It was not a conscious oversight but truly an oversight, and it was brought to light by a woman with a seat at the table who could relate to making those sacrifices and being overlooked.

I have watched a minority advocate detail things a minority associate did to promote the firm and the impact of that promotion. Those details, previously unknown by the room, carried significant weight. Everyone had already agreed this person was a rising star, so having some of the backstory clearly gave those in the room information to conduct a fair evaluation of the employee's compensation.

Both advocates pointed out factors that the others in the room were unaware of because, quite frankly, that additional information was not in their purview. Having women and diverse men participate in the process greatly improves it. Without this type of inclusion, significant perspectives and information may be lost or missed. The voices of women and minorities need to be at the highest level of the organization.

Having women and other diverse people in the room can also prove beneficial when a diverse or female associate is not elevated and there is disappointment. First, having women and diverse men in the room reduces the perception of an unfair evaluation. Second, the diverse leaders in the room have the cachet and credibility to go back to the person and articulate what happened and to assure them that their backstory was heard and they were treated fairly. Often women and other diverse people do not see many people like them at the top of the organization. Therefore, they are suspicious of the organization. Having someone like them who can explain a bad outcome leads to greater understanding and acceptance of the idea that the system is not rigged against them. This alleviates harsh feelings, helps with retention, and supports positive morale. Most employees understand logic and will get it if someone they identify with and have a degree of trust in explains the underlying circumstances.

The takeaway from having women and other diverse people at the top is that they understand certain circumstances that are not obvious unless you have experienced or been exposed to them. Further, they can give voice to issues that the majority white men do not normally face. Additionally, they can articulate to the disappointed employee why an adverse action was taken and assure them that the process was fair. When that is done by someone the disappointed employee relates to, it gives a certain level of transparency and credibility to the process. This adds tremendous benefit to firms and corporations.

I will end with a word to those fortunate enough to ascend to rarified levels in firms where career decisions are made: Do your homework, because your meaningful participation is critical. You are there for a reason. Draw on your experiences; do a detailed analysis. Learn the backstory. Remember that you are the voice for those who are not in the room.

Bruce A. McMullen

Career
Memphis Tennessee Office Managing Shareholder, Baker, Donelson, Bearman, Caldwell & Berkowitz, PC

Education
- JD, University of Tennessee College of Law (1996)
- MBA, Business, Georgia College & University (1991)
- BA, Economics, University of Georgia (1986)

Best Advice
Anything worth achieving has obstacles and challenges. Don't be discouraged when facing adversity; learn from it.

Personal
Bruce McMullen resides in Memphis, Tennessee. He is married to Judge Camille McMullen, and they have two children.

For More Information
https://www.bakerdonelson.com/Bruce-Anthony-McMullen
https://www.linkedin.com/in/bruce-mcmullen-048a018/

Discussion Questions

1. Discuss whether your experiences within your firm/company/legal community align with the studies that show the limited advancement of women in the profession.

2. What role can women attorneys play in advancing more women attorneys in your firm/company/legal community?

3. What benefits can be gained by increasing the number of women at high levels in your firm/company/organization?

4. In what ways have your identities (gender, race, sexual preference, etc.) shaped your experiences as a lawyer?

5. Have you felt pressure to assimilate within the legal profession and/or your firm/company? If so, how have you handled that?

6. Claire Gibson writes that women are being gaslighted about their experiences in the legal profession. Do you agree? Discuss.

7. Yendelela Holston discusses the misogynoir that Black women lawyers face. Have you faced this, or have you observed Black women lawyers who have had this experience? If so, what did you do?

8. In her essay, Sheryl Axelrod says that "by the time women leave the profession, they have often suffered a career death by a thousand cuts and finally, choose to go." Have you had these types of experiences or know others who have? How did you or others deal with these experiences? What could have been done to change the outcome?

CHAPTER 2

Understanding and Conquering Bias: Bypassing Barriers

More than 150 years ago, Susan B. Anthony declared that "women are in chains, and their servitude is all the more debasing because they do not realize it." Gender inequality and bias may have been more overt during Ms. Anthony's time, but, as the authors of the essays in this chapter discuss, these issues persist in the legal profession. Even in the 2020s, many women are unaware of the impact of gender inequality and bias until they are many years into the profession. To a certain extent, Susan B. Anthony's concern that many women are unaware persists.

To complicate matters, most of us are not open about the obstacles we face in the profession. These are topics many women attorneys do not enjoy thinking about, let alone disclosing to others. Unfortunately, the culture of not openly discussing issues relating to gender inequality and bias, and the micro- and macroaggressions these problems generate, only serves to perpetuate these problems.

This chapter focuses on bringing awareness to the biases that women lawyers face, ranging from "soft discrimination" to outright sexual harassment, in the hopes that shining a light will better prepare women lawyers for the road ahead. We need to work actively together—along with our male allies—to eradicate gender-based biases in the legal profession. These authors share lessons they've learned as they have overcome bias-driven hurdles and obstacles.

How Bias Holds Us Back and What We Can Do about It

By Andrea S. Kramer

The legal profession is dominated by men and operates in accordance with masculine norms, values, and expectations. In other words, the legal profession is highly gendered. As a result, women lawyers generally have a harder time advancing in their careers than do men. Women are given fewer career-enhancing opportunities; they are judged more critically than men; and their accomplishments are more often ignored or downplayed.

Women lawyers are routinely (if unconsciously) held back simply because they are women. To make this point, let's look at the Müller–Lyer optical illusion with which you might already be familiar.

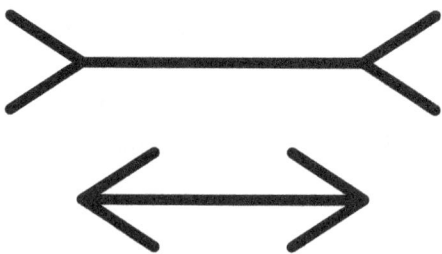

In looking at these two lines, we—all of us—see the top line as longer than the bottom one. It doesn't matter that we're told both lines are the exact same length. It doesn't even matter if we measure them for ourselves. Although we *consciously* know the lines are equal, *we don't see them as equal*. The same is true about gender stereotypes.

It doesn't matter that we consciously know women and men are fundamentally equal with respect to their ambition, talent, commitment, and competitiveness. Most of us (women as well as men) don't see them as equal.

I knew I wanted to be a lawyer when I was 12 years old. My parents had one friend who was a lawyer, so they arranged for him to have lunch with me. He spent the entire meal telling me why I didn't want to be a lawyer. He said there is a difference between "lawyers" and "lady lawyers."

Lawyers can be happy and successful, but lady lawyers can never be both. If I became a lawyer, he warned me, no one would ever love me; I'd never get married; I'd never have a family; I'd live out my lonely life without any friends or family.

Obviously, I ignored his advice. I've been an attorney for over 40 years. I was a partner in a major law firm for the past 30 years until I started my own firm on January 1, 2023; and I am the author of three books with my husband (Al Harris) on overcoming bias in today's biased workplaces. Two of our books address what women can do, and our third book, *Beyond Bias: The PATH to End Gender Inequality at Work*, is about interrupting and overcoming systemic gender bias.

The Goldilocks Dilemma

Looking back on the advice my parents' friend gave me so long ago—although offensive and clumsy—I must sadly admit that he had pointed to a very real double bind that women lawyers still face today. Al and I call this double bind "the Goldilocks Dilemma." Gender stereotypes about women are that they should be communal: warm, caring, sensitive to other people. Gender stereotypes about men are that they should be agentic: restrained, forceful, competitive. When women conform to the traditional communal stereotype, we are often viewed as pleasant and likable, but not competent or capable of leadership. If, on the other hand, we act contrary to this stereotype and we display agentic characteristics, we are likely to face negative reactions and backlash. We are seen as being too insensitive and too unlikable to be a leader. In other words, if we're too agentic, other people simply don't want to have us on their team. If we're too communal, people like us but don't see us as a leader.

Because of the Goldilocks Dilemma, whether we behave communally or agentically, we suffer negative career consequences. Some women try to play it safe by playing down their agentic characteristics to appear more likable. But this is a self-defeating strategy. The only way out of the Goldilocks Dilemma is to manage the impressions other people have of us. Women can do this by dialing up or down our agentic or our communal characteristics to ensure that we are being seen as both effective and likable in whatever situations we find ourselves. In addition, we can use nuanced and carefully honed communication techniques, what Al and I call "attuned gender communication," to overcome or avoid gender bias. These skills are the subject of our first book, *Breaking Through Bias*, now in its second edition.

To make my next point, let me share with you some observations about the origin story of my legal career. When I graduated from law school, I joined a small, 3-year-old firm with seven lawyers. I was to be the firm's only tax lawyer. The partners told me they would give me whatever resources and support I needed. The decision was right for me. I spent almost 15 years at that firm, and two things are most memorable. First, the partners kept all their promises to me, and I learned how to be a real lawyer. I became an equity partner, brought in my own clients, and chaired the firm's tax group, which had seven lawyers in it by the time I left.

Second, my being a woman had no effect on my professional development or advancement. I worked with a group of senior lawyers—all of whom were men, and not one of them ever made me feel that being a woman made a whit of difference to my career opportunities, acceptance into the senior leadership ranks, or ability to become a great lawyer. Growing as a lawyer is never smooth sailing, but gender bias was never the cause of the rough waters I encountered during that period of my career.

Because of the opportunities that firm gave me, the time came when I needed the resources of a bigger firm to meet the needs of my clients. When I left, I was apprehensive. I expected many differences, but the most disturbing one I encountered was the one I least expected: gender bias.

My introduction to gender bias and the Goldilocks Dilemma showed up in two (conflicting) ways. Because I joined my firm as a partner with my own clients, I was assumed to be too agentic, making me, unfairly, seem unlikable and difficult to work with. People whom I'd never met referred to me as "the dragon lady." I remember looking that phrase up in the dictionary and finding that I was seen as "strong, deceitful, domineering, fierce, and formidable." At the same time, because I was the mother of a 2-year-old daughter, people also assumed I was too communal and not committed to my career. When I was working with one of my colleagues on a project, for example, he would suggest that we talk about the project at five o'clock, if I'd "still be around."

At my new firm—and at all of the other large law firms and businesses I interacted with—I saw obstacles in women's career paths. I saw inconsistencies in the opportunities available to women as opposed to men, and I found unfair demands placed on women trying to be good lawyers while raising children.

Coming Face to Face with Bias

Coming face to face with the reality of bias taught me several things.

First, I learned that there are truly gender-neutral workplaces, but these are a precious few. By and large we work in gendered workplaces, where men run most of the organizations and make most of the career advancement decisions. Their decisions are often affected by conscious and unconscious bias.

Second, I learned that women cannot passively accept the current gender-skewed environment. We cannot wait for the legal profession to become gender-neutral. We need to recognize and counter the stereotypes and biases that conspire to hold us back. We can do this with attuned gender communication techniques and impression management.

Third, women come in all sorts of shapes and sizes, races and ethnicities, ages, sexual identities, and countless other social identities. Because of these differences, we need to confront and address the biases that affect women with intersectionalities.

Fourth, women lawyers face bias from not just our colleagues, clients, co-counsel, and judges. We also face systemic bias that is enforced in our organizations through biased practices, policies, and procedures. Interrupting and overcoming systemic bias is the focus of my book, *Beyond Bias*.

Fifth, it is not just men who hold gender stereotypes; women hold them too. As a result, we can hold ourselves back by buying into negative stereotypes about women. We must not get caught up in this self-limiting bias.

Sixth, the career problems women lawyers face are found in four deep-seated biases: affinity bias, gender bias, out-group bias, and status quo bias. These fundamental biases powerfully and pervasively influence people's attitudes and behavior and also shape organizational structures and practices.

Fundamental Biases

The four biases that lead to our gendered workplaces can be briefly summarized as follows:

- **Affinity bias:** Favoring the similar over the different.
- **Gender bias:** Valuing the masculine over the feminine.
- **Out-group bias:** Disparaging the different.
- **Status quo bias:** Resisting change to established practices.

Affinity Bias

Affinity bias causes men to prefer to hire, work with, and socialize with other men. It does not necessarily involve conscious discriminatory intent. Regardless of its motivation, however, affinity bias systematically disadvantages women simply because we are not "like" the men who make up the overwhelming majority of leaders.

Gender Bias

Gender bias causes individuals and organizations to prefer to see men in high-profile leadership positions while ignoring or undervaluing women's contributions. Both women and men hold gender stereotypes that are generally deeply embedded in individuals' perceptions of other people, often with little or no awareness of how these stereotypes affect our perceptions.

Because of gender stereotypes, we implicitly assume that certain characteristics are typical of women and of men simply because they are women and men. Gender stereotypes often lead us to automatically assume we "know" what someone is like just because we know their gender. As a result, we tend to overlook their actual characteristics by relying on our stereotypical (false) knowledge about them.

To take a simple example, as noted above, the common stereotype of men is that they are (and should be) agentic and that women are (and should be) communal. Consequently, our unconscious tendencies are likely to lead us to deal with men as though they are (or should be) leaders but to deal with women as though they are (or should be) caregivers or assistants. Thus, one study found that approximately 75 percent of people think "men" when they hear career-related words such as business, profession, and work, but think "women" when they hear domestic-related words such as family, household, and caregiving. Indeed, an overwhelming majority of people associate "men" with leader-related roles such as boss, CEO, and director. At the same time, people associate "women" with aide-related roles such as assistant, attendant, and secretary.

Out-Group Bias

Out-group bias leads men to exclude women from informal, career-enhancing networks. It is most often expressed through (intentional or unintentional) exclusion, incivility, harassment, and microaggressions. Although dominant in-group members can display favoritism (affinity bias) toward other in-group members, without having negative feelings about out-group members, there is a very thin line between the positive and negative feelings. There is another very thin line between feeling uncomfortable with out-group members and disparaging or expressing hostility toward them. These lines are likely to be crossed if members of an out-group are systematically characterized as "different from" and "not as good as" in-group members.

Unfortunately, this is how women are frequently characterized in relation to men because of gender bias. The combination of (white) men often being the dominant in-group *and* the prevalence and power of gender bias means that women (and people of color) are often a distinct out-group that can be easily subjected to out-group bias.

Status Quo Bias

Status quo bias expresses a preference for, or greater comfort with, the familiar. When people are given the choice between changing their current situations and leaving things as they are, most people choose to stick with the familiar. They make this decision even when choosing change carries with it a chance of achieving a better overall result. Thus, status quo bias can be thought of as a preference for "the devil you know" rather than "the devil you don't." And while there is considerable variation among people in their aversion to change, status quo bias is a powerful force of resistance to change. To overcome status quo bias, we must convince senior male leaders that *they* would personally benefit from ending systemic gender inequality.

Affinity, gender, out-group, and status quo biases underlay the gendered standards that foster workplace gender inequality. The key to ending such inequality is to identify techniques, practices, and initiatives that effectively interrupt these systemic biases.

Biased Treatment of Women

Women experience biased treatment relative to men simply because they are women. This biased treatment typically takes three different forms:

- **Prejudice**. An attitude or orientation that results in a less favorable view of, or regard for, members of one social identity group than for members of another social identity group.
- **Stereotyping**. Categorization of members of social identity groups based on the characteristics they are assumed to have simply because they are members of that group.
- **Discrimination**. Behavior toward, or treatment of, members of one social identity group less favorably than members of another identity group.

Attitudes, categorizations, and behaviors become prejudice, stereotyping, and discrimination when they have no objective justification and cannot be supported by empirical evidence or verifiable information. People display biased attitudes toward women because they have (unconscious) beliefs about the inherent characteristics of women. These unjustified attitudes lead them to treat women as "not as good as" men. Organizations are biased if their structures, policies, or practices result in the treatment of members of one social identity group in a way that is unjustifiably less favorable than the members of another such group.

Getting Men Involved

An important way to end gender inequality is to get men actively involved in the effort. As a group, men have greater power, resources, and status in society than women. Without men on the front lines—and not just as supportive bystanders—it is hard to imagine much, if any, progress will be made to end systemic bias in the legal profession. Men need to walk side-by-side with women. They need to be part of the efforts to disrupt the behaviors, processes, policies, and structures that currently prevent women lawyers from competing with men on equal terms. We cannot disrupt the systemic nature of gender inequality unless men are fully engaged.

Given the four fundamental biases I've mentioned above, men's lack of active involvement is not surprising. In the book Al and I are working on now, we identify at least six reasons that men of good will—the true believers—have not been actively working to end gender inequality:

- Men don't think gender equality is their fight.
- Men fear backlash if they join the fight.
- Men are apprehensive about saying or doing the wrong thing.
- Men are uncertain about how to get involved, what they should do, and how to go about doing it.
- Men think they are too busy to get involved in an effort that holds no personal payoff for themselves.
- Men are unaware of the harms that stem from sexism.

Each of these reasons can take up an essay of its own. With the limited space still available to me, I'll say a few brief words.

We need to work together to overcome men's reluctance. We need to provide men with a clear view of the discriminatory consequences of gender inequality; an understanding of the legitimate stake they have in advancing fairness; an appreciation of how they will personally benefit from the elimination of gender inequality; an understanding that they can advance gender equality by sponsoring women; and a willingness to advocate for their own rights, such as paternal leave and more work flexibility.

Women and men can work collaboratively to develop a sense of shared core values, common objectives, and respect for each other's differences. This requires a long-term commitment to promote, engage with, and extract value from diversity.

Conclusion

It is our responsibility to reform the legal profession so that women are evaluated and promoted comparable to men. Although there is much that women can do on our own behalf to break through gender bias, we cannot ignore the fact that structural reforms are also needed. We should not wait, however, for those structural reforms. We want to move up in our careers today. As I have briefly mentioned, through the use of attuned gender communication and impression management we can do a great deal to advance before the critically needed structural reforms are actually implemented.

We cannot simply tell ourselves to stop thinking in terms of stereotypes. This ignores the hard work needed to bring about much-needed reforms. Ending bias is everyone's responsibility, even if it is not anyone's fault.

Andie Kramer (Andrea S. Kramer)

Career

Andie started her legal career in a small firm, where she built its tax department from scratch. She moved to an international law firm, where she started and headed up its Financial Products and Derivatives Practice, served on its Management Committee and Compensation Committee, and started its Gender Diversity and LGBTQIA+ Diversity Committees. She is now the founding member of a boutique law firm where she advises clients on complex, high-stakes transactions involving derivatives, energy transactions, cryptocurrency and other digital assets, and environmental, social, and governance issues.

Education

- JD, *cum laude*, Northwestern University Pritzker School of Law (1978)
- BA, *summa cum laude*, University of Illinois Urbana-Champaign (1975)
- Certificate in Financial Accounting, Harvard Business School (2022)
- Certificate in Leading with Finance, Harvard Business School (2022)

Best Advice

Perfection is overrated. Don't hold yourself back in your career with fears that you won't be perfect. Sometimes you just need to jump in with both feet and do the very best you can.

Personal

In January 2023, Andie Kramer launched her boutique law firm, ASKramer Law (www.ASKramerlaw.com). She has been recognized for her thought leadership in cryptocurrency by the *National Law Review* (as both its 2020 and 2022 Go-to Thought Leader in cryptocurrency) and by *JD Supra* as the 2021 Readers' Choice author in cryptocurrency. Andie is a well-known leader in diversity, equity, and inclusion (www.AndieandAl.com); she is a Forbes.com contributor on gender equality; and she is the co-author of three books on gender equality in the

(Continued)

workplace with her husband, Al Harris. Their newest book, *Beyond Bias: The PATH to End Gender Inequality at Work*, was released in May 2023. For over 30 years, she has helped organizations become more diverse, equitable, and inclusive. Andie and her husband, Al, live with five rescue dogs and two rescue cats. Their daughter is a forensic pathologist in New York City.

For More Information
https://andieandal.com/about
https://www.linkedin.com/in/andiekramer
https://www.askramerlaw.com

Meeting and Overcoming Socioeconomic Barriers to Law Practice

By Mary A. Prebula

Like so many other women and minorities, I faced obstacles, many unique, to even having the courage to think I could become a lawyer, much less to have a career in law. But I believe in justice and fairness, and that belief has governed my life and my profession. I prefer to think of hurdles rather than barriers or obstacles. In my case, those hurdles were socioeconomic and what in reality were and are still class challenges.

When I reflect on my legal career, it is amazing to consider the sheer limits I faced because of my lack of socioeconomic and class status. Where we come from and how we grow up have an incredible impact on our lives. While most of this book focuses on issues in the profession, my focus is on overcoming those socioeconomic and related class barriers and getting to the belief you can enter that door, become an attorney, and succeed.

Hurdle One: Believing You Can Succeed

It is critical to believe in yourself; to believe you can succeed. This hurdle is often connected to socioeconomic status and is often overcome in small stages as we struggle to overcome the messages from those who tell us we can't succeed. My abiding message in this essay is: "If you work hard enough, you can be whatever you want to be." My mother, Josephine Peele Prebula, ingrained that message in my siblings and me. Find that rock, whether it is a parent, a mentor, or your own grit, and work hard. My brothers and I have often reflected on "what would Josephine say" or "do." We learned to believe in ourselves.

Through long, hard roads, my mother saw all three of her children become successful. Girls in my extended family simply did not go to college until after I did. I was the first in my immediate family to graduate from college, to obtain a master's and then a JD degree. My older brother had an accomplished military career. My younger brother obtained his college degree and has a successful sales career. I found that rock in my mother, in academics, and in hard work; that is the essence of how I ever dared to dream to become an attorney.

Hurdle Two: Lack of Money, Unfairness, and Unequal Access to Justice

No one in my early life predicted success—exactly the opposite. I was born in a tiny town in Pennsylvania. From my very early days, I remember my mother working from before I was awake until after I went to bed, whether at her job at the local lumber mill or tending to us. My father existed in name only and a few sporadic visits. We lived above a garage on the side of a mountain, living paycheck-to-paycheck.

Take lessons from those early messages. An early lesson of the unfairness of lack of money was when I broke my first pair of glasses falling in the snow and had to patch them together with a wooden toothpick for months because my mother did not have the money to repair or replace them. I was eight and was teased mercilessly over being too poor to fix them. My older brother often told the story, and said, in much more colorful language than this, that that was the day he knew I would not "put up with unfair."

Shortly thereafter, we moved back to eastern North Carolina where my mother was raised—the daughter of a tenant famer who had worked hard to buy his own farm—and still had family. Homeless and with just the clothes in our suitcases, we lived in an abandoned farmhouse, where we had no electricity, a well for water, and a wood stove for heat. We knew true hunger and often had no food of any kind in the house. Farming relatives helped us with donations, the opportunity to overpick or scrap an already-picked field, or a ride to the welfare office for stale government bread, cheese, and powdered milk the one day a week it was our turn.

I first experienced the harsh reality of these lessons when I saw how socioeconomics influenced access to justice and the legal system. A family member with no money and no attorney was going to jail while the doctor's son, charged with the same offense but able to afford an attorney, was being released. At literally the last minute, a lawyer took the case of my family member for a pittance and a few dollars a week, saving the family member from jail by having representation. That lawyer's actions became a model for me. That stark injustice forged my desires for justice and a legal career and to provide pro bono services where I could.

Hurdle Three: Low Expectations Based on Socioeconomic Status

One hurdle created by socioeconomic conditions that is hardest to overcome are the low expectations from those in authority. While many incidents can demonstrate the barriers faced by children of disadvantaged socioeconomic status, low expectations and prejudgments are demoralizing. You have to decide not to accept the judgment of others and prove to yourself your own worth and what you can achieve.

We were ecstatic when we moved into a federal housing project with water, electricity, heat, and no leaky roof, and Mom got on welfare. However, I quickly learned the reality that I was then "just a Projects Kid," and that would color how I was treated until I left for college.

I went to a new junior high school, and my new best friend and I were inseparable at school until her dad drove me home one day. The next day my "friend" told me that she could no longer see me because I was from the "Projects" and I was "not good enough" to be her friend. This incident was repeated in various forms throughout my high school years with teachers, parents, and other students, and it partially drove my goal to "make something of myself."

As a Projects Kid, little was expected of me, and a few incidents stand out. In school, I was tested for the chance for a scholarship to attend the Governors' School, a statewide summer residential school for gifted students. The principal called me in to his office and told me that I had made the highest score on the exam, but the school chose not to send me because the experience would be wasted on someone with such poor means and poor expectations. He told me my prospects were so low that it would not do me any good, and instead they were going to send someone who "might amount to something."

You have to fight your way out of believing these low expectations. I chose not to believe them, and I earned good grades. When the only way out is through academics and a college scholarship, "you might as well try for it," as my guidance counselor told me when I asked. He did nothing to assist me. I applied on my own to the University of North Carolina at Chapel Hill, researched scholarships, called repeatedly, and drove the scholarship office crazy. I was awarded the James M. Johnston Scholarship based on academic achievement and financial need.

College at Chapel Hill changed my life. For the first time, I was accepted for my academics, my accomplishments, for who I was, and not for where I came from or what my parents had. When that opportunity comes along, grab it and let it lead you to the next step in overcoming hurdles.

Hurdle Four: Proper Bearing, Attire, and Confidence

Your bearing, the way you carry yourself, your self-confidence, and even your attire can influence your path. You have to find your own way, your own legal style, and your own path, but you also have to fit into the system. One of my defenses in my youth was to adopt a hard veneer, showing that nothing could bother me and that I would stand up for myself; that defense has carried through and has given me an edge in the legal profession.

While it seems odd to talk about clothes today, we still need to be cognizant that attire is an issue for those who are socioeconomically disadvantaged. My full scholarship included a clothing allowance, so for the first time in my life I had new clothes that were not homemade, secondhand, or from a thrift shop, and they actually fit. It is amazing how clothes define you. I entered the legal profession when clothes were still very important, and women wore bows and pin-striped mock male suits. I was able to buy four suits, one of which I still have in my closet. Today, I support and contribute to charities and clothing drives that provide attire for women entering the professional world. Find your own style within this profession of ours and help others.

Hurdle Five: Fighting the Impulse to Accept That the First Path Is the Only Path

After obtaining a teaching degree, teaching high school, and obtaining a master's degree in education, I determined that I could finally go to law school. While I had more resources at this time, again I relied on scholarships and hard work, and I obtained admission and a scholarship to Emory University School of Law.

The lessons learned in overcoming early hurdles were essential in law school. Everyone in my law school class had been in the top of their college class. For over half of my class, family paid for their education costs, and they did not have to work as I did. Again, hard work was essential for me, and I approached law school as I would a job. Other than clerking, I devoted the entire day and well into the night to school and preparation. That work ethic has stayed with me—work until the job is done.

That hard work led me to work for a regional defense firm, an international corporate firm, a solo practice, a small partnership, and my small firm practice today.

This path is not always an easy one. You will receive criticism. Evaluate the lessons and the criticism, consider whether they work for you, and if they do, accept them and learn from them. A lesson always carried from my mother was to be respectful even toward those you oppose or with whom you disagree. Always stand up for what you believe in. Treat others with kindness, but do not tolerate mistreatment.

I handled criticism by expecting others to follow the same rules I was being asked to follow. I was told I had to wear a jacket to look like a lawyer; I told the male attorney in shirt sleeves to put his jacket on also (and I wear my jacket with clients most days). I was told I was not deferential enough; I said I treated those with respect who had earned my respect, partner or not, and I did. I was accused of being too arrogant; I said it was the result of years of hard work and confidence in my abilities. I was charged with being too proud of what I had accomplished; I replied that we have to be proud of what we accomplish so we can help our clients, other lawyers, our profession, and ourselves. I know males did not receive the same critiques, but I was never criticized for not working hard enough, for not being successful, for not winning cases. Perhaps I've mellowed over time, and I would meet such challenges less head-on today, but each of us needs to find the way that works and stay true to oneself.

Hurdle Six: When You Can't Find a Mentor, Create a Model and Be a Mentor

Until I entered the legal profession, I had no idea what being a mentor meant; I had no understanding of the concept. Based on where I came from and the path I took, I never had a mentor. I had the good fortune to work as a legal secretary between teaching and law school and to clerk in law school. In that short time, I observed many different attorneys, along with their styles, their creeds, and their ethics. Once I became a lawyer and joined a law firm, I worked regularly for certain partners, but none of them became my mentor.

So I created a model for what I would have wanted in a mentor. I started with the attorney who had helped my family member and then developed a model of what I wanted to be based on aspects I admired in certain individuals. I believe, and hope, that I have created a model and have been a mentor for my daughter, Ashley Frazier Heintz, who is also an attorney and for whom I was able to remove some of these hurdles because of my profession.

Whether I worked for a large defense firm, an international mega firm, or my own small and solo practices, I have often mentored other young attorneys. I am willing to answer questions, provide advice, share examples, and be a good example for younger lawyers coming into our profession. I have always worked at all levels of the bar, helped with pro bono activities, helped those more disadvantaged than I, and encouraged others to do the same and to keep our profession a noble one.

Lessons Learned; Obstacles Overcome

My goal has been to represent my clients diligently, fairly, and ethically, and to work toward fairness and equity. My career has been varied, and I have been fortunate to have handled cases for persons in every walk of life—including the unwed mother who now has child support, the disabled worker who now has income, the cancer survivor who now has insurance coverage, the worker who has received just compensation for employment discrimination, the sole proprietorships that have stood up to big companies, the mega corporation that has helped clean up a contaminated site, the small corporations that have resolved contract disputes, the family members who have resolved long-held feuds over land and possessions, the homeowners who have kept their land, free of false claims, and others. As an associate attorney, I have been blessed even to help represent former President Jimmy Carter in litigation relating to his presidential library.

Here are some of the lessons I have learned: you can overcome obstacles if you treat them like hurdles and not barriers. Hard work and taking one hurdle at a time will see you through to achieve your goals. You cannot do everything; you can only do the best you can with what you have and what you know at the time. Working for inclusion of women and minorities in our bar and in our profession is rewarding. Helping those in need is necessary to your soul. Trying to make a difference and seek fairness is meaningful and fulfilling. I have tried and hope I have made a difference in the lives I have touched.

I truly love the law and what I do. I am a better person because of the law. I love the hard work and the hurdles, and I love overcoming the obstacles my clients face every day. If the Projects Kid can do it, so can you. "If you work hard enough, you can be whatever you want to be." That is Josephine's legacy.

Mary A. Prebula

Career

Attorney, Prebula & Associates LLC, handling civil litigation, including contract and tort, business disputes, real estate litigation, family law, employment discrimination and harassment, fiduciary, and probate litigation. Previously Attorney, Jones Day and Hansell & Post

Education
- JD, Emory University School of Law (1984)
- MEd, University of North Carolina at Greensboro (1978)
- BA, Education, University of North Carolina at Chapel Hill (1974)

Best Advice

Know who you are and your capabilities and believe in yourself. Don't wait for doors to open: find a way and create your own opportunities to succeed. Be willing to work hard, to strive for your goals, to promote yourself, and to fight to achieve your own potential. Once you do that, then you can help others. And always have the same strong faith in yourself that your mother or your mentor has in you.

Personal

Mary A. Prebula is proud that her daughter chose to become an attorney as well and is now a partner at a major international law firm. Mary enjoys visits to the mountains and beach, foreign travel, and spending time with her daughter's family and four grandchildren. She believes that experiencing different cultures and environments and meeting with people from all backgrounds and in all walks of life enriches us and creates a better understanding of others.

Mary is active in bar matters and among many other things serves as the current Chair of the Formal Advisory Opinion Board of the State Bar of Georgia and Vice-Chair of the Judicial Procedure and Uniform Rules Committee. She is a Past President of the Georgia Association for Women Lawyers. Mary has received numerous awards, including Georgia's Top Rated Lawyers®, Tradition of Excellence Award 2013—State Bar of Georgia, General Practice & Trial Law Section, and Martindale-Hubbell© Peer Review Ratings—AV Preeminent.

For More Information
www.prebulallc.com

Turning Obstacles into Opportunities
By Hon. Abbe F. Fletman

What have I learned in my more than 40 years of working life? A lot. Here is my story.

In the fall of 1984, I was a pretty good newspaper reporter on a pretty good newspaper, but I had a plan. An acquaintance of mine was running for Congress. He would win, and I would be on my way to D.C. as his press secretary.

The voters of North Carolina, however, had other ideas. My candidate lost, and on November 7, 1984, I signed up to take the Law School Admission Test. I had my reasons, in addition to the kick in the pants I got when my candidate lost. While I worked for the scrappy afternoon newspaper and still enjoyed beating the morning broadsheet to a story, reporting had become rote to me. I also chafed at the restrictions placed on newspaper reporters. I thrive as a participant, not an observer, and I wanted to be involved in my community.

Fortunately, I got into a top 10 law school, the best-ranked in my hometown of Philadelphia, and so in the fall of 1985, I started as a law student at the University of Pennsylvania. Again, I had a plan—law review, clerk for a federal judge, and work for a public interest organization.

But I didn't catch onto how to take law school exams until the end of my first year. By second semester, with the help of a law professor, I understood that the key to good law school grades was to discuss the intersection between the facts presented in the exam question and the law. The light bulb turned on too late, though, so I didn't have the grades to make law review or to get the clerkships I wanted. After working at two legal clinics representing indigent adults during law school, I decided that work was too emotionally draining for me to do full-time. I was offered a summer associate position during an on-campus interview at one of the top firms in Philadelphia, and in 1988 I started my law career as a litigation associate. Litigation appealed to me because I can analyze information and write quickly, and I enjoy putting an argument together.

Four-and-a-half years later, I was garnering good reviews but getting little to no trial or even deposition experience. Looking forward, I also saw that the associates working for my mentor weren't advancing. My partner and I had wanted to have children from the beginning of our relationship, and once I had a stable, well-paid job, we started having our children. I was already thinking about moving to a firm where I could get some trial experience when I met another mother at the gym during maternity leave after the birth of my second child. She told me that her partner, a lawyer at a medium-sized litigation-driven firm, was looking for a midlevel associate. My resolve to change firms was reinforced when I returned to work and was told that the firm wanted me to work on cases that I had no interest in. I interviewed with a group of partners who had been frozen out of leadership at a big firm and had decamped to Firm No. 2. Firm No. 2 presented opportunities for me to get the courtroom experience I craved while maintaining a high-level commercial litigation practice.

This was a great move in many ways. I tried my first cases, took scads of depositions, and began to learn how to manage associates. This firm was known for its aggressive style, and I learned to stand my ground and be fearless. Firm No. 2 prized courtroom skills and paid for one of its lawyers each year to get an LLM in Trial Advocacy at Temple University. With the firm's financial backing, I started in the LLM program. It was no small feat, with two young children at home and still billing at least 1,900 hours a year. I think of it as the year I didn't sleep, but I learned the skills and gained the confidence that propelled my career forward.

I also learned not to take opposing counsel's aggressive style personally. In one case, opposing counsel wrote a letter calling me an unprofessional liar. It shook me, and, after consulting one of my mentors, I responded by refusing to talk with him on the phone so that he couldn't mischaracterize our discussions—all communications would have to be in writing. The animosity toned down, and after the case settled, opposing counsel asked me out to lunch. I realized that his name-calling was just a tactic.

While I developed my skills and confidence at Firm No. 2, 4 and a half years after joining, I hit another wall. The leaders of this firm were all in their 40s, intensely involved in their cases, and always looking over the shoulders of their younger partners. I was a nonequity partner nearing the time when I would be asked to buy into the firm. I was uncomfortable thinking I'd never have the last say even in cases I was trying, and I was uneasy with the idea of taking out a high-interest bank loan to buy into the firm. Also, the head of my department was abusive. I could look through boxes of documents and distill them to the 10 most important, but he would find the one document I had overlooked. I could write a brilliant brief. He would find the one paragraph that didn't fit. He would fume and yell, and I would take it. To make matters worse, I also was paid less than men with comparable positions at the firm.

Before I joined Firm No. 3, I wasn't really looking. I was unhappy and venting to a good friend who had been a partner with me at Firm No. 2. He suggested I join him at his firm. There was only one problem: the bully from Firm No. 2 had moved to Firm No. 3. As part of my negotiations to join Firm No. 3, I made it clear that I would not work for or with the bully. Nonetheless, a few months into my time at Firm No. 3, the bully approached me with an opportunity to work on a case with lots of international travel. The bully suggested that I would do the grunt work and he'd get the travel. I dropped the file on his desk, turned on my heels, and left his office. Shortly after, he came and gave me the case—to handle on my own. He never again gave me a problem.

I was halfway through the trial advocacy master's degree program when I moved to Firm No. 3, and part of my negotiation was for Firm No. 3 to pay the second half of my LLM tuition, which it did. As soon as I got the degree, the chairman of Firm No. 3 and the head of my department paid me a visit on a Thursday. They had a major jury case going to trial the following Monday and they weren't confident in the lawyer who was supposed to try the case. Three-and-a-half days later, I was opening to the jury. Keeping the verdict small and then halving it on appeal was viewed as a big victory, and other trial work followed.

Since law school, I had been involved in the LGBTQIA+ community and the greater legal community. I served as the first woman co-chair of the LGBT lawyers' organization and sat on the board of one of the city-wide LGBTQIA+ organizations. Because of my leadership roles, the chairman of Firm No. 3, who was very involved in Democratic circles, asked me to meet with a mayoral candidate—but not just any candidate. This candidate was known for being homophobic. In fact, a few years earlier, he had been one of the most vocal opponents of recognizing domestic partnerships. I almost said no, but I decided not to turn down the opportunity. I made a list of 10 policy changes the candidate would have to agree to in order to get my support. He looked me in the eye and agreed, and I became one of the five LGBTQIA+ people in a city of more than 1 million people who was willing to publicly support him.

After he won a contested open primary, I asked the chairman of the firm if I could take a leave and work full-time on the campaign. I had always been interested in politics and wasn't able to participate when I worked for newspapers. I wanted to see a big-city political campaign from the inside, and I thought I could help the candidate with my LGBTQIA+ connections. After he won the general election, I was asked to stay and work on the transition, which gave me a fascinating inside look at the appointment process. The chairman of Firm No. 3 had promised me that my leave would not affect my standing, and more importantly, my compensation at the firm. Firm No. 3 had a subjective compensation scheme where equity partners were awarded shares, whose value fluctuated. Compensation each year was a multiple of the number of shares owned. There also was a bonus pool. While I was in the top tier when I took my leave, and ahead of my female peers on compensation, when I returned, I started falling behind the men. The first year it happened, I saw it as an aberration. The second year, I talked with firm management and was assured it would be corrected. The third year, I left.

Before joining my fourth and final firm, I embarked on a "listening tour." I had lunch or coffee with every smart, successful lawyer who would meet with me. I asked questions to identify the best firms offering the highest remuneration and the greatest chance for a woman and out lesbian to advance, and I listened to the answers. One of my former partners whom I had lunch with told me I should join her firm. It was a medium-sized firm based in New Jersey with a solid reputation and a small Philadelphia office that the firm was seeking to expand. In the 35-year history of the firm, only one partner had ever left. I saw this as a strong sign of a congenial workplace, especially since one of my prior firms had a revolving door out. The only sticking point was their entirely formulaic compensation structure. Partners were awarded a draw for the coming year, and compensation was based on a complex formula that weighted origination; your own production, whether on your own cases or matters for the clients of other partners; and the production of other lawyers who worked on your matters. If the money coming into the firm over the year based on your efforts was insufficient to meet your draw, your draw was cut. There was no guarantee.

At that point in my career, I was mostly a service partner, doing excellent work on other partners' files. I was originating some of my own matters, but would it be enough to sustain me? I was the primary breadwinner for a family of four and was just 2 years away from my eldest child going to college, so it wasn't only my own survival I worried about. I'd had a lot of interest from other firms and a solid, guaranteed offer from one, but that other offer was a lowball I'd have to negotiate up. I was tired of the annual compensation fight at all my other firms, where I never felt I won, particularly when I compared my compensation to that of my male peers. So instead of doing the same thing and hoping for a different result, I took a risk and joined the formulaic, and therefore objective, compensation firm.

And it worked. Not only did one of the biggest clients at Firm No. 3 follow me, but in my first year at Firm No. 4, I landed a trio of high-profile matters. In the first case, I led a trial team in the successful defense of the marketer of a store-brand sweetener in a trade dress case where a national company unsuccessfully tried to enjoin my client's business. In the second, my team defeated an attempt by the U.S. Department of Justice to obtain federal observers to go inside voting booths during the November 2006 election in Philadelphia. In the third, I led a trial team representing women collegiate athletes in a Title IX case and stopped their university from eliminating two women's varsity athletic teams.

Eighteen years into my legal career, I was having a fine time—working on interesting cases, bringing in plenty of money, and doing good works on boards and in community and professional organizations, including the American Bar Assocation (ABA). Then my phone rang. One of the boards I served on was an LGBTQIA+ educational organization, and the executive director, a former practicing lawyer, called to say there was an opening on our local federal district court. There had never been an open member of the LGBTQIA+ community on the court, and he was encouraging me to apply.

I had not given the bench a lot of thought. But in talking with my friend, I thought, why not? So I filled out the 25-page questionnaire, participated in an interview with my senators' judicial nomination advisory committee, and was deemed qualified. The winds, however, didn't break my way, and the nomination went in a different direction.

So I put my head down and went back to my law practice, but I still thought about my next move. While I loved the courtroom and the challenge of putting a case together and the camaraderie of trial teams, I did not love the constant stress of where the next case or client would come from. I also didn't love the sheer amount of time it took to get, service, and keep clients. I looked for nonprofit organizations I might want to head. I applied for teaching jobs. I thought about my escape hatch.

During my search, I had never thought about the state bench. Most of my practice was in federal court, and in the infrequent times I was in state court, I wasn't interested in doing the things I saw the judges there doing. When I was a young lawyer, I was sometimes sent to state discovery court. This was one courtroom where hundreds of discovery motions were listed once a week. Once the uncontested motions and agreements were processed, a judge came out and heard one motion after another. This plaintiff wouldn't answer interrogatories. This defendant wouldn't appear for deposition. This plaintiff didn't produce complete documents. I remember musing that I couldn't think of a worse job than the one that judge had. Plus, I live in a jurisdiction where judges are elected, so the only path to becoming a state court judge was to run for public office.

This idea of becoming a judge, however, continued to grow on me, so in 2013, my family, friends, and I gathered multiples of the 1,000 signatures I needed to get on the ballot, and my odyssey as an electoral candidate began. Anyone in Philadelphia politics can tell you there are three things that get you elected: money, ballot position, and the endorsement of the Democratic Party. (In Philadelphia, Democrats outnumber Republicans by a 7–1 margin.) The common wisdom is that you can win with two out of three. Ballot position means where your name appears on the ballot in the voting booth. Those with the top spots get an advantage in a judicial election where more than 30 candidates are competing for 7 seats because voters, unless they are highly motivated for a particular candidate, rarely look beyond the first couple of rows. Ballot position is selected in Harrisburg, our state capital, by picking a number out of a black bag. Suffice it to say, I picked poorly. And because I picked poorly, the Democratic Party decided not to endorse me. After all, they want to endorse winners and a candidate with a bad ballot position is a bad bet for them.

Withdrawing from the 2013 race felt like failure, but I fortunately had the support of my family and friends and colleagues. Of all the people who contributed to my campaign, many of whom I met through the ABA, only two asked for their money back. I ran again in 2015 and won this time. In the interim, I was appointed to fill the unexpired term of another judge who had left the bench, so I started my judicial career in 2014. Since taking the bench, I have on most workdays been in the courtroom, where I dearly love to be. The work is intense—it directly affects the lives of the people who appear before me, and much of the work is in public, but the working hours are a fraction of the time I spent in private practice. Even better, I no longer have to worry about where the next case is coming from.

So, what have I learned in my more than 40 years of working life?

Lesson No. 1: If Plan A Doesn't Work, Pivot to Plan B

I like to tell the young lawyers I mentor that if you don't have a plan, you'll never get there, but just because you have a plan doesn't mean you'll get exactly where you hope to. All those years ago, I thought I was heading to a job on Capitol Hill on the coattails of a new congressman. When that didn't happen, I took another path—law school. Similarly, when I hit a glass ceiling at one firm, I went to another. And when I lost my dream of becoming a federal judge, I focused elsewhere, finding a satisfying career on the state bench.

Lesson No. 2: When an Opportunity Presents Itself, Grab It

When an opportunity comes and you don't expect it, take it. When I met the partner of a lawyer looking for an associate, I sent my résumé. When the chairperson of my firm set up a meeting with a known homophobe, I took the meeting. When a friend said, "You should be a judge," I listened.

Lesson No. 3: Take Risks

The legal profession is filled with well-worn low-risk paths. Go to a top law school. Clerk for a federal judge. Work as an associate at a big firm or do a stint at the U.S. Attorney's office. Make equity partner. Yet the women I know who are the happiest did something different, like starting their own firm, or running a nonprofit, or becoming a judge, even if it meant they put at risk immediate advancement or financial security. When I left my firm to work on a political campaign, I knew that I might fall behind my peers, notwithstanding the assurances of the firm chairperson. What I didn't know at the time was that I would make personal connections that would enrich my life and later pave my way to the bench.

Lesson No. 4: Stand Up to Bullies

Our profession is filled with lots of high-achieving lawyers with big egos, so it should not be surprising that some of them are bullies. What I've learned is that the only way to deal with bullies is to stand up to them. For years, I cowered when the head of my department screamed at me. When I found myself working with him again at another firm, I called him out when he wanted to assign me grunt work and take the cream for himself. My advice is the same whether the bullies are male or female and regardless of whether they're condescending to you because you're a woman.

Lesson No. 5: Cultivate Relationships

Life is a web of relationships, and you never know whom you can help or who might help you. If an acquaintance at the gym hadn't put me in touch with her partner, would I have left my first firm? If a friend hadn't thought I could be the first LGBTQIA+ person on my home federal court, would I be on the bench today? Always try to help others when you can, and rest assured that it will come back to you in multiples.

Lesson No. 6: Be Yourself

The most important lesson I can leave you with is to be yourself and embrace all your intersecting identities. I have many identities—wife, mother, judge, lesbian, and Jew, to name a few. My career path is an example of how a one-woman lawyer navigated the rocks of law practice. What I wish for any reader is that they find their own satisfying path and their own voice.

Hon. Abbe F. Fletman

Career

Judge, Philadelphia County Court of Common Pleas, Pennsylvania; Lawyer in Private Practice; Newspaper Reporter

Education

- LLM, Trial Advocacy, Temple University Beasley School of Law
- JD, University of Pennsylvania Carey Law School
- BA, University of Chicago

Best Advice

Take risks and cultivate relationships.

Personal

Hon. Abbe F. Fletman is married with two children.

For More Information

https://ballotpedia.org/Abbe_Fletman

Discovering Soft Discrimination: The Persistent Underestimation of Women in the Legal Profession and a Strategy to Contest It

By Diana Flynn

As I reflect upon almost four decades as a civil rights lawyer, it seems to me that official discrimination is usually based on a pernicious justification to give legitimacy to the harsher treatment of a group. Specifically, the targeted group is viewed as somehow different—and different in a way that makes its members less capable of participating in society on an equal footing. Such slanderous claims about enslaved Black persons were offered to justify enslavement and Jim Crow laws. While that is the most outrageous example of derogatory stereotyping, other groups, including women, have not been exempt. The perception that women have lesser or different abilities once led to the establishment of formal legal barriers to female success in our society and economy. These barriers were slow to fall. As recently as the early twentieth century, the Supreme Court tried to justify disparate treatment with assertions that "woman has always been dependent on man" and "in the struggle for subsistence, she is not an equal competitor with her brother."[1] In the Court's view, women's shortcomings were so severe that their freedom would pose a danger to others. Thus, restrictions placed upon a woman "are not imposed solely for her benefit, but also for the benefit of all."

While rhetoric softened over the years, for decades it remained respectable to argue that women were not able to participate effectively in large segments of society. In the 1970s, for example, federal government lawyers attempted (unsuccessfully) to justify female service members' inferior family benefits on the ground that military wives need more help than the husbands of women service members.[2] And in the 1990s, for example, the Commonwealth of Virginia sought to exclude women from the Virginia Military Institute—its premier military college—on the grounds that a less rigorous program is more appropriate for women.[3]

---

1. Muller v. Oregon, 208 U.S. 412, 422, 423 (1908).
2. Frontiero v. Richardson, 411 U.S. 677 (1973).
3. *Muller, supra* note 1.

Such discrimination supposedly protected women from the consequences of their inability to compete equally. The discriminatory regimes in these and other cases ultimately were held to be unlawful, but that has not ended the debate over the ability of women to perform equally in a variety of contexts. The legal restrictions may fall, but the doubts about women's abilities that led to them do not necessarily dissolve with the issuance of a judicial mandate.

To be sure, women's legal position in society and in the workforce has vastly improved. But vestiges of the philosophy that led to the earlier unabashed restrictions on women's participation in the workforce remain. A softer discrimination based on the underestimation of women remains persistent. The legal profession is not immune to this situation.

Far from it. Women lawyers know that they are underestimated. They know they must work harder to have their talents noticed. They know that solutions they offer often will be greeted with silence or skepticism. They know that equally (or sometimes less) qualified male candidates will often be thought of first when a promotion opening arises. They know men are more readily given the chance to assume new responsibilities when they are not as clearly qualified. They understand this all contributes to a system in which men remain disproportionately powerful in the profession and women have a steeper road to advancement.

Those who have not suffered this soft discrimination may think the problem is overstated. Indeed, it is in their interest to do so. And it is easy for doubters to select anecdotal examples to justify their doubts. There are cognitive advantages for both men and women to seek confirmation of their positions by choosing anecdotes. After all, where you stand often depends on where you sit.

But some of us know. *Some of us have seen both sides.* I am among those few lawyers with the perspective of having presented myself professionally for years as a man and then, following gender transition, as a woman. And I have personally experienced the different and preferential treatment previously afforded to me as a man that has not been afforded to me as a woman.

Gender transition has never been easy, and it still is not today. But a few decades ago, it was even more complicated. For some of us, transition on the job was delayed until all other pieces were in place, due to the lack of recognized legal protections and lack of understanding by employers.

As a result, there were occasions when medical, physical, and social transitions went forward before there was a formal announcement at work. This would mean that the formal change in gender identification on the job, for example, from male to female, could occur rather abruptly.

In my case, it was over a long weekend! To minimize the danger to my employment and my professional standing as a senior leader in the Department of Justice's Civil Rights Division, I waited for what I judged the right time and circumstances to change my name and adjust my official departmental gender marker to female on the Department's rolls. I also deferred the final changes in my in-office presentation until that point. Once the preparations were complete and the pieces were in place, I left on a Friday with one name, gender marker, and gender presentation, and returned on the following Tuesday with others.

I had been preparing for that Tuesday morning for years, and I thought I was ready for anything. I expected transphobia, and I did not escape that. But I was usually treated decently in that regard, even by the political leaders in a conservative administration. There was one large unpleasant surprise: the soft sexism of underestimation of women. And it was stark!

Let me provide an example. For most of my career, I was responsible for directing the appellate litigation program for the United States in civil rights cases. Frequently Civil Rights Division cases, or other cases affecting our interests, would come before the Supreme Court. Various Department of Justice (DOJ) divisions and other federal offices would have to work out a joint position and prepare a brief that was acceptable to the entire government. Meetings among those offices were frequently held for that purpose, and as Appellate Chief, I often represented my division. I attended one such meeting on my last day before my official transition. As had almost always been the case, I was treated with the utmost respect, and my views were carefully considered by those present. Points I made sparked expressions of agreement and even praise. I happily took this all for granted as we scheduled another meeting for the following week.

What a difference a few days made! Present at the next meeting was the same mostly male group that had attended the prior week. (They had been alerted to my transition to avoid awkwardness.) At the second meeting, I had the same long experience in the DOJ, held the same senior executive service position, and had the same significant role in the litigation we were discussing as I had had the prior week. But some things had changed. I had asserted my female gender identity, changed my name, and was presenting as a woman.

Not too far into the second meeting, we wrestled with a particularly difficult legal problem. I offered what I thought was a good suggestion. It was met with silence. After a time, one of the men present changed the subject and we moved on. But later in the meeting, a man made the same point as I had—he even used almost the same words! While I had been ignored when I offered the solution earlier, he was roundly congratulated for having solved the problem. We proceeded with the idea I proposed, but the effusive credit went entirely to the man who had repeated my thoughts almost *verbatim*.

While this treatment shocked and offended me at the time, the sad fact is that this same scenario has often occurred since. And I know few women lawyers who could not recount similar experiences. Society has conditioned many to expect less from women than from men. Many male lawyers simply are not listening, or at least they are not listening in the same way, when a woman offers a point of view. Over time, the fact that women are not afforded the same respect and attention in professional settings can manifest in many ways, and it can raise significant hurdles to professional success. If no one remembers that a creative or useful idea was yours, they also may not remember you for the next challenging assignment or the next promotion. Perhaps they will instead think of the man who repeated your point later in the meeting.

This pattern of women being ignored for offering an idea and men being praised for repeating it later became more pronounced and troubling as more women attained the opportunity to attend these interoffice meetings at the DOJ. This was enormously frustrating. But our increased presence has also inspired a partial solution.

Women attending these meetings began to take special care to acknowledge each other's contributions. After one of the women present made a good point, other women would expressly attribute it to her when they had the opportunity to comment. Thus, statements of agreement or praise now began with "As Amy said . . ." or "Becky made a great point about that earlier." This conscious attempt to lift each other worked!

While it did not result in perfect equity, it changed the dynamics of these meetings. We became harder to ignore. People began to listen to us a bit more and underestimate us a bit less.

A few years later, I learned that this very technique has been used by women in other forums when they suffered the same problems of systemic misallocation of credit. A *Washington Post* article reported that women in political offices at the Obama White House used the same approach when they felt their voices were being ignored. They referred to their mutually supportive efforts as "amplification."[4] Apparently, this worked as effectively in the political offices of the White House as it had in the Department of Justice.

Many other obstacles result from systemic underestimation of women in the workplace. And there are many ways women can cooperate in the workplace to alleviate it, particularly those of us in management or other senior positions. If women are less frequently chosen to make presentations, we can encourage them to volunteer or even request such presentations. If a woman is reluctant to apply for a promotion because of doubts about her qualifications—something far less common among men who may be interested in the same promotions—we can reassure her and encourage her application. Perhaps more importantly, we can encourage the selection committee to give her full and fair consideration. If female authors are not fully given their due in professional literature, we can be sure that we cite them and discuss their work in our own writing. The list goes on.

We have strong tools to counter the underestimation of women that pervades our workplaces. There is no reason that such tools cannot be employed in any office—legal or nonlegal—where women are ignored or where credit for their ideas goes elsewhere. When women work together for mutual support, it is possible for all to get more of the credit and respect that we deserve. Cooperation and mutual support are some of the best tools we have, and they can be effectively employed whenever more than one of us is present.

Pursuit of these strategies also is likely to garner the support of male allies. Few of the men who overlook the contributions of women do it

---

4. Juliet Eilperin, *White House Women Want to Be in the Room Where It Happens*, The Wash. Post (Sept. 13, 2016), https://wapo.st/3LUSqTi.

out of conscious bias or malice. When women note each other's value and amplify each other's views, decent men will pay more attention, even if they had not done so before. Some may even be distressed to find that talented and able women have been and are being overlooked. Indeed, such was the pattern at the DOJ and the White House.

Lawyers who have transitioned from male to female during their practice frequently say they were more surprised by the prevalence of sexism than by transphobia. For high achievers, one of the more difficult adjustments of transitioning to a female identity is to come to terms with the sudden casual and irrational underestimation of our professional abilities. Happily, although women remain frequently underestimated and sometimes ignored, we are a resilient and effective sorority that can work together—and with supportive men—to overcome such barriers and create a fairer and more efficient workplace for all.

Diana Flynn

Career
Practicing law in Saratoga Springs, NY; Long-time director of national litigation programs specializing in civil rights and constitutional law

Education
- JD, Yale Law School
- BA, *summa cum laude*, Political Science, University of Rochester

Best Advice
In career matters, don't be afraid to be your own advocate. But resist the temptation to be your own judge.

Personal
After 40 years of legal practice in New York City and Washington, DC, Diana Flynn is now semiretired and lives with her wife in Saratoga Springs, New York. She is an avid runner and gardener. In the warmer months, you also might find her watching thoroughbreds at the Saratoga Racecourse or casting unsuccessfully for trout in one of the many local streams.

For More Information
https://www.linkedin.com/in/diana-flynn-a1331235

The Systems Currently Addressing Sexual Harassment in the Workplace Are "Still Broken" and Need to Be Fixed

By Cory M. Amron

Thousands of women have told this or similar stories, now and in the not-too-distant past. But hopefully not in the future: "I was raped by a board member [of my nonprofit], who was allowed to voluntarily resign from the board, but [he] faced no other consequence and I am expected to still deal with him."[5]

In October 1990, a year before the Anita Hill-Clarence Thomas hearings catapulted the issue of workplace sexual harassment to the forefront of the U.S. psyche, the American Bar Association's (ABA's) first Commission on Women in the Profession—chaired by Hillary Rodham Clinton, and of which I was a member—published the initial edition of its guide to parental leave and alternative work-schedule policies, bundling a sexual harassment policy with these two policies.[6]

The parental leave and alternative work-schedule policies were published in response to testimony about barriers to women's advancement in the profession that the Commission heard in its inaugural national hearings during the previous 2 years. Sexual harassment was never mentioned publicly in these hearings, but we received tearful, whispered calls from women bringing their dreadful experiences to our attention. Including a sexual harassment policy and discussion in the Commission's guide was a not-so-subtle effort to educate the profession and encourage employers to implement policies about sexual harassment.

Then, in 1991, Anita Hill's testimony rocked the profession and woke up the country, bringing a once hushed topic to light. As the newly installed second Chair of the ABA Commission on Women, I fielded

---

5. All quotes are from respondents to Women Lawyers on Guard's (WLG's) 2019 nationwide survey on sexual harassment in the legal profession.
6. COMMISSION ON WOMEN IN THE PROFESSION, LAWYERS AND BALANCED LIVES: A GUIDE TO DRAFTING AND IMPLEMENTING WORKPLACE POLICIES FOR LAWYERS (ABA 1990).

many calls from reporters wanting me to explain what this "so-called sexual harassment" was; they weren't even sure how to pronounce it.

In 1992, the ABA's House of Delegates passed a resolution calling upon the profession to take action against this "discriminatory and unprofessional practice," recognizing that sexual harassment is a serious problem in the legal profession and must not be tolerated in any work environment. Many firms and companies heeded the call, conferred with their legal counsel, wrote policies to address sexual harassment, and some even instituted training programs. However, few delved into what was really happening in their workplaces to ferret out problems proactively.

Fast forward 25 years to 2017. You may recognize this year from the anguish and explosion of the "#MeToo Movement." Many industries and professions began shining urgent, targeted, laser lights on egregious incidents of sexual harassment within their workplaces. We even heard a few stories from the legal profession. Notwithstanding three decades' efforts to combat sexual harassment, we are still mired in this obstacle to women's[7] progress.

Many people (the great majority of whom are women) have been working on the issue of sexual harassment these past 30 years. Why has it not been more effectively eradicated? What can we do now to try to ensure that 30 years from today we do not experience another reckoning that our daughters and granddaughters are still being sexually harassed?

Women Lawyers on Guard (WLG), a national nonprofit of which I am the president, was determined to take action to address this problem. (See www.womenlawyersonguard.org for more information.) But how to do so and how to make an impact and not duplicate the efforts of others? We were convinced that some "outside-the-box" thinking was necessary.

So we conducted an informal "listening tour." What did lawyers think was happening in the profession *vis-à-vis* sexual harassment? We heard two distinctly different perspectives: Those who weren't being affected (or weren't affected any longer) thought that the problem was solved or at least under control with policies and training. But others (not just younger women) told us stories that would make your skin crawl—horrid incidents of sexual harassment and coercion happening now in firms/

---

7. The term *women* is intended to refer not only to cisgender women, but also to non-binary and trans people.

companies/government/academia/judiciary, in organizations that you would recognize.

We wanted to implement some "out-of-the-box" solutions right away! But we were told that lawyers would not accept the need to employ other, newer strategies unless they were convinced of a problem and a need.

With the assistance of Dr. Arin Reeves of Nextions Consultants, WLG created and deployed a nationwide survey of sexual harassment and misconduct in the legal profession. We received responses in proportion to the lawyer population in geography, race and ethnicity, practice settings, and so on. They were representative of the legal profession in every way, though we received more female responses than male, since this was an experiential survey (a deep dive into what people who are harassed have experienced).

Analysis of the survey results showed that people are still being harassed and continue to fear reporting and retaliation; 86 percent of incidents aren't even reported; and while some progress has been made in the "culture" of the workplace, those who are harassed are, for the most part, more profoundly impacted than those doing the harassing. In 50 percent of the incidents reported, the harasser suffers no consequences; in an additional 20 percent, the person harassed is not informed of the consequences. Conversely, many of those harassed reported significant economic, career, and psychological consequences, some of which were long-lasting.

Sexual harassment and misconduct targets women (and sometimes men) of all ages and at all career stages and in all levels of "power": from law students to, yes, law firm partners. From interns/clerks to, yes, judges. From staff to, yes, senior counsel, and even general counsel. Harassment and misconduct saps individual productivity and adversely impacts organizational economics at the very least, and, at the worst, destroys careers and organizations' reputations. A significant percentage of respondents indicated that intersectionality was a contributing factor to the harassment they experienced (i.e., the combination of gender and age, race, ethnicity, sexual orientation, or religion).

The survey findings led to the inescapable conclusion that the existing system for addressing sexual harassment in the legal profession is "still broken," which led to the name of WLG's report. Three decades after Anita Hill woke the country up and nearly six decades after Title VII of the Civil Rights Act was enacted, the legal profession has yet to implement effective strategies to ensure that no one suffers from such harassment.

I heard a quote the other day: "Statistics are human beings with the tears wiped away." That's certainly the case with the respondents to our survey. Their quotes describe the very difficult stories of some of the toughest moments of their lives—a window into their experiences that will give you great insight into this difficult problem if you have not personally experienced it. We received so many quotes that, while we reproduced some throughout the report as space allowed, we also devoted an entire Appendix to the many that would not fit. I have included some of them in this essay. "I am an employment lawyer and it happened at every firm I have ever been with, despite the fact the firm practiced employment law!"

Harassers may not remember or even recognize their harassing conduct, but it lives on in the memory of many, if not most, of those who are harassed. It continues to affect those harassed, sometimes profoundly and long after the behavior ends or they have changed jobs. Even behaviors that are not legally actionable and that some people pass off as inconsequential (called "sexual misconduct" in the report), can still have a profound effect on persons who have been harassed. The harassing situations diminish productivity and negatively affect the working culture—whether or not reported, whether or not investigated, and whether or not appropriate consequences were imposed.

I encourage you to read the full report of *Still Broken*, available at www.womenlawyersonguard.org/still-broken. To make matters worse, reports of backlash to the #MeToo movement indicate a potential to destroy years of progress for women in the legal profession, including valuable and necessary opportunities for mentoring, stemming from overblown fears of false accusations.

This is an auspicious moment. The #MeToo movement sparked the current tinder. The legal profession at large may believe that the sexual harassment policies and trainings that it has instituted over the last 30 years have dealt with the problem or that there has been no "backlash" to these movements. But that would be wrong. The strong, broad spotlight just hasn't reached the legal profession. And those who tell their stories are clear: much more needs to be done.

"I thought it was the price for being a successful female in a male-dominated profession."

So, what can be done?

Many forward-looking thinkers in the legal and other professions have envisioned a myriad of more effective ways to address sexual harassment specifically, as well as its more profound and ingrained cousins, gender discrimination and inequity. The legal profession has always been a microcosm of the greater society we live in—no better and hopefully no worse. Despite attempts to address disparate treatment of women, people of color, and other marginalized groups, people in these groups remain severely underrepresented in vast swaths of the legal profession.

Having experienced the problem firsthand, the respondents to the survey had many recommendations to make, including:

- Identify and call out problem cultures.
- Devise more tailored strategies.
- Create concrete intervention tools, for example, effective, in-person, bystander intervention training.
- Create more effective, and gradations of, individual accountability.
- Provide much more transparency (everyone knows through the gossip mill that this is happening; they need to know it was appropriately dealt with).
- Support work on this issue at an early age.
- Devise more options for independent investigations, reporting systems, and accountability; for example, implement ABA Model Rule of Professional Conduct 8.4; and provide secure, online reporting.

Many other ways exist to untie this Gordian knot. Here are two additional recommendations that form the cornerstones of WLG's newest initiative, Conversations with Men:

- Seek better understanding through frank and nuanced conversations.
- Develop active male allies (whose efforts are now mostly missing) in combating sexual harassment.

Society and the legal profession have, for the most part, treated sexual harassment as a "women's issue." Although men are also sexually harassed, all studies show that the overwhelming percentage of those who are harassed are women. But it's the entire workplace and profession that is impacted by this scourge. And although the label "sexual harassment," implies that sex or sexuality is the driving force behind this behavior, it is clear that it's the power imbalance and the abuse of that power in the workplace that fuel gender harassment. Women have been toiling to rid our profession (and society) of sexual harassment for decades. Men must now step up.

Research has shown that when men are allies for gender equity, progress advances dramatically: from 30 percent without men to 96 percent with men involved.[8]

With this research as a basis, the goal of Conversations with Men is to motivate male lawyers to become *active allies* in ridding our workplaces of sexual harassment. Here's how we have proceeded so far and what we have accomplished already; stay tuned for our report later this year.

WLG formed a Conversations with Men Expert Planning Task Force to assist with developing and conceptualizing the pilot phase of this initiative, including: Chai Feldblum (former Equal Employment Opportunity Commission [EEOC] Commissioner and co-author of the EEOC seminal report on sexual harassment in the workplace); Ally Coll, co-founder and CEO of The Purple Campaign (a nonprofit devoted to eradicating sexual harassment); James Sandman (former Managing Partner of Arnold and Porter and former CEO of Legal Services Corporation); Bobbi Liebenberg (volunteer extraordinaire who has devoted her entire legal career to eradicating gender discrimination); Nate St. Vincent (previously with Morgan Stanley, now General Counsel with Engine No. 1); Sarah Beaulieu (author of *Breaking the Silence Habit: A Practical Guide to Uncomfortable Conversations in the #MeToo Workplace*); and others.

We hired Dr. Arin Reeves to structure the Conversations curriculum and devise measurement tools, and Neil McGaraghan, a clinical professor

---

8. Matt Krentz, Olivier Wierzba, Katie Abouzahr, Jenn Garcia-Alonso, and Frances Brooks Taplett, *Five Ways Men Can Improve Gender Diversity at Work*, BOSTON CONSULTING GRP. (Oct. 10, 2017), https://www.bcg.com/en-us/publications/2017/people-organization-behavior-culture-five-ways-men-improve-gender-diversity-work.

of facilitation and mediation at Harvard Law School, to facilitate. We invited august individuals and organizations to join our Advisory Council and our Roundtable of Advisory Organizations.[9]

What about the male participants? We were pleasantly surprised that 40 (to date) incredibly diverse male lawyers who we and our networks nominated to participate in these Conversations enthusiastically and almost instantaneously agreed to take part. One told us: "I think that this type of creative approach is what is needed to help us make positive progress in our attempts to achieve equality."

Lastly, we created a step-by-step set of "Active Ally Actions" from which allies can choose, after they participate in two Conversation sessions, to help them embark on their journey to become the active allies our profession needs.

Conclusion

After 30 years of creating and deploying policies, procedures, and training programs to address the problem of sexual harassment, the legal profession and society at large have much work to do.

In light of the leadership role of lawyers in society and their awareness of and responsibility to uphold the rule of law, the persistence of this conduct after more than 30 years of attempts to address it and the failure to deal with its consequences are unacceptable.

The legal profession did not create this problem—it is ubiquitous in our society. But the legal profession is perpetuating it. The profession

"In every legal position I have held . . ., I have experienced this type of behavior and felt I needed to brush it off or minimize it in order to be 'part of the team' . . . I routinely observe other women laughing off such behavior for presumably the same reasons. I hope as awareness increases, we can all feel comfortable and safe in speaking up and refusing to tolerate such behavior."[10]

---

9. *See* WLG, *Conversations with Men: Uprooting Workplace Sexual Harassment,* WLG, https://womenlawyersonguard.org/conversationswithmen/.

10. *See supra* note 5.

needs to educate, create more effective policies and reporting structures, ensure adequate enforcement, proactively ferret out existing problems and toxic cultures, and address, discourage, and disrupt harassment before it reaches the level of impact. Written policies, "check-the-box" training programs, and anemic reporting systems are attempts to comply with the law, but they are not enough to root out long-standing, ingrained patterns of behavior and lack of accountability. And it is inexcusable that we are not engaging men as active allies in tackling this problem.

The time for action is now. We can and must do better.

Cory M. Amron

Career
President, Women Lawyers on Guard

Education
- JD, Harvard Law School (1977)
- BA, Psychology, University of Rochester (1974)

Best Advice
Make a plan, follow your own agenda and passions, not other people's; get out and network; and don't put up with crap.

Personal
Cory Amron retired from the practice of law in 2016. In early 2017, Cory co-founded and runs Women Lawyers on Guard, a national nonprofit network of all genders, harnessing the power of the law to protect equality, justice, democracy, and equal opportunity for all. Women Lawyers on Guard focuses primarily on sexual harassment, women's reproductive rights, and gender and workplace equity (see www.womenlawyersonguard.org).

For More Information
https://womenlawyersonguard.org/bios
https://www.linkedin.com/in/cory-amron-5778b2b

Sexual Harassment: The Interplay of Bullying and Bias in the Profession

By Francine Friedman Griesing

Throughout my four decades of practicing law, I have experienced, witnessed, and heard about a particularly insidious form of bullying and bias—sexual harassment directed principally at women lawyers and other women working in firms, law departments, government, and the judiciary. According to recent studies, offenders include colleagues, supervisors, clients, opposing counsel, and judicial officers. The targets of unwelcome conduct range from the most junior members of the profession to accomplished leaders, although younger people are more likely to be targeted. It appears that senior partners, general counsel, and judges are not immune from inappropriate conduct, including sexual harassment. Despite the pervasiveness of the problem, sexual harassment is often swept under the rug. Recent developments, such as the #MeToo movement, have drawn more attention to the issues. The focus here is on sexual harassment of women, but statistics show that men and nonbinary individuals in our profession also experience harassment.

Although I have been well aware of sexual harassment directed at legal professionals, to my knowledge the first global comprehensive study of the issue was not available to a broad audience until May 2019 when the International Bar Association (IBA) released *Us Too? Bullying and Sexual Harassment in the Legal Profession* (IBA Report).[11] According to the IBA website, the organization was established in 1947 to bring together bar associations worldwide to "contribute to global stability and peace through the administration of justice." Initially an affiliation of bar associations, membership later expanded to include individuals and firms. With over 80,000 individual lawyers, 190 bar associations, and law societies from over 170 countries, IBA has the wherewithal and clout to impact crucial issues affecting our profession and the legal system around the globe. Through its Legal Policy and Research Unit (LPRU), IBA engages in research to advance its objectives.

---

11. This report is available on the IBA's website at https://www.ibanet.org/MediaHandler?id=B29F6FEA-889F-49CF-8217-F8F7D78C2479.

IBA's interest in studying bullying and sexual harassment in the legal profession was triggered by the disturbing results of a survey conducted by research company Ipsos MORI and the Global Institute for Women's Leadership at King's College London, querying respondents in 27 countries about the top three issues facing women and girls. According to that survey, the top three challenges facing woman in order of respondent ranking were: (1) sexual harassment, (2) sexual violence, and (3) physical violence. Recognizing that lawyers are in a unique position to effect change through legislation and litigation, IBA felt lawyers needed to look at ourselves first. IBA undertook its own survey on the issues in the legal profession. Julia Gillard (AC, 27th Prime Minister of Australia, Chair, Global Institute for Women's Leadership, King's College London) reflected in her Foreword:

> the legal profession can only step up to this role with integrity if it makes sure its own house is in order. This is challenging in a hierarchical profession where the most senior practitioners still tend to be disproportionately men and advancement is often as much about networks as measurable merit. But it can and must be done.

In 2018, IBA and Acritas conducted the largest-ever global survey on bullying and sexual harassment in the legal profession. The process involved almost 7,000 respondents spanning 135 countries using 6 languages, working in a broad array of law-related settings. The results were disturbing but not surprising to many. The respondents, who held various positions in the legal field, were 67 percent female, 32 percent male, and 0.2 percent nonbinary/self-defined. The data showed that bullying and sexual harassment are rampant in the legal profession. About one-half of female respondents, one-third of male respondents, and almost three-quarters of nonbinary respondents reported being bullied in connection with working in the law. In addition, more than one-third of female respondents, 1 in 14 male respondents, and almost one-half of nonbinary respondents reported experiencing sexual harassment at work.

The survey did not define "bullying." If participants responded that they had been subject to or witnessed bullying, they were given a list of options to designate specifically the conduct at issue or to define it for themselves.

Examples included being given too much or too little work; being subjected to ridicule, demeaning language, or unwarranted criticism; being excluded or peripheralized; being threatened with job loss or physical harm; and being subjected to harmful rumors. Examples of sexual harassment cited by respondents included sexist, sexual, or sexually suggestive comments; unwanted, unwelcome, inappropriate touching and other intimate physical contact; and sexual assault. Even if one disagrees with the IBA Report's approach to defining the behavior being measured, respondents perceived this type of misconduct to be pervasive and intractable for people working in the law. According to then-IBA President Heracio Bernardes Neto, in his letter accompanying the IBA Report: "For the first time at a global level, this research provides quantitative confirmation that bullying and sexual harassment are endemic in the legal profession."

Equally troubling is the extent to which respondents observed bullying and sexual harassment at work and the reluctance of targets of and witnesses to this insidious behavior to speak out for fear of retaliation and career harm. Some respondents also perceived that the issues are so pervasive that there is nowhere to escape it. According to the data, 40 percent of female respondents and 32 percent of male respondents reported observing workplace bullying. The Report also concluded that bullying was not reported 57 percent of the time and that 75 percent of all sexual harassment incidents were not reported. The reasons for this silence should not be surprising. Generally, the perpetrators are in positions of power *vis-à-vis* their targets, and victims of misconduct fear they will lose their jobs or be ostracized within the profession, jeopardizing future employment. Also alarming is that for those who did have the courage to report bullying or sexual harassment at work, the response was dismal, often resulting in exodus from current jobs or the profession altogether. The IBA Report found that over 70 percent of those who reported workplace bullying considered the employer's response *insufficient* (33.7 percent) or *negligible* (38.2 percent). Further, 65 percent of people who reported being bullied at work and 37 percent of those reporting being sexually harassed left or have considered leaving their employment.

After reviewing these statistics and breaking them down further based on age, geography, employment setting, and position, the IBA Report discussed the ineffectiveness of common approaches for addressing bullying and sexual harassment, such as policies and training. According to the IBA

Report, policies and training do not suffice to prevent bullying and sexual harassment at the workplace. These strategies have faltered due to non-existing or unclear policies, lack of comprehensive training, inconsistent or inadequate enforcement, and woefully weak discipline. Acknowledging these widespread deficiencies, the IBA Report offered 10 recommendations as "starting points for ongoing discourse regarding how the legal profession can effectively and proactively address workplace bullying and sexual harassment." These recommendations are couched as what the legal profession *should* do, including among other things, promulgating, implementing, and training on more effective policies. Given the breadth of the misconduct, enforcement of antibullying and antisexual harassment policies must be more stringent and consistent. Powerful perpetrators must face genuine sanctions that impact their professional standing. Without enforcement with real consequences and meaningful protection against retaliation for reporting misconduct, this virulent problem will not abate.

You may be wondering how well this *global* survey represents what women experience in the legal profession in the United States, and whether it is an accurate reflection of where we stand today. The IBA research does break down some of the statistics by geography, and the results are not encouraging if you focus on just the geographic reach of the American Bar Association (ABA) membership. The United States and Canada, for example, rank fairly high in terms of incidence of bullying and sexual harassment in the law. However, we need not rely on the IBA Report alone to assess how things stand for ABA members or legal professionals practicing within ABA's geographic coverage. For that, we can turn to several surveys and reports by the ABA and others on the status and treatment of women in the profession.

The IBA Report noted that in 1989, a survey of female lawyers from 250 U.S. law firms found that 60 percent had been sexually harassed.[12] In 1992, the ABA adopted Recommendation 117, noting sexual harassment was a "serious problem" in legal workplaces. Since then the ABA has continued to tackle multiple issues facing women lawyers. The ABA website is packed with reports and resources on how individuals, firms, and other organizations can challenge the obstacles women face in the

---

12. *See* Nina Burleigh & Stephanie B. Goldberg, *Breaking the Silence: Sexual Harassment in Law Firms*, 75 Am. Bar Ass'n J. 46 (1989).

law, including sexual harassment. Fast forward three decades, and we are still trying to tackle this problem effectively, with state bar associations and the ABA conducting surveys and circulating strategy advice for targets and employers to deal with harassment head on. For example, in 2018, the ABA Commission on Women in the Profession published "Zero Tolerance: Best Practices for Combating Sex-Based Harassment in the Legal Profession" (the Zero Tolerance Toolkit), which is available online through the volunteer efforts of the Committee on Sexual Harassment and Gender-Based Bullying. It offers resources to professional groups, legal employers, and targets. But despite all the surveys, articles, and resources, the problem persists.

No one is immune from unwanted sexual harassment, regardless of gender identity. Below are common situations women encounter and strategies for addressing them:

1. A female law student working at a firm is approached by the male partner in charge of the summer associate program to have dinner with him alone "to get to know each other better." She is uncomfortable and unsure if the partner's intentions are entirely professional, but she is afraid to jeopardize a potential job offer. Over dinner, the partner refills her wine glass, urging her to "relax and have fun." At the end of the night, he kisses her, insisting that they "have to do this again."
2. A female partner is attending a firm retreat. A big rainmaker on the firm's management committee, with a reputation as a womanizer, asks her to join his table for dinner. He steers the conversation to her compensation and suggests that if she is "friendlier" to him, it could create opportunities for more high-profile work, client contact, and greater compensation. When she feigns ignorance of what being "friendlier" means, he suggests they go upstairs for a drink in his suite.
3. A female general counsel has served in her role for about a year when the CEO retires. His successor has made it clear that he does not think she is "up to the job" and that she "will have a hard time proving herself" to him. He tells her that she needs to accompany him on a cross-country trip to negotiate an important deal, but when they arrive, he tells her to "sit there and look pretty" and let

him "do all the talking." Later, he suggests they celebrate the deal by going dancing.
4. A newly minted female lawyer lands a coveted clerkship with a highly regarded judge. She is eager to prove herself, as she knows that a recommendation from this judge could help her land a high-paying job in the private sector. She is always dressed professionally. When she wears a tailored conservative pants suit, the judge comments that he prefers that she not wear pants so he can see her "shapely legs."

Women lawyers encounter these situations and worse. Usually, they involve a significant imbalance of power. The offender, having a higher position in the firm, has the power to impact the woman's current position and her future career. How many of us have been subjected to unsolicited comments about our appearance or our personal lives? How many of us have had a male colleague, client, or superior say or do something of a sexual nature in a professional setting? Far too many have suffered these indignities. Given the harsh reality of pervasive bullying and bias in the legal profession, what is a woman to do when faced with these challenges at the legal workplace, whether from peers, clients, superiors, adversaries, or judicial officers? This issue is painful and tricky to navigate, often compounded by the disparate authority between perpetrator and target.

Here are some actionable steps that women and allies can take to challenge this engrained problem:

- Know the applicable ethical and civility rules in your jurisdiction and your workplace policies; retain copies for easy reference.
- Push for training within your organization and the profession.
- Advocate for policies that require new hires to certify past issues of sexual harassment by them or certify that none exist.
- Insist that dispute resolution provisions not demand confidential arbitration, which, as of this writing, may become law.
- Advocate for settlements that do not muzzle victims from speaking out against the offensive conduct.
- Report the behavior via the applicable channels within your organization (e.g., anonymous hotline, HR) and be specific about the details of the incident.

- Keep a journal offsite documenting bad behavior and actions you have taken to address it and your employer's response.
- Call the offender out in writing, but don't stoop to that person's level. State the who, what, when, where, and how of what happened, and emphasize that you do not expect it to happen again. Keep it professional; you will lose credibility if you do otherwise.
- If the offender works with you or is a client, bring the offenses to the attention of your colleagues and seek their support. Observers of sexual harassment, both female and male, also suffer and may be willing to intervene.
- Consult a seasoned lawyer you trust outside your organization for support and advice.
- When an adversary engages in sexual harassment in ongoing litigation, consider whether to make a report to that firm's leadership or to file a motion for a protective order (if appropriate, given client interests).

There is no guarantee that these strategies will work. Sometimes, especially if your employer will not take meaningful action to stop the offensive conduct and impose discipline or even terminate the offender, you are faced with tough choices. You can stay and keep fighting, file a claim with the appropriate agency or court, or move on. We cannot sugarcoat the stress and potential career impact of asserting a claim inside or outside your organization. Unfortunately, the consequences can be harsh. There should be no shame if you opt to pass on fighting. Regrettably, if the situation is untenable, your best option given your particular circumstances may be to leave your position and find a setting that is more respectful. You can enlist counsel to support you in negotiating a separation that provides some severance to ease the transition or you can just move on. Having counseled many women on these options and having represented them in their transitions, I can say without hesitation that your health and physical safety must take priority. Unless leaders, regardless of gender, promulgate policies, organize training, conduct good faith investigations, condemn retaliation, and discipline offenders, harassment and bullying will continue. It is important to take action now by advocating to protect against sexual harassment, rather than expecting others to do so.

Francine Friedman Griesing

Career

Business Attorney, Litigator and Neutral, Serial Entrepreneur; Public Speaker and Author; Bullying and Ethics Expert

Education

- JD, *cum laude*, University of Pennsylvania Carey Law School (1981)
- BA, *magna cum laude*, Binghamton University (SUNY—Harpur College) (1978)

Best Advice

Become the best lawyer you can be because no one can take that away from you, develop a niche in which you are the "go-to" lawyer, and take control of your own career rather than rely on others to help you advance.

Personal

Fran Griesing is co-founder of Griesing Mazzeo Law, a woman-owned firm based in Philadelphia, with offices in Arizona, Florida, New Jersey, New York, and Ohio. She is a relentless advocate for diversity and elimination of bias in the legal profession and the advancement of women in law and business.

For More Information

https://www.griesinglaw.com/bio/francine-friedman-griesing
https://www.linkedin.com/in/frangriesing

How We as Men Can Make a Meaningful Difference in the Fight for Gender Parity

By Steven Velkei

I am in awe every day of the strength, resilience, and fortitude of women in law. Make no mistake. It takes those characteristics for a woman to succeed in what remains a predominantly male-dominated profession and one that bases its existence on maintaining the status quo.

The record is full of examples of how gender bias remains entrenched in so many ways, but the roots of that disparity need not be so elusive. How can one possibly have parity in the workplace when the expectations put upon each gender are fundamentally so different? I remember watching this disparity play out in stark form during the U.S. Supreme Court confirmation hearings of Brett Kavanaugh. I watched in disbelief and anger, candidly, as the nominated justice appeared belligerent and argumentative, while Dr. Christine Blasey Ford had to exercise restraint and dispassion while testifying about allegations of sexual assault. Had she behaved in any other fashion, she would have been accused of being too emotional, and her story would have been minimized and mocked. I have never forgotten observing her controlled restraint and her visible struggle to maintain her composure even while revisiting a past trauma, as compared to the reactions of the nominee. Unfortunately, those kinds of dynamics, albeit in a different context, are in play in some of the most basic interactions in the workplace.

Men can make a difference in this fight when we acknowledge two basic principles. First, we need to acknowledge that we do not know enough to make the right choices around establishing gender parity. That means acknowledging that men need to stop viewing these issues from their singular lens and recognize that the world can *and often does* look very different through the lens of a woman. Second, we need to acknowledge that men are in fact inherently biased. Every one of us is biased, including me, even if only unconsciously so. Acknowledging those two basic principles in our daily life only starts the journey—not finishes it—but they are essential predicates to making a difference and in my opinion are guaranteed to make a difference. Allow me to explain.

I strive to be an ally in the fight for gender parity. I am gay. I am married to a person of color. My mother is Hispanic and my father is first-generation American from Hungary. I understand how it feels to be treated differently, and I am all too familiar with the struggle to keep others from defining me in a way that makes me feel less. I have been the victim of discrimination and the target of countless stereotypes, assumptions, and microaggressions. I remember when I posed for pictures at one of my prior firms and the photographer recommended that I pose more like a man. . . . What??

My background and my connection, however, do not give me full insight into the unique experience of women in the workplace. But even though I consider myself an ally, if I am not careful, I could become part of the problem, woke or not.

As a man and even as a gay man, I benefit from a certain level of privilege that a woman does not get to experience. I am less likely, for example, to be the victim of workplace harassment. In contrast, one in every three women is the victim of sexual harassment in the workplace, and the vast majority of women never report it. I glide through any number of experiences that I take for granted in a way that a woman cannot. Those privileges skew my perceptions of the challenges women face. If I do not work hard to understand those experiences, I may make dangerous assumptions that will continue to foster gender disparity.

The New York Times columnist Charles Blow eloquently made this point in a column published on October 29, 2017, titled "Checking My Male Privilege." I have often cited it in speeches I give on gender bias. He writes that

> [w]hile [he] understands that all oppressions are, in some way, intersectional and connected to all other violence, that the empathetic connections of ally-ship are multidirectional and reciprocal . . . it remains a stubborn fact that it is hard to stay fully immersed in another person's pain. . . . No matter how many times you hear them talk about their struggle, and even when you feel deeply moved by the expression of it, unless you have experienced that same pain yourself, a gap remains.

I have previously joked that I began to understand women better once I started dating men (which happened later in life for me), because I got to experience firsthand at least some of what women experience. In that regard, I stepped into different shoes and realized how different that other perspective can be. In truth, those experiences helped me realize basic deficiencies or gaps in my experience and perspective, which then opened me up to listening better. Until then, I remained within my own version of male privilege, immune to any complete understanding. Charles Blow perceptively wrote in the aforementioned October 29, 2017, column: "I can't know what women experience in this country and indeed this world—not on a gut level or an experiential level—but I can learn the facts of those experiences. I can be eager to listen. I can advocate for cultural and policy changes that would make women's lives better."

If men can acknowledge that basic deficiency in understanding, it makes a solution, however imperfect, that much more attainable. In other words, I cannot look at this issue from my male perspective alone but must acknowledge and be open to the reality of another perspective. In the end, it comes back to the old adage, "Don't judge someone until you've walked a mile in their shoes." It requires throwing out basic conceptions about how women are supposed to act, talk, or behave in the work environment, and, inevitably, when those inner voices start going there, shining a light on it.

Years ago, the *The Washington Post* selected famous sayings in American history, all by famous men, and posited how a woman would have to say the same things.[13]

"Give me liberty, or give me death"	"Dave, if I could, I could just — I just really feel like if we had liberty it would be terrific, and the alternative would just be awful, you know? That's just how it strikes me. I don't know."
"Mr. Gorbachev, tear down this wall!"	"I'm sorry, Mikhail, if I could? Didn't mean to cut you off there. Can we agree that this wall maybe isn't quite doing what it should be doing? Just looking at everything everyone's been saying, it seems like we could consider removing it. Possibly. I don't know, what does the room feel?"
"I will be heard."	"Sorry to interrupt. No, go on, Dave. Finish what you had to say."
"I came. I saw. I conquered."	"I don't want to toot my own horn here at all but I definitely have been to those places and was just honored to be a part of it as our team did such a wonderful job of conquering them."

From The Washington Post. © 2015 The Washington Post. All rights reserved. Used under license.

---

13. Alexandra Petri, *Famous Quotes, The Way a Woman Would Have to Say Them during a Meeting*, THE WASH. POST (Oct. 13, 2015), https://www.washingtonpost.com/blogs/compost/wp/2015/10/13/jennifer-lawrence-has-a-point-famous-quotes-the-way-a-woman-would-have-to-say-them-during-a-meeting.

It is mind-blowing to think women are shackled by those kinds of constraints and expectations and how fundamentally inefficient it is to impose those kinds of constraints on half the workforce. But I know it to be true. I have found myself using the same kind of indirect and conciliatory language when facing certain group dynamics—as assertive as I can be and as committed as I am to advancing these issues. Sometimes it is just easier to get through a meeting that way, and you sacrifice just a little to get through it. But, over time, it gets tiring, and I expect I experience it far less frequently than women lawyers do.

Most men have the right intentions. They have meaningful relationships with women outside the workplace and they want to do the right thing. Men are constrained by their own lack of awareness of a basic deficiency in understanding, and they often tend to base policies on a misunderstanding of the issues. The first step toward making a more meaningful difference in eliminating gender bias is for men to admit that the gap exists and that they have to work differently to better understand women in the workplace. In other words, men need to acknowledge what they do not know.

Men also need to face the reality that they are biased. Let's face it. All of us are biased in many ways, and women only recently (relatively speaking) have reached basic milestones toward parity.[14] *The New Yorker* once ran an illustration taken from the satirist webcomic XKCD (featured on the following page), which captures the dilemma that women face in the workplace.

We are the sum of our experiences, both good and bad, and those experiences affect our unconscious self. And that part of us bases most decisions on "instinct" and "precedent," two scenarios where we bring limited, if any, intentionality. Without intentionality, bias will always creep into the equation. If we refuse to acknowledge it, we truly miss understanding the root of the problems surrounding gender parity.

---

14. A few statistics illustrate the point. It was not until 1983 that the Ivy League institutions were completely co-ed; *see* Genevieve Carlton, *A History of Women in Higher Education*, BESTCOLLEGES.COM (Feb. 22, 2022). It was not until 2010 that a woman, Kathleen Sullivan, became a named partner at an AM Law 100 law firm; *see* Sarah Mui, *Quinn Emanuel Makes Kathleen Sullivan Name Partner*, ABA J. (Mar. 11, 2010), and *Outstanding Women Lawyers: Kathleen Sullivan*, NAT. LAW J. (May 4, 2015). It was not until 2023 that women led just over 10 percent of Fortune 500 companies; *see* Emma Hinchliffe, *Women Run More than 10% of Fortune 500 Companies for the First Time*, FORTUNE (Jan. 12, 2023).

Source: *XKCD, "How it Works" (https://xkcd.com/385/)*

Recent studies report that only 14 percent of those surveyed acknowledge even having an average level of bias. In fact, the vast majority of those surveyed—85 percent—believe that they are less biased than others. That is just not statistically possible. We take comfort in our intentions, but we miss the impact of countless decisions we make that derive, not from intentionality, but from deep-rooted unconscious biases that we formed in childhood (i.e., heavily influenced by norms and values from decades ago). These include fundamentally basic decisions in the workplace involving hiring, work assignments, and retention.

In other words, values and beliefs that we may reject, if asked about them, can still affect how we react to a particular situation based on our subconscious mind. That point became clear to me when I visited the Harvard website to test my level of implicit bias as a gay man toward the LGBTQIA+ community.[15] I never expected the results that I obtained. I discovered that I have unconscious biases toward the same group with whom I identify. Those results opened my eyes to the complexity of the situations we face, but also gave me the perspective to approach these topics and discussions with utmost humility and without judgment.

The effect of these unconscious biases is real. Our unconscious drives our decisions daily, and important ones at that. It happens all the time in hiring decisions, work assignments, and even in performance reviews. We all as humans revert to those things and those people with whom we are

---

15. Visit https://implicit.harvard.edu/implicit/takeatest.html to take the Harvard implicit bias test.

most comfortable, but those who are most comfortable to us almost never include someone who is different from us. Because men overwhelmingly continue to pull the levers of control, women are operating at a distinct disadvantage unless we create processes that require intentionality.

That means we have to bring more intentionality into decisions that affect a lawyer's career, such as hiring, work assignments, and retention. I offer the following situation to illustrate this point. Many years ago, I was staffing a new litigation matter. A woman of color had approached me a few weeks prior and asked if she could be on my next matter. When I discussed staffing with a more junior colleague on the new case, I recommended we put her on the file. My colleague instead advocated for a straight white male. When I asked whether he had a negative experience with the woman, he answered no. When I pushed to bring her on, he pushed back again. "Why not bring [insert: another straight white male]," he recommended. The reality is that the decision had nothing to do with the female lawyer's capabilities. As he admitted, he had never heard that there was a problem with her work. Instead, he felt more comfortable with his particular choice and did not recognize his unconscious bias in the moment. The good news is that we brought the female lawyer on to the case, and she did a tremendous job. I often think about how different things could have been had I not had that conversation. That conversation took place in minutes, and it could have gone, and often does go, in a completely different direction.

Bringing intentionality to tackling these unconscious biases is the best approach that individuals in the legal field can take to advance greater gender parity. While we are starting to see meaningful change, progress is slow, and true gender parity is years away. One can look to any number of metrics when evaluating the change. For years now, I have followed the invaluable work conducted by top recruiting firm, Major, Lindsey & Africa, which tracks the compensation gap between men and women law partners. I have watched with consternation as the disparity in compensation grew over the reporting periods, even as law firms touted well-funded programs designed to reduce that disparity. Remarkably, the gap in compensation between men and women *more than doubled* between 2010 and 2018. I am pleased to report, however, that this upward trend has finally stopped, and over the last 4 years that gap has narrowed. See Figure 2.1.

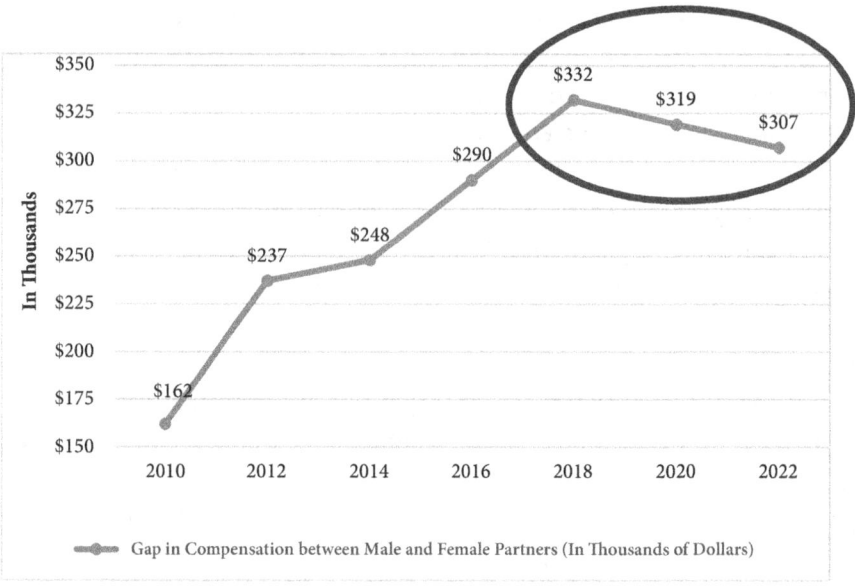

Figure 2.1 *Gap in Partner Compensation over Time*
Source: *Major, Lindsey & Africa 2018 and 2022 Partner Compensation Surveys*

Notably, the compensation gap between men and women narrowed by just 7.5 percent over the last two reporting periods, but it is now finally trending in the right direction. Let us celebrate even those small victories.

Over the last 6 years, I have been on a journey toward achieving a better understanding of these issues and myself. While I have made a host of mistakes and struggled with these issues repeatedly, I do not regret a moment of that process because I now can confidently say that I am better for it and better in my dealings because of it. To be clear, I did not do it alone. The women and men who are GOOD Guys (Guys Overcoming Obstacles to Diversity), a program designed by the National Conference of Women's Bar Associations to gain the support of men in the fight for gender parity in the law, provided invaluable support and guidance to me over that period.[16] My journey started in earnest when I joined that organization, and I credit so much of my recent professional development to it. Indeed, women lawyers inspired me to start my own firm. I connected

---

16. For more information, visit the National Conference of Women's Bar Associations website at www.goodguysinlaw.com.

with their stories of feeling marginalized and deciding to take control back by starting something different, and I followed in their path. I successfully helped women in Orange County gain access to comprehensive reproductive care, but only after I developed the tools to listen and gain a better understanding of what that actually meant for women. I have had more women mentors in recent years than male ones.

In short, men can make a meaningful difference in issues of gender disparity by following a few basic principles and, at the same time (speaking selfishly), can unlock experiences and connections that will strengthen, not dilute, their professional development.

Steven Velkei

Career

Trial Litigator, Velkei Law PA

Education

- JD, UC College of the Law, San Francisco (formerly UC Hastings College of Law)
- AB, Princeton University

Best Advice

Embrace the unique you and pursue what gives you passion.

Personal

Steve Velkei has been with his husband for 17 years and lives in the Hollywood Hills. He loves travel, vinyl, books, and hiking.

For More Information

https://www.linkedin.com/in/steve-velkei-464aa3177

Discussion Questions

1. Have you encountered explicit or implicit bias in your practice—either within your workplace or in your interactions with co-counsel and opposing counsel?

2. If you encountered bias in the legal profession, how have you responded to it? Consider whether your biases have affected someone's career.

3. If you experienced bias in the profession, have you shared your experiences with others? Why or why not?

4. What lessons have you learned from your experiences with bias?

5. Have you faced soft discrimination? If so, discuss your experiences and how you reacted.

6. What strategies can be used to combat soft discrimination? What strategies can we try in the future?

7. What unexpected opportunities have you experienced in your professional life? How did they compare to your plans for your career? How did you respond to those opportunities?

8. Do you have sexual harassment policies and trainings in your workplace? If so, discuss whether they are effective.

9. What can you do to disrupt sexual harassment in the workplace?

10. Have you experienced or witnessed sexual harassment? What do you want us to know? Discuss these experiences and the subsequent effects.

11. Do you know male leaders who are champions for diversity, equity, inclusion, and belonging? How are they manifesting their support, and how can we support them? How can we encourage other male leaders to follow their example?

CHAPTER 3

Hidden Hazards and How to Overcome Them

This chapter demonstrates the truth of Brecht's statement through stories of overcoming adversity. The authors in this chapter describe their journeys around hidden hazards to find joy as they

"If there are obstacles, the shortest line between two points may be the crooked line."

—BERTOLT BRECHT

became their authentic selves. Although each author faced a different type of obstacle—addiction, depression, anxiety, perfectionism, fear, shame, and guilt, to name just a few—the common theme of recovery, creativity, and courage brings hope to us all. Even when obstacles seem overwhelming and insurmountable, our own journey can lead to happiness in unexpected ways. These authors help us remember that we are not alone.

Redefining Obstacles as Opportunities for Growth

By Erika R. Bales

I often find that starting with definitions can help focus my thinking. Merriam-Webster defines obstacle as "something that impedes progress or achievement."

It has been my experience, both in my personal life and in my practice, that framing is one of the most important aspects of defining success, however success looks based on the situation. To me, thinking about an obstacle, much less confronting one, feels decidedly negative. Obstacles can be daunting or even insurmountable. Have I overcome obstacles in my life? By most definitions, assuredly. But that is not how I view my past or the circumstances that comprise it.

Was the man I knew as my paternal grandfather illiterate of both words and math? Did my father's mother drop out of high school? Was my dad a high school dropout who only got his General Education Degree (GED) so he could obtain a certificate from the National Institute for Automotive Service Excellence (ASE) and be an auto mechanic? Were my parents functioning alcoholics who would go into rages and have occasional physical fights, divorcing when I was 14? That same year, did I enter what was to be a series of emotionally, physically, and financially abusive relationships? All these questions are answerable in the affirmative. Did I overcome any of these hardships, or did I just live my life and incorporate these realities into my personal narrative?

My dad's biological father abandoned my grandmother and their three children to move to a nearby county and remarry. The man I would come to know as my grandfather joined the family in the 1960s. My father would tell me stories about how, when he and my grandfather would go to the grocery store together, my grandfather would basically have to hand over all of his money to the cashier and pray they would give him proper change back because he did not know how to count money. Only when I became an adult did it hit me how my grandfather, working as the janitor at the elementary school I would end up attending, must have felt washing lessons for children off of blackboards that as an adult he himself could not read.

Because of these experiences, my father was quite insistent that I focus on my studies, particularly reading and math. He would make me memorize lists of words for school spelling bees, going through them again and again. If I missed a word twice, I had to write it 10 times. If I missed it again, I would have to write the word and all of its definitions from the dictionary five times. Seldom did I miss a word a fourth time.

Now I live by words for a living and use them much in my personal life. My husband and daughter are both dyslexic. I spend a lot of time helping to sound out and spell, reminding them that words are completely made up and the supposed rules that govern them often make little or no sense. Do your best, then ask for help. There is no shame in not knowing something, but there can be in not asking for help.

My paternal grandmother is what most people would describe as "salt of the earth." She had virtually nothing in terms of money, but on the weekends she would go to garage sales, buy used kids clothes and toys by the garbage bag full, and deliver them to where her grandbabies lived. And, if push came to shove, she would give someone the shirt off her back if they needed it.

After my grandfather died, the factory jobs my grandmother had relied on throughout her life to support herself and her family began to dry up in our small Indiana town. She recognized that education was key to her being able to care for herself as she advanced in age. Consequently, when I was in high school, I had the privilege of helping her study for her GED. She passed on her very first attempt; I was never prouder of my family.

Although my dad was a staunch advocate for his children's education, his own scholastic past was a bit rockier. In the eleventh grade he dropped out of high school; I will never truly understand why he dropped out so close to graduation. Having observed my dad over the years, it is my lay opinion that he may also be dyslexic or have some other learning disability, and that it, combined with aching poverty and his inability to confront his own childhood abuses, helped push him out of traditional school. But he loved cars and is one of the very best mechanics I have ever met. A GED was required to get his ASE certification. So he got his GED on his first try and did what he needed to get his ASE.

My parents married young and were involved in the biker and van-er (i.e., people who live out of their vans) communities. Being exposed to these lifestyles helped form some of the fondest memories of my childhood; these communities were a large extended family, always there to help each other, no questions asked. Although there were some downsides—including exposure to drugs, alcohol, and other adult situations—the collective experience taught me valuable lessons about the potential dangers of controlled substances, drinking, and driving, and I learned to establish clear boundaries even with adults or people seen as having a superior position of authority. I also learned one thing that has come in very handy in my practice as an attorney: keeping secrets.

The social communities my parents were part of fostered a sense of security and taught me that respect is earned and not given. At the same time, there were interpersonal relationship structures that I had to process and, in some cases, chose to reject. Homosexuals were part of these clubs, and I do not recall any negative treatment of either them or their partners. Conflicts, on the other hand, were often settled through physical violence (fist fights). And once the fight was over, beers (or other alcoholic beverages) were had and the beef was squashed. That was true even between men and women. I was taught that if a woman was prepared to battle a man, she should be prepared to get hit like a man. This was not seen as domestic violence, which was actually discouraged in the groups.

My parents did not shy away from conflict, likely in part because of abuses in their own childhoods. Before their divorce, they fought frequently. It was not uncommon for my mom to scream herself hoarse. Although my parents never went to the doctor for treatment or formal diagnoses, I believe my dad once cracked a few of my mom's ribs, and, in another instance, broke bones in his hand trying to punch out his van window when my mom tried to take my brother and me from the house one night. My mom is no shrinking violet; she could definitely give as good as she got. Again, I have processed these situations and decided that in my life and in my family we simply keep our hands to ourselves.

My first serious boyfriend was 22 years old when I was 14, the same year my parents were separating and divorced. Clearly, this relationship was not appropriate and involved an extreme power differential—although I believe I was more mature than he was. My next serious boyfriend had been expelled from my school district by the time we met. For context, I was a band nerd, friends with the principal's kids, and had a job. This boy was in and out of juvenile delinquency halls. He was physically violent, emotionally manipulative, financially draining, and adept at gaslighting and isolation. During our relationship, I quit playing baseball, quit band, and avoided most of my friends. I had to keep the relationship a secret from my mom because she knew what a dumpster fire of a human being he was and would have done nearly anything to keep him away from me. Of course, as a young person who had not had the best examples of interpersonal relationships, I was sure my mom was wrong; she could not possibly understand our young love. In the end, she was completely right, but there was no way I could see it in the moment. It is so hard to be so wrong about something that you have allowed to consume your entire life.

By the time I realized how right my mom had been, I had thrown away the things that meant the most to me. And because I was sure this person was going to kill me, I fled my hometown and moved a six-hour drive away to another state. I had an unlisted telephone number and paid cash or used money orders for everything I could. Yet, somehow, he found my telephone number and called me. He told me that he was going to find me and finish what he had started; he was going to beat me to death. Surprised by my own rage, I told him that I would worry about that once he managed to get a car and hung up on him. I broke my lease and started crashing on couches of acquaintances to stay further under the radar. He never did find me. I have since learned that he has children, has been addicted to drugs, and has been in and out of prison.

It was because of him and that move to a neighboring state to escape that I met my husband when I went to apply for a job in a restaurant where he worked in the kitchen. My husband is a kind man who never expected a thing from me. Sadly, he was broken in his own ways and did not feel he deserved love from me. Despite our respective traumas, we loved each other and healed together. We continue to love each other and have been married for 22-plus years and managed to have two of our three children in our 40s.

I was lucky. I met the love of my life at 19 and, while that relationship was a sure thing, my career certainly was not. I have worked in residential home construction, for nearly every pizza chain, as a waitress at innumerable restaurants, bars, and cafes, and at temporary employment agencies.

Through one of those temp agencies, I found my first job in the legal industry. This job was with a solo attorney in a tiny town practicing out of the first floor of his townhouse. Recognizing my ability and interest, he bought out my contract from the temp agency, gave me a raise, and provided me with benefits.

From there, I would go on to work for other firms across the Midwest, working in various aspects of civil litigation while I attended Purdue University. My undergraduate degree is in behavioral sciences; I wanted to be an FBI agent specializing in serial killers. But during my studies, that specific goal seemed to fit my life less and less.

Over the years, I worked for some attorneys who were brilliant, inspirational. Others were walking examples of how not to conduct yourself as a lawyer—or as a human being. It got to the point where I decided that if the awful lawyers I had worked for managed to pass the bar exam, I absolutely could too. So my husband and I decided I would attend law school. And then I passed the bar exam.

To me, these were not obstacles to overcome or succumb to; they were simply my realities, trickling down over time. Immutable truths. Did these realities interfere with or slow my progress? Probably, but I will never know for certain. What I do know is that each of these circumstances individually and cumulatively made me who I am, polishing my edges like water shapes stone, affecting the decisions of my life.

I have no access to generational wealth and will likely not have any wealth to leave to my children. For me, there was no legacy admission to a top-tier school; a parent having a regular jail cell to sleep off their latest binge does not qualify one for much of anything except for hushed whispers or unwanted pity. It is my opinion that my overdeveloped sense of loyalty to family and personal responsibility have served me well and helped me meet my goals. Would I be who I am—a lawyer, businesswoman, wife, mother, daughter, sister, friend, and so much more—if my life had been any different? Would I be able to recognize myself if these obstacles had been overcome by those around me?

Is there more to my story? Absolutely. Were they obstacles as well? By definition, yes. I never viewed any of the foregoing as obstacles. These were simply facts—it was what it was. I had to figure out what I did and did not want for my life and set my goals accordingly.

Setting goals feels more positive than focusing on obstacles. Trying to forecast the potholes, speed bumps, and detours I might encounter along my path provided me with a sense of power. Potholes can be avoided. Speed bumps can be surmounted without bottoming out if you slow down. Detours can be followed and the destination may still be reached.

Perhaps the most important part of confronting any situation is to recognize those things over which you do and do not have control. You can never truly control someone else's behavior. All you can control is your reaction to it. You can never completely foresee what is to come. When whatever it is arrives, acknowledge it and incorporate it into the path toward your goal.

I frequently used positive spin messaging in my practice. If I could work magic, what would be the most perfect outcome? What is the worst possible outcome you would be willing to accept and still be willing to close this chapter of your life? Is there a "drop dead" issue or item about which you are simply not willing to negotiate and must achieve?

Conversations about goals should never be a one-and-done talk. Circumstances change. New or previously known facts emerge or become clarified. Client (and familial) needs can change dramatically in the blink of an eye. Changing a goal, or altering the path toward that goal, feels much more manageable when you recognize those things over which you do and do not have control and manage your expectations.

In short, in my experience, I have found that the best way to overcome an obstacle is to redefine it. Sometimes an obstacle is simply that: an obstacle. Acknowledge it and decide how it will impact the path to your goal. Is it a pothole you may fall into? A speed bump that will cause you to bottom out? Or a detour to follow? Obstacles feel big, monoliths of potential failure or jabberwockies to be battled. But a minor adjustment may allow you to avoid calamity and to reach your goal in the most expeditious manner based on your own, or your clients', cost-benefit analysis, considering where you (or they) are mentally, physically, or financially at any given moment.

The best way to overcome an obstacle may simply be to accept it and continue to move forward, one step at a time.

Erika R. Bales

Career
General practice attorney experienced in family law and real estate litigation, debt collection, and business assistance, The Law Office of Erika R. Bales, PLLC

Education
- JD, North Carolina Central University School of Law (2010)
- BA, Behavioral Sciences, Psychology Concentration, Purdue University (2005)

Best Advice
Listen to your gut. If something feels off, even if you cannot articulate exactly what the problem is, trust your instinct and try to extricate yourself from the situation as much as possible to seek help or advice. Although we are no longer chased by apex predators in our day-to-day lives, we still have that "lizard brain" reflexive part of our instincts that can really help us if we listen to it.

Personal
After a brief hiatus, Erika reopened her successful solo general practice to continue her tradition of helping members of her community navigate the complexities of modern life. Erika has published multiple articles on various topics over the years, including for the *ABA Journal*. She loves to share knowledge and in July 2023 gave a primer on compliance and security for *Creditor Collections Today*. Erika has three children between the ages of 15 months and 12 years and two fur babies (dogs). She has been married to her husband, Andrew, for nearly 22 years. Erika's hobbies include caring for her ever-expanding houseplant collection (especially her orchids), playing with her kids, and visiting estate sales and auctions.

For More Information
erika@erikabaleslaw.com
(888) 299-8675 (Toll free)

Learn How to Define Your Priorities and Use Them for Success: How to Get Unfrazzled

By Kate Ahern

It took me years to figure out why, despite becoming a time management rock star, I still felt like I was drowning. Law and life ask a lot of women. Opening your to-do list probably feels like when my toddler picks up a roll of toilet paper by the end square and it unrolls across the entire room like a medieval scroll. We typically attempt to handle the many demands of law and life in three ways: planning, organizing, and powering through.

>
> "There's just never enough time to keep up with everything!"[1]

You Plan and Organize

Think of your to-do list, your beautiful paper planner full of tasks *(ah, that new planner high . . . full of possibility and clean, unspoiled pages)*, calendar, time blocks, sticky notes, emails to yourself, phone reminders, the latest productivity hack, and so on. We're convinced that more organization, or more planning, or the right system, will be the panacea that finally gives us enough time to keep up with everything.

(Spoiler: Not so much.)

You Power Through

Next, we power through and try to be more focused, efficient, and productive because we're also convinced that mustering a bit more will power, discipline, or focus is the key to making it all fit.

(Spoiler: Also, not so much.)

---

1. Throughout this chapter, I'll share quotes from women I've helped. While this chapter is the story of my own journey, it's also the shared story of many others, and I'd like you to hear their voices as well. After you read this chapter, I'd love to hear from you, too!

We keep doing these same two things, partly because it's all we know. No one teaches us the skills we need to handle it all. Most importantly though, it's all we feel we can control. *Let's break the fourth wall and put that in bold; it's that important:* **Planning and powering through are all we feel we can control.** The gender bias women face every day makes it feel unrealistic to control the firehose of stuff coming at us, to stop, or to say no, so we plan and power through to try to make it all fit instead. Let's take three examples of how this unfolds in our day-to-day lives:

Guilt

Women are expected to be communal and nurturing and to take care of others. We're supposed to say yes, be responsive to others, and worry about what someone will think or feel if we don't take care of something. This particular flavor of gender bias leads us to feel guilty, pretty much no matter what we're doing. We always feel like we should be doing something else. Setting and enforcing boundaries triggers even more guilt.

"I have so much guilt related to each piece of time. If I'm doing one thing, I'm not doing another. Then I feel guilty that I'm not fully present."

"I . . . tried to do everything and wiped myself out. I either didn't cut stuff out or I did and then felt guilty about it."

"I'm a people-pleaser."

Guilt dials up the pressure to say "yes" to every ask and task. BUT WHAT IF the guilt you're feeling lacks credibility because it's external? What if that guilt is not a reliable internal indicator to follow but just a reflection of gender bias?

Perfectionism

Society expects women to be perfect. Our impressive, brilliant accomplishments are constantly undervalued—another gross flavor of gender bias. When we absorb those messages over a lifetime, we tend to internalize pressure to be perfect. In other words, we often assume that being a perfectionist is just part of who we are. However, while you may have a healthy drive to produce quality work and outcomes, the unhealthy perfectionism holding many women back is a result of years of gender bias and societal expectations. In other words, *the call is coming from outside the house!*

Perfectionism dials up the pressure to get an A+ in everything we do and makes it difficult to allow asks and tasks to take up only the appropriate amount of time and attention. BUT WHAT IF you are not really a perfectionist? What if your appropriately smart and thorough tendencies are just flooded with gender bias until they turn into a perfectionism problem?

"I lose so much time trying to do everything perfectly."

"I'm not good enough to do this."

"I'm just a perfectionist."

"Everything always takes me longer than I think it will."

Imposter Syndrome

Imposter syndrome is that awful feeling that you're really not as capable as your mountain of gold stars, degrees, and accomplishments suggests. The constant doubt of yourself and your abilities. The feeling that you don't really belong here. Those nagging feelings lead us to try to prove ourselves constantly. We struggle to rest or celebrate between the accomplishments that make us feel worthy, prove we can do this, or show we belong here. *Get those dots Ms. Pac-Man! Level unlocked, boom, accomplished; on to the next!*

Women are routinely assumed to be less competent, less committed. We face subtle, trivializing,

"I can't do this."

"These people are better/smarter/deeper/more impactful/more successful than me."

"I'm not smart enough to. . . ."

"I'm not going to make it as a. . . ."

"There's just something wrong with me that I can't do this; I'm different than everyone else."

"I'm an imposter and someone will find out."

gaslighting comments. We're also the subject of "benevolent sexism," which results in less challenging assignments and opportunities, to protect us from what others assume we cannot handle. It's not surprising we doubt ourselves. It would be a miracle if we didn't!

So-called imposter syndrome leads us to fill our time with lots of projects that don't serve us, get us the results we want, or take us where we want to go (looking at you, most committees I've ever been on). BUT WHAT IF imposter syndrome is not just an internal issue for you to solve? What if instead you're feeling the impact of a lifetime of gender bias?

Because we've internalized gender bias, it rarely occurs to us to do anything other than just try to fit it all in and get it all done. Remember Monica's secret closet on *Friends*? If you were busy watching *How I Met Your Mother* instead, let me catch you up. Monica was known for having it all together; her apartment and stuff were always perfectly clean and organized. But later in the series we learn Monica has a secret, mega-disorganized closet full of miscellaneous things she couldn't fit anywhere else. She needed people to think she had it all together, all figured out, so she was terrified someone would find out about the messy closet. (Could this metaphor be any more thinly veiled?)

You see, planning is like trying to organize that overstuffed closet. The planners, sticky notes, and lists feel great at first, but it will keep returning to chaos until you declutter. Powering through is like trying to muster an extra bit of discipline, throwing all your body weight against that closet door, willing it all to fit. It might work for a moment, but eventually the stressed hinges will break.

Meanwhile, the world's answer is throwing time management tips at us, but again, gender bias just turns time management itself into another attempt to cram all the to-dos into our closet, which explains why I hear women make statements similar to those quoted to the right.

"Time management? ... ugh. I tried and failed at that; it didn't work."

"Time management stresses me out."

"Time management doesn't feel approachable."

And so here we are with our overstuffed closets. Our needs are not getting met; we feel out of alignment with the life we want; we question our choices and our profession *(and feel guilty about those thoughts, of course).* Meanwhile, the life we worked so hard to build is draining the life out of us. We react by looking inside, beating ourselves up, asking *"Why can't I do this?"* or *"What's wrong with me?" Nothing friend, absolutely nothing is wrong with you! You are completely capable and absolutely amazing!* It's not you. Again, the call is coming from outside the house!

As women, we're pressured to pay attention to others' needs. As lawyers, we're pressured to respond to clients, to take on nonbillable projects and roles for the good of our firm or industry. But there's no one encouraging us to pay attention to our own priorities. *And ignoring your priorities + over-filling your closet = burnout.* Turning up the volume on your own priorities solves both parts of this equation.

When I got clear on my priorities, it felt like the moment when a 3D picture suddenly and clearly pops out of the Magic Eye puzzle. I realized how much of my time and effort was unnecessarily going to things that were not important to me, and I couldn't unsee it. That realization gave me life-changing insight and empowered me to help myself and other women navigate the pressures of gender bias and our profession.

Your priorities are the key to decluttering your closet. When you're clear on your priorities, you can always stop and compare all the asks and tasks against them and filter out what doesn't serve you. Your priorities act as a guide for choosing and acting every day on what's most important to you *(and that, lawyer friend, is what psychology tells us makes humans happy).*

If you're thinking, *"But Kate, it sounds great in theory, but how can I actually do that?"* or *"But Kate, there's really nothing I can put down or filter out; I've tried!"* Then please tell your resistance to grab a magazine and chill in the waiting room; we'll call it into the exam room in a minute.

True, using your priorities this way can be hard for four main reasons:

You Don't Know Your Priorities, What You Most Value, What Makes You Happy

This often happens to lawyers. I decided to be a lawyer at age 12; then I spent years following that path. *Get good grades in high school, overachieve, get into college, repeat in college to get into law school, repeat in law school to get into practice, repeat in practice to . . . um . . .* and that's where I got stuck. I was on the same path, head down, for so long I didn't pause to look up and think about what was most important to me. By the time I did, considering my priorities and what I really wanted felt difficult and strangely unfamiliar.

Solution: Get very clear on your priorities, and revisit them often.

You Confuse Goals with Priorities

Goals work best when they're a concrete way to act on your priorities. If you're hitting goals but are feeling unsatisfied, your goals may not be connected to your priorities.

Solution: Start with your priorities, then use them as a guide for setting your goals, a way to act on your priorities.

Everything Feels Like a Priority

When we're not clear on our priorities internally, we look around externally instead, and everything seems important. There's no filter. Plus, as lawyers, our brains are really good at justifying everything as a priority.

Solution: Know your priorities so you can clearly see what's important and filter your time and energy accordingly.

Your Priorities Are in Conflict with Biases and Other External Pressures

Once you're clear on your priorities, you'll likely see where they're in conflict with some of the gender bias and societal pressures. But there are other sources of pressure as well. Other types of bias, how you were raised, messages the world sent you as you grew up, the impact of these factors on your self-worth, and so on, can all get in the way when you attempt to align your time with your priorities. For example, my low socioeconomic status and first-generation college student experiences led me to try constantly to prove that I was worthy, to the exclusion of my own priorities.

Solution: After getting clarity on your priorities, examine what factors are most likely to get in the way.

Back to the waiting room! Okay, resistance, we'll see you now; hop up on the table, please.

Now Try Examining Your Own Resistance

Put it in the X-ray machine and see if you can tell what's really going on in there. Is it one of the above four issues in particular, or, more likely, a nasty mixed cocktail of a few of them? The more you examine where your personal obstacles are coming from, the more you'll see opportunities to save time and energy by filtering out what doesn't align with what's most important to you *(and the more those gender bias pressures will loosen their grip on you),* and the more you'll:

- take back control of your time and feel confident about how you spend it
- feel focused
- feel awesome about what you accomplish every day
- know when to say no, feel more confident saying no, and have less guilt and stress when you do say no
- notice things you don't need to be doing at all and things you're overdoing, where you're unnecessarily using a ton of time and energy to get an A+ in something that doesn't matter or get you to where you actually want to go
- disconnect, rest, take care of yourself, enjoy your life, and feel present with the people you love
- feel balanced (and know how to adjust if you tip out of balance)

I call this state "Unfrazzled," and helping women achieve it is my life's mission.

Friend, you're a highly educated, high achiever. You've probably been hitting the gas your whole life, and you're making incredible forward progress. But what if you get clear on your priorities and the obstacles in your way? What if you start aligning your time with your priorities? *For me, it felt like realizing the emergency brake was also on the whole time—no wonder I was*

"I feel more in control. Before, I would have tried to do everything and wiped myself out. I either didn't cut stuff out or I did and then felt guilty about it. [Kate's approach] helped me rein that in and make good decisions about my time. Things feel balanced now. I even feel better saying no, and I no longer feel guilty about it!"

drained! How much easier would it feel to drive where you want to go? How much faster would you get there? What would our profession look like if success as a woman lawyer felt this way—felt Unfrazzled?

That's my dream for all women lawyers.

You can use this chapter as a starting point to help you get clear on your priorities, navigate what's getting in the way, align your time with your priorities, confidently filter out the rest, and plan for taking focused action every day on what's most important to you, without feeling guilty, burned out, or haunted by what you feel like you should be doing instead. Also, connect with others so you have a regular, consistent escape from the culture that makes you feel weird, selfish, guilty, or like an outsider. It can supercharge your progress to be surrounded by others who make living an Unfrazzled life feel normal, expected, and respected, where people cheer you on for going after it!

Here's to your Unfrazzled future, and I'm pumped to hear from you![2]

---

2. Really. I'd love to hear what's going on with you. Feel free to connect with me at katieaahern@gmail.com, and let me know which of the obstacles above is causing you the most trouble right now or where you're feeling stuck. Talk soon!

Kate Ahern

Career

Unfrazzled Strategist; Time Management Mentor; Law Professor; Transactional Lawyer; Former AmLaw 200 attorney

Education
- LLM, Taxation, Boston University School of Law
- JD, Roger Williams University School of Law
- BS, Accounting, University of Rhode Island College of Business

Best Advice

Get clear on your priorities, align your time with them, regularly revisit them, surround yourself with others doing the same, and identify your frazzle factors that are getting in the way. Go outside, often.

Personal

Kate Ahern is a wife, mom, friend, breakfast-enthusiast, and giraffe-adorer. She is often found gushing over sunsets, joyfully crunching leaves underfoot, staring mesmerized up into tree canopies, or trying to change the world for women from her laptop in the corner of a coffee shop. She is more fun than her LLM in tax law might otherwise suggest.

For More Information

www.KateUnfrazzled.com

Drains on Personal Time

By Chancellor Anne C. Martin

It is funny to think about family as being a drain on personal time, and I would never characterize my caretaking responsibilities as a drain. If anything, the expectations of me away from my court, and formerly my law practice, act as a reality check for me regarding priorities and personal satisfaction. And I say that as someone who loves being a lawyer and who loves being a judge even more!

I grew up with two parents who were married for 58 years, until my father's death at the age of 83 last year. I have two siblings I like very much and parents who loved me fiercely and always told me I could be anything I wanted to be. I experienced the same insecurities, teenage angst, worries about being popular, and body image issues that all girls grew up with in the 1970s and 1980s. But I was always an exceptional student, a likeable person, and attractive enough that I could make things happen for myself with enough hard work and determination. I have grit and put significant effort into everything I do, for which I have been rewarded.

That is not why I was asked to write this article; that is probably a story to which many readers relate. Women who become successful lawyers and judges get there by working harder than many of their male counterparts and earn every bit of the accolades they receive. My story is about being a parent.

Becoming a parent has been the greatest joy, but also the greatest challenge, and in some ways brought me the greatest sorrow of my life. My son, who turned 18 last year, has Fragile X syndrome and autism. I had never heard of Fragile X until his diagnosis. We identified developmental delays before he was 2 years old, and he was diagnosed with autism at 3. The Fragile X syndrome was a surprise and a real punch in the gut. This condition results from a hereditary chromosomal irregularity that causes developmental delays and intellectual disabilities. Essentially, my son has a low IQ and will never be able to learn enough to live independently. Fragile X is a "cousin" to Down syndrome without some of the physical characteristics and associated medical challenges (although some challenges can develop later in life). Fragile X is the only known cause of autism. We learned my son had Fragile X when we did some genetic testing of him to qualify for a sleep neurology study at Vanderbilt. This inherited condition came as a significant shock to his dad and me, and to my family, given that my parents came from multi-kid families and I had many cousins from those aunts and uncles. There had never been any sign of this condition in our family, all of whom are biologically related. I was the nonmutated carrier of this condition, which we discovered came through my mother's family, all previously undetected in our large extended family.

I do not have words to describe the sadness and fear I experienced as a parent when I realized my son would never be able to be truly independent, much less go to college, marry, and have children, or be a successful adult as I defined that term. My mother and I have often spoken of the guilt we feel about passing on this trait, which was not then tested for in utero. My husband and I have since divorced but we remain dedicated to co-parenting and supporting each other and we have learned a lot since the diagnosis. Teachers, therapists, programs, and support persons have been true blessings to us and have helped us raise a wonderful, funny, curious, silly man-child of 18. Our son continues to amaze us with his somewhat innocent way of looking at the world, his quirkiness and repetitive questioning to those he meets about their pets and their children, and his joy at the few friends he has made.

As his mother—especially as a single mother—I have experienced a lot of grief along the way. Our friends with typical children the same age drifted away as they made friends with their kids' friends' parents, which became their new social circle. I continued to have a large network of friends, including them, with whom I spent time. We did not, however, have families we vacationed with or joined for barbecues or multigenerational dinner parties. My friends' kids did not find my son interesting. They thought he was annoying and weird. Most of them attended private school and did not experience non-neurotypical kids in the classroom. My son was a challenge and often had bad nights. We did not mix easily with others. Special needs kids with autism do not join in play or play appropriately, as do typical children. My son did not get asked to sleepovers, and we did not get invited to playdates. In the meantime, his dad and I continued to try different therapies and programs to help him develop skills and work through his social and cognitive difficulties. I cannot count how many teams, camps, and groups we were politely asked to abandon, or for which we soon realized that continuation was making everyone involved miserable and that we should quietly withdraw.

While all this was occurring, my career was blossoming. I was a ferocious commercial and employment litigator. I was at a large firm by Nashville standards. I was in leadership roles at my firm, the bar, and nonprofits. I had many clients, worked long, hard hours, and (almost) never let anyone see the stress I carried from responsibilities at home. Divorce and breast cancer were challenges I handled along the way while trying not to miss a beat. None of this was possible without a supportive husband (albeit one who eventually became an ex-husband), and great parents and other family. I felt that I thrived under pressure. I was making great money and bought expensive shoes from time to time. I convinced myself that I was the best mother I could be, because my economic success would provide my son resources through the end of his life after I was gone. I worked a lot and ran myself ragged, although it was very satisfying in many ways.

Just before my 50th birthday, I did an about-face. A judicial position became available that was my dream job. I was of the proper political persuasion to run for it, but an appealing candidate had already announced. I was handling some complex litigation that I needed to see through, and I was mentoring two young women lawyers I really believed in, for whom I felt I needed to stay at my firm. It did not seem possible that I could run for judge and potentially leave all this behind. Plus, I questioned whether I could be the mother I needed to be in that circumstance. Those barriers to running soon resolved themselves in various ways, and so I decided to run. After a brutal year-long campaign, I beat two primary candidates and was elected. I relished campaigning and loved getting to meet those I did not know, as well as visit unfamiliar parts of the Nashville community. I have never looked back and have figured out some things along the way. My friends really stepped up to help with childcare so that I didn't have to drag my son all over town (which, when I did try to do that, ended with both of us in tears).

Being a judge is stressful, and my chancellor role is extremely challenging. However, I have greater control of my schedule than I used to, and when I go home at night, unless I need to prepare for court the next day (which is more often than not), I am not on the clock the way I was with clients who needed to talk to me after hours. I am more *present* for my son. I am a natural at being an adjudicator, even though I can go toe to toe in complex litigation with the best of them. While I sometimes miss the highs and the lows, and particularly the client relationships of private practice, the public service I do as a judge is extremely satisfying. It is nice to work on my files without wondering whether I am adding value, whether the client can afford me, and whether the risk for the client is worth the potential reward. My job is to move the cases through and bring them to conclusion, however and whatever that looks like. I think my experience as a special needs parent has given me some gifts that I would not have otherwise gained.

First of all, I have developed very thick skin. As a special needs parent, people hurt your feelings all the time in ways you cannot imagine. Some people are cruel and small. Most, however, just don't know how to act when they see a child do something "weird," or they may assume a behavior problem when the origin is in a disability. That is not to say that special needs children should not be disciplined or have expectations set for them. It is just that the cognitive appreciation of what is appropriate, and the natural ability to read others' social cues and act accordingly, are sometimes missing. I will never forget my son at 5 or 6 years old slapping me in the face when I was entering Costco. I got a very "judgy" look from the greeter! Behavior therapists will tell you that the bad behavior is being used to get a reaction, and the thing to do is pretend it didn't happen and *not* react. It takes all the patience and will power one has not to react to such offensive behavior, but that is what I did. It is embarrassing, and people think you are a bad parent or a pushover, but that is not the case, and besides that, what they think is not your problem. My son probably has not thought of that incident again, but I have carried it with me for over 12 years!

My son was in daycare when he was little, before any diagnosis was made. Two parents wrote the school the meanest emails you could imagine, suggesting our 2-and-a-half-year-old child was committing a criminal act when he scratched a child to get her attention or acted out. They suggested that the state be contacted about our child to provide intervention or train us to be parents. The school showed the emails to me and arranged a sit-down to "clear the air." We did that, but it was apparent that those parents had no understanding of what we were experiencing. We removed our son from that program and hired a sitter until he was eligible for services through the school system. I carried copies of those emails in my purse for 6 months. They burned a hole in my soul. Eventually, my mother convinced me to throw them away because dwelling on them was not going to change those people or their insensitivity.

In addition to thick skin, I have reset my definition of success for my child, while continuing to celebrate the successes of my friends' typical children. While my friends were talking about what private schools their kids were applying to and how well they performed in testing, or all of the colleges that accepted them, I was genuinely happy for them, yet appreciated the small victories my son was having on the scale that was achievable for him, including having a meltdown only every so often, making a successful trip to a restaurant, or attending an event as a new experience. Those successes are important and deserve just as much celebration, but to most, they do not seem like a big deal. I am allowed to celebrate those successes and I do. This is not to say that my friends are not going through their own stuff. Raising kids is tough no matter what the situation. On the very positive side, my kid will never hang out with the wrong crowd and do drugs or drive drunk or have an eating disorder. I don't wish that on any of my friends, but those issues are a constant worry for most parents.

Finally, my special needs parent status has helped me to not sweat the small stuff, or at least not so much. I am still a very intense person. However, I am forgiving; I see the good in people far more often than the bad, and I spend less time being upset about what people did or why they did it and more time appreciating what I have. This outlook made me a better lawyer and makes me a better judge. My experience has changed me for the better. I would not wish this experience on anyone; indeed, worries about my son's happiness, safety, and future keep me awake at night. There are far too few resources for people with intellectual disabilities, and the programs that do exist are expensive and only available, seemingly, to people like my son who has parents with the means and ability to access them.

Getting back to the topic of drains on personal time, all of this is extremely time-consuming. Even for a judge, figuring out conservatorships and Social Security Disability at 18, and years of identifying programs, determining eligibility, and the assessments and evaluations that go with it all, is exhausting. This is in addition to the regular kid stuff. We do not have sports teams and lessons, but instead have therapy, Individualized Education Programs (IEPs), meal preparation, and we help with hygiene at an age when typical kids can do those things for themselves. My big, smelly 18-year-old is, in many ways, an immature child who needs a lot of assistance to get through the day.

I do not feel sorry for myself, but I am sometimes sad. However, my son has given me a gift that other parents never receive. I appreciate everything about everyone. I have an extremely positive outlook on life. I really like all types of people, and they really like me. I appreciate differences and see value in all persons, no matter how those differences manifest. And I have made personal and professional decisions that allow me to be the best mother I can be while also having an extremely satisfying and rewarding career. Some things at home definitely slip. Some things at work slip from time to time. But being sad all the time or seeking sympathy from others is a disservice to myself and disrespectful of my son. We are just fine and he is just fine—better than fine. I push hard at work and I have a heavy lift at home. That is a balance I have become used to and manage with the help of great friends and family. I do feel drained from time to time, but I would not be the judge that I am without my special son teaching me what is important in life and how kindness and empathy go a long way to being a better human.

Chancellor Anne C. Martin

Career

Chancellor, Davidson County Chancery Court

Education

- JD, Vanderbilt University Law School (1992)
- BA, Smith College (1989)

Best Advice

Treat everyone as you expect to be treated, lawyers and clients alike. The saying "what goes around comes around" is never more true than in the practice of law!

Personal

Chancellor Anne Martin has been an active participant, board member, and officer of many Nashville nonprofits and bar associations over the years. She loves the law and attributes her love for the profession to the excellent legal mentorship she received as a young lawyer. She enjoys being able to share the skills she learned from her mentors with aspiring students. To this end, Chancellor Martin was an Adjunct Professor at Belmont University College of Law where she taught a course in client counseling. She is currently an Adjunct Professor at the Nashville School of Law, teaching sales and secured transaction courses.

For More Information

https://www.tncourts.gov/courts/circuit-criminal-chancery-courts/judges/anne-c-martin

Overcoming Imposter Syndrome: Living for Yourself or for Others?

By Shayna M. Steinfeld

"Imposter syndrome is loosely defined as doubting your abilities and feeling like a fraud. It disproportionately affects high-achieving people, who find it difficult to accept their accomplishments. Many question whether they're deserving of accolades."[3]

"To be yourself in a world that is constantly trying to make you something else is the greatest accomplishment."

—Ralph Waldo Emerson

When my middle son was 23, he received a call from the Dean of his undergraduate business school, telling him that a donor was looking for a Chief Financial Officer for one of his new ventures. The Dean told my son that he had recommended him, and only him, 2 years out of school, with his only experience being with a consulting firm. My son's reaction was one of thanks and general willingness to pursue. He accepted the job, put together a team of contacts at the same level or higher whom he could reach out to with questions, and was there for 4 years.

My reaction, even now, would have been: "I can't do that, I don't have those skills." This would be despite the fact that I've been an attorney for 30 plus years, and I also have an MBA. I believe that part of the difference in reactions is a societal one; another is general personality. The focus of this essay is the "fraud" element felt by the high-achieving woman in the room.

There were differences in how my son was raised and how I was raised. This was intentional. I grew up in New Jersey and spent my summers with my grandparents in Miami Beach, Florida. My grandmother had a challenging personality. She loved us. No question about it. I later learned that, although she was quite beautiful and very smart (she graduated college and obtained two master's degrees), her mother, an immigrant from

---

3. Ruchika Tulshyan & Jodi-Ann Burey, *Stop Telling Women They Have Imposter Syndrome*, Harv. Bus. Rev. (Feb. 11, 2021), https://hbr.org/2021/02/stop-telling-women-they-have-imposter-syndrome (last visited Sept. 24, 2023).

Poland, had lost her first baby and was very superstitious about compliments. She would jinx the next three babies if she did something wrong in the universe. It would bring on the evil eye.

There's an expression in Yiddish, "*kein ayin hara*," which translates as "no evil eye." This phrase functions as a Jewish "knock on wood." "The origin of the phrase is the superstition that talking about one's good fortune attracts the attention of the evil eye, which loves to mess things up."[4] My great-grandmother apparently really believed in this superstition. Therefore, my grandmother never received a compliment, and others in my grandmother's universe were not received well when they paid her a compliment. My grandmother reacted to this upbringing by giving her three daughters and four granddaughters (I was the oldest), compliments with the "comma but clause"; things could *always* be better. What we heard and processed was that we were *never* enough, no matter what we did or accomplished. This impacted each of us in different ways.

I became the classic overachiever. I strived to achieve, overcome, and conquer my universe. It was internalized, but it was, as indicated, never enough because it could *always* be better. I could have gone to a better school; I could have worked for a better firm; I could have handled my career better. The list goes on. It was very difficult to look at my *curriculum vitae* and accept the achievements for what they were, and there have been many, beginning with the schools I attended and the firm with which I began my career.

With our three sons (now in their mid- to late 20s), we tried very hard just to let them be themselves and to challenge them to be the best they could be without any "comma but clauses." They were enough as long as they did the best they were able to do. They played year-round sports. They excelled on their own terms. They thrived in a very stable environment—home-wise and community-wise (okay, my oldest was a guinea pig and his environment was a bit less stable, as there were more changes as we were challenged to figure out how to parent). They have a confidence that I never had at their age. Is this because of their upbringing or due to being male rather than female?

---

4. Elizabeth P. Alpern, *The 3 Most Important Jewish Words*, JEWISH TELEGRAPHIC AGENCY, https://www.jta.org/jewniverse/2013/the-3-most-important-jewish-words (last visited Sept. 24, 2023).

When I got to my firm as a young associate, I was one of a few women in a male-dominated bankruptcy world. I looked young (I still look young). I would appear in court, and they would think I was 18. I would play it to my advantage because I was actually good at what I did. I would get a victory and go back to my office and tell folks about it. They would then get upset with me for bragging. The guys would do the same, but no one got upset with them. This is the corollary to the notion that women are "bitches" and men are just "aggressive." I would eat lunch with the secretaries and paralegals. I am still friends with a few of them 30 years later. They are wonderful people. I like them. It never occurred to me until recently that this wasn't quite right and that I should have been eating lunch with the male partners and male senior associates. They should have taken me under their wing and guided me rather than left me to my own devices as a young associate.

At Bankruptcy Section bar lunches, there would be only one or two women for every table of ten in attendance. There were never any lines for the women's room. The first women on the Bankruptcy Bench were only 4 years into their tenure. It never occurred to me that this should have been a red flag. I was happy with the practice area. It was fascinating to me. It was Code-driven and "new"; the law wasn't archaic. There was no Rule Against Perpetuities. There was minimal Latin (even "res judicata" and "collateral estoppel" have been replaced with "claims preclusion" and "issue preclusion," respectively). The cases needed to be argued based on recent case law. It was the most wonderful combination of all sorts of specialties and skills: litigation, corporate, and negotiation, while also pulling in a wide variety of other practice areas and using my business classes, such as strategy and financial accounting. Why worry about the lack of women in the arena?

I had the audacity to have three pregnancies as an associate. Some might think that this was not a good idea for a female lawyer career-wise, and those kinds of views feed into the "are you a fraud?" or "are you really as good as you think?" thoughts that can run through one's head on speed dial.

But it worked out marvelously well for our family. I have been on my own and in practice with my husband, a family lawyer, in a two-person firm, ever since our youngest son was born in 1997. I reach out to peers when I need to bounce ideas in a case. Younger lawyers reach out to me. I have been president of the Atlanta Bar Association and the Georgia

Association for Women Lawyers. I have served on the National Conference of Women Bar Associations, helping to create and implement one of its core annual programs. I have chaired the bankruptcy sections of the Atlanta Bar Association and that of the State Bar of Georgia. I was a founding "mom" of more than one bankruptcy group in Atlanta and I was instrumental in a legislative change for bankruptcy exemptions in Georgia for the first time in 25 years (they have since been changed again). I'm a co-editor of this book, along with its predecessor. I have published articles and another book, which is in its fourth edition. Did I mention that I am an overachiever? I have chosen a field that is male-dominated and that ebbs and flows with the economy. I am happiest when it is flowing. This means that for the society at large, the economy isn't going so well.

During the pandemic, the economy was held artificially at bay by the government, resulting in my world being slow. This meant that I had more time for self-reflection and self-doubt. When busy, there is less time for such considerations. Self-doubt robs me of confidence and joy. It is much better when confidence wins and I march through life full of the sureness that all is right with my choices. This is hard to do during a pandemic, when choices have been contracted.

When self-doubt kicks in, there's a term for it: imposter syndrome. There are various levels of it. Sometimes, it's mild and just means one should reflect, kick one's own tuchas, and become more positive. Other times, it may be more of a crisis, and more serious help should be sought. There are many out there who experience this phenomenon. In 2019, an Imposter Syndrome Research Study[5] showed that imposter syndrome could be costing British businesses billions, yet hardly any businesses had processes in place to identify employees who were struggling with it—or training to support them. How do you think American law firms are handling it? Here are a few key points:

1. Imposter syndrome affects both men and women. Research has found that both men and women are affected at similar rates, though they handle it differently. With women, it tends to make

---

5. Clare Josa, *Five Key Findings from the 2019 Imposter Syndrome Research Study*, LinkedIn (Sept. 24, 2019), https://www.linkedin.com/pulse/five-key-findings-from-2019-imposter-syndrome-research-clare-josa (last visited Sept. 24, 2023).

them less likely to seek out opportunities to shine or to apply for promotions and pay raises they know they deserve. They are more likely to deflect praise and, instead, highlight their faults.
2. No business is immune.
3. Imposter syndrome is a driving factor in star performers leaving present situations and in stalled personal development. It is the "last taboo" of the personal development world.
4. Imposter syndrome damages an individual's own performance, a team's dynamics, and a firm's productivity and profit.
5. Imposter syndrome is one of the drivers in the gender pay gap and gender-related glass ceilings, which also includes a lack of equality in leadership roles, even in firms with proactive policies in place to address this problem.

My guess would be that if imposter syndrome was studied in the law firm environment, we would find that it impacts how cases are assigned and how client contacts are managed given what is already known about how it impacts the business world. This would be an area that would be interesting to dig into a bit deeper.

In some situations, imposter syndrome is an actual mental health issue and requires treatment. In these cases, it may be present alongside depression, anxiety, low self-esteem, and social dysfunction. In these situations, women often feel alone in their feelings, and group therapy may be incredibly helpful.[6] Those who have mild cases need to focus on their own accomplishments, daily meditation, and mindfulness exercises, which can work marvels for self-awareness.

Dr. Gerald S. Drose, an Atlanta psychologist and author of the novel *Bird Gotta Land*, offers the following advice for handling mild cases of imposter syndrome:

1. **Figure out where it originated.** If you can recognize it as a "story" being told by your kid-self rather than the "truth," you can work

---

6. Dena M. Bravata, Divya K. Madhusudhan, Michael Boroff, & Kevin O. Cokley, *Prevalence, Predictors, and Treatment of Imposter Syndrome: A Systematic Review*, 4 J. OF MENTAL HEALTH & CLINICAL PSYCH. 12–16 (2020), https://www.mentalhealthjournal.org/articles/commentary-prevalence-predictors-and-treatment-of-imposter-syndrome-a-systematic-review.html.

to uncover the origin of the story. In so doing, you should develop some empathy for that child who was doing her best to simplify and understand a complex world.
2. **Understand the protective function of the story.** It's designed to keep you small and safe. Forgive that part of you! Thank it for trying to protect you, and assure it that you are now strong enough to handle the potential negative feelings that come from not being perfect.
3. **Become aware of when the imposter syndrome is sabotaging you.** When you are avoiding, procrastinating, and underperforming, you are engaging in a self-fulfilling prophecy.
4. **Rewrite the narrative in the here-and-now.** Pushing yourself out of your comfort zone and trying things that you did not believe you could do will help you collect more accurate data about yourself. This new data can be used to update the story and rewrite the narrative.[7]

Change can come from within. Create a Diary of Accomplishment and track your personal successes. For yourself: Be positive. Self-care is incredibly important. Do something for yourself—just because. Don't chase that ever-elusive external reinforcement of achievement; do it for yourself and only for yourself. Carve out 15 or 30 minutes in your day, each day, just for you. The external reward will never be there. Do what you do for you, not for someone else. That "someone else" is always impossible to please. Personally, I could never make my grandmother happy, and it took me too many decades to figure that out.

---

7. Gerald Drose, *Imposter Syndrome: Challenging the Faulty Narrative*, OFFICIAL WEBSITE OF GERALD DROSE (Nov. 10, 2021), https://www.birdgottaland.com/post/imposter-syndrome-challenging-the-faulty-narrative?fbclid=IwAR2LY_ZRv8p_wozzY-9Ce3p0FzG9ITwxs8UshPoOpfZa0_41P7CgC4RET5t4 (last visited Sept. 24, 2023).

Shayna M. Steinfeld

Career

President, Steinfeld & Steinfeld PC; Board Certified by the American Board of Certification in both Consumer and Business Bankruptcy Law

Education

- JD/MBA, Emory University School of Law (1990)
- BA, History, Emory University (1990)

Best Advice

In Shakespeare's *Hamlet*, Polonius said, "To thine own self be true." You can't help anyone else—clients, children, a spouse, and so on—if you haven't prioritized yourself. Put yourself at the top of your "to-do" list.

Personal

Shayna Steinfeld is a past President of the Atlanta Bar Association, the Georgia Association for Women Lawyers, a past Chair of both the Sole Practitioner/Small Firm and Bankruptcy Sections of the Atlanta Bar Association, and Chair of the Bankruptcy Section of the State Bar of Georgia. Shayna has been a frequent lecturer, locally, nationally, and internationally, and has authored several articles and other publications, including *The Family Lawyer's Guide to Bankruptcy*, which has been published by the ABA Family Law Section and is now in its Fourth Edition. She is a co-editor of *Her Story: Lessons in Success from Lawyers Who Live It*, published by the ABA Litigation Section, and she is a co-editor of this book, *Her Story 2: The Resilient Woman Lawyer's Guide to Conquering Obstacles*. Shayna has three sons, who are now between 25 and 30 years old. She practices law with her husband, Bruce, a family lawyer. For fun, Shayna's hobbies are traveling, scrapbooking, and researching family history (genealogy). She loves when these hobbies overlap when she can travel to places on the family tree and create a book about them (per branch) for her children.

For More Information

https://www.steinfeldlaw.com/shayna-steinfeld
https://www.linkedin.com/in/shayna-steinfeld-474a779

From Fear to Trust: Lessons from My Recovery for the Legal Community

By K. Brooke Welch

Fear

My heart was beating, a deer caught in the headlights. I'd broken an invisible rule, and there would be serious consequences. The senior associate, who would later be Partner, gave me a dressing down. My unforgivable action as a new associate? I left at 10 p.m. when most of the team stayed until the wee hours on a time-sensitive case. I spoke with the *wrong* senior associate, who gave me permission to go home. I didn't talk to *her*. I didn't intuitively grasp her strict hierarchy.

That's the moment when I let a destructive force start to dominate me. Fear. I vowed never to make that mistake again. The constant fear of not meeting expectations drove me for years. It would amplify stress and anxiety. It would undermine my sleep. It would prevent awareness of a looming well-being crisis.

Fear would take my authentic self and contort me into an unrecognizable person. Fear ignited and fed a drive to be "better than," while constantly fearing that I was "less than."

This is a story of the triumph of trust over fear. Trust in ourselves and our community.

Fear Is a Cancer in the Legal Profession

Manipulative and powerful, fear takes on many forms. It replicates, over and over, like any cancer. Fear of criticism. Fear of failure. Fear of embarrassment. Fear of not being good enough. Fear of being fired by a client. Fear of losing a case.

Fear thrills at pain, self-doubt, and shame. Fear takes you outward for approval—anything to avoid the imagined consequences. Fear delights in throwing you off-kilter, robbing you of clarity and equilibrium. Fear affects individuals, clients, and teams.

Fear warps and pervades the practice of law.

We try to escape fear by exerting illusory control in the form of perfectionism and tangible billed hours. We believe a baffling lie that our safety lies therein. Yet we arrive at the result we most fear. We threaten the greatest resource for our legal profession—ourselves.

From Confident to Catastrophe

I joined Big Law as a dynamic, highly recruited graduate with a multidisciplinary joint degree from a top law school and graduate international relations program. I felt confident in my accomplishments: brief writing awards, facility with international travel, communication in multiple languages, and recognized leadership skills.

I loved adventure and the results of going off the beaten path. It all started when I was 17 years old. I left home to be an exchange student in Brussels, Belgium. I experienced serious emotional distress leaving the nest, but I returned speaking French. I chose to study abroad in Valencia, Spain, I won an award and traveled solo across Western Europe.

Going to work in Paris without a job? Getting on a ferry to Albania by myself? Choosing to do a joint degree? Doing an internship in Bangladesh? Anxiety was inevitable, but ultimately worth it. I trusted myself.

I decided that working at a top law firm in New York City was the next frontier. I would not "stay safe" and choose to work in a smaller city or less prestigious firm. It was exciting! It would be an intentional challenge leading to a desired outcome. I would have money and prestige. I would pay off my loans. I would join the elite.

But, like many women, I came into my legal career on merit, following the rules of getting good grades, going to the right schools, and excelling in *that* system. I didn't know how to navigate the Big Law culture, strategize, make the right connections, advocate for myself, or do the right nonbillable work to refine skills.

I was naive and unprepared. I thought I was invincible. I didn't anticipate my crippling susceptibility to fear. I could never have imagined the devastating consequences.

The Transition

After the heart-stopping experience of my first "dressing down," I floated without an anchor, wounded. Delegating your career to the whims of assignments, supervisors, assigned mentors, and haphazard skill-building doesn't work. Intentionality is invaluable. I didn't understand this at the time.

A lull in work left me vulnerable to unstrategic assignments. A mega, high-stakes, domestic litigation needed bodies to review documents in a different office. I was "loaned" to the case. I feared that my reputation was already at stake. I had to prove that I could "cut it." I didn't know that it would be a one-way door.

Fear told me that my survival depended on pleasing people. For me, that meant thrilling my new supervisors with high billable hours, perfectionism, and a willingness to excel at less desirable projects.

Jump? Okay! How high? No assignment was too low and no expectation was too high. Fear of criticism preceded any other priorities. I would do anything to avoid rejection and humiliation. I would work any hours.

Fear also meant the stress of competition. My self-worth was tied to approval, which felt scarce. I had to "toughen up" and sharpen my elbows. Slowly, I learned to fight for it. I learned to maneuver. I bought into the ethos of winning through endurance. If my workhorse colleague was still in the office, then I was, too.

I embraced a "work hard, play hard" mentality. I was in New York, right? The bars closed at 4 a.m.! Oh, how I loved alcohol as a release at the end of the day. I needed an outlet for the stress of unreachable perfection, elusive expectations, and unwinnable competition. If self-worth comes from external sources, so does self-soothing.

Like fear, alcohol is cunning. And it is so easy to be shielded from awareness and accountability in our alcohol-infused legal profession. Weekly kegs and drinking rituals at law school. Summer associate programs chock full of boozy events. The default happy hour for social bonding. Holiday parties, after parties, and after-after parties.

As workaholism narrowed my personal life, alcohol became my primary extracurricular activity. Drinking fit into my schedule. I could work until 11 p.m., angling and achieving, and then go to my favorite Irish pub for camaraderie until 1 or 2 a.m. An initial experiment turned into a daily habit.

Over time, I started to revel in my growing identity as a high-earning badass in New York. I lived in the city near Central Park. I hobnobbed with artists, musicians, and eccentrics at the pub. The firm covered or subsidized so many expenses, as long as I worked past 10 p.m.

My workaholism seemed to be paying off. Week after week, month after month, I dedicated 70-plus-hours a week to my work. Alcohol facilitated that schedule, adding color and relief beyond the office. I added in Paxil for anxiety and Klonopin to sleep.

Meanwhile, I didn't pause to be present with myself or my career. Was this working for me? Was I building the relationships and skillset that mattered for long-term success? What kind of work would be fulfilling? Where could I be of service in the legal community?

I didn't ask myself these questions. I couldn't zoom out and see the bigger picture while laser-focused on pleasing partners during the day and drinking at night. The billed time and number of post-work drinks added up, instead of new experiences and connections with a purpose.

I didn't do pro bono projects. I didn't participate in Bar Association or community leadership. I didn't attract and excel in meaningful, visible work in the New York office. Assigned mentors did not transition into sponsors.

Without focus and centeredness, I couldn't advocate for myself. Long hours and alcohol helped me avoid self-reflection. I envied my well-placed colleagues advancing in their chosen practice, but I felt powerless. I was isolated from quality relationship-building in my own office.

On the positive side, fear can produce some phenomenal short-term results. I worked with truly exceptional attorneys in the mega litigation case. I ultimately excelled in one of the best factual defense teams in existence. The joint defense team respected me. I was chosen to support the Global Head of Litigation for the Mock Trial. We won Summary Judgment.

Finally, I got the long-sought approving nods during my annual review. But now what?

The Bottom

As the mega-case wound down, reality set in.

I was exhausted. It was like exams—you can work your bottom off and deplete your reserves. Then, afterward, your body senses the permission to release, and you get sick. It's like a pact. Your body promises to get you through a tough time, and you promise to let it demand healing afterward.

But what if your "exam period" doesn't last a couple of weeks and instead lasts over 4 years?

Unfortunately, there is no quick cure for an extended depletion of well-being. I opted for a new start and leveraged my joint defense relationships for a lateral move. I was relieved and optimistic. I took time off, did an amazing road trip, and bought my very own (expensive) home outside of Washington, DC.

But I had fundamentally changed. Fear and alcohol had morphed me into a bizarre combination of excellence, ego, ambition, and delusion. I would have short-term wins in my new job, but my ego was out of control. I started to get in trouble with colleagues and clients.

My behavior screamed with red flags, but I couldn't see it and my supervisors did not intervene. Well-being programs and policies were rare at the time.

I didn't know it, but I was devastatingly sick in mind, body, and spirit. I was unrecognizable from the open, friendly, dynamic, woman who started her Big Law career with naivete.

Trust over Fear: Recovery

A stunning, unexpected, spiritual journey rocked my world. I reached a point where all the training in perfection and control could not save me. The opposite did. I can only describe it as Grace, doing for me what I could not do for myself. Surrender.

I couldn't think my way to recovery. And I lost the strength to rebel. So I showed up for doctors, therapists, mentors, and support groups. I took their suggested actions. Without a guaranteed outcome, I made progress. I learned to trust the process. I healed, slowly and imperfectly. And I started to trust others.

I intuitively discovered a life-giving tool rooted in creating openness to new experiences and connections. I now call it the "tiny adventures path." Instead of disruptive, major challenges, I adopted a gracious approach that fooled my fears.

I could try new things with a spirit of experimentation. I could make mistakes while celebrating the joys of discovery. I welcomed intentionality and spontaneity. By getting just beyond my comfort zone, I started to be present and trust myself.

And so much happened just in my yard. I tried gardening for the first time. I planted flowers and watered them daily. I watched some thrive and others die. I removed old, entrenched, bushes with my Dad. I gave a massive butterfly bush to my neighbor. I created new designs and then changed them again. I thrilled in the colors of my hydrangeas. I pruned my rose bushes.

I discovered that Morning Glories like to take over. My tomato plants did, too, but they tasted authentic, powerful. I removed the dead debris each spring to start again.

Dormant trees in my front yard sprouted peaches. I talked to my neighbor while I tended them. I visited a local "peach guy" I had found on the internet. I learned to make simple, delicious, peach cobbler that I shared with others.

I created a covered area that housed my purple bike with a basket. I rode along the Potomac River, smelling the water and pausing to pray.

I sought connection. I potted flowers and put out chairs to welcome people on my porch. I dug out huge raised beds to make room for a little table. I sat there to commune with the wonder. I invited others to my little garden. I bought seeds from Mount Vernon during a "tiny adventure" with a friend. I hosted cookouts and learned to grill hamburgers, while creating a space to nurture community.

I learned that I can show up and put in the work, but I don't control the outcome. Change doesn't happen on my timetable. All experiments don't succeed. I don't like everything. I can change course and be okay.

Freedom came from humility and from compassion replacing ego. Connection overpowering isolation. Seeking instead of escaping. Selfishness transforming into service.

Trust as a Tool for Our Legal Community

What is your favorite work memory? After reflection, I have a few. They all have something in common: trust.

Friendship

My best friend at work in New York started as a stranger. We met as summer associates and lucked into neighboring offices. I experimented with popping into his office, taking a break from my lasered concentration. Over time, our comfort level grew. We shared our silliness as well as our frustrations.

I distinctly remember him calling me one day. He had just left the doctor's office with life-changing news. He was in tears. Looking back, I'm so honored that he trusted me. We trusted each other. Years later, I would reciprocate with a call to him about my own surrender.

Our bond, nurtured from nothing, served our well-being in extraordinary ways.

Guidance

I will always be grateful for a partner who guided, instructed, provided pointed feedback, and awed me with his exceptional writing. I worked directly with him on our final Summary Judgment brief for the mega case. I was poised for criticism and judgment that I experienced so many times before. After all, my brief-writing skills were underdeveloped. Instead, he treated me with respect and encouragement. As a team, we excelled, and we won.

Collaboration

I will never forget my client's walking up to me with an orchid, crying. We both cried as we exchanged my orchid for her Green Card. This win was against all legal, factual, and political odds. A miracle backed by innumerable hours of dedicated collaboration.

She was a trauma survivor, trained to be suspicious. Collecting the key evidence and translating her story into words required listening and insight. I showed up, and she showed up. Our trust and relationship turned the impossible into the possible.

Trust and Excellence

Trust is a protective force. It's not fear that wins, but trust.

We can build trust in our work dynamic. When we initiate and nurture a space for connection, we create powerful possibilities. Our careers and businesses thrive when it's safe to have a voice, try new experiences, make mistakes, and ask for help.

We can make well-being simple and diverse. We can get creative and experiment. We can do "tiny adventures" for both occupational and personal growth.

We can create systems that detect distress and offer solutions with compassion and support.

And we can bring intentionality and consistency to strategic planning for everyone.

With trust, we reach our greatest excellence for personal well-being, professional development, teamwork, and client service.

We can do this.

K. Brooke Welch

Career
Founder & CEO, Tiny Adventures Path; Team Connection, Lawyer Well-being, DEI-B

Education
- JD, University of Virginia School of Law (2002)
- MA, Law and Diplomacy, International Economics, The Fletcher School at Tufts University (2002)
- BA, University of Virginia (1995)

Best Advice
Our journey as legal professionals is a marathon, not a sprint, with many different paths and opportunities. By getting just beyond our comfort zone with (tiny) new experiences and connections, we cultivate our well-being and trust in ourselves.

Personal
Brooke Welch lives in Richmond, Virginia, to be closer to family. You can find her doing "tiny adventures" either solo or with family members, friends, and her Tiny Adventures RVA Sober-Friendly Social Group community.

For More Information
https://www.linkedin.com/in/k-brooke-welch

Grateful to Be a Sober Female Lawyer

By Jessica R. Blaemire

I spent 20 years of my life and the first 9 years of my law career actively drinking. I was absolutely convinced for most of those 9 years that my seemingly endless capacity for booze was an asset to my legal practice. Almost every firm and client event seemed to be dripping with red and white wine, and sometimes with beer and liquor. I could hold my own and then some. And, I believed, the legal community cheered me on.

Admittedly, I did not need encouragement to drink. My inner anxiety and alcohol's apparent ability to ease my overactive brain provided plenty of encouragement on their own. Like so many of us, I was an overachiever and perfectionist as far back as I can remember. In high school I made straight As. I sang in the chorus and made honors choir. I played softball on the state championship team. I was a class officer and president of the National Honor Society. I competed in our school's annual pageant and was selected "Miss Congeniality." (To this day, my mom reminds me it was the most important award.) Yet, I walked through the halls of my Virginia high school feeling insufficient. I feared I would fail the next project. I was scared I would choke in the middle of my solo or drop the ball when fielding a line drive. I questioned whether people really liked me.

My first drink—not counting the sips of beer my godfather gave me under the Christmas dining room table around age 3—was at age 14 in the middle of this pubescent distress. I was the youngest player on the varsity high school softball team. I was invited by a good friend to attend the varsity sports teams' spring party. One parent would be there, but he was a "cool" dad who drank with the kids. I arrived and was surrounded by the players on the varsity baseball and soccer teams. They were tall, popular, and moved with an ease I didn't personally know. I walked upstairs and grabbed an R. L. Stine book off the shelf. Then a friend encouraged me to head downstairs and handed me a drink. I grabbed the solo cup not caring what was in it. From the first quick gulp, I latched onto alcohol's ability to calm my spinning brain. It tasted like relief. My doubts were still there, but I didn't care about them as much. I spoke to the cute boys without concern. I fell down the steps in front of some of them and bounced back up feeling unshaken. I felt confident. In the drunken haze, I could finally believe I was liked and accepted. I am not sure how many drinks I had that night among a selection of Boone's Farm, Zima, wine coolers, and whiskey. I didn't get sick or black out, and I woke up the next day with a very mild hangover. This, I thought to myself, I need to do again. This is definitely okay.

Thankfully, most of my high school peer group did not drink. I had a healthy respect for my mom and a fear of getting caught. Accordingly, I made it through high school indulging in this escape only one or two times a year. Whenever I did, I surprised myself and those around me with how much I could ingest and still function. It never occurred to me to be concerned about this. To the contrary, I was proud. Drinking, I believed, was another thing at which I excelled.

I went to a competitive public college in Virginia. My group of friends there studied seriously but partied just as seriously. Binge drinking on weekends was the norm. Among my group of friends, even though we all drank to excess, my ability to "keep going" made me stand out from the crowd. I took the worm. I challenged a marine to a vodka-shot contest. Every social situation, including my first meeting with my now-husband, was laced with alcohol. And, looking around me, my drinking did not seem that different than others'. Even though it is true that I often pre-partied before the pre-party, I justified to myself that I could "handle it." I had the highest grades in my friend group, so I was okay.

My drinking progressed from "every social situation" to "almost daily self-medication" by the time I began law school. In my last semester of college, my anxious mind betrayed me, and my negative worries escalated. I started obsessing about falling out of love with the only person that—to this day—I have ever truly loved. One negative worry spun into a million. My brain—addled by too many romance novels, unbalanced by the birth control pills I had started, in a weird zone because I was engrossed in an honors thesis on manic depression involving interviewing people who were often in manic phases, and of course, affected by alcohol—finally broke. The obsessive-compulsive disorder (OCD), which had always lurked in me and kept me checking stoves, doors, and alarm clocks throughout my youth (I broke at least two), flew to the surface. I got very sick.

I was officially diagnosed with OCD in March 2003. My form of OCD is one where persistent negative thoughts barrage my brain. It is sometimes called "Pure O" because there is no obvious compulsion. I mentally try to "fix" the obsession by pushing it away with a different thought. The obsession may be realistic (i.e., "What if I fall out of love with my boyfriend?") or totally ridiculous (i.e., "What if I forget how to read?"). I started on medication and began cognitive-behavior therapy. At first, I also stopped drinking because the doctor told me not to drink on the new medication and I was a rule-follower. A few weeks after my diagnosis, though, I found myself faced with a formal dance. Dressed in a long gown and holding the hand of the man I loved, I wanted nothing more in that moment than to *stop thinking* . . . so I drank. The negative thoughts were pushed away with each glass of cheap wine and cheaper vodka. I enjoyed my evening with a quiet mind. Morning came, and so did the obsessive thoughts. My thoughts spun so fast I rushed to the hall bathroom. I couldn't breathe. I thought: "I can never drink again." Yet the temptation to quiet my mind was too strong. That night, and so many nights after, I had another drink. When I was drinking, I felt okay.

In law school, I was drinking almost daily. This seemed normal in the company of my law school classmates. The line between academics and partying was blurred as students rolled a keg into the law school courtyard on Thursday afternoons. At my top-10 law school I was no longer the hardest drinker in the room. The mythical summer associate who got drunk and jumped in the Hudson at a law firm event? That person was in my law school class. THAT is what someone with a problem looked like. Not me. I wasn't close to jumping in the river. I wasn't drinking alone, or during the day, and I was at a top law school. I was okay. Not for a second did I think my drinking was an issue, even as fights with my significant other increased. I focused on what I saw were the fun times and explained away the bad times. Drinking allowed me to connect more easily with possible employers. At a summer event at a New York country club, I was the only female invited to hang out with the senior (male) partners on the terrace, because I told them how much I loved whiskey. It also allowed me to push away the fact that I didn't love the academics of law school like I had loved undergrad, and that I didn't feel like I fit in with most of the law students who seemed very privileged and focused on monetary success.

And when I worried that my exam or paper wasn't good enough, drinking calmed the concerns so I could turn in decent work.

I entered the practice of law in Chicago in 2006. Chicago is a wonderful city for a budding alcoholic. Drinking felt like the city's official pastime, and we were able to walk everywhere. On the work front, my ability to consume large amounts of alcohol was praised by my colleagues and by clients. I connected with a junior partner over beer at the original wings restaurant in Buffalo, New York. I bonded with clients over martinis and whiskey in Vegas and was invited to exclusive after-parties. I had wine dates with female partners whom I admired and respected. I was hired by a boutique law firm after bonding with a partner over a specific crisp Italian white wine. This same partner later tasked me with "keeping up" with a client as I was one of the few people who could drink as much as she could. She had drunkenly fallen and broken a bone on a golf course the year before. I was instructed to drink as much as she did and make sure she did not get into any trouble.

Drinking (or the promise of a drink) seemed to allow me to work later and not notice the tiredness and the burnout. As always, it numbed my anxiety enough so I that I could finish the brief, presentation, or contract without being overcome by fear of failure. With that drink, I felt like success. Or at least, I was still okay. Even though more and more nights ended blurry and slurring. Even though my marriage was starting to crumble. Even though by 2009 I had given birth to my first daughter and worried what would happen if she needed me in the wee hours of the morning when I was highly intoxicated. Even though I had to drink more and more to keep the fears at bay. Even through increasingly during the day my anxiety was worse as the alcohol left my system, and the doctor-prescribed medication could not keep up with the mental gymnastics my brain was performing. The only solution I saw for the anxiety rebound was another drink.

Alcohol was what I turned to even as it was destroying me. Eventually, any benefit I received from drinking was replaced by the harm it caused. I was at a great place in my career. I hadn't been arrested. I didn't have a DUI. I had a car, a home, and a husband. I had a beautiful daughter who was smart and happy and loved me. On the surface it looked like I was holding it together. Underneath, I was on the verge of divorce, I was not the mother I knew I needed to be, and my anxiety was consuming my waking (and sleeping) moments. Alcohol could not keep the fears at bay long enough to justify the destruction it was wreaking.

In 2013, I received some devastating news about my marriage. I wasn't all to blame, but neither was he. My marriage almost ended. Realizing how disconnected I was from myself, my husband, and my daughter inspired me to begin to "really try" to curb my drinking. My second pregnancy—an unplanned result of my husband and I working to rebuild our relationship—turned out to be an amazing gift in setting me on the path to sobriety.

After my second daughter was born, I spent a year convincing myself I could still drink normally "sometimes." I didn't keep alcohol in the house, but I continued to drink at some work events and social events. When I drank, even if I limited it to one or two drinks, it was all I could think about. A therapist asked me why I hadn't stopped completely, and I had no good response. My last two drinks were a few weeks after that therapist's question. I had two beers (not even my favorite deep red wine) at my mom's retirement dinner. After the dinner I stopped at the local Walgreens with my older daughter. While there, I almost grabbed a bottle of wine to take home. At that moment a light miraculously switched on in my head: I was playing with fire. No matter how much it looked like I was controlling it and drinking normally, I could never really control it. That was June 30, 2015. I am very grateful that I have not had another drink since that date.

In sobriety, my OCD medication and therapy are actually effective. When anxiety does pop up, I journal, meditate, or walk. I talk to another alcoholic. I read sobriety memoirs like *Drinking a Love Story* by Caroline Knapp or *A Girl Walks Out of a Bar* by Lisa Smith. I work daily on not trying to control everything and everyone. I make gratitude lists. I try to let things go instead of allowing them to build a resentment I may want to drink over. I let negative thoughts drift in and drift back out. I stay present even in hard situations. I take each day—and sometimes each moment— one at a time. I am okay.

I can now see that drinking—while it allowed me to connect with others on the surface and put a bandage over my anxiety—was not the aid to my career that I thought it was. Sobriety has helped my profession in ways

I never imagined. I set healthier boundaries at work. I delegate and admit that I can't do it all. I seek out constructive criticism. I never thought to do this while drinking; there would not have been enough alcohol in the world to overcome my fear of being less than perfect.

I am still occasionally thrown off and overwhelmed by feeling like my work won't be good enough. I felt that way with this essay deadline looming. But I no longer drink to make it fade away. I turn to my new tools. Having talked with other sober lawyers, I know many of us have this fear. This allows me to move forward. With the help of a sobriety toolbox, I have stayed sober through a major role change at my firm, the death of my grandmother, a family member's relapse, and a pandemic. When difficult things occur in work or in life, I stay present and remember that, for me, a drink will only make the bad moments worse.

There are many of us who struggle, and I am so grateful for those before me who have shared their paths to sobriety. I learned there were other sober lawyer moms. I learned there were other sober lawyers at my firm. There are quite a few of us on this side of the addiction fence. But there are still so many caught in active addiction. A recent study released by the California Lawyers Association and the Washington, DC Bar found that more women lawyers are reporting hazardous drinking than in the past. In fact, more than *half* of the women surveyed reported risky drinking behavior.[8]

Between law firm events promoting drinking and the pandemic's putting even more burden on women's (especially mothers') plates, it was no surprise to me when I read the report. Almost immediately after I stopped drinking in 2015, I was faced with pressure from the legal community to drink. My office hosted a red wine and whiskey tasting that July. I skipped it. I also skipped happy hours and other opportunities to bond with my colleagues and the partners at the firm. I became highly aware that almost *every* legal event pushed alcohol. This still seems true to me today despite

---

8. Justin Anker and Patrick R. Krill, *Stress, Drink, Leave: An Examination of Gender-specific Risk Factors for Mental Health Problems and Attrition among Licensed Attorneys*, PLOS MED. (May 12, 2021), https://journals.plos.org/plosone/article?id=10.1371/journal.pone.0250563 (last visited Sept. 24, 2023). *See also* Melissa Heelan, *Women Lawyers More Stressed, Drinking More than Men, Study Says*, BLOOMBERG L. (May 12, 2021), https://news.bloomberglaw.com/us-law-week/women-lawyers-more-stressed-drinking-more-than-men-study-says (last visited Sept. 24, 2023).

the efforts of many bar associations and firms to combat the stigma surrounding mental health and addiction.

I am very grateful that my office has made mental wellness a priority. Among other things, it has a wellness task force, it hosts panels on mental health and addiction, it encourages partners to share their wellness (including addiction) journeys, and it no longer hosts alcohol-focused and themed events. This is not universal. Just this week two different women's bar associations sent me emails about their annual fundraisers; both are wine-tastings.

As I began writing this essay, I was interrupted by a call from a client's in-house counsel. We are working on a tough matter. My client asked: "Is it too early for a nap or day drinking?" I totally agreed with her on the nap, and I sidestepped the drinking remark. Seven years ago, I would have relished the opportunity to connect with a client on this level. Seven years ago, I would have felt like a good lawyer for sharing the "work hard, drink hard" attitude. Seven years ago, I would have thought this was okay. No, I would have thought it was great. Now I reframe the conversation. Now I bond over something else—crime podcasts, puzzles, vampire romance novels, parenting, Girl Scouts—it is an almost endless list that does not involve drinking. I am incredibly grateful, and I know I am not alone.

Jessica R. Blaemire

Career

Senior Legal Analyst, Bloomberg Industry Group, focusing on Legal Operations, Attorney Well-Being, and Attorney Development; Former commercial litigation attorney with over 15 years of practice experience

Education
- JD, University of Virginia School of Law (2006)
- BA, Sociology, American Studies, College of William & Mary (2003)

Best Advice

Take all things one day at a time, focus on the present moment, and do the next right thing.

Personal

Jessica Blaemire is mom to two wonderful girls, ages 13 and 8. She has been married to her college sweetheart since 2006 and is grateful for the ups, downs, and everything in between. She is a Girl Scout Leader certified in archery, tomahawk and knife throw, slingshot, and canoeing. She is a lover of music, reading, comic conventions, tattoos, hiking, puzzles, and cats.

For More Information

https://www.linkedin.com/in/jessica-blaemire

Confronting and Defeating Anxiety on a Journey to Inner Peace

By Janet E. Sobel

I was born in 1943, grew up in the 1950s, and graduated from a California state college in 1965, the year I got married and started teaching elementary school. In the 1970s, I had two children and got

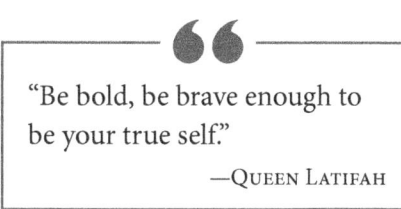

"Be bold, be brave enough to be your true self."

—Queen Latifah

divorced before the decade was over. In 1980, I started UCLA Law School as a single mother, graduated Order of the Coif, and passed the California bar exam in 1983. Somewhere along that unexpected path, I began to struggle with anxiety that I didn't understand, let alone know how to manage. My anxiety was driven by fear of failure, with two children to support and no belief in my own abilities. I had the outward appearance of confidence, while fighting the inner fears that haunted me at night.

Although, in retrospect, none of my fears ever came to pass, I spent most nights awake with worry of the worst that could befall me. The fears seemed fully real and sensible when they came upon me in the middle of the night. Fortunately, once the sun came up, I was positive, cheerful, outgoing, and tireless. I felt I was two people—and the sun made all the difference. I tried therapy after my second child went off to college, but my therapist was uninspiring.

My story is about how I dealt with the debilitation of anxiety over economic insecurity, which was made worse by my unhappiness with being a trial lawyer. I loved law school but was miserably unhappy with my job and saw no good way out. The bottom line is that I instinctively felt that I was living a lie somehow, that I wasn't meant to do this. Like all people, my personal history doesn't tell the whole story, because our history doesn't define us. We are influenced by our past experiences, but we are not defined by them. I was a study in the anxiety that comes from living a life that feels at odds with what I wanted to be. Bob Dylan wisely said, "A man is a success if he gets up in the morning and gets to bed at night, and in between he does what he wants to do." True, of course, for women, too.

The truth is that getting a professional degree is no guarantee that you will enjoy that profession. When the profession is law, things can get pretty complicated. For one thing, the state licensure brings duties that are vast and not at all intuitive; the idea that we must put the interests of strangers ahead of our own, especially when they can be selfish, irrational, and demanding, is hard to take. For another thing, women find themselves in a profession dominated and controlled by men, often ones who don't understand a woman's world. Worse, women are not getting equal pay, let alone equal say. And the pull of motherhood cannot be denied.

Because I love to speak publicly on topics that rouse my passion, I was a natural for litigation, which is what I did. But I soon became jaded at the uselessness of what I was doing, and I felt that my entire life was constructed of aggravating problems. In short, I was a bundle of unsatisfied desires, without any inkling about what I really wanted from my life.

I knew one thing for sure: that I was searching—searching for peace of mind, for my life's meaning, for a way to escape the inevitable anxiety that arrived every night. Thankfully, I began to look inside myself, introspecting about what I enjoyed and what I hated, and I knew I needed to find greater happiness as a lawyer. I often asked myself, "What can I do with my law license that pleases me?" Flash forward: I did find the answer to my law career, but I also discovered that resolving my career didn't by itself resolve the nighttime anxiety, which I knew by day was irrational. As my story plays out, I finally defeated my nightly anxiety by outsmarting the imposter's voice inside of me that tried to destroy my peace.

Throughout millennia, wise teachers have instructed that life is a school, full of lessons; that the purpose of life is to find what we are meant to be and do. I believe the unhappiness I felt as a lawyer was what forced me to search for my true self. That search guided me to look inside myself and to do the hard work of self-discovery—against the backdrop of a career in the law, a career that has many branches upon which to sit and do good works. I also believe that the happiest people use their talents to serve others and that being a lawyer affords us the opportunity to do exactly that.

What I found when I assessed my own frailties is that, for me, my anxiety and its accompanying sadness and dissatisfaction were not solved merely by changing what I did for a living. However, changing what I did for a living was a necessary, if not sufficient, step on my road to finding the harmony that human beings require for a happy life. That is, I knew I couldn't find my peace of mind while holding a job I hated. First, I had to change my career path, to free myself from the daily demands which prevented my efforts to introspect. I had to get off the merry-go-round to get grounded.

What I discovered during my unhappy career is that the satisfaction we glean from being lawyers is up to each of us to find in our own way according to what is uniquely us. If our careers are unsatisfying, we need to make changes to our own lives. Living a lie about who we are and what makes us satisfied professionally can only lead to anxiety and depression. Don't we know that to be true?

There's a parable that resonates with me. It is about the Native American grandfather who tells his grandson about the two wolves in each of us: one is angry, full of hostility, mean, and selfish, and the other is kind and good and full of love. The grandfather explains that the two wolves fight with one another all the time for control of our souls. His grandson asks, "Grandfather, which wolf wins?" His grandfather replies, "It depends on which one you feed."

That was me, fighting with myself. I decided I needed to change what I did with my law license if I was to find inner peace. So, after about 18 years of being a litigator, I asked myself what I enjoyed doing the most as a lawyer. The clear answer was quick to come: I enjoyed talking with people about their legal claims and helping them to find a way to resolve their issues—short of litigation, if at all possible. I decided to stop litigating, work out of my home, and charge people only $75/hour for that service. Eventually, I raised my rate to $100/hour, but I had no interest in charging what the traffic could bear; I enjoyed making my services affordable to people with smaller problems. I called my practice "Counseling at Law," and I made a modest, but doable, income for the next 20 years, which brings me to now.

That shift in my career was the beginning of my new identity as a lawyer. I stopped feeding the "warrior" wolf because I knew that the conflict of litigation was not good for my inner self. I came to realize that some lawyers can handle life as a litigator without getting so caught up in it. But I wasn't that lawyer, and coming to terms with my own limitations was a first step in promoting my own mental health. I knew I needed to change the life I was living to be more in accord with my true self. The rub is that it is a difficult undertaking to know your inner self. Most people, including most lawyers dealing with anxiety, aren't asking themselves these questions. I can't deny the conviction that women are more willing to introspect than their male counterparts, who notoriously are loath to ask for directions. Indeed, isn't asking yourself who you are the ultimate request for directions?

Many of us struggle with private demons and some level of emotional issues that we hide from the world. No one can give us inner peace; we have to give it to ourselves. Counseling and therapy can help, of course, and so can prescription medications. But our search for inner peace is, at its core, in our own hands—because no person, no matter how close, knows us like we know ourselves. We think something like 99.99 percent of our thoughts inside the private walls of our own mind, shared only with the Universe (or with a Creator, according to one's own beliefs).

One article that I read recently got my wholehearted approval: an insightful piece by a law professor having to do with the crucial need lawyers have for self-awareness.[9] He is so right. We don't learn self-analysis in law school, which is designed for the adversarial nature of the legal profession that is the backbone of the legal system itself. Once we get into law school and pass the bar, we are in for a wild ride that we are ill prepared to take. When I started my first job at a well-respected, large firm, I felt as though I knew nothing—and I was right. I learned a lot during my first few years, but not about my inner self.

Experienced attorneys are spending their time trying to become excellent at lawyering; consequently, the need to find our true center core can fall to the wayside. Women lawyers can get caught up trying to be mothers and wives while pursuing legal careers, and that is not always easy to manage. When I worked in a firm setting, I never (not once) talked

---

9. *See* Patti Alleva, *Wholeness: Thoughts on Law Teaching, Lawyering, and Living*, 94 NORTH DAKOTA L. REV. 289, 290 (2019), citing DEBORAH KENN, LAWYERING FROM THE HEART 67–68 (2009) (describing teaching to the "whole person" in the clinical setting and noting her expectation that third-year law students "show up for the clinic" with "their entire person"). *See also* Alli Gerkman & Logan Cornett, *Foundations for Practice: The Whole Lawyer and the Character Quotient* 2 IAALS (2016) (emphasis omitted) (concluding that successful new lawyers are neither "merely legal technicians ... nor ... cognitive powerhouses," but persons who "come to the job with a much broader blend of legal skills, professional competencies, and characteristics that comprise the whole lawyer"), https://law.und.edu/_files/docs/ndlr/pdf/issues/94/2/94ndlr289.pdf.

about how hard it was to meet my responsibilities to my children at the same time I tried to bill enough hours to "succeed" at the firm. I carried that guilt with me because the needs of my firm and my clients always came first—until I decided that the firm life wasn't for me.

For a long time after leaving the firm life, I felt the guilt that came from putting my clients' needs first, but one day a good person asked me to rethink my assumptions about whether I should feel guilt—which was driven by the feeling that I had let my children down. On reflection, which is always a valuable exercise, I realized that children don't necessarily suffer when their parents work harder than life requires. They may complain, but that doesn't mean they were injured. If I had been then what I am now, I am sure I would have taken a different path. But that's not how my life played out. I was who I was, burdened by a need to excel in a calling that was not in harmony with my inner self.

But the truth is that all of us (including our children) have to play the cards we are dealt. My children got me for a mother, with all the benefits and detriments that came with me. As I was living my life in real time, which is the only way we can live it in this time-driven reality, there were too many times when I had to work instead of giving my children the attention they wanted. It is comforting to realize, in the retrospection required to see our lives in perspective, that they came out okay; actually, better than okay—outstanding, in fact. As children of divorce, they bounced between Las Vegas and San Diego, spending time with divorced parents, and they had to bear the consequences of that disruption. I wasn't a stay-at-home mom, but I was a fighter and a survivor, and both of my children are as well—strong, independent, self-reflecting adults.

I have spent the last 20 years trying to find myself. The search was surprisingly difficult but worth it. Regret becomes an enemy if it keeps us from finding the truth. But it is correct that the truth sets us free. I used my anxiety as the motivating factor to find my way to peace. I was willing to acknowledge my unhappiness as a lawyer but unwilling to throw away the value of my law license. I committed myself to finding something I could do with my law degree that would add value to the lives of ordinary people and to using that something as a way to make myself a better person, more likable to myself.

I put aside the fiction I used to read, and I spent my time reading the nonfiction works that have become staples across the world. For my own inner venture, I found helpful the works of Don Miguel Ruiz, Jack Canfield, Napoleon Hill, Norman Vincent Peale, Rhonda Byrne, Paramahansa Yogananda, Thích Nhất Hạnh, the Dalai Lama, and others. I took up meditation, yoga, and mindfulness training, and I changed the friends I kept. I looked at my own life and asked myself what felt good and what didn't. I began to spend more time volunteering to help others and started to examine my own self.

Change doesn't occur overnight; that's for sure. It's a slow process, but the anxiety that haunted me is gone. Finally! For me, going to law school was an exciting adventure, but practicing law was a struggle until I began my Counseling-at-Law practice. I am proud to be a lawyer, even if I don't practice in the traditional way. Lawyers in the United States generally appear full of confidence, rarely admit they are wrong about anything, and wear a mask that belies their fears. For me, that mask hid me from myself, and I spent a long time trying to get rid of it. Looking at myself took courage—and I am grateful I finally did.

My unhappiness as a lawyer was a part of me, and my life couldn't have been otherwise. I encourage all lawyers, especially women lawyers, to be true to themselves, whatever that might mean and wherever that may lead. The quest for inner truth is the most important one we undertake.

Janet E. Sobel

Career

Counselor-at-Law, Private Practice

Education

JD, University of California, Los Angeles, School of Law (1983)

Best Advice

Read Don Miguel Ruiz's *The Four Agreements* and make a promise to be unrelenting in applying the four agreements to yourself. Perhaps it's a very good thing that practicing law can lead to the very kind of misery that permits us to see ourselves in a clear (though sometimes harsh) light. Our discomforts allow us to discover who we really are, deep inside, because they help us to realize that we are out of touch with our inner core; *The Four Agreements* can give us the tools to find that truth. Be fearless in looking at yourself because coming to understand the truth of who you really are will truly set you free. Or, simply, as Winston Churchill famously said, "Never, never, never give up."

Personal

Janet Sobel leans heavily toward the serious side of life; she is curious about the world and what makes people tick. She has a few close friends, shares her small home with her indoor rescue cat, likes to play Mahjong, will drop everything for someone who needs her, and expresses her opinion more than she should. She was raised in the 1950s in the San Fernando Valley and likes that she remembers things like her first pair of pantyhose (which she thought would never catch on because one run and you have to throw both sides out). She likes small parties, good movies, lively conversation, and spending time alone thinking her own thoughts.

For More Information

https://www.linkedin.com/in/janet-sobel-07182611

Suicide: Returning from the (Nearly) Dead
By Eric C. Lang[10]

Trying to Die

Every semester, Philosophy 101 students across the world read Camus, and almost all of them are stunned by Camus's declaration about suicide. A very small number, though, find familiarity with the sentiment and assume everyone else does too. I know this because the day after my suicide attempt, the therapist in the "special hospital" asked me whether I had considered suicide before. I answered,

> "There is but one truly serious philosophical problem, and that is suicide. Judging whether life is or is not worth living amounts to answering the fundamental question of philosophy."
>
> —ALBERT CAMUS, *The Myth of Sisyphus*

"you mean other than the thoughts people have about it every day?" Her face told me all I needed to know.

What reason would I have had to question these thoughts, which had been with me for as long as I could remember? We—especially those of us who spend our career in courtrooms—live an outcome-judged life. Do well in school—get praised and get into a good college. Do well in college—get praised and get into a good law school. Do well in law school—well, you get the idea. I did well all along: state debate champ in high school; student body president in college; graduating at the top of the class in law school. Follow all that with a career of courtroom success, and the praise of others affirmed that I had a great brain. Why would I have any reason to question the thoughts being constantly thrown at me by that brain?

One particularly bad day, that great brain convinced me that dying would be better than living. I reasoned that, because of any number of factors, I was of no value to anyone, but that my life insurance policy was of great value. (I hate to encourage others, but it is a myth that there is a blanket exclusion in life insurance policies for suicide, something I researched

---

10. Suicide attempts occur among both women and men; few are willing to tell their story publicly.

before my attempt.) Deciding to follow a pile of pills with a glass of vodka seemed logical, if not brilliant. This was an exercise of the daily math—that day was the day the numbers said that life was not worth living. It is fortunate that I turned out to be a much better lawyer than a pharmacist.

From there I got to spend a few days in the aforementioned special hospital, where I was quickly and correctly diagnosed with bipolar disorder. The hospital had a program for professionals with such challenges, and I spent a year in weekly group therapy with other lawyers. At the same time, my doctor spent a year and a half getting my drug cocktail just right. (That time frame is normal.) Compliance with that medical regimen, coupled with regular therapy, is now a part of my life.

Predicting and Preventing

Suicide is an issue in our profession. Though the statistics about attorney mental health and suicide are imperfect, I feel confident that we all know more than one attorney who has died by suicide or has attempted to do so. Dean Prosser's words ring true. This is a very taxing profession that takes its toll on even the psychiatrically strongest among us.

Let's take a step back and ask whether there was anything that could have prevented me from attempting suicide. First, to all of you who have lost someone to suicide and are tortured by thoughts of what you could or should have done, the answer is likely *nothing*. A person who truly wants to die

>
>
> "Your lawyer in practice spends a considerable part of his life doing distasteful things for disagreeable people who must be satisfied, against an impossible time limit and with hourly interruptions, from other disagreeable people who want to derail the train; and for his blood, sweat, and tears he receives in the end a few unkind words to the effect that it might have been done better, and a protest at the size of his fee."
>
> —William L. Prosser, *Lighthouse No Good*[11]

---

11. William L. Prosser, *Lighthouse No Good*, 1 J. of Legal Ed. 260 (1948).

instinctively knows how to mask that desire.[12] The morning of my attempt I was in my office with five or six others. While taking the pills, I put some playoff baseball tickets up for sale (to leave more money behind). There was no outward appearance that anything was wrong. My own belief is that, for the most part, those who can be stopped want to be stopped.

Indeed, the standard lists of suicide warning signs[13] are, in reality, of little help. Are we really expected to hear someone talk about "wanting to die"? What ability do we have to see people "making a plan or researching ways to die"? Undoubtedly, if these signs are present, there is a problem to which to react. But it is a rare person who answers "how are you" with "preparing for death by my own hand." No one in my life would have noticed those things from me.

Lawyers can, however, manifest behavioral changes that could be viewed as signals of problems. Calls that are unreturned (or slowly returned); changes in quality of written product; and repeated extension requests (or outright missing of deadlines) all can signal potential issues. The existence of objective indications may only be cold comfort. We deal with so many different people that no one person can detect a pattern.

Prevention, therefore, does not depend on what some outsider observes or says, but rather on the vulnerable persons themselves. In retrospect, there were many things that I could have seen that I did not. For me, it was not the quality of the work that I actually performed. Rather, it was a predominance of almost silly things I did not get to (and then hoped would disappear as I put my head in the sand) which should have alerted me to a bigger issue.

I could have done a better job of paying attention to others who noticed and raised things with me. Just a few months before my attempt, I was working on a tough case that went to trial. It was pretty clear we had won, but there were 12 folks who disagreed. Right after the surprising verdict, the judge's clerk approached me with the last words an attorney

---

12. I say that as if it is established fact, when actually it is an anecdotally driven opinion. For obvious reasons, we cannot study those who "succeeded" in taking their own lives. My view is based only on my conversations with others who have attempted and "failed."

13. These signs are taken from the National Institute of Mental Health but are representative of lists that can be found all over the internet. *See Warning Signs of Suicide*, NAT. INST. OF MENTAL HEALTH, https://www.nimh.nih.gov/health/publications/warning-signs-of-suicide (last visited Sept. 24, 2023).

wants to hear: "the judge wants to see you in chambers right away." The judge sat me down, told me I was the best lawyer he ever saw (let's call that "blowing smoke"), and then told me I was about to go through some tough times, having lost a case that I won. I guess he spent 5 to 10 minutes calming me down, even though if you asked me whether I needed to be calmed down, I would have said no. I should have—but did not—treat the experience as a caution flag.

This is where the great brain, the outcome-judged profession, and the bipolar disorder come into the picture. Though bipolar disorder manifests itself differently with different people, the concept is relatively simple—there are ups (mania) and downs (depression). For me, the mania (which I did not know was mania) was my strength. It was my ability to get the job done well, no matter what. The depression was my down time—my affect was not staying in bed; rather, it was doing something mechanical—like cleaning my office or working on forms. As long as I got the job done, what did it matter? I often tell a tale of two opposing lawyers, each with 30 days' notice of an important evidentiary hearing. Lawyer 1 prepares 4 hours a day following a plan—research, drafting, rehearsing, revising, and so on. Lawyer 2 is lost in thought for 28 days, but "inspiration" hits and fuels 2 days of getting ready. Lawyer 2 wins. Lawyer 1's client takes no solace in Lawyer 1's perfect process; Lawyer 2's client is ecstatic that Lawyer 2 was so efficient. Our profession rewards Lawyer 2; therefore, Lawyer 2 does not know there is a problem.

Thus, I did not know I had a problem. Some of the "silly" things I missed were not just silly but were quite unethical. My brain told me that although I was causing problems, I could solve them. I was wrong. This brought me to the point where taking my life "made sense" to me. The ethical lapses caused a 2-year "vacation" from practice. The psychiatric explosion that was the suicide attempt would have knocked me out for a couple of years even without the mandatory time off.

Recovering

> JOSH: You said you diagnosed me in five minutes. What was the diagnosis?
> STANLEY: You have posttraumatic stress disorder.

> JOSH: *Well, that doesn't really sound like something they let you have if you work for the President.*
>
> . . .
>
> STANLEY: *No.*
> JOSH: *Why not?*
> STANLEY: *Because we get better.*[14]

We do get better, but the thought is incomplete: we get better when we try. The first part of trying is mechanical: if you are thinking about your own death or if you have attempted to take your own life, go to the doctor (in this instance, a psychiatrist). If you were experiencing extreme physical symptoms, you would get them treated because you feared harm. Treat nonphysical symptoms that threaten harm in the same fashion. The doctor will start the process of determining the right regimen of medication. Know that it will take a while, for there is a great deal of trial and error. Chances are that some of the things you try will have no impact, and some will have a negative impact. Be patient, because once the "meds" are right, there will be a difference.

Medication, however, is no more a solution for mental health than a crutch is for a broken ankle. The medication helps you do other important work—therapy. Whether group therapy, individual therapy, or both, talking about how you are doing at any given time will create a baseline for a third party (the therapist) to notice the kind of signs described above. One personal view: although it is possible to "just" see a psychiatrist every few months to keep your prescriptions current, do more than that.

Having dealt with the "easy" items—taking pills and keeping appointments—the real work truly begins. And when you start this work, you will come to the realization that your (my) conclusion that no one really needed or wanted you in the world was wrong. People will come out of the woodwork to do what is needed to keep you alive. Your family

---

14. Some may know the reference, some may not. It is from *The West Wing* episode, *Noel*. Josh Lyman, the Deputy White House Chief of Staff to President Bartlet, engaged in an act of self-harm and exhibited other questionable behavior, triggered in part by the suicide of a fighter pilot. Stanley was the psychiatrist brought in to help Josh. Though Josh's situation involved PTSD and self-harm, as opposed to suicide, the concept of getting better is universal.

and your close friends will surround you with love. For every person who shocks you by disappearing, there will be two or three whom you never expected to come forward to ease your pain.

From the time of my "vacation" until the time my brain was fully capable of practicing law, I had to find ways (other than the practice of law) to put food on the table. But during that time, the support I received from my professional relationships was overwhelming. A number of lawyers hired me to do nonpractice legal work. A number of other people found ways to involve me in their businesses other than the practice of law.

One story stands out above the others. Long ago, I successfully represented a client who was starting a business and had been sued by his former partner. I sent him a bill, and he told me that my bill was too low (it was). I told him this was the right bill for him to receive at that point in his business life. Go forward about 15 years to the time of my issues. I received a check from him, along with a note: "here's what you didn't charge me; it's the right time for you to get it." *You learn that people care about you, and it saves your life going forward.*

When I was able to practice again, the old clients and old referral sources were there for me. The first matters I received were, well, simple—small contract breaches, collection matters, and the like. I was being tested, and that was fine. I passed those tests and am now handling the very cases I was handling at my peak so many years ago, but . . .

But self-awareness governs me in a way it did not before my attempt. While I might want to spend 100 percent or more of my time working on high-paying, high-stakes, business disputes, I now know that I cannot.

Although I know I would enjoy that for the moment, taking on that workload would be a recipe for long-term disaster. Instead, I try to limit the most difficult work to no more than half my workload and to keep the other half focused on less intense matters (or as second chair on the more intense matters).

Learning to say "no" is an important step. Mania leads you to believe you can do anything and everything. You can't. When you fail, and when suicide is on your mind, your internal math leads you to conclude that your life is not worth it. My most extreme "superman" story from before the attempt: I coached a 5:30 p.m. Little League game on a Wednesday, took a late flight to New York for a 9 a.m. hearing, and grabbed a flight back to coach a different team on Thursday. Now I know that just because I *can* do something does not mean I should.

My final step has been to try to destigmatize suicide. I have spoken on this subject to groups of a couple of dozen (small county bar associations) to more than 1,500 (the Georgia Chief Justice's Commission on Professionalism). Each time I speak, I urge people to be open about their own experiences, so that those who believe that suicidal thoughts are normal (and in line with what they learned in Philosophy 101) can become aware of the challenges they face.

Eric C. Lang

Career
Trial Attorney and Legal Strategist; Leading Speaker on Attorney Mental Health

Education
- JD, High Honors, University of Florida Levin College of Law (1990)
- BS, Economics, Wharton School of Business, University of Pennsylvania (1987)

Best Advice
I've become fond of saying "there's a way to be, be that way." This touches everything from rounding up your tip to the server to pretty much never denying a request for an extension to respond.

Personal
Eric Lang grew up in Florida but has spent his entire professional life in Atlanta, Georgia (that is, since 1990). Eric and his wife raised three children there, with the full complement of extracurricular activity and family fun. With the kids now scattered around the national map, there is more time to focus on "his own" activities, which include all things baseball, food (both its preparation and consumption), and trivia competition. Eric also acts, from time to time, as lay clergy at his synagogue. Though he doesn't define himself by his mental health, for the purposes of this publication, he felt it's worth noting that he tried to take his own life in 2012, which revealed a lifetime of undiagnosed bipolar disorder, which led to self-awareness through therapy and medication. Since then, he has become a very frequent speaker and writer on attorney mental health.

For More Information
https://www.linkedin.com/in/ericclang

Discussion Questions

1. What are your priorities? How are you aligning your time with your priorities?

2. What is standing in the way of your living an "Unfrazzled" life?

3. What hidden hazards do you face in your life? How can you frame those situations so that they feel more like speedbumps than barriers?

4. Has imposter syndrome impacted your practice? If so, describe its effects on you and your practice.

5. Does fear affect your decision making? If so, what are you afraid of? What changes would you make in your professional and personal life if you did not have any fear?

6. Many of the authors describe using tools such as meditating, journaling, and going for a walk to protect their mental wellness. What self-care tools are you using each day? What are some tools you would like to try?

7. What do you like to do just for yourself? How often do you make the time to do it?

8. How has the pandemic changed the way you practice law? Which of these changes would you like to make permanent?

9. What changes can your workplace make to support mental health and wellness? How can you be a part of those changes?

10. Which of the essays in this chapter most resonated for you?

CHAPTER 4

Going Places We've Never Been Before: Succeeding at the Business of Law

Career paths change; we adjust. Challenges present; we persevere. The stories in this chapter provide strategies for navigating our careers with a focus on the business side of our careers, while also providing useful tips for confronting the obstacles that come with it. In these essays, the authors share their insights on time management, building a book of business, creating your brand, negotiating compensation, and being a strong manager, as well as sharing their stories and lessons learned on dealing with inexperience.

An Unanticipated Career Path to Greater Opportunities

By Gwen Keyes Fleming

I'm a planner. So much so, that when I was 16 years old growing up in New Jersey, I planned my *entire* life:

- I would get married at 24 (after meeting my husband in college or graduate school out of state);
- We would have our first child at 26 (it would be a boy);
- We would have our second child at 28 (it would be a girl);
- And I would live out the rest of my life as a successful working soccer mom living in suburbia and driving her BMW SUV into "the city" where I would work at a six-figure job as a financial expert after getting my MBA.

CRAZY, right? While some of my plan has come true (which I'll describe more later), I often think about what my response would have been if God had given me an advanced copy of the "Book" referenced in Psalm 139:16 that outlined HIS plan for me. I think the conversation would have gone something like this:

> GOD: I'm going to send you to an All-Women's College . . . in New Jersey. Instead of getting your MBA, I'm going to send you to a city and state you've never been to in order to get your law degree from a school you've never heard of before. You will not meet your husband in school and instead of working in a silk-stocking firm practicing corporate law, I'm going to have you serve as a local prosecutor in a city nationally known for its high crime rate (Atlanta circa 1994). Instead of a six-figure salary that gives you financial freedom, you will scrape by barely affording to pay your law school loans. Then, after 5 years, I will have you run a very hotly contested primary election for Solicitor General in DeKalb County, Georgia. You will raise less money than your annual salary and your youth and lack of experience will be highlighted at every turn. The person who encouraged you to run will

withdraw his support and ask you to leave the race so the "establishment's candidate"—a man—can win without challenge. But in the end, you will make history as the first African American and first female Solicitor General of DeKalb County, Georgia. It won't be easy, though, because within your first year, you will have to quell an opposition-fueled rebellion within the office and replace your entire leadership team.

After things settle down and you win reelection without opposition, I'm going to have you run a second hotly contested political race against a well-liked and well-funded incumbent. Your fiercest competitor from the first race will reemerge as a primary contender, and both men will challenge your integrity as well as your competence and besmirch your reputation at every chance on the campaign trail. People will openly challenge your audacity to run, claiming women aren't constituted to make tough decisions about whether to seek the death penalty in a criminal case. But in the end you will prevail, becoming the first African American and first female District Attorney (DA) of DeKalb County and one of the first elected African American female DAs in the state of Georgia. And just when you think your election put to rest everyone's archaic thoughts about what a woman can and cannot do, when you finally get married (at age 36) and have your first child while in office (at age 37), the press will question whether your maternity leave is a disservice to the citizens who elected you!

THEN after securing your reputation in criminal law . . . I'm going to have you reinvent your career TWICE! This pattern of firsts will continue as you are appointed by President Barack Obama to be the first African American Regional Administrator (RA) for the U.S. Environmental Protection Agency (EPA) in Region 4 and the first African American female Chief of Staff for the agency where you will learn a completely new area of law after practicing for 17 years as a prosecutor. The local papers will write extensive stories about your lack of qualifications, but I'll show you how to turn what others want to use to tear you down into your greatest gift: You'll use your newness in the environmental space to help the experts be more inclusive and translate the science and their expertise so that others in communities—who like you do not have advanced degrees in biochemistry and environmental science—can understand and apply the concepts to protect their families from pollution. After serving as the RA for 3 years, Gina McCarthy will ask you to be her first Chief of Staff as she becomes the Environmental Protection Agency (EPA) Administrator during President Obama's second term. This, once again, will make you the first African American woman to serve in this role as you move your family to Washington, DC, leaving behind the communities and support systems that helped you through so many chapters of your career. While you'll have several successes in this role, including organizing the first ever senior leadership training on unconscious bias, you'll often be beleaguered by imposter syndrome and consider returning "HOME" after only 6 months on the job.

You'll persevere for the next 2 years, and the second reinvention will occur when you are appointed the first African American Principal Legal Advisor for Immigration and Customs Enforcement (ICE) in the Department of Homeland Security (DHS) and lead a team of 1,000-plus immigration lawyers in 60 offices around the country. This position will truly test your leadership skills and your ability to manage a decisive (and not always agreeable) client team for the first time in your career, and it will serve as a glide path for your transition from administrative roles back into the active practice of law.

Within 3 years of launching your private sector career, you will become the first African American member of your firm's Executive Committee. At a small firm you'll learn how to manage achieving billable hours targets while conducting the necessary business development to get new work. You will also learn how to set healthy limits in both your professional and personal life. Finally (at least in terms of what is known thus far), you will go on to become the Co-chair of the domestic Environmental Practice at one of the largest law firms in the world—a title that is held by only two other African American women (to date).

When God finished reading these pages of "His Book" to me, after picking my jaw up off the floor, I probably would have said:

"Hmmm, No disrespect God, but no thanks! I know there have to be firsts in all kinds of places and professions, but I cannot do that. It's too hard, and someone else is more qualified. There's NO WAY I can learn a whole new area of law once, much less twice while still raising young kids. Plus, I have no interest in politics, no influence, no husband, no money because I have no husband, and I'M NOT GOING TO AN ALL GIRLS' SCHOOL!"

Looking back, I see that I was just terrified to dream bigger than what I planned at 16. And what I planned was heavily influenced—some would say even limited—by what I could see at the time. It's ironic that God used my limited vision to expand not just my own notions of what was possible for women in several fields, but the visions of others as well. As I look back over my career, I've learned a few lessons along the way that I now try to share with others:

1. Don't succumb to your fears. Be courageous. Get out there and do it!
2. Recognize your place in our communal pyramid.
3. Recognize that things that look like setbacks are actually setups for success.
4. Have a plan, but don't be afraid to deviate and reinvent yourself. You'll get to where you're meant to be if you're patient and recognize one fact: It's all a process.

Don't Succumb to Your Fears. Be Courageous. Get Out There and Do It!

My favorite quote is the following by Marianne Williamson:

> Our deepest fear is not that we are inadequate. Our deepest fear is that we are powerful beyond measure. It is our light, not our

darkness that most frightens us. We ask ourselves, "Who am I to be brilliant, gorgeous, talented, fabulous?" Actually, who are you not to be? You are a child of God. Your playing small does not serve the world. There is nothing enlightened about shrinking so that other people won't feel insecure around you. We are all meant to shine, as children do. We were born to make manifest the glory of God that is within us. It's not just in some of us; it's in everyone. And as we let our own light shine, we unconsciously give other people permission to do the same.[1]

Running for office is a TERRIFYING experience! You are constantly putting yourself and your views out there, and you often receive biting criticism in return, not to mention the constant rejection you receive making fundraising calls! When I ran for Solicitor General and District Attorney, several people—other women and people of color—told me I hadn't "paid my dues" or wasn't qualified. But I couldn't let that stop me; I had to keep going. I didn't know if I was going to WIN (at the time), but I knew I had to RUN. When chided that I "had big shoes to fill" in reference to my male predecessors, I found the courage to quip back "Maybe . . . but I'll be wearing SLINGBACKS instead of WINGTIPS!"

This brings me to imposter syndrome. In varying contexts, it's the (false) belief that you don't belong to sit in the position you hold, a belief that can lead to an extensive amount of anxiety and stress. When confronted with my own insecurity and bouts of imposter syndrome on the campaign, my internal mantra became a combination of Deuteronomy 31:6 and the old Nike commercial: "Be strong and of good courage" paired with "Just Do It!" Over the years, I have come to learn (with much therapy and work) that imposter syndrome is less about me and my skills and instead is rooted in widely held and often internalized patriarchal notions of who should hold certain positions and be given certain opportunities. I now counsel younger women who are entering leadership or other positions as firsts (or not), to have the courage to be themselves and recognize that this is their opportunity to make their mark using their own gifts and on their own terms. The sentiment comes from my own personal experience when my management team at the

---

1. MARIANNE WILLIAMSON, A RETURN TO LOVE: REFLECTIONS ON THE PRINCIPLES OF "A COURSE IN MIRACLES" (Harper Collins, 1992).

Solicitor General's Office threatened to resign in protest of my deploying a different leadership style than the one used by my predecessor during his 16 years in the office. After trying to cajole and compromise to try to get the holdover team to stay and work with me, I finally said to myself: "ENOUGH! I may lose reelection for this, but at least I'll lose it on my terms. LET THEM GO!" Honestly, it was my first leadership challenge and I did not know how things would turn out, but I knew that I couldn't be something I wasn't or change myself to fit someone else's notions of what I should be.

Years later, after being reelected to my second prosecutorial position—without opposition—I received a letter from one of my early detractors. In an attempt to bestow a compliment, he claimed that I had "evolved into a competent DA." In actuality, I was competent all along; HE'S the one who actually evolved by recognizing that just because something HASN'T been done before because of someone's "inside the box" thinking doesn't mean it CAN'T be done by someone—especially a woman—who dares to dream "outside of the box." As they say: "Well behaved women rarely make history!" Here's to all of the past and future ill-behaved women who beat back imposter syndrome to shape this country and change others by having courage, standing tall, and, as encouraged by Nike, "doing it!"

Recognize Your Place in our Communal Pyramid

Another favorite quote is by Benjamin E. Mays: "Every man and woman is born into the world to do something unique and something distinctive and if he or she does not do it, it will never be done." This quote reminds me of cheerleading with friends growing up where we used to build "human pyramids": I would stand shoulder to shoulder with another cheerleader, and someone would stand with one foot on my shoulder and one foot on the shoulder of the young woman standing next to me. We would keep building in that fashion until we reached our desired height (or until the coaches and medical teams told us to get down). The point is that I had to be standing in the right place for the pyramid to grow to new elevations. This view isn't just a hope of what can be in the future; it's also homage to those who came before me and upon whose shoulders I stand. Without the sacrifices and bloodshed of the late Congressman

John Lewis and so many others in the civil rights movement, I would not have been elected to any of my positions. There are now seven elected African American female District Attorneys in the state of Georgia. This is just a subset of the other people of color serving as prosecutors, public defenders, and judges in a state that saw its first African American prosecutor in 1968 (the year I was born) when Lewis Slaton hired now-retired federal judge Clarence Cooper to handle criminal cases in Fulton County, Georgia.

Similarly, without Congressman John Lewis, we would not have elected Barack Obama, the first African American President, in 2008. Without President Obama, Lisa Jackson would not have been nominated and confirmed as the first African American Administrator of the EPA. And without Lisa Jackson, I would not have been appointed as the first African American EPA Regional Administrator in the Southeast. Each of the aforementioned individuals stood in their right place—sometimes at great personal sacrifice—and as a result were part of the communal pyramid that helped change the way environmental justice and environmental policies were handled in the South.

These and other diversity-focused changes in almost every industry bring to mind the Sam Cooke song, "Change Is Gonna Come." That statement is true only if women recognize their opportunities to be incremental parts of that change and stand in their right place, maximizing their "unique and distinctive" opportunity.

Recognize That Things That Look Like Setbacks Are Actually Setups for Success

Let's face it: no matter what you choose to do, you will experience setbacks. For example, despite my best efforts, I could not find a law firm in Atlanta that would hire me as an intern my first summer out of law school. Similarly, after graduation, I wanted to secure a coveted judicial clerkship. However, after applying for a job with almost every judge in the Atlanta metro area—state and federal—I could wallpaper my room with all the (very polite) rejection letters. These "failures" were devastating to absorb at the time, but I now realize that they were simply "redirections" toward what I was meant to do.

Specifically, since I could not find a paying job after my first year, I volunteered my time at the Fulton County District Attorney's Office that summer. There, I met a host of mentors who not only helped launch my 17-year career in prosecution, but also with whom I remain close personal friends today. While I didn't work as a judicial clerk, serving as the elected prosecutor in both local and state courts allowed me to work with (although some of them would say "for") a fantastic group of state court and superior court judges in DeKalb.

Whenever I get frustrated or disappointed by an unplanned outcome in my career, I recount these experiences, but I also think of my father, the late Andrew J. Keyes, and his experience as a Tuskegee airman at Moton Field in Alabama in the 1940s: Dad always wanted to be a pilot. This desire was born out of bonding experiences he had as the only son of his father of humble beginnings. They would watch the planes take off from the recently opened Newark Airport in New Jersey in 1928. When the Army Air Corps opened the training program to African Americans in 1940, Dad headed south and started his training in 1944. After weeks of diligent course work and challenging test flights, he "washed out" and failed the program. Rather than returning to New Jersey, Dad regrouped and became the Sergeant in charge of the Control Tower. In this role, he was responsible for safely landing not just one plane, but *all of them*.

Remembering that Dad's (and my own) apparent setbacks and failures were actually pathways to greater opportunities helps me stay positive, maintain my confidence, and ask "what's next?" instead of "why (not) me?"

Have a Plan but Don't Be Afraid to Deviate and Reinvent Yourself. You'll Get to Where You're Meant to Be If You're Patient and Recognize: It's All a Process

As I said at the start, the plan my 16-year-old self imagined has come true in some respects:

- I was married, albeit at the age of 36 instead of 24;
- My first child was a boy, followed by his younger brother 2 years and 3 weeks later (to the day);

- I live in the suburbs of Virginia and travel into Washington, DC, where I work in a high-powered, high-paying job as an environmental lawyer;
- Both boys' love of soccer has me traveling around the country cheering them on from the sidelines; and
- When I was the DA, my office confiscated a 2005 candy-apple red BMW SUV that I got to drive on work-related business!

This is proof that not only do plans and dreams come true, but also that they can become something bigger and better than you ever imagined. While there were turns and twists, challenges, and career wins, as well as losses and lessons learned along the way, I feel like I'm exactly where I wanted to be.

Gwen Keyes Fleming

Career
Partner, Co-chair, Environmental Practice Group, DLA Piper LLP (U.S.)

Education
- JD, Emory University School of Law (1993)
- BS, Finance, Douglass College at Rutgers University (1990)

Best Advice
Do your homework, and then don't be afraid to use that historic information to charter a new career path that embraces your authentic self. Just because it hasn't been done before, doesn't mean it can't be done BY YOU.

Personal
Gwen Fleming is a frequently requested speaker on many topics, including leadership, diversity, environmental justice, and equity. She serves on the Board of the Environmental Law Institute, supports several local community causes, and enjoys traveling—especially to cheer on her sons in their favorite sports activities.

For More Information
https://www.dlapiper.com/en-us/people/f/fleming-gwen
https://www.linkedin.com/in/gwenkeyesfleming
gwen.keyesfleming@us.dlapiper.com
(202) 799-4419

Accessing Opportunities and Experiences to Succeed

By Sharonda R. Williams

I grew up in a rural parish in southwest Louisiana where people thrive on hunting, fishing, raising cattle, working in the oil industry, and wearing camouflage. I was the only African American girl in my high school graduating class. Opportunities to become a successful lawyer as an African American woman in that environment were few and far between—regardless of my intellectual capacity and achievements. Not only that, the unfortunate reality is that the legal profession remains male-dominated. According to the 2022 *ABA Profile of the Legal Profession*, women still make up only 38.3 percent of all lawyers.[2]

In my experiences with several male lawyers in my home area of Louisiana, I was viewed as nothing more than a "little girl" who might need instruction—even after over a decade in practice. Unfortunately, talented women lawyers are still confronted with the same preconceptions when they walk into a room in any city or state. Under those circumstances, it is often difficult to access opportunities that will enhance resumes and advance careers. Male lawyers still often give preferential treatment to other men when assigning important cases or clients. Women lawyers often must take additional steps to increase their own professional profiles so that they will have greater opportunities.

As a young lawyer, engaging in bar association (whether local, state, or national) and community activities was critical to my ability to engage with professionals outside the walls of my law firm. Naturally, this provided access to different opportunities. I viewed it as part of my law career development, even though it was difficult to balance with the demands of law firm practice. Engaging with bar associations gave me the opportunity to meet experienced, well-known lawyers and judges. Eventually, true, sustained involvement in those associations allowed me to become a leader in those organizations and to have speaking opportunities. Those

---

2. *2022 ABA Profile of the Legal Profession*, Am. Bar Ass'n (July 2022), https://www.americanbar.org/content/dam/aba/administrative/news/2022/07/profile-report-2022.pdf (last visited Dec. 14, 2022) (*citing* ABA National Lawyer Population Survey).

leadership and speaking opportunities allowed me to gain access to and to become familiar with a wider range of lawyers and judges, locally, statewide, and nationally.

In addition to bar associations, identifying and joining boards of nonprofit organizations allowed me to contribute to the community in ways other than providing legal services. Becoming involved in arts organizations and social services organizations has been incredibly enriching. And nonprofit boards are generally diligent about ensuring that its members have diverse professional backgrounds. It provided the opportunity to get to know business leaders who were nonlawyers. As a young lawyer, the idea of joining a nonprofit board seemed a little intimidating, but I did a nonprofit board training to lessen my anxiety about it. That board training also gave me great insight into issues related to proper board governance, which, as it turns out, has been useful even in assisting clients in my legal practice.

Another avenue to consider, but to be considered carefully, is joining organizations that focus on policy or politics. I joined a couple of politically oriented organizations early on in my career. It was fun to participate with groups of people who generally shared my political views. Those types of organizations have to be carefully considered, of course, because the clients who pay your legal fees may not be pleased about certain organizations. So, tread lightly with these organizations and assess the political atmosphere at your firm before becoming active in them.

And it goes without saying that finding a great mentor within your law firm is always smart. If one is not available in your firm, finding a mentor outside of your law firm can be great. Other women lawyers often refer work and include their friends in great opportunities. If you are able to find a great mentor who can provide you meaningful work in great cases, those experiences will be the best foundation for not only your legal career but also for additional opportunities. A managing partner who allows you to argue important matters in court and engage directly with clients is invaluable. I was fortunate enough to have that mentoring as a young lawyer, and it gave me the chance to work on complex and high-profile matters and to meet business owners and leaders who needed our services.

As a result of all those experiences, I was asked to take on different roles in both the legal profession and the community. Through those experiences, I was able to leave private practice and to become a government attorney, which was never an aspiration or anything I ever considered. This became possible not only because of my legal experience but also because of my involvement in bar associations and community and political organizations.

For many lawyers who are in private practice, the idea of becoming a government lawyer sounds preposterous. And for lawyers who graduated at the top of their classes (like me), unless there was a true passion for public service, those lawyers invariably aimed for jobs at large law firms rather than the lower-paying government jobs. After I graduated from law school, I worked for a state appellate court judge in southwest Louisiana whose opinions—both legal and otherwise—I greatly value, and he said to me "find a job that you love and the money will come later." With that in mind, I left the partnership at my law firm and took the leap into government practice, which, of course, was a pay cut. But it was my most valuable professional experience to date in terms of how much I learned about the law, management, and politics.

That experience provided knowledge of areas of the law that I would have never encountered in my private practice, which opened additional opportunities when I returned to private practice. When I returned to private practice, I had opportunities to get political subdivisions and public agencies as clients because I now had knowledge of issues unique to public entities. I have worked on land-use and zoning cases in my private practice because I learned those issues while in city government. In short, becoming a government lawyer, although it was not planned and, in some ways, not encouraged, provided me with additional and unique legal knowledge and experience and opened the doors to clients I would otherwise never had gotten.

To gain access to opportunities requires stepping beyond the walls of your law firm to gain exposure to others in the profession and the community. Once you have done that, making thoughtful decisions about what roles and opportunities you take is critical, and those decisions may best be guided by which relatively intangible benefits can be obtained by assuming those roles. Take on important roles where you can highlight your legal prowess and intelligence; it will allow even more opportunities to come your way.

Sharonda R. Williams

Career

Attorney; General Counsel and Director of Government Affairs, Loyola University New Orleans College of Law

Education
- JD, Loyola University New Orleans College of Law (2001)
- UNC School of Medicine (1998)
- Xavier University of Louisiana (1994)

Best Advice

Approach every situation with grace and patience.

Personal

Sharonda Williams currently serves as General Counsel and Director of Government Affairs for Loyola University. Prior to that, Sharonda was Special Counsel at Fishman Haygood, LLP, in New Orleans. Sharonda served as City Attorney for the City of New Orleans from May 2013 to November 2015. As City Attorney, Sharonda was the lead attorney handling the most comprehensive police consent decree in the history of the United States. At the same time, she represented the city in another consent decree aimed at reforming the Orleans Parish Jail, which was then recognized as one of the worst prisons in America. Both of those consent decrees required Sharonda to engage in negotiations with the United States Department of Justice on a near daily basis. Sharonda also was the lead attorney representing the city in settling a more than 30-year dispute relating to back pay and pension issues for the New Orleans Firefighters. Sharonda served as Chief Deputy City Attorney from October 2011 until May 2013. Prior to joining the City of New Orleans, Sharonda was a partner in the general litigation section at Sher Garner, where she handled cases ranging from construction disputes, medical malpractice, insurance coverage disputes, entertainment law contract negotiations, and intellectual property licensing issues to bankruptcy adversary proceedings. Governor John Bel Edwards recently appointed her to serve as a Commissioner for the Board of the Port of New Orleans. She has served

(Continued)

as the Chair of the Board of Commissioners of the Regional Transit Authority and the Chair of the Louisiana Judiciary Commission (appointed by Governor Kathleen Blanco), as well as being involved in numerous other professional and civic organizations.

For More Information

https://www.loyno.edu/academics/faculty-and-staff-directory/sharonda-r-williams

https://www.linkedin.com/in/sharonda-williams-7b099b4

My Blueprint to Success: Conquering Inexperience and Embracing Challenges

By Tamara P. Nash

Navigating the legal profession has been a process of creating my own blueprint and then trusting the blueprint to guide me. Often I struggle with feeling like I am starting from scratch or even behind the mark. I am a first-generation college and law school graduate, a woman, and a person of color. These intersecting identities often collide with the dynamics of the legal profession, which can exacerbate the challenges and barriers that already exist, specifically, finding (and being recruited for) employment opportunities, securing leadership opportunities, case assignment, and retention efforts.

My identity is proudly rooted in my status as a first-generation college and law student. However, I didn't always carry this identity so proudly. Initially, this identity was yet another reminder of not being enough. I grew up knowing few (to no) examples of professional women setting and achieving their own goals. Frankly, I maintained the mentality that if I graduated high school, that would be my greatest success. Academically, I struggled in high school. In my freshman year, I earned only a few credits. However, a twist of fate provided me with a second chance. My junior year, my family moved to a smaller community, and with the move I found an amazing mentor who was quite literally a game-changer. With guidance, I found my place within my high school. I became a student leader, made up missing credits, and even secured a scholarship for college. After graduation, I attended a local college and thrived. While in college, I realized my goal of attending law school. Of course, it was incredibly difficult. I didn't know where to start, and I didn't have anyone to ask. In spite of these challenges, I was fortunate enough to find many opportunities to learn, grow, and gain experience. Each experience has given me a chance to refine my blueprint and develop strategies I utilize to feel empowered and prepared to "hit the ground running" in new situations and challenges.

Throughout my career—in law school as a first-generation law student, as a judicial law clerk, as a federal and state prosecutor trying my first felony jury trials—I found myself thinking, "we all have to start somewhere, right?" But figuring out where to start or even how to start can often be overwhelming. So, where do we begin? Well, I recently had to remind myself of this answer. A few months ago, I left my practice as a career prosecutor and entered the world of academia. As you can imagine, the two worlds could not be more different. I felt the weight of inexperience and pressure of high expectations against me. In many ways, I felt paralyzed by the fear of making a mistake, failing to meet expectations, or not rising to the occasion. Ultimately, I figured out where the starting point was: it came after honest self-reflection and a reminder that self-doubt and fear are often not rooted in accuracy.

I would like to share the reminders I have for myself, as they were my starting point. They have become essential to my blueprint and continue to be helpful, sometimes daily.

- **Embrace Vulnerability!** Learning to be vulnerable is a process that can be uncomfortable and, yes, sometimes even painful. It starts with our revealing ourselves to the possibility of more— the willingness to take risks and expose ourselves emotionally to others. The concept applies to both our interactions with others and ourselves. Some people think of this concept in big ways, but what if we broke it down into smaller, more tangible pieces? When we permit ourselves to be candid, express concern or fear, or take a leap of faith, we slowly build our own confidence while also gaining the confidence of the people around us.
- **Take Risks!** I know, but hear me out! Maya Angelou has a wonderful quote that says, "Courage is the most important of all the virtues, because without courage you can't practice any other virtue consistently. You can practice any virtue erratically, but nothing consistently without courage."[3] I encourage you to allow courage to guide your decisions and empower you to say yes! Take every opportunity you can to grow and learn. When the opportunity presents itself, write the brief, second-chair the trial, depose the witness, take the opportunity. Each new skill will build your foundation. Trust me, you will learn as you go! Rarely will a time come when you feel 100 percent prepared. So, I encourage

---

3. Maya Angelou, Speech given at Cornell University Convocation (May 24, 2008).

you to just jump in! I also want to remind you that you will make mistakes, and that it is okay. Remember to extend yourself grace, learn from the mistake, and keep moving forward. Stacy Abrams said it beautifully, "[n]ot only must we stop telling ourselves no, we have to internalize our right to make mistakes and to use error as an entry point to more knowledge." As you move forward, your confidence will grow.

- **Celebrate Authenticity!** I encourage you to celebrate being unapologetically yourself and sit in the realness of who you are. Be true to yourself in all circles—fully authentic. Remember, you are good enough for the task and you are capable of conquering the challenge. When we walk in our own light and bring our best, most true self to the table, our best work shines through. This power implicitly gives those around you permission to also be vulnerable and authentic. When I think of being authentic, I smile and think of a quote by Amy Poehler: "if you can dance and be free and not be embarrassed, you can rule the world."
- **Cultivate Your Network!** Find your squad of dynamic, honest, and true individuals, whom you can call upon when needed (or even better, meet regularly) to gain perspective, advice, and counsel in a space that is trusted and authentic. These relationships are precious and invaluable, and they require attention and nurturing; each of us needs the others at different points in our life for different things. I have used my network as my personal champions. I have forced them to listen to countless speeches and opening statements. They have helped me script my requests for raises and job offer acceptance. This network will help build your confidence, develop your intuition, and cover your blind spots. Remember, we all owe a duty to enrich our community and lift up those around us.

As you are taking all these steps to cultivate your skills and grow, I want to share one of the best pieces of advice I have ever received. Keep a record of all your accomplishments—I call this my "I love me file." In this file, I track all my notable accomplishments, my substantive work, and my leadership opportunities. I also include copies of emails from supervisors or colleagues that compliment my work or progress. Not only does this serve as a great reference for future professional opportunities, it is a great reminder to you of your progress and growth when you need one.

You may notice that these reminders may seem very basic and maybe even somewhat fluid. That is intentional! I have found that intentionally focusing on a few reminders—aspects of life that you can control—is much more powerful than spinning out trying to control the uncontrollable. Ultimately, advice for overcoming obstacles is that, while obstacles and adversity are almost certainly guaranteed in life, those who love us and who are cheering us on from the sidelines do not require or want perfection. So, being your best in the moment is all that is required. Give yourself permission to be imperfect, make mistakes, and learn throughout the journey. Find freedom to pursue opportunities, to grow, and to gain meaningful experience. In this space, you will let go of the doubt and the need to control, and you will thrive. In this space, you will find confidence in yourself. Once you believe in yourself and your potential, you can leverage your strengths, understand your weaknesses, and maximize your skills and resources.

I can assure you that these reminders, when practiced, have a profound impact on how you live your life. They will empower you to live big—to allow yourself to take up space. Your journey may get difficult and it may get uncomfortable. You may even be unsure where to start. However, I can assure you that it is worth it. More importantly, it is necessary. Celebrate every new opportunity to learn, make a mistake, fail, and try again. You are your own North Star.

Tamara P. Nash

Career
Director of Experiential Learning and Lecturer, University of South Dakota Knudson School of Law (Vermillion, South Dakota)

Education
- JD, *Honors*, University of South Dakota Knudson School of Law (2013)
- BA, *magna cum laude, Honors*, Social Sciences, Wayne State College (Wayne, Nebraska)

Best Advice
The best piece of advice I try to live by (and would like to share) is when it comes to matters of principle, be firm like a rock, and when it comes to matters of style, be fluid like the stream.

Personal
Tamara Nash is a first-generation attorney. She is a former President of the South Dakota Young Lawyers Section (2018–2019). Tamara also served as Chair of the American Bar Association Young Lawyers Division (2023–2024). For fun, she enjoys traveling, baking, audiobooks, and spending time with her family—especially her niece, Harper.

For More Information
tamarapnash1@gmail.com

Gamechanger! Redesigning How to Practice Law

By Laura Hartnett

It was a windowless conference room, tucked in the middle of the smelly floor with new clients I was meeting for the first time in person. I had changed roles within the corporate legal department for a change and to expand my skillset.

"I've never seen this from a lawyer before."

—*My client said with a stoic face*

Years earlier, I had morphed from health care litigator to insurance attorney. You know, the answer *no one* gives in the small-group first-year writing class when you go around and say what kind of attorney you want to be after graduation. Most people say "I want to practice constitutional law!" only to later discover that means working for state government pay, opening handwritten letters from inmates complaining that their constitutional rights had been violated. (The other popular answer was "international law." I still don't know what that means. I think document review in Toledo, Spain, must be just as bad as document review in Toledo, Ohio.)

I did not say "insurance lawyer" that fateful first day of law school; I said "tax lawyer." Telling people you want to be a tax lawyer does not get you invited to parties. But I didn't need keg parties; what I already knew about tax law was that it gave you a process. If this, then that. Over this threshold, use this number. My parents had a pediatrician's medical handbook when I was a kid. Does the child have a fever? Go to the box on the right. Is the fever over 102? STOP. Call the doctor. That's how I thought of tax law. Only more fun because you look for exceptions and loopholes. Avoid the winding paths and find the direct path to reducing tax burden.

In the conference room with my clients, I was still resisting the insurance law I now practiced. I had tried to avoid it by practicing in other areas for an insurance company—internal investigations, litigation, technology—anything so that I didn't have to learn the ins and outs of insurance law. Insurance law is a suffocating patchwork quilt of confusion made up of 50 separate state regulations. Then you layer blankets of applicable federal laws over the top. And over that, add fluffy duvets stuffed with the whims of state regulators who will enforce their laws to wildly different extents. It's suffocating and I wanted no part of it.

I wanted the tax law I never ended up practicing. If this, then that. Follow the diagrams. A chart.

A chart, maybe. . . . My new clients had questions about interacting with insurers through all the new, hot methods—texting, apps, chatbots. Insurance customers in all 50 states, maybe also abroad. These new-fangled technologies aren't something even recent insurance regulations address head on. A chart.

When I was a litigator in private practice, we had a client ask for a chart. They wanted us to look into our proverbial Magic 8 Ball and predict what would happen in key litigation involving another company they were considering acquiring. They asked us to rank the risks: high, medium, low. Even better if we colored in our predictions: red, yellow, green.

The partner on the case started sweating and pearl-clutching, "Red, yellow, green? We can't possibly boil down our complex legal opinion to red, yellow, green!" "But that's what they asked for," I said quietly and confused. Weren't we trained as associates to give clients exactly what they asked for? Wasn't that "good client service"? Before law school, I was a management consultant delivering complex ideas in slide decks and charts. I figured we could at least color-code a legal opinion if the client wanted it.

But even when it was my turn to be the client as in-house counsel, I didn't ask outside counsel for a color-coded chart either. I called outside counsel with my complex insurance question. "Do you want a memo?" they would ask. "Sure," I agreed, not even considering there might be other options.

They gave me the memo: 10 pages and single-spaced. The real answer, the whole lynchpin to the complex insurance question that I needed to flag for my clients, buried somewhere on page four.

My eyes glazing over at pages of words, most of which weren't central to my legal issue, I realized that I wanted a chart. A red, yellow, green, color-coded chart of all 50 states showing me what to do. I could compare and contrast the laws. I could see which states I had to flag for my clients and which states would be a regulatory walk in the park. I could show it to my internal clients, point, and give them an answer.

But I know why outside counsel never suggested a chart. We're trained to write beautiful, lengthy, legal poetry. (If prose is considered "ordinary language," then legal writing cannot be considered prose.) We set forth all the historical background, explain the facts and legal landscape, detail every last risk, and reach a conclusion carefully tempered by disclaimers. To boil these intricacies down to a chart or even to omit any one piece is unthinkable. Some might even say the word that makes attorneys shudder: unethical.

I honed these legal poetry skills as a litigator, spending an inordinate amount of six-minute billing increments and hundreds of dollars making what associates called "happy/glad changes." Do we use "happy" in this sentence? Let's try replacing it with "glad." No, no, let's change it all back to "happy." Did it matter? It turns out that no one cared.

I'd leave work, pick up my daughter from daycare, eat dinner with my family, and log back in to find these kinds of changes from partners. Partners that would not-so-helpfully add a comment in the document for me to make the change rather than making the change in the document itself. And why hadn't I updated all the happys to glads ASAP? So I would delete their comments, make the changes, and return it to the partner. Then do other legal work until I couldn't keep my eyes open. I'd get up at 5:15 a.m. to get to yoga by 6 a.m. and be at my desk before 8 a.m. with a sense of calm, only to have it slowly and steadily erode throughout the day.

It got so bad that my spouse said to me in a matter-of-fact tone, "Do you know I've done the dishes every night for two months?" He cooks so I do dishes. It's fair and plays to each of our strengths. I think chips and guac is a meal. It all started when he kindly offered to do dishes—realizing that if I did dishes, it meant I wouldn't start my evening work until later, which meant I wouldn't finish work until even later, which meant getting to sleep even later. We settled into a routine that way. I failed to notice where I had given up even trying.

I also failed to notice he was up for tenure. He spent that summer pouring his life's work into a binder to be judged by a committee of academics who would decide whether he was worthy to be granted a position for life. Teaching is his passion and he's damn good at it. But it would shake anyone to their core to think you could be cast away if a mere binder didn't live up to unwritten expectations.

I failed to notice my daughter. The 18-month-old blossoms as her world expands daily, walking turns into running, words coming online by the second, the delight in her eyes, and the moments of lip-quivering sadness. It's impossible to give a squirmy toddler a bath and check emails at the same time.

I had spent so much time that summer making absurd editorial changes and writing overly detailed risk memos rather than giving the client the red/yellow/green they asked for that I failed to notice my life. I wasn't practicing law in a dynamic sense; I was dressed up in lawyer's clothes, playing the part, and I didn't recognize myself anymore.

That's when I knew two things had to change—both my career and how I practiced law. A few months later I changed my career for an in-house legal position, but I hadn't yet changed *how* I practiced law. Until the windowless conference room on the smelly floor.

"*I've never seen this from a lawyer before*," my client said when I showed him the color-coded chart I created. I was confident that the areas in green presented no legal risk, the areas in red would take our company to task if we did what the client wanted, and the yellow—well, those had some risk but were palatable when paired with potential mitigations I listed in another column.

My client was thrilled.

The meeting didn't take as long as we had scheduled since we could dive into the real issues immediately. I delivered answers faster than they expected. They were able to go back to their team and begin programming into the system exactly what we discussed.

They said "thank you." And they meant it.

And that was the moment that forever changed how I practiced law.

I didn't know until that day that all along I had been playing the role of a lawyer, doing what lawyers are expected to do. Writing my lengthy memos, finding the perfect words, overdelivering for clients, making sure I returned all phone calls within a few hours, always and in all ways available.

I had learned it didn't work for me and it didn't work for my clients. It took becoming the dreaded insurance attorney to try something different.

I don't know which pisses me off more: That we keep lawyering in ways that our clients don't want. Or that we keep lawyering in ways that don't even work for ourselves.

For every woman I know who has left the practice of law, left the partnership track, or left rising through the ranks, it wasn't one thing, one reason, or one incident why she left. It was a death by a thousand cuts. It wasn't one late night or one snide comment about leaving early for a child's doctor's appointment, it wasn't one annual review that told her absolutely nothing about her progress, and it wasn't a lone sexist comment while she was pregnant.

There were many nights when she went home at 6 p.m., and many nights when she went home much later. There were many supportive, kind mentors who listened to her cry in their office, and there were many who cut her down with a glance and a so-called greeting.

Psychology teaches us to use an intermittent reward system to keep behavior going. If the dog gets a treat every time it rings the bell, it may get bored and stop ringing the bell. But if the dog rings the bell and sometimes gets the treat and sometimes doesn't, it will keep ringing the bell.

The practice of law keeps women docile and showing up through the same ongoing system of inconsistencies and mixed messages.

- We support work-life balance! You can have meetings all day in the office and then take your computer home to log on at night.
- You have 4 months of paid maternity leave! Of course, we might email you. And you'll need to second chair this case if it goes to trial during that time.
- You can go part-time! We'll pay you for 4 days a week of work, but here's 6 days' worth of work.
- These featured women made partner, even while on maternity leave! Look at their smiling faces! They have the rare spouse who stays home, or they are miserable or they haven't been on a real, unplugged vacation with their family in years.

I didn't have to entirely change my career. And I strongly believe other women don't have to either. We just have to change how we practice law. We have to cut through the inconsistencies and mixed messages and take a stand for what works for us and against what doesn't.

We change how we practice law through three steps:

1. **We Empathize with Our Clients, Our Colleagues, and Most Importantly Ourselves**

We stop assuming clients want a detailed memo and their call returned in 2 hours because that's what lawyers who started practicing 40 years ago told us to do. We ask better questions of our clients to get to know them as humans beyond their legal request. What are their goals? What do they fear? How do they work best?

And we ask the same questions of ourselves. What do we want—I mean really, really want? What do we fear? How do we work best? We get honest and start from understanding ourselves as humans before lawyers.

2. **We Explore New Possibilities.**

Lawyers are some of the most creative, problem-solving, people in any profession. Don't believe me? How did you create that coherent winning argument stringing together the disjointed pieces of evidence? How did you draft that contract to get exactly what your client wanted without having the other side blow up the whole deal? Creativity and problem solving. We apply those same skills to how we work, brainstorming new ways to practice law and deliver solutions for our clients that delight them.

3. **We Experiment and Try New Things.**

We start small and try a little something. Try delivering a chart, try declaring "no meetings" on Thursday afternoons, try sending video walk-throughs of the drafted contract instead of scheduling yet another meeting. We get feedback because we're willing to be wrong. Because it just might be the right answer. Or the next thing may be. And we celebrate. We shout it from the rooftops with our legal sisters, our firm, our group, our division, our section, our team. *I did that. We did that.* It inspires all of us to start again. It inspires empathy.

I believe women are uniquely positioned to take these three steps and thrive in the practice of law. Women and historically excluded groups have been pushed to the edges so much that we can see the whole picture. We can stand up and say, the administrative burden is too much, we can automate this. The quarterly meeting we've held for years is pointless, let's make it a status report. The legal memo is dead, we're giving our clients a one-page slide with our legal opinion. Just watch them call us first for all their additional legal work.

This is how we grow, how we expand, how we take over. How we deliver more value for our clients, not less. How we save ourselves time and energy. How we save ourselves. We stop the thousands of cuts, one cut at a time, finding a better way that helps us lean into our potential.

Hearing more clients delightfully exclaim, *"I've never seen this from a lawyer before"* becomes how women redesign the practice of law.

Laura Hartnett

Career

Founder and Legal Consultant, Law by Design LLC; Legal Innovation Advisor, HIKE2

Education
- JD, William & Mary Law School (2010)
- MPP, Management, Finance, and Leadership, University of Maryland (2004)
- BA, Leadership Studies/Political Science, University of Richmond (2002)

Best Advice

Overcoming obstacles isn't about the legal advice, the numbers, or even who is involved. Overcoming obstacles is about storytelling—the story you tell yourself, the story you tell your clients, the story you tell your team. You get to write the story of how you get through the challenge.

Personal

Laura Hartnett is the founder of and legal consultant at Law by Design. She has over 15 years of experience as a management consultant, litigation attorney for national and international law firms, and in-house counsel for a Fortune 100 company. Today, she teaches lawyers how to redesign their practice of law from a human-centered approach, one that works better for both lawyers and clients. She is also a yoga addict, karaoke enthusiast, and proud mom of two creative girls.

For More Information

www.laurahartnett.com
https://www.linkedin.com/in/laurahartnett

Building a Personal Brand to Grow Your Career and Bring Personal Life Satisfaction

By Katy Goshtasbi

Women lawyers, and really all professional women, are facing the strongest headwinds they have experienced in decades. They are struggling to integrate their professional and personal lives. Many are unsure what "voice" they should bring to the workplace. For some women lawyers, the pandemic upended their views of themselves, their work life, their relationships, and their true purpose and meaning in life. Many are looking for new and creative ways to stay engaged in a career, but in one that they find more fulfilling. They are looking for a new definition of success—one that is based on *who* they are, not *what* they do.

>
> "She was a girl who could not wait. Life was so interesting she had to find out what happened next."
>
> —Beverly Cleary[4]

It took me 7 long and painful years to discover my own personal brand. My journey involved lots of tears, confusion, anger, aggravation, and fear. It was a process of letting go and trusting myself. If there was a difficulty in getting to the ideal personal brand, I faced it. I grappled with it. I yelled at it. The one thing I never did was give up. The personal branding programs and books that do exist are not individualized enough to really identify a woman's natural talents, abilities, and strengths precisely.

Throughout my own discovery process, I wondered how I could help other women lawyers uncover their own personal brands to achieve personal happiness and professional success just like I had—but without all the pain and difficulty I had gone through.

I have coached more than 850 female professionals across many industries (law, health care, academia, financial services) in finding their authentic personal brand. Despite the outward trappings of success—a decent paycheck, an impressive title, a husband or partner, and maybe some children—I hear over and over again a disturbing level of discontent. They are quietly, and sometimes overtly, unhappy. And they don't

---

4. Beverly Cleary, Ramona the Pest (Harper Collins, 2006).

know why. Many struggle with a set of core issues: low self-confidence at work and in relationships, fearful of standing up for their true value, tired of not being recognized for their unique self, and not believing happiness is a worthy goal. They don't understand that their personal brand, or "why," is at the core of finding happiness and success with work and in life.

I can relate, because that's how I felt most of the 15 years I practiced as a securities lawyer in the highest echelons of the Washington, DC legal profession. Until I decided I could not be a securities lawyer anymore. It was highly stressful, and I was finding it more and more unfulfilling. Being a lawyer is a very noble profession. It just wasn't mine anymore. For years, I had been searching to find my purpose, and securities law was no longer my purpose.

But what was I supposed to do with my life? Who was I, and how could I serve others and do so in a way that was natural to me and left me happy and fulfilled and excited at the end of the day? Was this goal even possible?

Let's skip back and I'll share my story of who I am so this all has more context for you. I was born in Iran in 1972. At the age of 6, the revolution swept through the country. Not being Muslim, we felt we had no real choice but to leave Iran. We packed two suitcases. I still remember the day so well. My mom and dad decided my dad would stay in Iran, while my mom, sister, grandmother, and I would leave until the unrest died down—likely 2 weeks.

Fast forward: 2 weeks turned into a lifetime. We all know how the story of the Iranian revolution has ended thus far. We stayed in America, and I grew up in Indiana. I put myself through undergrad, studying finance and accounting. As a good immigrant, you are always taught to maximize the gift that you have been given being in a great country like America. So my obvious (and only?) choices were to become a doctor, lawyer, or engineer.

Being a doctor was out of the question. I couldn't stand the sight of blood. That was easy. I ruled out engineering really fast, too. Numbers bored me. But being a lawyer was always exciting and fascinating to me. I had always been an entertainer and I had a gift for conversation and communication.

I decided to go to law school. That was how I wanted to save the world. Really. I put myself through law school. I was an average law student. Law school for me didn't always feel like I was getting skills that would serve me in my actual legal career. But I did love the rigor of law school. I also loved the courses that allowed me to apply real-world thinking to solve real-world problems. Bioethics and the Law was one of my favorite classes and I scored top paper. I loved grappling with the ethics of being in control of another's health decisions.

I remember the day I sat in my first Securities Law course. I immediately knew I wanted to be a securities lawyer. I was not really sure what that would look like, but it felt right. Just like how I had used my intuition to know I was meant to be a lawyer, I used my intuition to guide me to become a securities lawyer and to practice in Washington, DC.

I started out practicing for the Indiana Secretary of State in the Securities Division as an Enforcement attorney. I got to chase the corrupt meat locker salesmen—the men who were duping money out of so many. Those same people later went on to become the stars of the movie *The Wolf of Wall Street*.

My biggest dream was to move to Washington, DC and practice securities law. It was all I ever focused on. I told everyone, including my boss, Brad, the Securities Commissioner of Indiana at the time. I stepped into that dream in early 1998 when Brad came to me and said there was a job opening at a trade organization for states' securities laws in Washington DC. One opening. Thirty-five applicants. I put my name in. I flew to DC and interviewed. I got the job. I was focused and clear on where I wanted to practice securities law.

I moved to Washington, DC, without knowing anyone. I was excited and very nervous. I was bright-eyed and eager. I learned how to be a lobbyist on Capitol Hill. I learned how politics worked. I, along with two colleagues, one at the Financial Industry Regulatory Authority (FINRA) and one at the U.S. Securities and Exchange Commission (SEC), set up the registration system for investment advisors. I soon set my focus on being a lawyer at the SEC. Again, there was one opening and hundreds of applicants. I got the job. The years at the SEC were a dream come true for me. I got to work with brilliant lawyers—all of them out to help save the world. Enron happened, and I learned how to be an even better lawyer. I gave back. I grew.

I soon got the itch again. This time, one of my SEC colleagues left to go to a law firm. Six months later, he called me and asked me to come interview at the firm. I did. I got the job. I practiced there for 2 years. All the while I kept wondering what my life was about. At this point in my career, I had the privilege of having worked at many lucrative jobs. I kept wondering if this was meant to be my purpose in life. The nagging question would not stop.

I figured if I changed jobs, the nagging question would stop. I was getting three to four headhunter calls per week. I was a woman lawyer in a man's world with a skillset very few lawyers, let alone woman lawyers, had.

At this point, I decided I was ready to go in-house. I picked up and moved across the country to California, where my family had relocated years before I even started law school. In-house practice was everything I expected. Except it had a lot of drama. The workplace was very toxic and there was so much jockeying for power it was frightening. The worst part was that I saw people not accessing their full potential. People turned a blind eye to this fact all the time. I was frustrated. My stress level went through the roof.

My gastroenterologist told me I had to stop practicing before my stress killed me. I thought he was crazy and completely impractical. But something of what he said stuck with me. So I quit my job after realizing that I drafted prospectuses all day only to go home and throw my own prospectus away.

This was 2 years before the Great Recession. No one was re-creating themselves. Everyone thought I was nuts. So did I. But I really felt like I had no choice. My health and my desire to serve my purpose were more important.

While I stopped practicing, I never felt like I left the world of law. I focused on a different way of "being" within the legal community. I am not advocating that women lawyers leave the practice of law. Quite the opposite. My hope is that you read this and realize you want to stay a lawyer, but with good reason and an intentional plan to succeed, building a strong brand to get you there.

Over the last 12 years working with my clients, I developed the Emotional Resonance Factor to give women lawyers a clear blueprint to unearth, define, craft, and reinvent their brand. At the core of this approach is helping women discover their own unique emotional connection to happiness that needs to resonate through their personal brand.

The rules of the game, as I see them and have taught them for 12 years, are the following:

- **Know Thyself.** So many women lawyers confuse their roles as mother, daughter, wife, lawyer, with their identity as a human being. If you do not know who you are, you can never enunciate with clarity, let alone convince anyone else to stop and take notice of you, promote you, give you clients, or become your client. Knowing yourself takes bravery and a willingness to excavate, identify, and heal the rubble. Too many women lawyers stay so focused on the substantive work that they are buried under it. Knowing the real you allows you to accept the real you. You can then live an authentic life, sharing the best parts of yourself with others. At this point, you are ready to CREATE a brand that resonates.
    - Start by asking yourself:
        - What about my childhood needs to heal?
        - What's my story of why I really became a lawyer?
        - What are my natural strengths and talents?
        - What are the dark sides of my natural strengths and talents?
        - Why do I want to serve others?
- **Know Thy Emotions.** When I was in Washington, DC, I used to see so many woman lawyers wear pant suits so they could look like my male counterparts. As women lawyers, we were starting to lose our sense of identity and our biggest gift—being a woman. Without owning your womanhood, Queendom, and the ensuing emotions, we are robbing the world (and ourselves) of our greatness.
    - Start by asking yourself:
        - How much time do I spend on myself?
        - How much value do I place on who I am (as opposed to what I do as a lawyer)?
        - How often do I give myself permission to be angry, happy, sad, joyful, funny, etc.?
        - What would be the one thing I would do if I could do anything for myself for an hour? Do I do it? Why or why not?

- **Communicate Thyself.** Knowing yourself and your emotions is one thing. Being able to communicate, both verbally and nonverbally, is the equally important part of your brand equation. What good is knowing yourself and your emotions if you cannot communicate it to your audience? It's meaningless if your audience does not appreciate you and your brand.
- **What Makes You Really Tick?** Understanding what makes you tick is the foundation for a successful personal brand. Just like any other career, practicing law has its highs and lows. You must have strategies for dealing with the low points of your practice. Vices are generally where we turn; a glass (or two) of wine, chocolate, gossip, reality TV. None of these things really helps invigorate us. Knowing exactly what uplifts you and elevates your mood, allowing you to thrive, is the answer for weathering all aspects of your practice.
- **How Do I Scale My Brand?** You and your brand must keep growing. That is the pursuit of life, no matter what you "do." It's all about taking your personal brand to the next level to grow your career and business AND personal life satisfaction. I suggest every lawyer take one day each quarter to stop and reflect on the trajectory of their brand and career and personal life, implementing measurable actions and markers.
- **Where Can I Create Impact with My Brand?** Here is where professional women discover how to serve their purpose and make the world a better place. Being a lawyer is noble and may feel like you are having real impact. That's the hope. However, I have discovered that when women lawyers find a way to serve their community out of passion and purpose, their world (and their brands) organically grow and shift, leaving them satisfied beyond words. They almost develop a healthy glow that attracts admirers and fans and clients organically with grace.

Katy Goshtasbi

Career

CEO, Founder, Consultant, Trainer, Professional Speaker, Puris Consulting, Securities Lawyer; Former Chair: ABA Law Practice Division; Former Chair: ABA Law Practice Division Diversity, Equity, Inclusion, Belonging Committee; Author, *Personal Branding in One-Hour for Lawyers* (American Bar Association 2013); Fellow, College of Law Practice Management; Former Board of Directors, Group Legal Services Association

Education

- JD, Indiana University Robert H. McKinney School of Law (1997)
- BS, Business, Indiana University—Kelley School of Business (1994)

Best Advice

Never forget you are a woman, first and foremost. You matter. Bringing ALL of you to your entire life is key: you will be happier and feel more whole and authentic.

Personal

Katy Goshtasbi was born in Iran and immigrated to the United States. She and her husband have a nonprofit charity, Josie's Home, that brings attention and resources to three overlooked populations: senior citizens, senior dogs, and aged-out foster kids. Katy lives in San Diego and has a love of animals and dark chocolate. She used to teach yoga when she practiced law.

For More Information

www.purisconsulting.com
www.katygoshtasbi.com
https://www.linkedin.com/in/katygoshtasbi
katy@purisconsulting.com

Time Management Challenges

By Beth-Ann E. Krimsky

I can't give you more time, but let's discuss how to make the most of the time you have to achieve your career and other goals.

First, who am I, and why should you believe me? I am a trial attorney who has been practicing full-time since graduating from law school in 1989. I started my career at a large New York firm, and I had the unique opportunity to practice in the sports and related entertainment law field. I had a tremendous experience there, even with the long hours, as I loved what I was doing and had great mentors. As a result, I rarely noticed the amount of time I spent doing it. However, my soon-to-be husband, who was becoming a dentist with very regular hours, certainly did. Early on at Proskauer, the firm held a retreat and significant others were invited. Part of the program was to discuss how those "others" may feel a need to adjust to the time restrictions their spouses and significant others were about to experience. Mind you, this was before we had cell phones or remote access, so our hours were largely spent in the office. While some thought the seminar was too much or even scary, I thought it was honest. I appreciated that the firm not only recognized that the demands placed on our time were a bit unique, but that they also explained to our significant others that it was not just their spouse's desire to achieve or ego that kept them at the office late; it was the firm's expectation. (Whether that was right or wrong was not really considered to be an issue back in 1989.) I was grateful my soon to be spouse "got it" and knew I would be working this way from the start, whether the firm required it or not.

Despite what one may have expected, when I moved to South Florida to a completely different firm, the challenge as to time and needing more of it never changed. No matter how we try to set time boundaries, to be the attorney and person you want to be takes time: time you need to learn about your current cases; time to develop existing and new clients; time to mentor others; time to keep up with the ever-changing law and court rules; time to give back to your community; and yes, time to share with your family, which although listed last here is not necessarily what should be last but often turns out that way.

So back to why me. Shortly after starting my career in New York, I became engaged to be married. After 3 years there, we moved to Florida, and I joined what was then the largest Florida-based firm. Over the years, we had three sons, one while I was an associate attorney, one while I was a nonequity partner, and the last after I had become an equity partner. Juggling motherhood along with a progressing career that now includes chairing our litigation division nationwide and still working on a full caseload I still genuinely enjoy, has given me a few insights into how to manage my time to fit it all in—as well as how to thoughtfully create and use my resources.

Your Partner (Not in the Law)

Whatever you feel about her, I believe Sheryl Sandberg was right when she told the Barnard graduating class of 2011 that "the most important career decision you're going to make is whether or not you have a life partner and who that partner is. If you pick someone who's willing to share the burdens and the joys of your personal life, you're going to go further."[5] Now this does not mean you must have a life partner, but rather, recognizes that those who do may have an easier time or that it is important for you to gather other types of resources or support.

I know firsthand that so much of what I have been able to accomplish using my brain, talents, and resilience is because of the amount of time I have been able to devote to my career and community. My husband of over 30 years has always encouraged me to be the lawyer I wanted to be and helped to make it possible for me to have the necessary time to devote to our community. His understanding of how I seek to practice, as well as his own enjoyment and willingness to be so involved with our children's lives, has made a huge difference to all of us. I am convinced that having their father so involved, as well as seeing their mother advance in her chosen career and in the community, enriched our children and helped them learn that they can decide what is important to them as they chart their own careers and find their life partners. I fully recognize the external

---

5. Sheryl Sandberg, Speech given at Barnard College Commencement (May 17, 2011). *See* https://barnard.edu/headlines/transcript-speech-sheryl-sandberg.

forces and extraordinary demands on my time, and I try to make conscious choices to live within those confines or seek help either to change it or to make it happen. My support system of my husband, friends, colleagues, legal team, and assistants help me do that every day.

What Is Your Most Productive Hour

Next, find the best time of day for you. I am neither a scientist nor a health guru—very far from it. But I have known my entire life that I have had the same "most productive time," and thus, I have always tried to attack the hardest and "deepest thoughts required" work in what I have learned is my most productive time: early in the morning—really early. This is not to say I cannot work well at other times—especially when the constant adrenaline of a litigation is flowing. However, I do know that I sometimes can get double the amount written, more documents reviewed, or even a more in-depth focus in the 6 a.m. to 9 a.m. time frame than in the later hours. In addition, there are far fewer interruptions in those early hours. I also learned early on that I am much less productive at night or with no sleep. I firmly believe a rested brain is far more productive. Thus, it is far better for me to take a nap or break or to go home to sleep and get up at 4:30 a.m. if need be than to try to pull an all-nighter. Indeed, one of my most terrifying career moments turned into a great teaching lesson about sleep. As a second-year lawyer, I had an opportunity to help prepare an expert witness for an emergency injunction hearing. It turns out that due to the compressed time schedule, many of us had been awake for well over 24 hours. As a result, during the witness preparation session, I fell asleep. I was mortified and scared when I woke up and realized it. Rather than being fired (which is what I feared), the senior partner came to my office the next day, closed the door, and thanked me. He told me he was trying to figure out how to tell the junior partner that the direct examination he was practicing was dull and boring, but because I fell asleep, he was able to say, "If you made Krimsky fall asleep, what are you going to do to the Judge?" Find your best work cycle and try to build your day around it—even if it means blocking out "working hours" on your computer calendar. It is also a good idea to let others you work with know your best time to work so your entire team can maximize its production.

If It Is Not Working, Do Something Else

There will always be times when you intend to be at your peak or to get something done, even in what may usually be your prime working hours, and you want to tackle a challenging project, but you sit before an empty page or stare at your screen and nothing happens. Sometimes, as long as you are not on a filing deadline, it is okay to acknowledge it is not working today and do something else, even if it is administrative or business development or other less challenging items. We all get writer's block or mentally seek to avoid some important task at times. Just accept it, so you are not wasting time and getting even more frustrated. Then, do something else on your project or task list until you get back on track.

Combine Tasks

In my world, I believe it is truly necessary to be involved in the community for many reasons—helping others and sharing your skills at getting things done. People ask me all the time: why and how do you fit it all into so little time? I do it first because I believe in it. I believe in real community service—rolling up your sleeves and participating. I was raised by parents who had very little financial net worth and who did not have professional business development responsibilities, but who were very involved in their community, primarily by devoting time, even though both of my parents also worked six or seven days a week for long hours.

As to the how? I make the time and combine it with both my family and work social team-building efforts. I am grateful I had the experience of setting up charity carnivals with my dad or some other project with my mom or siblings, as our community service was also our family time, and we worked on projects that were meaningful to all of us. I have carried that over with my husband, children, and legal career. Thus, my husband and I engage in volunteer activities of interest to our entire family. For example, we are very involved in raising funds for childhood cancer research in part because we have a son who was diagnosed and survived leukemia at a young age. We know that good science and medicine can help others facing similar challenges. So, when we organized events, our entire family pitched in at all ages—even if it was setting up food at a 5K run at 5 a.m. or labeling invitations to a gala. Everyone has a role and some way they can meaningfully contribute. Indeed, as our sons have gone off to college, they've had their fraternities host similar events for causes they wanted to support.

As for legal skills, when our sons did debate or participate in mock trials at school, I would volunteer to help the more formal coaches. Similarly, my husband would volunteer to teach about dental education. Thus, we were helping the community at large while still spending quality family time. I also include my law firm family in many of my community projects, as it is great team-building. I enjoy spending time with our lawyers and staff outside the office—there is nothing like a tug-of-war at a charity event in matching firm shirts to get even closer. Again, combining work social events with charities helps me do both at the same time.

Find Allies on the Parent–Teacher Association

I knew I would never have time (nor frankly the inclination) to be class mom or president of the parent–teacher association (PTA), but I also knew that attending meetings or parent social events was not how I wanted to use my time. I thus had friends who loved their class mom roles who kept me informed and suggested when the most productive time would be for me to help at school while also affording me the opportunity to spend more time with my children. One of those programs was called Meet the Masters. I would research, or have help researching, master artists like Rembrandt and Picasso, and write up a story about their lives to teach in my children's classrooms once a month for an hour. I also would bring supplies to do a basic art project on these artists. This project gave me an opportunity to know my children's classmates while giving my kids a chance to be proud their mom could use her public speaking skills to engage with their friends and do a fun project. The teachers also appreciated the break and the much-needed art supplies. The end of the year thank-yous and photos from those students over the 10 years I was able to do that in each of my three sons' classes are priceless to me. Even though my children are now 19, 23, and 26, I still have those memory books, and my sons still keep in contact with some of those same friends who mention those projects. Thus again, I was able to help serve our community while also spending more time with our children.

Middle of the Night Notes and Inspiration

Similar to the tip that you should simply give in when you don't get inspiration in your "prime time" is the tip to write down any inspiration at whatever time it comes. I was told early on in my career to keep a notepad and pen *not* by my bed, but in the bathroom. That way, should you get an idea in the middle of the night, you have to walk to write it down so it will be coherent and not just scribbly lines. I do that to this day. I am not sure if the ideas come from some external inspiration or from just my brain not shutting off, but some of them have been the best ever. Although if my pad runs out, I have been seen coming into the office with notes on the back of a napkin or paper plate.

Business Development

The time to develop business is another combined effort. First, I find the best way to do it is to have happy clients refer you to their colleagues or have adversaries notice your work and call you for the next matter. All of that requires you to spend time to be the best lawyer you can be. The other part is also about the community. While engaging with your community, you have the opportunity to showcase your skills (public speaking, organization, and judgment) to the precise people who are most likely to hire you (other business leaders). You also can serve as a go-to resource about any topic, not just the law. Again, devoting time to what you already love to do will set you up as someone who can be trusted to do her best on all tasks, so it will engender confidence in clients reaching out should they have a legal matter.

While I still cannot give you more than 24 hours in a day, I do hope these tips will resonate so you can apply at least one of my life experiences to make the most of the time you do have. Being conscious of how to maximize your time will help you navigate your practice and personal life more calmly and with greater success. And please, don't forget to get a good night's sleep.

Beth-Ann E. Krimsky

Career
Partner, National Litigation Division Chair, Greenspoon Marder LLP

Education
- JD, Harvard Law School (1989)
- BA, Political Science and Economics, University of Rochester (1986)

Best Advice
My best advice to overcome an obstacle is first to stay calm. Then, assess the nature of the obstacle and consider what resources are available to you to overcome it or to work around it in a suitable fashion.

Personal
Beth-Ann Krimsky has been married to Dr. Peter Krimsky, a general practice dentist, for almost 32 years. They have three sons, one who is a litigation attorney, one who is an advertising copywriter, and one who is in college at Syracuse University Newhouse School of Communications. Beth-Ann is involved in her community by primarily serving as Vice Chair of the Memorial and Joe DiMaggio Children's Hospital Foundation in Broward County, Florida and on the Executive Board of Ramat Shalom, her synagogue. She previously served as President of the I Care I Cure Childhood Cancer Foundation for 13 years. The foundation's mission is to fund better and less toxic treatments for childhood cancer and has now become part of Alex's Lemonade Stand. Beth-Ann lives in Florida and enjoys spending time in Vermont and traveling.

For More Information
https://www.gmlaw.com/attorneys/beth-ann-krimsky
https://www.linkedin.com/in/beth-ann-krimsky-9653274

Where to Work: Flexibility and Advancement in a New Day and Age

By Heather Linn Rosing

The COVID-19 pandemic has been horrific, taking lives, upending lives, disrupting the economy, wrecking physical and mental health, and much more. As a small silver lining, tragedy can also be a tool to gain wisdom. I think that the pandemic has taught us a lot about how to appreciate our lives, our family, and friends, and how to work smarter, in innovative ways. We have broken out of molds in the work environment that, for many, were not very healthy. I write today to share my thoughts on how we have evolved and how a new work dynamic promotes not only wellness, but also the advancement of women in the law. Let me start by first recalling the pre-pandemic work environment for lawyers.

When I first started practicing law in San Diego, California, approximately 26 years ago, everyone was expected to be seated at their desks at 8 a.m., wearing a suit, and we did not go home until 6 p.m. Leaving early was viewed as "sneaking out."

There was also an expectation that all workers would come in on weekends. Indeed, if we go even farther back in time, my dad's small family law firm in Waukegan, Illinois, was open on Saturdays from 8 a.m. until noon, just like it was on a weekday. This was commonplace in the industry.

To be fair, this arrangement was dictated by the reality of our work-related tools at the time. Back in the 1980s and 1990s, there was no real ability to "work remotely" because the technology just was not there. Your early-generation computer was enormous, heavy, and permanently affixed in your office. Mobile phones were literal bricks that you had to lug around in a special over-the-shoulder bag. You and your secretary needed to be right next to each other, so that you could verbally convey all the instructions, and she could physically take possession of the dictation tape.

The technology progressed, but the work arrangements did not change that much. In the 2000s, most of us acquired truly portable mobile phones, allowing us to easily talk to clients and colleagues even when we were not in the office. We abandoned our DOS computer systems for the much cooler Microsoft Windows, and ultimately we acquired laptops. Yet the traditional arrangement of coming into the private practice office every day remained relatively unchanged. It was common for the law partners to walk around the office to see who was there and remind those who were not of their obligations to the firm. When attorneys were running a little bit late or leaving a little bit early, they would enter or leave through a back door, hoping to avoid scrutiny and chastisement.

I recall in the 2000s that travel in the practice of law exploded. Attorneys would take cases in other counties and states, far away from the home office. Litigators would travel a half-day to go to a mediation office to try to settle the case, or to a courthouse in another county, even for the most minor hearing. Depositions took attorneys far and wide, as did client meetings. There were many animated conversations within the profession about how best to get from point A to point B—the train, driving, an airplane? What was easiest? And, gosh, isn't that gridlock on the highway back from the court appearance just maddening!

The dress code for attorneys remained very formal. I remember in law school in the early to mid-1990s, I had this lovely pant suit. I attended a moot court event, and I was told it was not appropriate attire for a woman lawyer. (Yes, I did say the 1990s. And it was in Chicago!) I started at my first law firm (also my current law firm) in 1996 and quickly assumed a management position because I was interested in being part of the development and growth of the organization. I joined the Board of Directors in approximately 2006.

I recall that we would debate the office dress code at the management level. Until the pandemic, we would have *never* considered allowing leggings, shorts, sweatpants, T-shirts, blue jeans, flip-flops, or other clothes or footwear of that casual caliber. I also recall, though, always feeling that the women's suits that I wore every day were not very comfortable for my body. Traditional cut blazers were designed for men and never quite accommodated women with larger breasts. And, in San Diego, the traditional wool suit was just too hot! Despite the fact that pantyhose would inevitably rip the second or third time we wore them and that they were scratchy, women were expected to wear them (certainly to every court appearance; no bare legs for you!). Notwithstanding these discomforts and the readily apparent lack of true need to dress up to sit at our desk and work all day, we persisted with the longstanding traditions in lawyer attire.

Although I do not believe many of us fully appreciated it at the time, these work-environment traditions—developed at a time when the profession was almost all white males—held women back, particularly women who elected to go through the childbearing process and have children. If a woman was going to have a child, she needed to commit to be at the firm, full-time, in the office, until a date certain, at which time she would go on leave. She would then have her leave, and, on a date certain, come back full-time, in the office.

When I started with my firm, there was only one other woman attorney, and she was about to have her baby. She quickly realized that there was not even a maternity policy in place, and she worked hard to get one established. I recall other women in my early years of practice going out on maternity leave and expressing a desire to come back part-time. Part-time schedules were generally frowned upon, and remote schedules were unheard of. I will never forget how two incredibly talented part-time women (both of whom had recently had children) were assigned one small office *together*, with their desks facing one another. You are part-time? Okay, you still need to come to the office, but you and another woman who just had a baby need to share one small office. What? (Fortunately, that was the last time the firm ever did that. We have progressed into an amazing organization that actively advances women in the practice of law.)

It was widely discussed at Lawyers Club—our local San Diego Women's Bar Association—that having a child, taking leave, and coming back part-time was perceived as taking oneself off of "the partnership track." Unquestionably, there were many women who overcame that stereotype and went on to become highly successful partners in prestigious law firms. But some women, discouraged or tired, retired from the practice of law or left private practice for friendlier legal jobs with enhanced work-life balance.

Fast-forward to April 2020.

We all remember what it was like when we began to realize the extent of the pandemic and the consequences of being exposed to the early variants of COVID-19. It was like the beginning of an apocalypse, with great uncertainty and great fear. How easy was it to catch the virus? Will I die if I catch it? What is the death rate going to be? Out of necessity and in compliance with state and local mandates, we almost instantaneously pivoted to working out of our bedrooms, kitchens, home offices, and even garages.

To credit the legal profession, we quickly figured out how to do our jobs in the new environment. Lawyers are nothing if not problem solvers. Zoom—what is that? I better learn it very quickly because this is how I am going to interact with clients! Court appearances? It is just awesome that the courts are devising systems to appear remotely. I will learn that as well! Filings? I am definitely stepping up my game with the e-filing. Mediations? Wow, turns out I *can* settle through a computer. My various committees and board commitments? We are going to keep on meeting, but now I will do it from home in my super comfy sweatpants.

And guess what? The profession of law quickly ascertained that many tasks and events that we previously *thought* could only be done from the office, or after traveling hours to be someplace in person, or in a formal suit and tie, could be effectively done in very different ways that blew the last 100 years of practicing law completely out of the water. The implications were mind-blowing—decreased or no commute, found time rededicated to health and family, massive efficiencies for clients, increased access to justice and the courts, enhanced ability to work outside of one's traditional locale, and much more.

Of course, there was (and still is) a tremendous amount of discussion about the countervailing considerations in doing your job on a remote computer. It is hard to mentor younger lawyers if you do not meet them face-to-face. It is very challenging to develop bonds within an organization as a new employee if you do not get to meet your teammates. Some court appearances definitely require looking the judge in the eye. Some cross-examination is just more effective in person. And some lawyers and some clients (though not too many, as we have seen) will disrespect the remote system and try to take advantage of it. These considerations are, indeed, tremendously important and will continue to shape how we practice law in these modern times.

The lovely part of it is that a balance *is* being struck. Lawyers—and the people who work in law-related organizations—are figuring out what can be done remotely and what should be done in person. The courts are figuring out that as well. And it is working. The success has been surprising and astounding.

And what does it mean for women? I think it means a lot. You can now be pregnant and not worry about commuting and coming into the office in an uncomfortable and overpriced maternity suit. If you are bloated, tired, nauseous (I was all of these things), you can roll out of bed and login, working at your own pace. After you have the baby, you can much more easily balance family and work. And this is not only for women, of course. This is for all parents. Being a parent of a young child, while also being a lawyer, just became a little bit easier, which, as anyone with a young child knows, means a lot.

And, because remote working has been normalized and traditional 8 a.m. to 6 p.m. schedules are out the window, part-time lawyer arrangements have blended into the new work schematic. There is no longer a bright line between full-time and part-time, or in the office and not in the office. Instead, we get the job done, and we do it right, on our own schedules. I believe that women lawyers will thrive with this flexibility and see that advancement within private practice no longer requires conformity to the antiquated model that preceded the pandemic.

And me? (This is, after all, *Her Story*.) Before the pandemic, I was definitely at my desk every day, in a suit, with few exceptions. I was also one of the first people back in the office after the pandemic hit. I only live a few minutes from work, and I really like my office space. But I also made changes. I started to come to work in these awesome yoga pants. I purchased exercise gear for my office. I moved entirely out of my individual office with the door into a glassed-in conference room for at least 6 months. I started walking to work from time to time. Each one of these small changes made me feel so good. Like I was doing something for myself.

My law firm was featured in the *ABA Journal* for quickly devising a pretty cutting-edge remote working policy that was designed not only for the pandemic, but for after the pandemic as well. We put criteria in place, of course, and we constantly strategized on events and initiatives to get people together in person. We also recognized that many of our employees have not only embraced, but tremendously prefer, working from home, at least from time to time. Our remote working policy is not only an adaptation to a new environment, but a tool to promote health, wellness, and ultimately, retention. I look at it this way: we want that valuable employee to work here. What does the employee want? How can we make this into a two-way conversation? Maybe the employee does not want to drive 30 minutes each way every day (and gas prices, right?!). Maybe that person has a parenting plan that benefits from flexibility. Maybe the person is exercising more without being required to sit at a desk in the commercial office building all day. Maybe the employee has a medical condition that is more easily addressed at home.

Somewhat ironically, while I have been a huge proponent and promoter of our remote working policy, I still come into the office every day. But like our other valued employees, I now have a choice in flexibility, if I need it or want it.

I love the stories that I hear from our profession on this topic. A lawyer going to Florida for a couple of months to be with her elderly parents, while still practicing full-time law in California. Another lawyer moving back to Connecticut to be with his family that he missed, while servicing his California clients remotely. A new mother who was able to come back to work—something she wanted to do—much sooner because she could work part of the time from her house. A law firm employee achieving her dream of homeownership by moving across country to a place where houses were more affordable, while still maintaining her job with the California law firm. The list goes on. They are happy stories that make me smile.

So, while it may sound a bit canned or trite, it is truly a new day and age, and I hope it sticks. If we continue to adapt thoughtfully to this new way of practicing law, I believe that it will improve our lives, and, in particular, help women finally achieve equal footing in the profession.

Heather Linn Rosing

Career
Shareholder, CEO and President, long-standing Chairperson of the Complex Litigation and Professional Liability Department, Klinedinst PC

Education
- JD, Northwestern University Pritzker School of Law (1996)
- BA, Broadcast Journalism, University of Illinois Urbana-Champaign (1993)

Best Advice
Do not wait for somebody to offer you an opportunity. Figure out what it is that you want, and what will make you happy, and go for it. If you live your career by this principle, combined with a solid work ethic and a commitment to helping others, you will go far.

Personal
Heather Rosing lives in San Diego, California, with her pug, two cats, husband, son, and twin daughters. She enjoys her job as CEO of Klinedinst PC, where she has worked for over 26 years. One of her goals is to figure out how to modernize the law firm model as a means of promoting the health and wellness of all employees, proactively advancing women and diversity, and best serving the clientele. When she is not working at Klinedinst PC, or on her bar and philanthropic activities, she enjoys being with her friends, traveling, walking, and reading. She wishes that she had more exciting hobbies!

For More Information
https://klinedinstlaw.com/profiles/attorney/heather-rosing
https://www.linkedin.com/in/heatherrosing

Demystifying Rainmaking: A Practical Guide to Building Your Book

By Kristin Housh

The term *rainmaking* conjures up visions of shamans communing with deities, willing rain to fall with song and dance. Indeed, that is where the term originated—from the rain dances performed by Native Americans in the southwestern United States, particularly during times of drought.[6] In the business context, a "rainmaker" is someone who fosters new streams of cash flow by what appears to be, at least for most of us, pure magic.[7] Let me assure you, however, that rainmaking (at least in business) does not require any magical powers. Anyone can become a rainmaker with targeted community involvement, consistent social engagement, and a dash of confidence.

When I was a junior associate at one of the highest grossing law firms in the world, my idea of a rainmaker was a gray-haired partner (let's face it, a male partner) who generated tens of millions of dollars in originations each year based on his social connections alone. He did not perform the actual day-to-day grunt work of being an attorney. He surrounded himself with an army of more junior "workhorse" partners and their associate underlings to do that. He was usually off hobnobbing with C-suite executives and general counsel of Fortune 500 clients, playing golf at the country club or at his second home in Palm Springs. How did he manage to amass all this social capital? Maybe he was born with some supernatural pull, or maybe it was just luck. Regardless of the source of his success, he was revered by the firm as a proliferator of business. And when he deigned to grace the hallways of our office, we lowly associates were awash with a mixture of awe and resentment. Business just seemed to fall effortlessly into his lap. And he profited off the blood, sweat, and tears

---

6. *Rain Dance*, INDIANS.ORG, http://www.indians.org/articles/rain-dance.html (last visited December 19, 2022); Lisa Earle McLeod, *What Sales Rainmakers Do Differently*, FORBES (Apr. 16, 2020), https://www.forbes.com/sites/lisaearlemcleod/2020/04/16/what-sales-rainmakers-do-differently/?sh=1b693625f144.

7. Barclay Palmer, *Rainmaker: Definition, Traits, How to Become One*, INVESTOPEDIA, https://www.investopedia.com/ask/answers/08/rainmaker.asp (last updated December 28, 2022).

of the rest of us. (Okay, no blood, but definitely a lot of sweat, tears, and late nights in the office.) Based on this (mis)perception of a rainmaker, I would have never imagined that I, a female attorney in my 30s (and just recently elected to the partnership), would ever be considered one, let alone be asked to write an essay on rainmaking.

The idea of myself as a generator of business began to form when I was a fifth-year associate. I had just lateraled to a different law firm—another Am Law 100 firm, however smaller in terms of both the number of attorneys and annual revenue than the behemoth law firm where I embarked on my legal career. Upon making that career move, I finally made time to do something else—something important that kickstarted my eventual rise to partner: I involved myself in the San Diego community. For the first 5 years of my career, I barely took a day off. My life was all but completely consumed with work. When I finally emerged from the work pit I had buried myself in, I embedded myself in several local organizations. I sat on a couple of nonprofit boards and presented regularly to other attorneys and judges at a local inn of court. I also joined a peer-to-peer advisory group made up of a variety of professional women from attorneys and accountants to news correspondents, business owners, and everything in between. We met monthly to process and find solutions for roadblocks we were facing in our respective careers and lives. I took solace among this brethren of successful women. We not only bettered each other emotionally and spiritually, but we also helped each other in more tangible ways—by becoming a booming referral network.

In addition to involving myself in community organizations, I got out of the house and spent time with (drumroll please . . .) **actual people**. I said "yes" to social invitations, even when I would have rather stayed at home. I really listened to people and became their sounding board.

My first origination came from an unlikely source—my financial planner. He and I spent time together not only studying my finances, but also straying off topic into a variety of professional and personal matters. During one of our working sessions, I (finally) told my financial planner about my legal practice, which, at the time, consisted largely of health care fraud investigations and litigation. To my surprise, he revealed that his mom worked for a cardiology medical group and that they had just received a government subpoena. This medical group became my very first client. A tiny flicker of an idea flashed in my mind—maybe I could generate my own business? I liked that thought.

My next client was a lot bigger and, again, arose from an unexpected place. One Saturday afternoon I dragged myself, begrudgingly, to a good friend's daughter's birthday party. I did not have any children, so the idea of spending a coveted weekend day watching children play pin-the-tail on the donkey, or whatever kids do at birthday parties these days, was not very enticing. Also, I am an introvert, and social gatherings tend to drain me. Despite this, I went. And I am sure glad that I did. At the party, I ran into a friend whom I had not seen for a few years. While the kids played in the front yard, my friend and I caught up. She shared with me some good news and then some bad news. The good news: she had created a burgeoning liquor brand. The bad news: Her company was the target of multiple lawsuits brought by plaintiffs who had come out of the woodwork claiming that they were entitled to equity, as is typical when a venture becomes successful. As President John F. Kennedy famously noted: "[V]ictory has 100 fathers, but defeat is an orphan."[8] I recall telling her: "This is literally what I do." (My practice had changed after I lateraled to a new firm. I was now representing parties in what I refer to as "business divorces"—lawsuits involving, among other things, breach of contract, corporate governance issues, and partnership and shareholder skirmishes.)

For weeks, I mulled over whether or not I should follow up with my friend and ask for her business. She was already being represented by another firm. What could I possibly offer that the other firm could not? And at the time, the idea of asking someone for business was downright cringeworthy. Finally, I mustered up the courage to send a text to my friend offering to give her a second opinion on the lawsuits, if she was interested, and reiterating that business disputes are my specialty. I very much expected her to tell me, "thanks, but no thanks." To my surprise, however, she said yes. That happenstance reunion at a child's birthday party and a follow-up text message spawned a multiyear-long business relationship and several litigation and transactional matters. The tiny flicker of an idea had officially morphed into a full-fledged belief: "I can actually do this."

---

8. John F. Kennedy, News Conference (Apr. 21, 1961).

Other referral source and client relationships blossomed thereafter, for example:

- I befriended a husband-and-wife team who own and manage a small boutique law firm in Orange County. I referred a family law matter to their firm a few years ago. They returned the favor in spades. Every few months, I receive an email from one of them asking if my firm can handle a matter for one of their clients. It does not always pan out. But it is a numbers game—eventually something lands.
- I found my way into a San Diego circle of young entrepreneurs, largely by way of a close friend who owns a local printing company and has clout in the entrepreneur community (notably, she also became a client). I attended the group's events and parties—again, despite my introversion. And I worked the room: I asked questions and took a genuine interest in their businesses, and they told me about their problems, which sometimes included their legal issues. I offered advice if the legal issue fell within my area of expertise, or, if not, I introduced them to one of my colleagues who could help.
- I made mental notes of attorneys I had litigated against who were professional and effective, and whom I respected (a remarkably short list—but I will save that for a different essay). Whenever I needed co-counsel or my firm was conflicted out of a matter, I referred the business to one of the attorneys on my short list. And, slowly but surely, they began to put my name on their respective short lists of attorneys to whom they referred business.

In the spirit of full disclosure, building my book of business has not been all puppy dogs and rainbows. Sexism is unfortunately alive and well in the legal profession. I have lost business because of my gender. I have been told, in essence: "I would love for you to handle this matter but . . . it would be more effective if we had [fill in the blank older man] representing us because . . . " "the judge is a sexist" or "opposing counsel does not respect women." These potential clients always assure me that *they* are not sexist, but, unfortunately, this is the world we live in; so, regrettably, they are forced to kowtow to the patriarchy this time. There are days when I almost feel like they are right—for example, the time when opposing counsel repeatedly interrupted me while I was deposing a witness to tell me how to take a deposition (because clearly I was not able to do it on my own—insert eye roll), or the time when the judge allowed opposing counsel to berate me while pointing aggressively at me for 30 minutes in open court. On those days, I swallow my anger, tears stinging the corners of my eyes, and I wonder if this profession is for me. And then I remember that I am really good at this, and better, more fulfilling days are ahead. I hope you, reader, remember this too, even in the darkest of your professional hours.

So, back to the question at hand: If it is not magic or luck, how exactly do you build your own book of business? A book of business is built on three main pillars: (1) community involvement, (2) social engagement, and (3) confidence. Each pillar must not only be carefully crafted at the outset, but must also be regularly reinforced in order to maintain a successful and long-lasting book of business. In other words, once you build your book, you cannot rest on your laurels. You have to go back to the pillars and reinforce, reinforce, reinforce.

Pillar 1: Get Involved

Select one or two organizations that you have an interest in and that put you in front of the movers and shakers in your community. Look at the composition of the organization's board and leadership. Are there any executives or general counsel? How about other attorneys who could be referral sources? Be selective about the organizations with which you become involved (after all, we attorneys have limited time to spare). Then, be consistent and deliberate about your involvement—show up to the meetings and events, invite potential clients or referral sources in the organization to coffee or lunch, offer to present on a topic that highlights your legal expertise and will be useful to your fellow organization members, and so on.

Pillar 2: Say "Yes" to Social Engagements

This does not mean you have to go to everything—being able to say "no" to events that do not serve you is an important skill indeed. However, you should be aware that the more events you attend, the more likely you will connect with someone who will give you business. For example, if I had not attended that children's birthday party, I would probably not have reconnected with an old friend and won her business. If you have to pick and choose which social events you say "yes" to, select those that will give you an opportunity to actually sit down and meaningfully chat with people who will likely have business to refer to you. For example, a seminar might not be the best event to sink your time into because the speaker will be addressing a captive audience and you will not have much of an opportunity (if any) to converse with other attendees.

Pillar 3: Be Confident

Or at least act like someone you admire who is confident (i.e., fake it until you become it). Tell others what you do, as specifically and memorably as possible, and then ask for their business.

- Explain your legal practice to your friends, family members, and acquaintances. What types of clients do you support? How specifically do you help them? Come up with a punchy opener to use when you are telling people what you do (often referred to as an "elevator speech"). A good friend of mine, and a powerhouse rainmaker, introduces her practice as follows: "I do birds and bunny rabbits." This opener is more interesting and memorable than "I do environmental entitlement work." Not to mention, this one-liner is far more likely to elicit follow-up questions and meaningful conversation. Always remember: People cannot refer business to you if they do not know or cannot remember what it is that you do.
- Do not be afraid to ask for work. Or be afraid but still ask for work. Had I given in to self-doubt and not sent that follow-up text to my friend, I would almost certainly have missed out on years' worth of business.

Contrary to what I believed as a junior associate, there is no magic involved in rainmaking. You do not have to be lucky. Nor do you have to be blessed with innate business development prowess. The vast majority of the time, business does not just fall in someone's lap. Top rainmakers do not become top rainmakers by sitting around waiting for someone to call. The ability to "make it rain" is available to anyone who, with some patience and grit, lays the foundation for and then consistently fortifies the three pillars of business development: community involvement, social engagement, and confidence.

Kristin Housh

Career

Partner in the Business Trial Practice Group, Sheppard Mullin Richter & Hampton LLP

Education

- JD, *cum laude*, University of Texas School of Law (2012), *Texas Journal on Civil Liberties and Civil Rights*, Submissions Editor
- BA, *magna cum laude*, Sociology and English, University of Southern California (2009), Phi Beta Kappa

Best Advice

The saying "it's not personal, it's just business" is nonsense. Business is deeply personal—so, embrace it. Do not be afraid to reveal your innermost self to your clients and business colleagues. Share your story and listen to theirs. Human connection is everything. It will get you ahead in life and in business, and you'll feel better too.

Personal

Kristin Housh lives in Encinitas, California, with her two cats, boxer dog, and husband. In addition to representing her clients in complex business litigation matters, she represents a variety of pro bono clients, ranging from inmates denied constitutionally adequate medical care to a class of asylum seekers illegally turned away at the U.S.–Mexico border. She is also active in the San Diego community and is dedicated to public service and promoting diversity. She sits on the Advisory Board for the American Bar Association's Immigration Justice Project and on the Host Committee for Equality California's annual fundraiser. In her free time, Kristin enjoys shredding the powder (on skis), wine tasting, exploring national parks, and observing big cats (especially cheetahs).

For More Information

https://www.sheppardmullin.com/khoush
https://www.linkedin.com/in/kristinhoush

Building a Book of Business: Sometimes the Only Person in Your Way Is You

By Jennifer Olmedo-Rodriguez

A book of business is something that we build over the course of our career. It is ever changing and ever expanding. Each lawyer is going to approach client relations differently, with one's own philosophies on growth and relationship building. While this skill comes naturally to some, for others it takes time to develop and refine the interpersonal skills needed to establish these relationships. There is no right or wrong way to build a book of business, but as women, we often face additional challenges. Learning from those challenges helps us grow and advance not only in our careers, but on our path of personal development. It is an organic process that should never cease.

Making Life Happen—A Family Tradition

I come from a family of change-makers. My parents fled Cuba for the United States in the 1970s with one goal: to escape oppression and provide their future generations with opportunities we would not have had otherwise. They wanted to give our family a life of freedom with the ability to obtain an education and provide an even better life for our future children and grandchildren.

As a young girl, I heard stories of their journey and watched as my parents and grandparents worked multiple jobs to ensure that my sister and I could achieve more than they had. My parents were determined to send my sister and me to college and worked tirelessly to ensure that we learned the importance and privilege of an education. The determination, grit, and commitment they modeled for us is something I aim to instill in my own two boys.

It is why I was able to graduate from college early with honors at the age of 20, becoming the first member of my family to earn a college degree and head off to law school. I took the opportunity my family provided for me and made my dream of becoming a lawyer a reality. My family's sacrifice taught me that you have to get out of your own way and let yourself pursue your aspirations even if the odds seem stacked against you.

Certainly, there will be help along the way, but your actions dictate your success. In the field of law, especially, you cannot be afraid to take risks, and learning to look at things from different perspectives is key.

My Two Barriers and How I Overcame Them

As I reflect on my career, I have come to realize that there are different types of barriers that we face as women: external barriers imposed upon us and internal barriers we impose upon ourselves.

When I started my career in commercial litigation, I was 23 years old. I am the first to admit that I was young, and I certainly looked it, too. I was short and petite and a first-generation Cuban American. It did not take me long to learn how challenging it is for a young lawyer to pitch for work in this high-stakes area of the law.

Instead of letting those challenges deter me, however, I decided to change how I viewed them, and I made a conscious decision to look at client development from the client's perspective. Just like us, clients have someone they need to answer to, and, as a result, they must also be able to explain their choices in representation and counsel. When a client hesitates to hire a young lawyer, it is not necessarily personal. They are making that decision with their company's best interests in mind. Once I reframed the situation, I was able to better understand the challenges young lawyers face when developing business and set out to overcome them. I quickly realized that I needed to show prospective clients that, despite my youth, I had the knowledge and ability to best represent their interests.

To do that, I leaned into the deep bench of talent and experience at my firm, Buchanan Ingersoll & Rooney. I quickly found allies who were more than willing to lend their "gray hair," so to speak, to proposed client teams when I set out to pursue opportunities. Do not hesitate to tap into the gravitas of your firm—many times you will find that the senior lawyers are more than happy to help young lawyers develop business. When faced with similar external barriers, understand that you can only control what is in fact in your control. Change your perspective. At times, you are the one and only thing standing in your way to success. Instead of waiting for others to act, force their hand through your own actions.

Sometimes, however, the barriers we perceive as being external are actually internal ones that we impose upon ourselves. After pouring everything I had into my education and my work, I had my first child a mere 4 years into my career. The prospect of balancing my demanding career with motherhood presented what seemed like an insurmountable challenge. I struggled navigating being a new mom and giving my work the attention I had given it prior to becoming a mother. At the time, I struggled to find mothers at national law firms whom I could model—women who had found the balance between motherhood and their career. I felt overwhelmed and isolated. I felt that it just could not be done—that I had to choose: either motherhood or my career as a partner at a national law firm.

I will be forever grateful for the opportunity I had to take a step back from my fast-paced, high-needs practice and transition to a small firm to work from home doing regulatory work while caring for my infant son. What we did for months or, in some cases, years, due to COVID-19 was practically unheard of 15 years ago. I relished that time, but, after a few short years, realized that I very much missed the career I had always envisioned and worked toward. I wanted to do both—be a mom and have the career I dreamed of having. But first, I had to give myself permission to do both. After some intense self-reflection, I decided to continue growing in my career and returned to my firm, where I have been ever since.

Reflecting upon my decision to take a step back, I realize that many of the barriers I perceived to being a mom and a commercial litigator at a national firm were self-imposed. I was trying to model two ideals that I had internalized: what I thought it meant to be a good mother and what I thought it meant to be a good lawyer. My predispositions and, at times, exacting and unattainable standards presented perceived barriers that perhaps were not really there. No one told me that to be a good mom I had to leave my job. I jumped without anyone pushing me. By thinking that I could only be one or the other—either a great mom or a great lawyer—I did not realize that I could be both and give myself permission to do exactly that. Now, I strive to be that example for other lawyer moms in my firm and beyond. With a strong support system, some creativity, and a little bit of self-forgiveness (i.e., you need to cut yourself some slack at times), you can excel at both.

As much as I needed my clients to believe in my capabilities, I first had to believe in myself as a working mom. In a society that has historically undervalued women and people of color, it is true that sometimes we must work twice as hard to achieve the same level of success as our counterparts. But we should not let this deter us from pursuing our goals and passions.

As we travel our individual career paths, each of us comes across people who uplift us. It is important that we, as women, strive to do the same for others in return. We may need to work harder, but that just makes our success that much sweeter. Empowerment from others has had an immense impact on my career and my personal growth journey. I never foresaw my current position leading my firm's Miami office in my career trajectory. I was not working toward it. Truthfully, it was completely off my radar. In that same vein, I have never thought of myself as a "rainmaker." I have, however, forged strong relationships with clients over the years. I attribute my success to the simple adage: hard work pays off. My clients see the grit, commitment, and work ethic I bring to their cases, and they value it. The support I received from my colleagues, clients, and network, however, cannot be overemphasized. Now, as a leader, I strive to support, elevate, amplify, and advance others in my firm. I truly believe that it takes a team effort to build a successful office—let alone a successful firm. Our collective client relationships make our office and, by extension, our firm successful. I make it a priority to emphasize the power of our group and the potential we have when we collaborate and support one another. No one person can do it all—the success of one advances the success of all.

Personal growth and business development are essential for the overall success of the group and the firm. However, you are not competing with your colleagues. You are competing with yourself. While it can be hard to tune out the outside noise, do not necessarily try to emulate what others do. Look inside yourself and identify your strengths—what do you bring to clients; how do you connect with others? Do not let someone else's achievements impact your confidence. While they may have found success one way, you will find it in your own way.

My Lessons on Rainmaking

Building a book of business takes time. For most of us, it is something we develop throughout the entirety of our careers. There are a few lessons that I have picked up over the years that have helped me forge genuine relationships and create business development opportunities for my firm.

Your Network Is Something to Nurture

One thing I wish I had appreciated at the beginning of my career is the power of your personal network. The relationships you build throughout your whole life—not just when you start your professional life—have the potential to shape your career in many ways. Your network goes as far back as your primary school and high school days. That is when you start meeting people and building relationships. Just like you, those acquaintances grow in their own careers. Those personal relationships are immensely valuable. All of them—childhood, high school, college, graduate school, and personal relationships—are starting points for building your reputation, establishing your brand, and growing your professional network. All can lead to potential business development opportunities.

Appreciate and nurture each relationship you build along the way because each one is valuable. Your friends, colleagues, clients, opposing counsel, and personal relationships from every stage of your life can impact your career. Now, as we start coming out of the isolation brought about by the pandemic, it is more important than ever to nurture your network. You never know when someone in your network might be able to help you or when you might be able to help them.

Opportunities Are All about What You Do with Them

Strive to exceed expectations. I have always been driven by the philosophy that some people may be smarter than me, but no one is going to work harder or care more than me. It is something I picked up watching my parents and grandparents work extremely hard to provide opportunities for our family. But opportunity is all about what you make of it.

Every time I have a chance to work with a new client, I cherish it. I give everything I can into building that relationship—to demonstrate the value I bring to their business and how important their work was to me. Once you get in the door, it is on you to take advantage of that opportunity. Make sure you do all you can to foster that relationship and show the client that you are the best person for the job. When you provide clients that level of investment, they will do the same for you.

Professionalism Is Key to Building Successful Relationships

Many people misinterpret what it means to be a good litigator or trial lawyer—acting aggressively, abrasively, or unreasonably, all in the name of achieving the optimal outcome for the client. But that is a mistake. Of course, it is your job to represent your clients' best interests and ultimately achieve their desired outcome. But you can do so while being both forceful and respectful of your opposing counsel. Those lawyers are also your peers and an important piece of your network. By developing a professional reputation for being a tough, yet reasonable and professional, adversary I have fostered relationships with opposing counsel that have led to additional opportunities down the line not only for me but also for my clients. Establishing good working relationships with opposing counsel can lead to more efficient litigation and resolution of disputes—saving your clients money and time. On the other hand, the best compliment you can receive is when your opponent sends you a case.

Your professionalism and the way you work are extremely important when you are building a book of business. A good lawyer understands their clients' goals and wants to win. An outstanding lawyer feels their clients' pain and is dedicated to finding the best solution. When you approach a case with this frame of mind, you will see that many times (though admittedly, there are exceptions) working *with* your opposing counsel will lead to better outcomes than working against them. Developing a reputation for integrity, excellent work, professionalism, *and* reasonableness helps you build relationships with your peers, broadens your network, and potentially leads to business development opportunities in the future.

The core tenet of business development is relationships. Relationship building is critical to bring in new clients, to keep them satisfied, and to help make you successful. Nurturing your relationships is the best way to develop business and move up in your career. I attribute my success to the strong relationships I have built *and* sustained along my life. Always strive to ensure you do not burn any bridge. You will be surprised how many times you encounter the same person as you travel along your career path.

I found my allies at the beginning of my career by nurturing and developing relationships and demonstrating to the more experienced lawyers at my firm that I was committed to learning, growing, and honing my skills. Usually, that is all it takes to build a dedicated coalition of people who are ready and willing to support and advance you as you grow. As women, allyship is incredibly important. Relationships I have formed with other women lawyers have been some of the most rewarding. I have encountered supportive mentors and colleagues who have grown into my most trusted advisors. Women benefit greatly from the support and encouragement of other women. I am committed to paying it forward. We have an obligation to raise each other up, amplify each other's voices, and promote and celebrate each other's successes.

My parents taught me from an early age that I had the power to achieve my goals, no matter how lofty they might be. As I reflect on where I came from and what I have achieved, I feel great satisfaction knowing that I have validated the sacrifices my family made for me and my sister. I have tried to make the most of every opportunity given to me. Many times, women can serve as obstacles to themselves, myself included. We should be mindful of the way we approach perceived barriers—whether external or self-imposed. When we see another woman who is afraid to take a risk or bet on herself, step up and encourage her, elevate her, advance and promote her.

This is one of the most valuable lessons I have learned in my career. I believe it has made me a better leader, a better colleague, and a better lawyer. Together we are a force to be reckoned with and can achieve great things. Better yet, we are just getting started.

Jennifer Olmedo-Rodriguez

Career
Shareholder and head of Miami office in the firm's Litigation section, Buchanan Ingersoll & Rooney PC

Education
- JD, *Honors*, University of Florida Levin College of Law (2002)
- BA, Political Science and Government, Florida International University (1999)

Best Advice
Take an active role to support another woman lawyer that crosses your path—whether by mentoring a young associate, providing advice to a young mother struggling to balance a budding career with the 24-hour demands of child-rearing, or genuinely celebrating the success of a seasoned colleague or friend. By doing so, we can work to provide a network of support that ensures the success of women throughout the legal industry.

Personal
As a first-generation Cuban American, Jennifer Olmedo-Rodriguez grew up hearing stories of how her parents and grandparents fled Cuba and worked multiple jobs to ensure that future generations—she, her sister, and her cousins—had new opportunities. At the age of 20, Jennifer became the first in her family to obtain a college degree. Shortly thereafter, she was awarded a full scholarship to attend the University of Florida Levin College of Law. Jennifer sees herself as working to validate the sacrifices her family made by coming to this country in search of the American Dream. For her, family honor transformed the desire to succeed from a selfish goal into a validation of her family's sacrifices and legacy.

For More Information
https://www.bipc.com/jennifer-olmedo-rodriguez
https://www.linkedin.com/in/jennifer-olmedo-rodriguez-43151b3a

How to Negotiate Your Compensation—Even When You Don't Want to

By Lee Tarte Wallace

In 2014, a hacker group dove into the databases from Sony Pictures and discovered gossip gold. Among other embarrassing tidbits, the film studio was paying Oscar-winning actress Jennifer Lawrence only 7 percent of *American Hustle*'s profits, while her less popular male co-stars were collecting 9 percent. After the hack, Lawrence spoke for many women when she said she had avoided negotiating because she did not want to appear "difficult" or "spoiled." "I would be lying if I didn't say there was an element of wanting to be liked that influenced my decision to close the deal without a real fight," Lawrence said in an interview for Lena Dunham's weekly newsletter, *Lenny*.

Lawrence is not alone. Many women avoid negotiating their compensation packages because they feel uncomfortable, and studies show they are not simply avoiding conflict; negotiating carries consequences for women that men may not experience. Fortunately, you can successfully negotiate your compensation by determining your priorities, carefully preparing, and using proven negotiation strategies.

Women Need to Negotiate Their Compensation

A 2007 study found that half of male MBA students negotiated the starting salary for their first job, while only one-eighth of women did.[9] Employees who negotiate their starting salaries wrangle, on average, an extra $5,000.[10] While $5,000 may not seem like a large amount in and of itself, the simple act of asking for more money for the very first job out of school can make an enormous difference across a career. "A 25-year-old employee who enters the job market at $55,000 will earn about $634,000

---

9. Hannah Riley Bowles, *Why Women Don't Negotiate Their Job Offers*, HARV. BUS. REV. (June 19, 2014), https://hbr.org/2014/06/why-women-dont-negotiate-their-job-offers.
10. Michelle Marks & Crystal Harold, *Who Asks and Who Receives in Salary Negotiation*, 32 J. OF ORG. BEHAV. 371–394 (2011), https://onlinelibrary.wiley.com/doi/abs/10.1002/job.671.

more over the course of a 40-year career (assuming annual 5 percent raises) than an employee who starts out at $50,000."[11]

Moreover, women who do not ask for the extra salary may find that the increasingly disparate pay affects their job performance: "Our perceptions of unfairness, whether factual or not, can breed envy and discontent and lower productivity."[12]

> "[W]e tend to be highly driven by status concerns—that is, we care a great deal about how we measure up to others. Finding out that someone you consider to be a peer is earning more than you do could cause you to be less satisfied with your own accomplishments and also more displeased with your organization."[13]

Women Pay a Price for Negotiating Their Salaries

Before you kick yourself for not negotiating an extra $5,000 back when you took your first job out of law school, recognize that women may have good reason to avoid negotiating their compensation. "In repeated studies, the social cost of negotiating for higher pay has been found to be greater for women than it is for men. . . . [I]n most published studies, the social cost of negotiating for pay is not significant for men, while it is significant for women."[14] In other words, a woman's decision not to negotiate may be "based on an accurate read of the social environment. Women get a nervous feeling about negotiating for higher pay because they are intuiting—correctly—that self-advocating for higher pay would present a socially difficult situation for them—more so than for men."[15]

So, while it makes financial sense to negotiate your compensation package, you admittedly are navigating a minefield when you do.

---

11. Harvard Program on Negotiation Staff, *Salary Negotiation: How to Ask for a Higher Salary,* HARV. L. SCH. PROGRAM ON NEGOT. DAILY BLOG (Aug. 21, 2023), https://www.pon.harvard.edu/daily/salary-negotiations/negotiating-for-a-higher-salary.
12. Harvard Program on Negotiation Staff, *Discussing Salary at Work,* HARV. L. SCH. PROGRAM ON NEGOT. DAILY BLOG (Mar. 7, 2023), https://www.pon.harvard.edu/daily/salary-negotiations/so-how-much-do-you-make-nb.
13. Id.
14. Bowles, *supra* note 9.
15. Id.

Strategies for Successfully Negotiating Your Compensation

You may feel stuck between two competing ideas: that you will miss out if you do not negotiate your compensation and that you will harm your career if you do. Fortunately, by thinking broadly about what "compensation" means to you, carefully preparing for the discussion, and using proven negotiation strategies, you can successfully negotiate your compensation.

Think Beyond the Number

Salary is always relevant, but it is far from the only metric you care about. Before you start the negotiation, consider what matters to you about your next job so that you can focus your negotiations on the most critical points. Given that you will pay a price for negotiating, you want to negotiate for the things that matter most. As a bonus, nonfinancial requests may not carry the same consequences that negotiating for salary does.

Your Long-Term Career Goals

Unless you are closing in on retirement, chances are your next job will not be your last. Ask yourself the all-important question: where are you headed? What is the next job you want, and is this job the best way to reach that next job? If this job is the straightest path to your ultimate goals, the salary may not be as important.

Work Culture

In some jobs you will be paid well, but you will also be working late into the night and on weekends; at other jobs, employees work from 9 a.m. to 5 p.m. and have no idea what the office looks like on a Saturday (admittedly, these jobs are rare in the legal field). In some workplaces, employees eat out together nearly every day; in others, employees bring sack lunches and eat at their desks. Some companies have elaborate parties at every possible occasion; others have a single, perfunctory party around the holidays. Chances are that you prefer one style over the other, and which style depends on your personality.

If you do not know much about the workplace culture, at least explore some of the basic questions that you can ask before you take the job. What will you be doing? With whom will you be working? What is the custom around lunches? What are the typical hours? Why did the person who had the job before you leave?

Intangible Points of Value

You may be drawn to a job for reasons that have nothing to do with the salary, like the great benefits or retirement package, proximity to where you live, or the ability to work from home.

Your Present-Day Values

When I was in law school, people compared notes about what their first jobs would pay and how many billable hours they would be required to log. Frankly, as young and inexperienced as we were with the working world, we did not know enough to ask other questions. As you gain more experience, the metrics that seemed all-important to you when you were 25 may no longer be as important. You need to assess the job offer based on your current values, not the ones you held when you were in your 20s.

Salary is never irrelevant, but you may also be very concerned about the hours you will need to put in, how much you will have to travel, whether you will get to take your own depositions, or where you will be allowed to work.

When you have thought through each of these factors, prioritize them in your mind before you begin to negotiate. If the job is a stepping stone to the career you want, you may be willing to work in the physical office because that serves your goal, and you may be willing to take less pay. You may be willing to trade more hours for the flexibility of selecting your own hours, working from home, or receiving a higher salary.

Prepare for the Negotiation

You can increase your chances of success and boost your confidence by preparing for the negotiation in advance. Preparation is even more important if you are particularly nervous about the upcoming conversation or if you innately dislike conflict.

Research

Your negotiations are far more likely to be fruitful if you have research to back up your positions. You will state your positions more confidently because you will know they are based on solid facts. Just as importantly, you will feel more confident as you negotiate, since you will be convinced that what you are requesting makes sense and is fair.

You will get the most accurate information if you directly ask people within the firm what they make. Historically, however, researching compensation has been difficult because of the taboo on discussing salaries in the workplace. These unwritten rules have had a greater impact on women, who tend to be relatively undercompensated.

Fortunately, the rules have begun to shift. In 2014, President Obama signed an executive order preventing federal contractors from prohibiting employees from discussing compensation. Additionally, sites like OpenDoor allow people to post salary information anonymously. Am Law, too, has been ranking large firms according to compensation for some time, although the figures typically focus on compensation for partners. If you are unable to find information specific to a firm or company, you may be able to find more general information about salaries in your area for people performing the type and level of work you are seeking.

Even if you have difficulty getting specific salary information, you ought to be able to find answers to basic questions about salary negotiations. For example, is the firm or company willing to negotiate salary at all? Does the firm try to meet the salaries offered by other local firms? Is the firm willing to negotiate other factors, such as working from home or billable hours? Is the firm flexible in some areas, such as where you work, but dead set on other requirements, such as the number of billable hours?

Pegging Your Demands to Outside Standards

If you want to persuade someone to adopt your point of view, you have to make it logical from the other person's perspective. As you prepare, you should look for objective standards other than your own personal desires. If you peg your demands to what you want, you are not offering the other parties a reason to give you what you are asking for.

By researching the company, job description, salary, and benefits this firm offers to other employees and by comparing each of those factors to the benefits and pay other companies offer, you will boost your ability to make reasoned, logical arguments about why you are asking for certain things in the negotiation. You will be able to tie your demand to objective standards that are not simply related to your own personal wishes. This approach will then give the other person the ability to accept your position without betraying their own sense of logic and fairness.

Confidence

Confidence makes a difference in how you negotiate and what happens when you do. If negotiation does not come naturally to you, you can boost your confidence with preparation and practice.

Training

For some people, negotiation is effortless; for the rest of us, we have a lot to learn. A negotiation class may boost your skill level and your confidence at the same time.

If you remain unsure about what you should request in the negotiation, consider asking a colleague for a second opinion. You may get additional information, and you also will build your confidence that what you are requesting is both reasoned and fair.

Negotiation Strategies

If you are negotiation-averse, it may be tempting to prolong the time you spend on evaluation and preparation. Eventually, though, you have to plunge into the negotiation fray. Several proven strategies, such as reframing how you view the negotiation and the parties, will help you as you negotiate. Here are some pointers:

Negotiate for Others

Studies suggest that women can negotiate powerfully and without repercussions when they negotiate for others. "[W]e love it when women negotiate assertively for others. It's just when women are negotiating assertively for themselves—particularly around pay—where we find a backlash. . . ."[16] In fact, this sort of thinking comes naturally to women attorneys, since we represent clients on a daily basis.

---

16. *Id.*

If you can reframe your thinking about the negotiation, you may be able to remove some of the repercussions and increase your confidence at the same time. For example, instead of thinking of your salary negotiation as something you are doing to benefit you personally, think of yourself as representing the people in your life who will be affected by the outcome. Your child may want to attend a private music college, your parents may need help with the cost of assisted living, or your husband may be dreaming about a cabin at the lake. Recasting the negotiation as a situation where you may be able to achieve positive outcomes for people you care about and "represent" can change your way of thinking as you negotiate.

Legitimize Your Reason for Negotiating

You may find the other side is more receptive to a negotiation if you give them a reason for you to negotiate that makes sense from the other side's perspective. When Sheryl Sandberg negotiated her compensation package with Facebook, she explained: "'Of course you realize that you're hiring me to run your deal team so you want me to be a good negotiator.' Sandberg wanted Facebook to see her negotiating as legitimate because, if she didn't negotiate, they should be worried about whether they'd made the right hire."[17] Note that Sandberg did not try to justify her requests based on her own needs. Instead, she adopted the employer's perspective and explained why the employer would want to hire someone who would be willing to negotiate hard.

Affirm Your Commitment to Organizational Relationships

Professor Bowles warns that women should "communicate [their] concern for organizational relationships" as they negotiate.[18] In other words, even when you are negotiating your own salary, your employer needs to be convinced that you remain committed to the company. For example, Sheryl Sandberg told Facebook, "This is the only time you and I will ever be on opposite sides of the table."[19]

---

17. Id.
18. Id.
19. Id.

Ask Questions

When you are negotiating for a salary, by definition you are negotiating with someone who has a power you do not have: the power to set your salary. Power differences can be particularly challenging when women negotiate.

Instead of directly opposing what the other person is suggesting, ask questions. The answers will help you discover what is important to the other people in the room—and after all, negotiations are a process of persuading people that what you are suggesting makes sense from their point of view.

Conclusion

In the years following the Sony hack, Jennifer Lawrence told *60 Minutes*: "It was my own mentality that led me to believe that I didn't deserve to be paid equally," and "I worked too hard to get here to be stupid about it."[20] Just like Jennifer Lawrence, you are in a position to negotiate because you spent years toiling to reach a spot where you have valuable skills and experience to offer. By evaluating your priorities, carefully preparing, and applying tested negotiation strategies, you can successfully negotiate a fair compensation package that considers the skills you have to offer, and that will make a long-term difference in your financial outlook and overall job satisfaction.

---

20. Bill Whitaker, *60 Minutes: Jennifer Lawrence's Surprising Trip to the Top of Hollywood*, CBS News (Feb. 25, 2018, 7:07 PM), https://www.cbsnews.com/news/jennifer-lawrence-surprising-trip-to-the-top-of-hollywood.

Lee Tarte Wallace

Career

Mediator, Attorney, BAY Mediation & Arbitration Services; Owner, The Wallace Law Firm LLC

Education
- JD, Harvard Law School (1987)
- BA, English Literature, Minors in Math and Economics, Vanderbilt University (1984)

Best Advice

Getting business is your job even when nobody tells you it is.

Personal

Lee Wallace is a past president of the Georgia Association for Women Lawyers and a past chair of the Product Liability section of the Georgia Bar. She loves following lawsuits in the news, public speaking, and ice cream, not necessarily in that order. Lee has authored dozens of articles on legal-related topics and mediations and has edited a book on Medical Malpractice. She has two children.

For More Information

https://thewallacelawfirm.com/attorney-profile
https://www.linkedin.com/in/lee-wallace-attorney-mediator

How to Manage a Team Effectively: Advice from the Field

By Tiffany J. deGruy

As lawyers, we are often told that we aren't good at certain things—namely, math, science, and structuring a sentence without trying to be impressive by dropping in Latin phrases. Many of us (this author included) did not go to law school so that we could become a manager. We had no desire to become human resource directors or to oversee the workloads of others. But, inevitably, the job of a lawyer is to zealously represent her clients. Often, the client's interests can be most effectively advocated by having more than one member of the legal team. And, thus, as our careers progress, many of us are somewhat surprised to find ourselves leading those very teams.

The most appropriate way to begin this essay would likely be to find a quote from a military general aimed at empowering the next generation of team leaders. One little problem: I know nothing about military generals. So, we will go with a quote from a Harry Potter book: "If you want to know what a man's like, take a good look at how he treats his inferiors, not his equals."[21]

First, an introduction. I am a litigator by trade and have been practicing for over a decade as outside counsel to large organizations. Most of the cases I have handled in my career have been on the defense side and include claims alleging damages with high dollar ranges. The teams involved in these multifaceted cases often involve dozens of lawyers spanning offices across the country (from both my firm and others). On teams such as these, managers are not just the senior lawyer on the file, or General Counsel of the organization. Rather, as trial tasks get divided, even junior members can look up and suddenly find themselves leading teams with very little guidance or training.

Advice on how to manage teams is not a novel idea. In fact, similar guidance covers the shelves of nearly every airport gift shop. While I am not the first author to write on this subject, I offer my experience here, describing what has and what has not worked for me over my career.

---

21. J. K. Rowling, Harry Potter and the Goblet of Fire (Bloomsbury, 2000).

In forming my advice, I surveyed a group of associates, paralegals, and assistants and have included their anonymous feedback in the paragraphs below. Finally, I offer my perspective on how the skills I developed leading trial teams help when managing those on your personal teams.

Following is my practical advice from the field.

No Disrespect

The first point should be obvious, although sometimes it is not. While disagreements and hard conversations are inevitable, a team cannot function if there is yelling or disrespect. When members feel disrespected or fearful regarding when the next blow-up will occur, they are unable to do their best work. The senior members on teams should also do what they can to ensure that no one is treating others with disrespect, including opposing counsel, senior management, and clients. The management consultants Steve Gruenert and Todd Whitaker once said that "[t]he culture of any organization is shaped by the worst behavior the leader is willing to tolerate."[22] This is also true of teams. Do not tolerate disrespect, even if that means making sacrifices or having difficult conversations.

Plan Ahead to Prevent Avoidable Time Crunches

Ask yourself what can be done now to set your team up for success later. Members should not be asked to consistently manage avoidable time crunches. Be purposeful about assigning tasks as soon as possible to allow your team to fit the projects into their calendars. Do not let something sit on your desk if all you need to do is spend a few minutes communicating the assignment to your group. Try not to be the bottleneck. It's easy to fall into the delayed communication trap when the time demands on the manager are high. Of course, there are situations where time crunches cannot be avoided and teams must pull together, stay up late, miss that personal event, and come together to perform for the client. However, poor planning that turns into regular emergencies for junior members should be avoided. Prioritize finding time for feedback that allows the

---

22. Steve Gruenert & Todd Whitaker, School Culture Rewired: How to Define, Assess, and Transform It (2015).

junior member to incorporate your changes before there is a time crunch. Often, spending time answering questions up front can avoid last-minute explosions and will ensure that the project runs smoothly.

Communicate Clearly and Directly

Communicate clearly and directly with your team. If a 30-minute meeting can be avoided with a 10-second email or message, send the message instead. However, include an invitation to meet to discuss the issue in case there are questions. Often complicated tasks can be better explained face-to-face or over the phone rather than by email. Particularly with new team members, do not assume they understand the instructions. Provide detailed directions and offer to meet to explain them.

Include members consistently from the onset of a matter. It can be very difficult to be asked to fulfill a task when you have not been included enough to understand what is going on. Explain the big picture of how specific assignments fit into the larger goal. It can be hard for members to successfully complete tasks without understanding how those tasks fit into the puzzle. When the larger picture is explained, members can take ownership not only of their limited roles, but also of the project as a whole, and they are then more likely to find other ways to help meet or exceed the team's goals or deadlines. Include members on communications and on larger deadlines. The more the group knows about what is happening, the better they can anticipate the next steps or forecast problems. Communication makes everyone's job easier.

Messages asking "someone" to handle a task can be confusing and leave open the possibility that no one will handle it. One thing that has helped my teams is to use the @ symbol in Outlook to tag members and let them know a task is on their list. This also helps with inbox triage since you tend to quickly glance at your inbox and see messages with task assignments.

Be sure to communicate not only timelines but also client preferences, billing requirements, and the like. If possible, try to send one message rather than a stream of messages providing individual thoughts, feedback, and edits.

Communication is a two-way street. You should not only learn to communicate effectively; you should also learn to listen. Check in with your team regularly to get updates on their tasks and discuss ideas for next steps. Listen to team members when they identify problems they are encountering or explain limitations in their time capacity.

Set Realistic Deadlines

Set realistic deadlines and honor them. The more that teams are encouraged to meet deadlines, even internal ones, the more likely the project will be successful. But do your best to avoid creating fire drills for the sake of fire drills. False deadlines when there is no urgency to review the work product only creates issues down the line. It is important not to downplay the amount of work needed for a task. Asking for a minimal amount of time and then confiscating an entire work week is difficult for members to accommodate. Of course, the unpredictability of litigation is not surprising. But downplaying the amount of time needed—whether that is done due to a lack of forethought or the desire to be liked by the group—is not helpful.

Be Approachable and Responsive

As a team leader, it is important to be approachable and responsive. Having a good attitude is so very important. No one wants to work on a team with a leader with a bad attitude. Being approachable and responsive will help your group function to the best of their abilities. Often, this advice is easier said than done when the pressures of life (and emails upon emails upon emails) pile up. Teach your team how you work best. What is the best way for them to get your attention? Would a standing weekly meeting help everyone get the quick answers they need? Do you find it difficult to read long emails and instead ask for a few bullet points at the top of emails? Are there new technological advances that could help with communication? Be sure you are not the source of delay for those working under you.

Simple Gestures and Kindnesses Go a Long Way

Feeling valued is essential. Late nights and short tempers can sometimes be part of the job. However, showing each member kindness no matter where they fall in the pecking order is essential. A simple "thank you" or "well done" can be the difference between a functioning team and a nonfunctioning one. Figure out what motivates your team members. Often, there are better motivating factors than the "wrath" of a senior member. If you see someone on your team struggling, don't ignore it. Even humorous comments can hint at an underlying issue that's important to explore. One very kind leader I have worked with went to the trouble of calling a hotel where a junior member was staying during her first vacation after a long, hard stretch of work to send a bottle of champagne from the team. Ask yourself what small gestures you could offer to make members feel valued. Maybe it is sending a note of encouragement to someone, bragging on them to their boss, or sending a thoughtful gift for every member—even the very junior ones—after the conclusion of a matter.

Be Careful How Credit and Blame Are Distributed

Give credit to the entire group for their contributions, no matter how small. A victory includes all the members. However, when the team fails or makes mistakes, the leader must step forward and take ownership. While mistakes will certainly happen, it is important for the leader to take responsibility for them, whether it be with the court, opposing counsel, or the client. Leaders should never blame those under them in a public setting. Yet, after the dust settles, it is important to work together to find a way to learn from those mistakes to ensure those mistakes will not be repeated. As part of that postmortem, it is important to consider how leaders might have contributed to the group's difficulties by lack of oversight, by creating time crunches along the way, or for some other reason.

Be Cognizant of the Life Experiences of Those on Your Teams

All teams are different. Find out what motivates yours and what doesn't. Getting to know their life outside the office will help you craft a workspace that is as inclusive as possible. Be cognizant that the life experiences of those on your teams may be different from yours. Diverse life experiences and life stages will help you provide your client the best service. Get to know your members on a personal level. If a member has young children, think about asking before you schedule a late afternoon meeting on Halloween. If working at odd hours allows you to spend your personal time in the manner you would like, consider whether a less intrusive way might accomplish that goal. Off-hours emails are inevitable, but it helps when those messages expressly state whether the email needs an immediate response, such as labeling the email "non-urgent," "tomorrow/Monday," or "when you return from vacation." Alternatively, consider setting a delay on the message so your team member does not receive it until business hours. Put the holidays that are celebrated by your team on your calendar to remind yourself to be respectful on those days even if you don't personally celebrate the same days. If a member has a sick parent, a death in the family, or a personal emergency, don't wait until they ask you to help reassign their work; ask them proactively whether another member should temporarily pick up a task. If the answer is no, respect that response and avoid making judgments about what you would want if you were in that situation. Encourage "blackout periods" where members can have a pause from the constant communications. Encourage vacations and allow your teams to truly be offline (unless there is a real emergency).

Fail and Try Again

Learning how to manage a team does not happen overnight. As your tenure grows and roles shift, there are new skills to learn. The job of a leader is to delegate, give clear direction, and lead the group. These skills can be learned. Watch what other leaders around you are doing well. Ask questions. Join a leadership development organization. Fail. Try again. Fail. Try again.

Building strong team management skills can help in your personal life as well. In addition to my role as a litigation team leader, I am the co-manager of a team that includes three children and a dog acquired during COVID. Whether that communication is with your household supporters, partner, children, or other caregivers, using the management skills that you have honed at work can help your home environment be successful as well. While it will certainly not be effective to send an email identifying daily tasks for your toddler, in leading a household, good communication is essential. Consider how you can effectively communicate expectations. Be mindful that your personal teams are often not as hierarchical as litigation teams may be. Try to avoid treating your friends and family like you are the task master; instead, collaborate to make family decisions. Responsiveness on the home front often looks like giving your friends and family your full attention when interacting with them and attempting to avoid distractions as much as possible so you can be present for those around you. And, of course kindness is key on the home front as well.

In conclusion, team cohesion can produce better results for your clients or business units. It can also lead to less burnout and help retain talented team members. Of these many tips, in my experience, the most important are responsiveness and a good attitude. If you are unsure where to start, think back to what you wish you had in a team leader when you were a junior member, and be that kind of leader for someone else.

Tiffany J. deGruy

Career

Litigation Partner, Bradley Arant Boult Cummings LLP

Education

- JD, The University of Alabama School of Law (2008)
- BS, Political Science, Auburn University (2005)

Best Advice

Never stop learning and growing as a person—whether that be in your legal practice, family life, or the person you are on the inside.

Personal

Tiffany deGruy lives in Birmingham, Alabama, with her husband, three amazing children, and their pandemic-acquired dog. When she is not litigating, spending time with her Woman Advocate Committee friends, or leading her firm's women's initiative, Tiffany is a foodie who loves travel and a good glass of wine.

For More Information

https://www.linkedin.com/in/tiffany-degruy

Discussion Questions

1. Do you struggle with time management? If so, discuss some time management tools you can adopt going forward.

2. What are some ways you can bring creativity into your practice? What is stopping you from experimenting with your own "color-coded chart"?

3. What is your brand? What brand do others impose on you? Do you want to develop or change your brand? If so, what steps can you take to develop or change your brand?

4. How do the essays in this chapter affect your thoughts on business development? Are you a rainmaker? Do you want to be a rainmaker?

5. Discuss your efforts to develop relationships that can mature into clients. Should you change your efforts? If so, how?

6. Are you fairly compensated for your work? Have you ever negotiated for an increase in your salary? If you set your own fee structure, are you appropriately charging for your time commensurate with your experience and with your competition? Discuss the reasons for your responses to these questions. How important is salary when evaluating what is most important to you in a job?

7. Whose management skills do you admire? What makes those skills admirable? Do you act similarly when given management responsibilities?

8. Discuss your or others' experiences with managing in a time of crisis. How did you or others overcome the crisis?

9. How has the pandemic changed your work life, personal life, and work-life balance? Was the change an improvement or not? Any corrections needed? During the pandemic, did your view of yourself or your work-life balance change? How?

10. Reflect on the trajectory of your brand, career, and personal life. Consider if adjustments are needed.

11. If you are in the middle of a challenging situation at this time, how can this make you a better lawyer or otherwise turn into a positive experience?

12. Discuss any unexpected turns in your career path. Should you make a turn in your career path? If so, what will you do?

13. What risks have you taken in your career? How did these opportunities impact you or your career? Do you regret any risk not taken? What would have happened had you taken that risk?

14. What uplifts you and elevates your mood when you are experiencing high stress levels, difficult situations at work, or low points of your career?

15. Do you celebrate achievements? If so, how do you celebrate?

CHAPTER 5

Own Your Unique Career Path and Be True to Your Genuine Self

When we experience obstacles in our career paths, we should stop and examine them. Perhaps the obstacles stem from careers, practice areas, co-workers, and other circumstances that are not aligned with our authentic selves. Who are you really? As lawyers, we spend significant time learning about our clients and their stories so we can effectively represent and advocate for them. As litigators, we spend months understanding the evidence that develops and fleshes out our client's story, and then preparing the most compelling way to present our client and their story, either through dispositive motions or at trial. As in-house counsel, we spend years understanding the various internal departments or external stakeholders or constituents driving the client's "identity." But how much time do we spend reflecting on who we are? How does that awareness align with our identity as women lawyers and the work we do?

The essays in this chapter hope to inspire you to search for your identity, lean into your authenticity, and experience the joy and career successes that come from being true to yourself. You will see how some fabulous women attorneys carved out their own unique career paths from a seed they found along the way that gave them joy and resonated with their authentic selves. In these essays, you will also see attorneys overcoming obstacles by being resilient, maintaining perspective, believing in themselves, and succeeding, notwithstanding (in one case) a naysayer who was merely speculating on an outcome. Sprinkled in these essays, as well, you will find advice on managing your career path by forging your own path, finding a community to support you, and becoming involved in activities outside of the law. Lastly, should you find yourself on the wrong and inauthentic path, here you will also find tips on how to change your path. In the end we hope you will find authenticity. As actor and comedian Amy Poehler says, "You attract the right things when you have a sense of who you are."[1]

---

1. Amy Poehler's Smart Girls, *Letting Go: Ask Amy*, YouTube (Dec. 6, 2012), at 2:10, https://www.youtube.com/watch?v=4iCHN-PzUlU.

An Undeterred Dream: Five Tips from a Practical Dreamer on Managing Your Legal Career Paths

By Deborah Enix-Ross

Langston Hughes's poem, "Dreams," has influenced me for as long as I can remember. Perhaps the reason is Hughes's connection to Harlem, the New York City neighborhood where I was born and raised. Everywhere I turned, whether school, church, after-school activities, or social clubs, I saw and felt the spirit of the Harlem Renaissance[2] and the promise of what I could be, if only I had the courage to dream and the desire to achieve and believe in myself. Seemingly impossible dreams were a part of my family's ethos. I was almost 7 years old when Dr. Martin Luther King Jr. delivered his "I Have a Dream" speech.[3] His words carried the hopes and dreams of my parents (who were raised in the segregated South) that their daughter living "up North" could achieve what they were denied.

>
> "Hold fast to dreams, for if dreams die, life is a broken-winged bird that cannot fly."
> —Langston Hughes, "Dreams"

It's been a long journey from being a daydreaming 7-year-old to becoming President of the American Bar Association (ABA), the world's largest voluntary association of lawyers. Throughout my career and service to the Bar, I learned the following lessons, which I hope you find useful.

Embrace Who You Are

I always describe myself as "just a girl from Harlem" who hopefully made good. I am a wife, a mother, and a lawyer. I am also a loyal friend, a woman of faith, a woman of many interests, and someone who is always looking to contribute where I can with whatever skills I have.

---

2. *Harlem Renaissance*, History.com (Jan. 11, 2023), https://www.history.com/topics/roaring-twenties/harlem-renaissance (last visited Sept. 21, 2023).
3. Dr. Martin Luther King Jr., "I Have a Dream," (speech given during the March on Washington, Aug. 28, 1963).

My parents, like a lot of African Americans of their generation, were part of the Great Migration[4] from the South to the North, in their case South Carolina and Tennessee, because they believed they would find better opportunities in the North, perhaps for themselves, but more importantly for their children. They settled in New York, in Harlem, north of 125th Street. Harlem was essentially segregated when I grew up. It was an area the rest of the country feared and avoided. During my teen years, I witnessed the start of the devastation of the crack cocaine epidemic. Many of my classmates and my peers succumbed either to the lure of making fast money by selling drugs or the temporary relief of using drugs to escape. I did not. Why? My community told me that I could be anything I wanted to be. This gave me a sense of "yes." I could be a lawyer even though I did not see any lawyers around me. I knew I could be whoever I wanted to be because my parents, teachers, and faith leaders encouraged me. When I stepped out of that community and into a world in which I faced obstacles and at times outright hostility, I felt confident that I could do more than just endure. I felt full of hope and aspiration.

No, I do not have the traditional educational pedigree or experience of many in the legal profession. But no one else has my experiences either. I am grateful for the obstacles I faced early in life. They made me strong, determined, and self-reliant, and they brought me to where I am today.

It is important to embrace and value our differences.

Forge Your Own Path

To say I have not followed a traditional path in the law is an understatement. I began as a legal services attorney and went on to practice in a variety of settings, including as the American representative to the Paris-based International Chamber of Commerce (ICC) International Court of Arbitration, the World Intellectual Property Organization's Arbitration and Mediation Center in Geneva, Switzerland, Price Waterhouse, and my current firm, Debevoise & Plimpton.

---

4. *The Great Migration*, Brittanica.com (Sept. 8, 2023), https://www.britanica.com/event/Great-Migration (last visited Sept. 21, 2023).

One advantage of being a lawyer is that we have flexibility in choosing our practice settings and areas of focus. Although my career path may seem disparate, dispute resolution is the thread that runs throughout my career choices. I have always taken the long view of the possibilities of what my legal career could be. It took me 7 years to achieve my first job in international law. It was not easy for people of color to practice international law, and I was not at a big law firm. But I just kept pushing forward because I knew it was what I wanted to do. I knew that I had skills and talents that could be used in international arbitration. This should be a lesson for all of us who feel stuck or feel that we are moving at a slow pace. If you are lucky, your legal career will be a long one. Sometimes you have to take the road less traveled.

Where you are now does not dictate where you will be in the future.

Write Your Own Definition of Success

I had a nontraditional career path in part because I never let anyone define what positions I should or should not take. My guiding principles have been: what skills do I have to bring to the position, and how will I leave it better than I found it? As a lawyer, I consider my career successful because I have been able to have an impact. As ABA President, I am combining my dispute resolution experience with my interest in promoting civics, civility, and collaboration for the ABA's Cornerstones of Democracy initiative.

You are the only person who should determine what is a suitable position or career choice for you.

Find Your Community

Forty years ago, I graduated from law school and soon after attended my first ABA meeting, which was held in San Francisco. I spent my graduation money on ABA membership fees, the flight, accommodations, and meeting registration fees. Why? Because I wanted to be around the best, smartest leaders in the legal profession, and I thought they could only be found in the ABA. When I think about it now, I recognize I was so determined to be a part of this association and the legal profession that I went to a meeting alone at my own expense and just walked into a room and tried to figure it all out. Not knowing any other members, I made my way to events hosted by the International Law Section. That was my first home in the ABA.

At first, I was the youngest person at bar associations meetings, or I was the only woman, or I was the only person of color. Sometimes I was all three! But I persevered. The sense of community I enjoyed in Harlem stayed with me and later I found professional communities, including at bar associations.

It is in community that we can find guidance and solace.

Lift as You Climb

Madeleine Albright famously said, "There's a special place in Hell for women who don't help other women."

Throughout my career I have used my positions to support and promote women lawyers. I placed the first woman on the arbitration panel of the U.S. National Committee of the ICC International Court of Arbitration, was a founding member of ArbitralWomen, an international association dedicated to bringing together women international dispute resolution practitioners, and established the Women's Interest Network and Women's Interest Group in the ABA and International Bar Association, respectively.

"Lifting as you climb" also presents opportunities for lawyers to demonstrate and emphasize the importance of lifting civility in the profession. Civility and the rule of law are closely intertwined. Lawyers are guardians of the rule of law. It is imperative that lawyers appropriately embody civility in all we do, because civility inspires confidence in the rule of law. The perception of incivility between lawyers, and between lawyers and judges, is dangerous to democracy and the rule of law. The public will not trust the legal system if it does not believe that lawyers and judges are honest, ethical, and civil in their interactions.

Bar associations are uniquely positioned to emphasize relevant programming that demonstrates to the rest of the country, indeed the world, the way to engage in civil discourse. Bar associations are critical to defending democracy and the rule of law. As officers of the legal system, lawyers and judges play a special role in the preservation of a democratic society. When lawyers engage in challenges with respect for both sides, we instill public confidence in the justice system and the rule of law. That is how we lift as we climb.

Lifting as you climb means not only creating opportunities for other women and young lawyers in particular but also lifting the profession and in turn society.

I began with one Langston Hughes poem, and I'll close with another poem of his "Mother to Son."

> Well, son, I'll tell you:
> Life for me ain't been no crystal stair.
> It's had tacks in it,
> And splinters,
> And boards torn up,
> And places with no carpet on the floor—
> Bare.
> But all the time
> I'se been a-climbin' on,
> And reachin' landin's,
> And turnin' corners,
> And sometimes goin' in the dark
> Where there ain't been no light.
> So boy, don't you turn back.
> Don't you set down on the steps
> 'Cause you finds it's kinder hard.
> Don't you fall now—
> For I'se still goin', honey,
> I'se still climbin',
> And life for me ain't been no crystal stair.

Keep climbing, keep lifting, keep working hard, and hold fast to your dreams!

Deborah Enix-Ross

Career

Senior Advisor, International Dispute Resolution Group, Debevoise & Plimpton LLP

Education
- JD, University of Miami School of Law (1981)
- BA, Broadcast Journalism, University of Miami
- Diploma in Comparative Law, Parker School of Foreign and Comparative Law of Columbia University (1989)
- Certificate in International Law, London School of Economics (1979)

Best Advice

Embrace who you are, forge your own path, write your own definition of success, find your own community for guidance and solace, and lift up others as you climb to success.

Personal

Deborah Enix-Ross also served as chair of the ABA's policymaking House of Delegates and as chair of the ABA Center for Human Rights. As chair of the ABA International Law Section, she co-founded the Women's Interest Network and worked with the International Bar Association to create its Women's Interest Group. Deborah always describes herself as "just a girl from Harlem" who hopefully made good. She is a wife, mother, loyal friend, woman of faith, and someone who always looks to contribute where she can with whatever skills she has.

Be Authentic: Navigating Complex and (Sometimes) Paradoxical Identities

By Michal Rogson

I am an externally cis-gendered, internally genderqueer, feminist, lesbian, observant Jewish lawyer. Those who like categories can put me in a whole bunch! But this represents both an advantage and a challenge. In this highly divided and divisive world we live in, where so much of community is about identity politics and the resulting echo chambers, at least I have a plethora of options. I can connect to many different people on a wide variety of issues. But the challenge lies in synthesizing these identities, sewing the seams between the contradictory pieces of me. We like to talk about authenticity as if it's a linear, two-dimensional thing. But human beings are incorrigibly paradoxical.

I chose to be orthodox at the age of 15. I use the term *orthodox* to mean the Jewish community with an originalist approach to Jewish law. I'll be using the term *observant* (which is how I identify today) to mean committed to Jewish law without allegiance to any specific community. Although they were not orthodox, my parents sent me to orthodox Jewish day school and high school to make sure that I had a solid background in Hebrew language and Jewish cultural heritage. They were somewhat horrified when I decided to identify as orthodox.

Many of my early adult decisions were born out of that identification. I had skipped a grade, so I graduated high school a month after turning 17. I wanted to move to Israel immediately, but my parents insisted they would only support such a move after I finished college. So I crammed 4 years of study into 3, one of which was spent as a gap year in Israel. After graduating from UCLA with honors at the age of 20, I did what I had set out to do: I moved to Israel.

And this is where the second part of my formative identity began. I returned to the women's college I had attended in my gap year in Jerusalem to get my master's degree and met a disarmingly charming tomboy. This was the first time I had to synthesize contradictory authenticities. I was an orthodox Jew, but I also was clearly attracted to another woman. My first task was to identify what Jewish law had to say about this. Interestingly, this is where women's invisibility in Jewish law (because they are generally objects rather than subjects of the law) turned out to be a saving grace. There was some general censure of lesbian practice (expressed in an exhortation to men to keep their wives away from women "who are known to do this"), but there was no explicit prohibition. Of course, law and lived reality often diverge. So, while this alleviated my initial concern, it was meaningless in the greater communal context. Lesbianism was strictly anathema in the orthodox community, whatever the texts might say.

It took many years for me to even start to synthesize these two fundamental pieces of my identity. While attending and graduating from the law school at Hebrew University in Jerusalem, I continued to try to date men in the orthodox world, but it never worked out. Meanwhile, in something of a cliché, I discovered the indie-lesbian folk music scene and developed friendships with other queer women in online communities centered on that music. I even got myself a guitar and started writing and performing folk songs! So there I was, half orthodox, half lesbian, all lawyer (and some folksinger!). I knew who I was, but I had nowhere to *be* who I was. The orthodox world would never accept me as a lesbian. And the rest of the world would be (and is) challenging to navigate while maintaining my orthodox observance (i.e., keeping kosher and observing the Sabbath, when one cannot travel or use money). So, without fully understanding what I was looking for, but knowing I needed something different, I went in search of a place where I could be my authentic self. I moved to New York.

It was a difficult decision. I had sacrificed so much to move to Israel, and I had built a good life there. I had graduated from one of the top two law schools in the country, and as an English speaker I was in demand in the corporate legal world where the Israeli tech boom required legal support. In America, I was alone in a new state with a law degree from a university no one had ever heard of. But it's remarkable how motivating the need to find a community that will accept all of a person can be. I think I recognized even then that I would never be able to be wholly myself without community. I could not have articulated it then, but I knew what I needed—a place where I didn't have to dissemble or put energy into worrying about what people would think, where I could see myself reflected and validated in others. And let me say—once one finds that place, it's very difficult to accept anything less than that ever again. It's like a foam mattress. Once a person takes it out of the box, it is never getting put back in.

I found an apartment in New York and enrolled in the LLM program at Benjamin N. Cardozo School of Law. I simultaneously enrolled in a religious program that was providing ordination-equivalent education to women. I synthesized these two areas of study and mixed in my LGBT focus in my Master's thesis titled "When the Shoe Doesn't Fit: The Gendering of Individuals with Ambiguous Genitalia in Jewish Law." I was living my authentic life, trying to synthesize all my pieces, but I still didn't have a lesbian community until a chance meeting led me to an unexpected resource.

I had just finished shopping at Fairway when I bumped into someone who stopped and said, "Wait, Michal?" It was a woman I had met several years prior in Israel. We had bonded but had not kept in touch. We chatted briefly and then she asked me, "So, are you going to Sheitelstock?" I looked at her dumbly. What was a Sheitelstock? For reference, the word "sheitel" means "wig" in Yiddish. Loosely translated, "Sheitelstock" was a play on "Wigstock." She was shocked that I hadn't heard of it and insisted that I attend with her. She said it was a dance hosted by a Jewish orthodox lesbian organization for the holiday of Purim. She had me at the words "Jewish orthodox lesbian organization." That existed? It did, and boy was it eye-opening! The first thing I saw as I walked in was a woman I had known in high school, taking tickets at the front table with her partner. Inside, I bumped into another woman I had known in high school, dancing with her girlfriend. Women and some men, many of whom came from orthodox Jewish backgrounds, gathering in honor of the Jewish holiday of Purim and dancing together. I was no longer alone.

I don't know if finding community does the same thing for everyone. But I can tell what it did for me. It helped me face my identity, my authentic self, and accept it. It gave me the confidence in my own identity to give others in my life the opportunity to accept that authentic self. I came out to my roommates and to old friends from high school. I lost some people along the way, which was sad. People who were secretly uncomfortable drifted off. Most people were surprisingly supportive. It gave me the courage to own my authenticity and make autonomous choices. It even gave me the courage to start dating—openly. Which of course posed another problem.

I had obtained a job with a small midtown firm owned by an orthodox male lawyer. He hired from within the orthodox community, so the bulk of the attorneys were orthodox men. For a time, I was the only female lawyer at the firm. By then I had started dating my girlfriend (now my spouse), and it was difficult trying to hide that. But I knew the game; I had played it in Jerusalem. There was no way to come out in that environment; it simply would not be accepted, so I had to dissemble. The experience was made easier by the fact that my girlfriend's name is gender-neutral. Being able to refer to her by name eased the burden of the "Pronoun Game" a bit. For those who aren't familiar with the term, the *Pronoun Game* is what LGBTQIA+ folk do when they don't want to out themselves by using pronouns when referring to their partners. It's not easy to keep pronouns out of sentences (try it!), and it gets fishy if a person uses proper names too much. So there are calculations of what can or cannot be said, and how to say it. It's utterly exhausting.

And then one Saturday night my girlfriend and I were on a subway when we found ourselves face to face with one of the orthodox male lawyers from my office. I thought, "crap, the jig is up." My girlfriend had borrowed my spandex tank top to wear under her men's button-down shirt, which was hanging open, and there could really be no doubt whatsoever about her sex. That is, if one looked past her general masculine presentation. I will never know whether he did, or did not, look past her masculine presentation. He chatted with us amiably until he got off and then told everyone at work that he'd met my boyfriend that weekend. This lawyer was a bit absent-minded and may well have simply not "seen." Or he saw and understood immediately what I was hiding and supported me. I will never know. But what I did know was that I did not want to continue having to live a bifurcated life, having to hide a fundamental part of myself for a significant part of each day or worry about the consequences of discovery. So I began to look for a new job.

When I found one, the very first thing I did was use a pronoun. I used pronouns as often as possible, just to make sure there was no confusion. I was pronoun-happy—literally! It was like ripping off a bandage—I was nervous, but boy, did it feel good not to have to hide or dissemble. I promised myself I would never do it again, and I never have. Sort of.

Because I've learned that little in life is black and white. There are LGBTQIA+ folks who militantly believe that one needs to be out to everybody all the time. I respect them and recognize that this is what their authenticity demands. I have a different perspective, probably born out of my relationship with my mother. My mother is a child of holocaust survivors and has two traits that I've discovered are fairly common among that group: paranoia and negativity. Every time I would tell her about something that happened, she'd ask why I hadn't done any number of things differently that might have yielded better results. These responses made me feel bad, and that wasn't good for me or for our relationship. And then I realized that I did *not* need to be radically honest with my mother. She did *not* need to know everything. Am I less authentic with her simply because I don't share everything?

I face that same question in my current position, where I am responsible for "rainmaking" from within a limited group of clients. Cultivating relationships within a finite group can be challenging when some members of the group are patently uncomfortable with (or downright disapproving of) queer orientations. Depending on people's internalized biases, disclosing sexual orientation can alter their perceptions entirely, and then, as my experience has shown, they actively depart or quietly slip away. But as a relationship builder for my company, I owe a duty to my company to retain and cultivate such clients. Furthermore, my queerness wouldn't impact the quality of service they're receiving, so why should I create an opportunity for it to be factored in? It's interesting, because I can actually connect to many of the people for whom my queerness would be an issue using the other fundamental piece of my identity—my religion. I've had many fascinating discussions on value systems and ethics with people that I choose not to come out to. Again, the question is: does this make me less than authentic?

Obviously I would argue that it does not. I don't expect every woman with a breast cancer diagnosis to throw that into a conversation, no matter how central to their lives that experience may have become. I similarly do not expect pansexuals or swingers to throw that reference into a conversation. Why are their sexual proclivities any of my business, even if it is a core piece of their identity? I don't think authenticity needs to be radical in order to have integrity. Each of us is multifaceted. Like jewels, we show different sides of ourselves to others all the time. The light may not always bounce off all the facets at once, and that's perfectly natural. Though when it does, it is glorious.

The practice I've developed with clients is therefore to wait until the context or nature of the relationship creates an opportunity to come out to them and suggests that it would not harm the relationship. Admittedly, this approach has its drawbacks. I have one client with whom I've developed a long-distance friendship over the last decade. He is a devout Christian and some of his comments over the years lead me to believe that my coming out to him would subtly, but negatively, affect our friendship, so I have chosen not to. Does this make the friendship inauthentic, based on a lie? Only if the friendship is premised on my assumed heterosexuality. I would like to believe it's premised on our affinity and interest in everything from religion to economics to home remodeling. I have given him my authentic self. I just haven't given him *all* of it. If I can do that with my mother, is it any less authentic in a work environment?

So what does it mean to live authentically? Ultimately, I think it's about self-awareness and self-acceptance. In my experience, finding a community where a person sees the whole self reflected and validated is a critical tool for reaching self-acceptance, but I'm sure others have their own paths to that space. It's only from that space of self-awareness and acceptance of all the (sometimes contradictory) pieces of oneself that each can then engage with the world authentically.

But does someone have to bring the "authentic" self to the workplace, as so many articles suggest? Well, yes and no. I do not believe that a person needs to engage in radical candor in the workplace or anywhere else. Each person should absolutely bring their authentic self to the workplace. But it is entirely up to every individual to decide which facets the person chooses to shine the light on. If I was going to promote "radical" anything, it might be radical acceptance. I think about the young genderqueer folk today who wake up one morning feeling masculine and the next feminine. They present us with their different authentic selves each day and highlight the basic truth—that our "selves" are not linear. We don't always make sense. Many of us spend thousands of dollars a year on therapy trying to smooth out the seams of our own contradictions. Maybe the best thing we can do for authenticity is to learn how to simply accept our own contradictions and then accept each other's. If we can do that, maybe we can create spaces that allow people to bring more of their facets everywhere they go. Including at work.

Michal Rogson

Career

Vice President of Commercial Surety, Court Bond Specialist, Skyward Specialty Insurance

Education
- LLM, Advanced Legal Studies, Cardozo School of Law (2001)
- Talmud, Drisha (2001)
- JD, The Hebrew University of Jerusalem (1999)
- BA, English Literature, University of California, Los Angeles (1994)

Best Advice

In the film *The Sound of Music*, there's a moment where Maria says, "whenever God closes a door, somewhere he opens a window." Similarly, a wise man once taught me that when a river changes course, it diverts its original flow to a new course, thereby reducing what it contributes to the original course. Change is not easy; it can feel restricting or even blocking. But a boulder in the middle of the river can create something new. It's valuable to remember that there are always other options, different ways of looking at the same thing. Obstacles may be opportunities in disguise.

Personal

Michal Rogson is current co-chair of The Woman Advocate Committee of the ABA's Litigation Section and past co-chair of the LGBT Law and Litigator Committee. She has an LLM, with a twofold focus on gender theory and alternative dispute resolution. After practicing as a corporate and insurance plaintiff and defense litigator, she went in-house with a specialty surety insurer. She is an expert on appeal bonds, litigation bonds, and fiduciary bonds, lecturing often, authoring various articles and guides on the subject, and serving as subject matter expert. Her hobbies include singing, dancing, acting, and writing Jewish-themed spoofs of popular music and making videos of them, including a guide to Hannukah sung to the tune of "Despacito" (look up "Nes Asita") and the Purim story set to the musical *Hamilton* ("Hamalkah"). Her favorite part of legal conferences is finding other lawyers who can sing and rap so they can get up in their suits and surprise the unsuspecting local karaoke crowds.

Be Resilient: Lessons from Reviving My Family's Business

By Stephanie Stuckey

"You've never even run a lemonade stand. What makes you think you can run our family's business?"

My father's words hung thick in the air like a *New Yorker* cartoon caption. Only I didn't have a witty reply like the ones that graced the magazine's pages. Emptiness filled the room.

He was right. I hadn't run a lemonade stand. Or a business. I thought about my years working as a public defender. My clients were as tough as their chances of winning. *Facts are facts. You can't change them.* But you *can* change how you present them. That's the secret that I had learned from hours of watching trials during my lunch breaks. I had been a legal groupie, observing skillful courtroom theatrics whenever a big case was on the docket.

My father's question sat there, demanding an answer. I thought of those cases on my lunch breaks 25 years ago. *Keep your emotions in check and speak slowly. Words have the power to convict or acquit. And when the judge asks you a tough question, pause.* The pause is uncomfortable, but it's also an incredible show of control. Like, *I've got this. I'm just waiting for my moment.*

I paused. Then, voice steady, I knew what to say. "Maybe I've never run a lemonade stand. But I can run Stuckey's."

I thought of my grandfather, W. S. Stuckey Sr., who founded the business in 1937. He grew it from a roadside pecan stand to a nationwide chain of stores that became a staple of roadtripping families. At our peak in the 1970s, we had over 350 stores in 40 states along every major highway in the country.

My grandfather had wanted to be an attorney. He looked to education as his one-way ticket to a better life. He was in his third year of law school at the University of Georgia when cotton hit bottom in 1931, and he was summoned home to help save the family farm.

It was the Great Depression. Jobs were scarce, but pecans were plentiful. It was a bumper crop year, so he borrowed $35 from his grandmother, retrofitted an old Ford Model T to haul pecans, and started selling them off Route 23 in Eastman, Georgia. From those humble beginnings, my grandfather created the first roadside retail chain that became synonymous with the Great American Road Trip.

But he'd sold the company in 1964, and it was sadly trashed by decades of outside corporate owners who didn't get our quirky Southern brand, known for pecan log rolls, kitschy souvenirs, and colorful billboards urging motorists to "pull over here."

After the sale, there were decades of outside owners of Stuckey's. These were large corporations that were more focused on the bottom line than on continuing the legacy my grandfather had built. He wasn't just interested in roadside stores that offered gas, quick snacks, and souvenirs. My grandfather wanted to celebrate the joy of taking a road trip and exploring America. The sense of community he'd built was lost over the years.

In 1985, my father had the unexpected opportunity to buy Stuckey's. At that point, the number of stores had dwindled from 368 to 100. The franchisees were unhappy with how the company had been managed and were threatening litigation. This was too much aggravation for the owners to manage, and they approached my dad about taking what was left of Stuckey's. Although preoccupied with his other business ventures at the time, my father took on the challenge of reviving the family business. His other business interests—like running Dairy Queen franchises—were more profitable. But he managed to keep the Stuckey's brand alive by pairing it with his Dairy Queen locations. Decades later, when he and his business partners retired, they left Stuckey's—with a mere 65 franchised locations—to be managed by only a handful of remaining employees. After a decade of dwindling resources, the company was six figures in debt and at risk of bankruptcy.

That 80-plus-year history is what led my father to lecture me, at age 53, about my lack of qualifications to run a lemonade stand—much less a failing business venture.

But I thought of my grandfather on that lonely stretch of rural road during the Great Depression. He was a hustler with a chip on his shoulder. And that's what it takes for you to make it—people telling you that you can't do it—especially if it's the people closest to you. Like my grandfather, I had something to prove. And that was proving that his legacy wasn't going to be shuttered stores on the side of the interstate, fading memories of family vacations long past.

I believe that comebacks are possible, that we have the power to change our story, and that we can pivot at any age. Even at the age of 53; actually, especially at the age of 53.

I left a career as an environmental attorney and advocate to become CEO of Stuckey's with zero experience running a company. I had to learn how to read a balance sheet, manage inventory, source merchandise, and a myriad of other skills needed to successfully turn a venture around.

I purchased Stuckey's in November of 2019. We were six figures in debt, with our only assets being a rented warehouse full of inventory, some of which hadn't turned in a decade. We didn't own or operate any of the 68 franchised locations still standing, and our franchise agreements were woefully out of date and out of compliance with the law. And we had less than 10 employees.

Yet I sank my life's savings into this business venture that two financial advisors had warned me against purchasing. Instead, I listened to the third advisor who cautioned that it was risky but worth it. Like me, he recognized what wasn't on the balance sheets. And that was the value of the brand. Not just the trademark, but decades of fond memories that people had from stopping at Stuckey's and experiencing the fun of taking a road trip. That was worth more than any asking price.

Despite all the challenges, within 2 years, we were able to restore Stuckey's to profitability, closing out 2021 with almost $13 million in gross sales and $2.5 million net. While we still have a long way to go to revive the company, we're trending in the right direction and continuing to gain momentum.

I'm often asked the secret to our comeback success, and it can be summed up in one word: resiliency. Most folks don't fully understand that word. They think of it as the ability to bounce back, but that's only half of the equation. The other half is the ability to bounce back *better*. To be truly resilient, a person needs to learn from the challenges and become stronger as a result.

Here is a real-life example from my grandfather. When he was just getting the business underway during the 1940s, he had several locations and was doing well financially. Then World War II hit, and gas was rationed, forcing him to shut down his stores. And he couldn't sell his candy either, as sugar was also in short supply. To survive, my grandfather had to make a 180-degree pivot. He changed his business model to manufacturing. That enabled him to get sugar from the U.S. government, provided he made candy for the troops. So, he transitioned from making candy onsite at his stores and serving food directly to customers to mass production for mess kits going to the front lines. He had to learn about food packaging and preservation. These skills enabled him to create a new line of business. When the war ended, his factory made candy boxes for department store gift sections, for example for Rich's in Atlanta. And, thankfully, gas was no longer rationed, so he reopened his stores and started up his retail operations again.

The lesson I took from my grandfather was to build back stronger in tough times. He embraced the change and used it as an opportunity to expand into manufacturing. That enabled him to rapidly scale his stores when the war ended. Those early years for Stuckey's were the very model of resilience.

I like to say that I'm rebuilding my family's brand by learning from the past, not living in it. With so much rich history, these lessons help inform my strategy, which is centered on the concept of being resilient.

Like my grandfather, when I bought Stuckey's in 2019, I had to make a hard assessment of where there were opportunities to drive revenue, despite the challenges I was facing. He faced the rationing and supply chain issues of War World II. I faced similar constraints caused by the COVID-19 pandemic lockdown. I realized that the path to profitability was in manufacturing. For over 50 years—since my grandfather sold the company—Stuckey's had been outsourcing our branded products to third-party manufacturers. Not only were we dealing with a high-margin structure, but the quality had suffered. The nougat in our famous pecan log rolls wasn't as light, the pecans not as fresh, the flavorings artificial. We needed to take back that aspect of the business to deal with the supply chain issues caused by COVID-19 and to restore the reputation of our brand.

Thanks to favorable government loans for small businesses in rural communities, we secured financing to purchase a pecan shelling and candy plant outside of Augusta, Georgia. That has made all the difference. We've been able to scale from a couple hundred retailers selling Stuckey's pecan snacks and candies to almost 5,000 stores.

This turnaround hasn't been without its pain points. Emotionally, I've always been attached to the brick-and-mortar stores that our family operated for decades and that established Stuckey's as a national brand. But that was in our past. I had to embrace the present reality if I was going to save Stuckey's. Taking a hard assessment of our finances, plus learning not only to accept, but embrace, change was the most critical lesson I learned.

This book is focused on attorneys, so I want to stress how important my legal training has been to my professional success. Starting my career as a trial lawyer representing indigent defendants taught me how to stand up for tough causes and persuade others. Developing a case for trial is like the process of raising funds for a business. You must break down the facts, apply the relevant law or financial principles, and drive that to a persuasive conclusion. Law school engrained in me the importance of paying attention to the facts and coming up with hypotheticals of what could go wrong. Preparing—and overpreparing—are the hallmarks of a good advocate. Those of us who've had to present hard cases before a jury know that firsthand.

My journey is far from over. It is a continuing evolution, with other pivots no doubt in my future. I hope someday to be able to revive a handful of Stuckey's stores that will celebrate the fun of the road trip and pay homage to my grandfather's legacy. But, for now, I'm slowly reviving the family business, one pecan log roll at a time.

In closing, I'd like to share a few points that have been helpful to me and will hopefully be of value to you.

Know the Purpose

Have a sense of purpose. When challenging times hit, being grounded in a strong faith in why a person is doing what that person is doing is essential. That purpose can't be simply to make money; it must be bigger than that to have lasting value. For Stuckey's, we're not just selling pecan snacks and candies, we're celebrating the fun and adventure of exploring America by car. We're all about reviving the road trip and connecting people with places to create lasting memories. That's how a brand has sticking power. And that's how people survive tough times.

Be Okay with Rejection

If someone is afraid of getting a "no," that person will never take the risks needed to succeed. I often think of a "no" as a "not now" and focus on how I can tweak my delivery, pricing, product quality, and the like, to land a deal. Shifting the response to rejection as a learning experience yields a stronger and more resilient result.

Build a Balanced Team

It's important to be surrounded not just with people who complement individual skillsets, but also with those who complement emotionally as well. A more high-strung and energetic person needs a few laid-back, chill folks in the room to provide balance. Warren Buffett said in an interview that one of the key factors he looks at when acquiring a new company is the emotional intelligence of its leadership team. That can't be overstated enough. People who are able to withstand tough times on an even keel are the people who are wanted for any team.

Know You're Not Alone

The entrepreneurial journey is about being alone together. Strong networks exist that support female entrepreneurs. So, don't be shy about asking for support. And when you are successful, be sure to give back to young women starting out in their careers. We need to form a pipeline for more women heading up businesses and fulfilling their entrepreneurial dreams.

I'll close by saying that my father telling me I couldn't run a lemonade stand was a low point for me. But it was also the moment I realized that I had the passion and drive to be successful. I'm now grateful for my father's tough love, as these are the moments that define us. Use the tough times for what they're intended to be: opportunities to bounce back stronger and be resilient. Know that there are many women out there rooting for others to succeed.

Stephanie Stuckey

Career
Chair, Stuckey's Corporation

Education
- JD, *cum laude*, University of Georgia School of Law (1992)
- BA, French, The University of Georgia (1989)
- French, Vanderbilt University (Freshman-Junior Class)

Best Advice
You are never too old to reinvent yourself.

Personal
Stephanie Stuckey is CEO of Stuckey's, known for generations as a highway oasis serving up pecan log rolls and kitschy souvenirs. Founded in 1937 by her grandfather, W. S. Stuckey Sr. in Eastman, Georgia, Stuckey's grew into over 350 stores nationwide by its peak in the 1970s. The company was sold in 1964 and sadly declined for decades under a series of corporate owners. Fortunately, Stuckey's returned to the family in 1985 under the leadership of W. S. Bill Stuckey Jr. and is now being continued with Bill's daughter, Stephanie.

The company acquired a pecan shelling and candy plant in Wrens, Georgia, in January 2021 and has been scaling production of the Stuckey's branded snacks and sweets, including the iconic pecan log roll, to be sold in almost 5,000 retail stores nationwide. Stuckey's also operates a distribution center in Eastman, a fundraising business, a corporate gift program, and an online store.

Stephanie received both her undergraduate and law degrees from the University of Georgia. She worked as a trial lawyer, was elected to seven terms as a state representative, ran an environmental law firm, served as Director of Sustainability for Atlanta, and taught as an Adjunct Professor at the University of Georgia School of Law. Stephanie purchased Stuckey's in November of 2019 and assumed the role of CEO. Stephanie's achievements include being named one of the Most Admired CEOs of 2022 by the *Atlanta Business Chronicle*, 100 Most Influential Georgians by *Georgia Trend* Magazine, and a graduate of Leadership Atlanta. She serves on the corporate board for Bealls, a Florida-based retailer with more than 550 stores.

The Stuckey's story has been featured recently in *The New York Times* Sunday Business Section, *The Today Show*, and *The Washington Post*.

When she's not running Stuckey's, Stephanie enjoys road tripping with her two kids, Robert and Beverly, and pulling over at every boiled peanut stand and the World's Largest Ball of Twine.

For More Information

https://www.linkedin.com/in/stephaniestuckey
Instagram & Twitter @stuckeystop
sstuckey@stuckeys.com

Maintain Perspective When All Is Not Well

By Heather Torres

It is my family—in its broadest definition—that enables me to maintain perspective and stay grounded. The opening line of my law school personal statement was, "My family is my life's passion." It was a direct, clear, and foundational start to an essay that was meant to give the reader a sense of who I am and how I could contribute to law school campuses and the legal profession. My mentors from the Graduate Horizons program, an intensive graduate school preparation program for American Indian, Alaska Native, and Native Hawaiian students,[5] instructed me to make a short but impactful opening statement that would immediately draw the admissions team's attention amid reading a sea of highly competitive applications. I am not sure how well it worked, as I was on a waitlist for my top choice law school and was admitted just a week and a half before orientation (which was likely due to factors such as my less than stellar Law School Admission Test [LSAT] score), but I come back to the personal statement now as I reflect on the topic "Maintaining Perspective" and consider how my family support system has been able to keep me in check and on track as I pursue and grow in my career and personal life.

In my statement, I expanded on my definition of family. For me, family is broader than blood or any concept of the nuclear family, and it includes relationships with those with whom I worked, who lived in the same community as I did, and who were my close friends. Reflecting on the definition, I realize the source of that understanding came from my parents. Growing up, they told me and my younger sister, Christina, that we were to put "family first." That meant that despite being studious, year-round competitive athletes, we showed up to every family gathering, big or small; we volunteered our time at local community organizations and the community center, Lytle Creek, in downtown San Bernardino, California, where my parents met, where I took my first steps, and where my mom spent the majority of her professional career; and we joined my parents as they engaged in the caretaking of their parents, siblings, and friends. They modeled for us how to be caretakers, good friends, coaches, and community leaders.

---

5. Visit the Graduate Horizons website at https://graduatehorizons.org.

My understanding of family played a huge part in my ability to persevere through law school and in how I continue to look at my career. For example, when I started law school, since I had come off the waitlist just a little over a week before orientation, I had no place to stay; I did not have books; and I was not as financially prepared as I hoped; but I could not pass up the opportunity to go to my top choice school. I started as one of six Native American students in my year, and the first semester humbled me quickly—very quickly. I was able to maintain perspective because, thankfully, I still had friends in Los Angeles, so I was able to crash on their couches during my first weeks of law school. They were a small comfort as I was thrown into an environment that was meant to chew me up and spit me back out.

By October, I really hit my breaking point. I would vent mostly to my mom about all the challenges I faced, how oppressive the law school environment was, and how maybe I was not cut out for a legal career after all. And just as swiftly as law school humbled me, my mom quickly and formidably realigned me. She reminded me that I wanted to be a lawyer not just for myself, but so that I could be in a better position to advocate for others. She reminded me that I was privileged, but, more importantly, that I was deserving of my place there. She reminded me about who I was and where I came from—a tough girl from the Inland Empire, a descendant of boarding school survivors, a big sister, and the first in my family to pursue a law degree. She gave me perspective. She renewed my strength to build my family there at the law school—to make new friends, to engage with my professors, and to find a way to be of service. That is just what I did.

From October on, I did what I needed to do to survive and ultimately thrive in that environment. I set up my own definitions and goals for success based on my perspective, disregarding what the school had in mind or general notions of what a "good law student" was supposed to be. I took advantage of every opportunity to become a better advocate, particularly of tribal sovereignty. I interned with the Senate Committee on Indian Affairs, spent a summer at a Southern California law firm in its Indian Law practice group, completed an externship with the Indian Child Welfare Act court in Los Angeles, and volunteered my time in clinics focusing on tribal and education rights. I built my family at the law school through my involvement in the Native American Law Students Association, La Raza, and the Critical Race Studies program, and even the broader campus community through the Graduate Student Resource Center. I never pushed myself to engage in unhealthy behaviors to make the grade. I asked the dumb questions and I answered honestly in class. I was purposeful in choosing my professors and courses. I made it through law school, completed bar prep (twice), and launched a full-time legal career in 2019.

I entered law school wanting to be an academic. I was not even sure I wanted to take the bar exam. In my personal statement, I wrote that I saw myself as a professor, a dream highly influenced by my career in higher education before law school. However, after my various work experiences throughout law school, I found myself thinking about a new direction. I wanted my license and I wanted to do policy work. Specifically, I wanted to work with tribes or tribal organizations that would help defend, exercise, and strengthen tribal sovereignty. I wanted to help tribes do the internal work needed to create systems of governance and care that reflected their tribal values and worldviews. Is there an organization that does that work? Yes, and it happened to be right there in my community in Los Angeles. It was a familiar place. I had interned there as an undergraduate, and UCLA law alumni worked there at the time. It is where I work now, the Tribal Law and Policy Institute (TLPI).

After law school, I was awarded a fellowship at TLPI, during which I researched and contributed to publications and other materials used for training and technical assistance provided to tribes across the country. TLPI supported my studying for the February bar after I found out I did not pass the July exam. Due to timing and other circumstances, an offer of employment may not have been possible at the end of my fellowship. I also questioned whether I could positively contribute to the organization without my bar license. This questioning was mostly all in my head, of course. TLPI has attorneys on staff, but a majority of the staff are non-lawyers skilled in the fields of public policy, victim advocacy, juvenile justice, and child welfare. More importantly though, I possessed skills outside of the legal acumen allegedly measured by the bar exam. I learned from thought leaders in federal Indian law and critical race theory during law school. I was a strong researcher and a solid team player. I could build good relationships with "clients" and partners. There was also a values match with TLPI: its philosophies powerfully matched my own and aligned with the work I wanted to pursue.

Having to take the bar exam a second time was difficult. I graduated from a top law school and I took a bar prep course. I thought I did all the things students were supposed to do to prepare, but it was not enough. Frankly, I did not do everything *I* needed to do to learn the material. I needed more time. I needed more practice. To say I was fatigued and traumatized from law school is an understatement. I should have taken time off to start to heal after graduation. I needed time to re-center and reconnect with myself. I highly encourage taking that time to heal when you are pushing through a tough situation, personally or professionally. We can get so caught up in surviving or moving on to the next benchmark that we forget to care for ourselves. We can lose sight of our value.

Following the fellowship with TLPI and post-February bar, I returned to higher education in an administrator-level position. I worked at the University of Redlands as Director of Native Student Programs (NSP), a program I founded as a coordinator prior to law school. I felt ready to put my new advocacy skills to work and continue to build NSP and serve the local Tribes and urban communities in Southern California. I loved my work in higher education. I thrived in an environment where I got to work with students and their families, with tribal leaders and education programs, and with other student services professionals. I planned to be with NSP for a few years to solidify the program within the institution and to grow its impact in the Southern California Native community. TLPI reentered the picture with other plans, giving me an opportunity to start my legal career.

An opportunity to join TLPI staff as a Tribal Justice Specialist came to me less than a year into my time at Redlands. With the bar under my belt, I was prepared to heal from my law school experience and contribute again to higher education. I thought my new path was to return to an old path with new skills. I spent a lot of time reflecting on the opportunity. I questioned whether I was "ready" and if I would be abandoning a program that I had built. My concerns were primarily external. Would I be doing a disservice to NSP? To the students? I reached out to my parents and sister and to my peers in both higher education and law for their guidance. Resoundingly, their advice was to use my gut and to contend with harmful thoughts in my head that were rooted in fear or doubt. They asked me how I felt when I was first approached about the position. Was I excited, nervous, or disinterested? Why? They challenged me to do deeper heartwork and to sit with those feelings. Did this opportunity align with my values and where I saw myself in the future? Those questions were critical in leading me to the choice of returning to TLPI as full-time staff and starting my legal career. Fortunately, my commitment to and care for NSP was recognized by others and I was asked to serve on the advisory committee for NSP as a representative of the university's tribal partner, the San Manuel Band of Mission Indians, after I left the Director position. I still serve on the committee today and have sustained relationships with my relatives in Native higher education. I have found that others pick up on genuine investment and care, perhaps leading to unexpected activities, interests, and friendships.

In 2019, I started my first full-time job as an attorney, working for a Native-operated nonprofit led by its Executive Director and co-founder who had built an extensive network over decades of work in Indian country and in professional spaces like the American Bar Association (ABA) and the National Native American Bar Association (NNABA). I felt honored to be joining the staff. The work environment was (and still is) invigorating and exciting. Professional development opportunities like leadership opportunities within the ABA and NNABA were encouraged. I went from working for a predominantly white institution to a Native-centered organization. I felt that difference. I joined in an agile position, one that could float across TLPI's various projects with a focus on managing some subawards and contract work. This allowed me to dive in on specific projects, which kept me on my toes and pushed me to be comfortable with adapting quickly. By the end of my first year (and at the start of a global pandemic), I was promoted to Program Director and part of the organization's management team. To say I have learned a lot about nonprofit management and organizational leadership during the last 2 years is an understatement.

Rereading my law school personal statement, I see it has some core truths that show who I am. That makes me think that I did hit the mark my mentors were pushing me to meet. I value my relationships and feel a responsibility—not in a burdensome way—to care for everyone with whom I am in a relationship. I wrote in my introductory paragraph, "With that [familial] bond comes a responsibility to represent my relatives and protect their future endeavors. My mission is to be a strong, community-grounded Native American advocate, making my family proud in all I do because I am a reflection of them." That is still my mission. I can return to this statement to ground myself and maintain perspective when I have to make a tough decision, when I am not doing my best at work, when I am struggling, when I am volunteering my time, when I am thriving, and when I take some time to reflect. I encourage creating or thinking about a personal mission statement. Has it changed or should it change since first entering the profession? Are there core values that have been relied on to maintain perspective to get to today's place and tomorrow's goal? Are there people or places that have had a great impact and influence?

I hope sharing my journey resonates with women entering the profession. It has been 4 years since I passed the California bar exam and I feel fortunate to have my family in this work, particularly of Native attorneys. I am still healing, still growing. The process is a life-long one.

As we continue to see women rise as leaders in all sectors, not just law, I am excited for us to care for one another and to offer creative and loving solutions to challenges facing our society. If someone ever feels like their self or purpose in this work is being lost, I humbly offer the following tips to help maintain perspective:

- Identify the people and places that have shaped you. They (or their cherished characteristics) can be grounding in moments of uncertainty.
- Cultivate a core support network that can be trusted with goals and feelings. Emotions are just as powerful as, if not more powerful than, ambition.
- Conduct a self-inventory of skills and values periodically, particularly in moments of doubt or uncertainty.
- Be your own barometer. Define success in context. If that means engaging in interests or activities outside the profession, do just that.
- Learn to trust in self and intuition. Be open to opportunities that might not have been envisioned.
- Grow family, and relatives, in this work.

"Once you know who you are and where you come from, you gain a sense of belonging. Your sense of belonging brings you to your sense of responsibility, and when you have taken care of that, your sense of peace."

—ELLA MULFORD (DINÉ), as quoted by Wilma Mankiller in *Every Day Is a Good Day: Reflections by Contemporary Indigenous Women.*

Heather Torres

Career

Program Director, Tribal Law and Policy Institute

Education

- JD, Critical Race Studies Specialization, University of California, Los Angeles—School of Law (2017)
- MA, Collaborative Educational Leadership, Fielding Graduate University (2014)
- BA, *cum laude*, English, American Indian Studies, University of California, Los Angeles (2011)

Best Advice

Obstacles will come, but there is always a path through or around them.

Personal

Heather Torres (she/her) is a former board member of the National Native American Bar Association and volunteers her time to other organizations, including as a Trustee for an up-and-coming Tribal College in Southern California, California Indian Nations College. Heather also regularly speaks with local youth and community organizations to share her personal and education journey. In her down time, she enjoys watching reality TV and sports, singing karaoke with friends, and playing board games.

For More Information

Heathertorres.esq@gmail.com

The Best Advice I Didn't Take: Lessons in Getting Involved Outside of the Office

By Katie Larkin-Wong

I was standing at a bus stop on Van Ness Avenue in San Francisco, headed home after the post-3L ritual the summer after graduation—a bar prep class. I called my mom, as I often did during those rides home.

"Hey Mom, you won't believe the email I just got. They are asking me if I would consider being President of Ms. JD."

Mom knew that throughout law school I had been active in Ms. JD, an online community for law students and early-career women lawyers. After participating in nearly every program Ms. JD offered, earlier that Spring they had asked me to join the board. I had fallen over myself, so excited that the organization thought that I could contribute more! I had only been on the Board a few months when they asked me to consider taking on the Presidency. It was incredibly flattering that the Board put its trust in me, but I wasn't sure that it was the right time to take on what was potentially a very big responsibility.

"Wow, honey, that's so exciting!" came her first response. "How are you feeling about it?"

"I don't know. Honored, obviously, but I guess I'm a bit worried that I shouldn't take on something that could be very time consuming before I start my job." I was slated to be a first-year associate at a big firm in October 2011. And even before starting, I didn't feel I had any career security because I had just watched the classes above me have their offers rescinded and delayed. We talked for a while about why I was excited about the role, about what it would mean to be able to contribute to advancing women in the profession through the organization, and about my concerns about taking it on as I was starting the infamous "Big Law" job.

Although my mom was a lawyer, she had never worked in Big Law. She came to law later in life—I had flown back from my sophomore year of college to see her sworn into the Montana State Bar. She had practiced as a law clerk and then as a State Appellate Defender. What she knew of Big Law was based on my summer experience and what she'd read. I distinctly remember my call to her before summer recruiting started when she told me, "Honey, I can't help you here anymore. I just don't know."

As a result, she tended to be cautious in giving me advice; but this time was a rare exception. After we'd talked for a while, she said, "I don't know, Katie, you're going to be adjusting to a lot. New city, new job, a lot of new responsibilities. I'm not sure now is the right time for you to take on a leadership role like this."

When my mom told this story, she would laugh and say that she should have known that was the moment I would take the opportunity. "Telling her she can't do something is the surest way to ensure that Katie does it" is something she used to say frequently. But she would also admit that this was her best-intentioned advice that she was glad I never took. Being part of Ms. JD opened up an entirely different part of the legal profession for me and taught me the value of getting involved outside of work.

While this vignette is the first one that comes to mind when I think of getting involved outside of the office, it is not the last. Over the next 5 years that I served as President of Ms. JD, I forged new relationships with women outside of the organization who would serve as lifelong mentors, and others who served with me who remain longtime friends. I also learned a lot that ultimately paid dividends as I advanced in my career at the law firm. I've gone on to seek out other opportunities outside of the office, serving on other nonprofit boards, seeking other leadership positions within the ABA, and sometimes just taking a few hours off in the morning to serve breakfast at the soup kitchen downtown. If I were to bottle those vignettes and opportunities into the dividends that involvement outside the office will pay, I would offer these:

Reground to the World Outside of Law

I still remember being incredibly stressed the morning a friend asked me to join her for her annual birthday tradition—serving breakfast at Glide, a soup kitchen in the Tenderloin district of San Francisco. As I rushed to the soup kitchen that morning, I was occupied by concerns that I might miss an important email or call while serving meals to San Francisco's homeless community. How stupid that concern seemed an hour later as people began coming in and I bustled around the dining room, clearing empty plates and engaging with those who had come in for a warm meal that morning.

Sometimes law, including our pro bono work, can be an ivory tower endeavor. Getting out into the community—even for an hour or two—can remind you that there is a reality outside of your office walls, and this thought can reground you. But it doesn't have to be a morning at the soup kitchen. Consider spending time at a local school, tutoring one night a week, or coaching a local team. Reconnecting to the things that were loved before becoming a lawyer can help a person remember who she is and maybe show that her problems are, quite frankly, very first world. And, it should go without saying that learning to draw healthy boundaries (i.e., protecting an hour or two a week for something outside the office) makes for better lawyers.

Find a Board of Directors/Mentors/Sponsors

Many think pieces have been written telling women to develop their own Personal Board of Directors. Personal Boards of Directors are supposed to be people who understand who we are and are willing to advise us in areas where we need to grow. But if we never get out of the office, who will these people be? Only individuals from our own organization/firm? Maybe a few from law school or undergrad? That could yield a potentially singleminded view of the world!

One of the biggest things I gained from involvement outside of the office is a group of incredible mentors who are central to my personal board of directors. I turned to them when I wanted advice from someone outside my firm. I sought their guidance when I was considering moving in-house. And they were some of the first people I emailed when imposter syndrome kicked in after I decided to throw my hat in the ring for a spot on the ABA Board of Governors. I trust these men and women because they know me, my goals, and the things I value in life. And for many of them, we never would have crossed paths if we had not become involved in organizations outside the office.

Expand the Network or Better Yet, Make New Friends

I can't deny it: there is something special about friendships forged by fighting together for something they believe in or by creating incredible programming that people value. They are made through late nights and hard work. And they are people you can rely on. The friends I made from the early days of Ms. JD cheered me on when I got married, squealed with excitement when I became pregnant with our "Ms. JD Baby," and were there when my mom passed away unexpectedly. We also supported each other professionally, recommending one another for other boards, submitting nominations for various awards, and being there for one another when our professional lives weren't going quite as planned. There is power in a network, and outside involvement will broaden that network. It may also bring some lifelong friends.

Learn Something New

Guess where I first learned about search engine optimization (SEO) or how to pitch an organization, or when I first started thinking through how an *organization* (as opposed to me personally) balances a budget? All of this happened for me when I got involved in organizations outside the office. I learned a ton about SEO and branding when we rebranded Ms. JD and redid our entire website. I was also forced to learn how to pitch our organization to firms as we sought sponsorships. That process paid dividends when I had to think about how to write the various versions of my firm bio for pitches. As I have joined other boards, I've considered not only the skills I could offer them, but also the skills I wanted to learn. I've leaned into opportunities to learn more about finance, an area that I feel less strong in, through my work outside of the office.

Finally, Take the Challenge to Rewrite the Mental Schemas

When I was talking to my mom at the bus stop that day, I was flattered but also scared. I was focused on all of the things that could go wrong, but I wasn't thinking about all of the opportunity. Even when I accepted the role, I did so because I thought I could give something back to an organization that had given me so much.

I've since learned that if I'm a little bit scared of something, it probably means I should take it on. When I was scared that I was shooting too high by running for the Woman-at-Large seat on the ABA Board of Governors, my husband reassured me: "Go in and be unapologetically yourself. If you lose, you can be comforted that it wasn't the right fit. If you win, you have a mandate to do it your way."

So, the first thing I told the committee was that I had faced a heavy dose of imposter syndrome when the call went out for nominees. But then I took a deep breath, took a step back, and thought about what I could bring to the table. Then I told them what I thought I could offer, and guess what? They agreed.

There are a million reasons to find opportunities outside the office. Start small. Find what it is that brings happiness and fulfills something that is not available in the office, maybe something that is better preparation for the office—and build from there.

Katie Larkin-Wong

Career
Associate General Counsel, Competition and Regulatory, Meta Platforms Inc.; Currently Board Emeritae (Former President and Chair of the Board of Directors) Ms. JD; Woman Member-at-Large, ABA Board of Governors

Education
- JD, Northwestern University Pritzker School of Law (2011)
- JD, Georgetown University Law Center (1L)
- BA, Government, Psychology, Women's Studies, Claremont McKenna College (2006)
- American University Center of Provence (2005)

Best Advice
"Get comfortable being uncomfortable. That's where you'll learn." In my career and life, I try to run toward experiences that scare me a bit, for that means I'm taking on something new and challenging. Succeed or fail, you're guaranteed to learn.

Personal
Katie Wong lives in the Bay Area with her husband, Jono, two children, Kieran (5) and Declan (3), and their rescue dog, Wes. When she's not running between gymnastics, ballet, piano, soccer, or a playdate, Katie loves to get outside and enjoy everything the Bay and its surroundings have to offer. If she's not in the Bay, you'll likely find her family in Montana (where she grew up), New Zealand (where Jono grew up), or on another traveling adventure, learning about the world through food, culture, and language.

For More Information
https://www.linkedin.com/in/katherinelarkinwong

From Big Law Commercial Litigation Partner to Art Museum General Counsel: The Unexpected Path to a Second Act Dream Job

By M. Thérèse Vento

Like many good women lawyer stories, this one has elements of youthful ideals; dream jobs; coping with reality, overload, and attempts to find balance; success; questioning; tapping into the strengths of being true to oneself; finding joy; irony; and an unexpected open door that, in retrospect, was meant to be.

Does this story have a happy ending?

The Seeds

The seeds for my career transition from Big Law commercial litigation partner to art museum general counsel were planted more than 30 years before—long before I even knew there was such a thing as an art museum general counsel. I had always enjoyed the arts, having studied ballet and piano, attended symphonies, and visited museums of all kinds for decades: the right-brain kinds of things. But making a living through the arts world wasn't even an option. I did not have the talent to perform, but I appreciated and marveled at the artistic talent of others.

I did, however, have the ability to write, to advocate, to be intellectually curious, and to think logically, so I majored in journalism and spent some time writing for newspapers and being a panelist on a broadcast public affairs television series. I won an internship to work as a press aide to a senator in Washington, DC, at a most eventful time in our nation's history. I was there when *Roe v. Wade* was decided and when Richard Nixon had his second inauguration with the Watergate scandal developing. It was heady stuff for a young journalism major, and I decided then that I wanted to eventually come back to Washington, DC, as a Supreme Court news reporter at the highest level. But to do that, I needed to go to law school.

The Law

There weren't a lot of women attending law school back in the 1970s. I was met with a lot of skepticism about my decision, especially from my very traditional father. He thought the only reason I wanted to do this was because my boyfriend at the time (who eventually became my husband) was also going to law school. My father eventually acknowledged that I was serious about this but told me repeatedly that I should feel free to drop out of law school at any time, and that there would be no shame in that. (He later came around on this topic when a friend of his was upset and told my father: "It's daughters like yours who prevent sons like mine from getting into law school.")

I enjoyed law school, including moot court. After I won the book award for trial advocacy, I started to rethink whether practicing law and helping to make the law, instead of writing about legal decisions from afar, would be a viable career that I would enjoy. Before deciding, I clerked for a federal district court judge in Miami for 2 years, during which I observed talented trial lawyers and had a bird's eye view of how the courts work. I thought, "I can do that." And I did. Out the window went the plan to cover the Supreme Court, and in came the journey to a partnership in Miami's oldest law firm as a commercial litigator. But there were a few things I never completely left behind: my news reporter's need to dig into the facts and inquire in such a way as to get people to let their guard down and respond; and my love for the arts. The former would come in very handy when taking depositions and researching and investigating, getting to the bottom of what didn't pass "the smell test" in an opposing party's case, and then making sense of it all by presenting the story to the court.

The Arts

As for the arts, serendipitously, when I was a new partner, my law firm was celebrating its 75th anniversary, and I was asked to research and recommend a way the firm could celebrate in a way that would be positive for both the law firm and the community. My love for the arts led me to cold-call and knock on the door of the new Center for the Fine Arts (CFA), and I learned that they were hoping to bring a Picasso exhibition to Miami but did not have the funds. Fast forward, and, at my suggestion, my law firm and a few of its major clients sponsored the exhibition. A few years later, I became the youngest person to join the CFA Board of Trustees. I did not fit the profile of a traditional trustee, but I had a passion for its mission and a strong work ethic.

The Pro Bono

As any lawyer who sits on a nonprofit board can attest, the lawyer becomes the most likely candidate to be assigned anything legal for that institution. That was true for me. As a litigator, I did not have the expertise to work on bylaw revisions or contract analysis, but I had good friends who did. I had been very active in the local and state bar associations and knew several good-hearted partners at multiservice law firms who agreed to do projects for the museum pro bono. I tapped a number of them and spread out the work so as not to be a burden to any one law firm. Over the course of decades, they wholeheartedly participated. I learned from them, and they became what I affectionately call my "pro bono law firm."

The Mission Change

In the midst of all of this, the CFA changed its mission from being a showcase for traveling exhibitions, to being a museum that collects art, which then triggered the name change to the Miami Art Museum. My mission had changed, too. Right before the opening of the Picasso exhibition, I became a first-time mother—the first partner in my law firm's long history to have a baby. The challenges came fast and furious over the next few years. Juggling marriage to another lawyer, motherhood, a full-time (and then some) litigation practice, bar association duties, trustee duties, and pro bono legal work for the museum was exhausting. And then I had another baby.

The Reckoning

I would be lying if I said I didn't have moments of wanting to chuck it all. I resigned myself to not being extraordinary in each of those roles all of the time, and instead recognized that I could be very good at them, but not all on the same day. And that was good enough. I did some self-reflection and focused on the things that meant the most to me—my family, my career, and the museum. I burned a lot of midnight oil, but each one of those aspects of my life gave me joy. I had a caring and supportive husband; two bright, funny, and good children (who both ultimately became lawyers); a challenging but fulfilling career; and a creative outlet—or at least my pro bono legal work was for a creative place where I had a role in transforming our community into a quality artistic destination.

I had my day job, which I enjoyed and which paid the bills, and my night job after the children were in bed, doing trustee and pro bono legal work for the museum. Slowly, over the years, I learned from my friends who did projects for the museum in specialties other than litigation about contracts, trademarks, employment law, construction law, nonprofit law, and myriad other areas involved in running a business.

The Discovery

I also discovered a nationwide museum attorney community and began attending the annual American Law Institute-Smithsonian-sponsored "Legal Issues in Museum Administration" conference, sometimes on my own dime. I was like a sponge trying to absorb a waterfall of topics that were new to me: art law, museum law, museum best practices, and all the aspects of the other areas of law that touch on running a museum. The museum community attorneys were collaborative, generous of spirit and knowledge, and so, so smart. I was in heaven.

The "New" Museum

Eventually, the Miami Art Museum constructed a new building, designed by renowned architects, right on Biscayne Bay, and it quadrupled its exhibition space and staff. Its art collection grew. It added a restaurant/café. In a short while after opening at the new location in 2013, it became an iconic place for contemporary art, inclusive community dialogue, and thoughtful creativity. As a thank you to a major donor who kept the building project going during a major recession when the capital campaign pledges of many other donors were jeopardized, the museum was renamed the

Pérez Art Museum Miami (PAMM). Throughout this period, I continued my practice with the law firm and my pro bono legal work for PAMM.

The Dream Job

About a year after PAMM opened at its new location, the director of the museum told me that if I ever wanted to leave private practice, he would love for me to come to work as the museum's first in-house counsel. At that time, although I found his offer enticing, I was concerned about the difference between private practice and nonprofit salaries. A few months later he mentioned it again. I was really torn. But becoming the General Counsel of PAMM would be my dream job. If it went to someone else, I would regret that forever. My husband and I had long talks about it and how we could make do. And we made it so. I resigned from the law firm (but still have many ties and friends there) and resigned as a trustee after serving the museum as an officer and executive committee member for 27 years. I was named a Trustee Emeritus. I then started as the museum's first General Counsel and have never looked back.

The many years of doing the job from afar, with no expectation of it being any other way, had prepared me for a second chapter that unexpectedly has enriched my life in all of the important ways. I finally have a legitimate outlet for my creative cravings—my office is in the museum building, and I just have to walk down to the galleries to enjoy the art. I work with creative people who are fun to be with. They see the world differently. Part of my job is to help them understand risk and to work with them to proactively find solutions to issues, which are respectful of their vision while still consistent with legally protecting the museum. That is not something that is taught in law school or that is even often found in a litigation practice. When I review contracts, gift offers, and prospective policies, my goal is to find a way to "yes."

The Transition

When I first started in-house, there was some distrust among the staff that I would be a "spy" for the trustees, and they were wary of being seen "in the lawyer's office" because they thought that meant they had done something wrong. They had no model for an in-house attorney. Both the staff and I, as well as the trustees, were new to this dynamic. I had to learn to interact with the staff differently than when I had dealt with my corporate clients and their in-house counsel while in private practice. There was no shortcut lingo or legal mind meld between counsel. I had to learn to slow down, listen, and understand more. They had to learn to come to me *before* making decisions and signing documents. There were some bumpy transition rides. Even the trustees had to recognize that my job had changed and that I represented the institution and had to put that first, over the friendships I had on the board. Over time, the staff and trustees have come to see me for who I really am—an ally helping to make the museum great, identifying and meeting best practices, and helping to keep them out of trouble.

I brought a lot to the table, having the perspective of a trustee as well as a lawyer, and having had many life experiences and excellent legal training. But they have made me a better and more well-rounded lawyer. As General Counsel, I work with every department and every aspect of the museum.

I work closely with the Chief Operating Officer of the museum. We are a symbiotic team as so much of the business side of the museum has legal aspects. He learns from me, and I learn from him.

I work closely with the curators, registrars, and collection management staff as we negotiate with donors, artists, galleries, and vendors, and ensure that artworks that come into the permanent collection are properly accessioned. They learn from me, and I learn from them.

I work closely with the development team as we navigate capital campaign or endowment pledges, sponsorships, donations, and legacy gifts of funds and art. They learn from me, and I learn from them.

I work closely with the trustees—my former colleagues—on preparing and keeping current all of the numerous policies and procedures that an accredited art museum must have and must comply with; addressing conflicts of interest; providing legal advice at board and executive committee meetings; assisting with governance and nonprofit law issues; and helping to provide historical perspective due to my more than 35-year relationship with the institution. They learn from me, and I learn from them.

The Irony and the Ending

I am often asked what advice I have for lawyers who want to have a job like this. There are not that many of these positions, but I tell them that if they follow their passion with action, perseverance, generosity, and some luck, and perhaps provide pro bono legal advice, they will put themselves in a position where they will be in the right place at the right time. Every step on my winding road to my second chapter dream job was a good experience in and of itself. If it had ended there, it would have been a quality career and a life very much worth living. But little did I know at the time that those opportunities to learn outside the traditional box gave me the skills needed to be able to say "yes" when, ironically, the museum came knocking back on *my* door. Life had come full circle.

Does this career change story have a happy ending?

Decidedly, "yes."

M. Thérèse ("Terry") Vento

Career

General Counsel/Senior Director of Legal and Government Affairs, Pérez Art Museum Miami, Miami's flagship contemporary art museum

Education

- JD, *Honors*, University of Florida Levin College of Law (1976)
- BS, *High Honors*, Journalism, University of Florida

Best Advice

In the face of obstacles, calmly trust in yourself and keep the big picture in mind. Hurdles along the way are not only expected and part of life, but are the source of wisdom, strength, growth, and experience in the long run. And if as a result you chose to take a different path, embrace it—because sometimes the road less traveled leads to unexpected joy.

Personal

Terry Vento is a left brain/right brain person who has married the practice of law with her love of the arts through her role as General Counsel of the Pérez Art Museum Miami. She was named Top In-House Counsel 2017 by the Dade County Bar Association; was honored by the *Miami Daily Business Review* with its Professional Excellence Award in 2020 for Solo In-House Counsel; is profiled in the book *Beyond Julia's Daughters: Women in Miami-Dade History 1975–2000* (Her Story of Florida 2006), which celebrates women of vision who have made exceptional contributions to Miami-Dade County's history; and is profiled in the book by Paula Black, *A Lawyer's Guide to Creating a Life, Not Just a Living* (Black Box Publishing 2018).

Terry has been married for more than 46 years to an attorney. She has two children (both her son and daughter are attorneys) and three grandchildren. She enjoys attending arts and cultural performances, baking, modified cross-fit workouts, tandem bicycling with her husband, family time, and reading.

For More Information

https://www.linkedin.com/in/m-therese-vento-bb67a85
tvento@pamm.org

Career Transitions: Interval Training for Life

By Amy Ragen

About 10 years ago, I received a phone call from a friend who had just been at an event led by Microsoft's General Counsel, Brad Smith, where prominent lawyer and author, Anne-Marie Slaughter, talked about interval training as a successful model for career planning, particularly for women. My friend explained that, following Slaughter's speech, Brad had called out one of his Women-Owned-Business-Enterprise outside counsel firms as an example of how the Microsoft legal department values this model of interval training. Apparently, it was the firm I founded, Ragen Swan PLLC. I was flattered, but I also realized at that moment that, in fact, I had engaged in this kind of interval training during my career and didn't even realize it. This essay tells my story of managing career transitions in the same way that an individual might interval train for long-term health and fitness as articulated by Slaughter.

>
> "Athletes have long understood that the best way to get into peak condition is to engage in interval training. You go all-out for a period of minutes, then slow down for the same number of minutes before going at it again. Going 100 percent all the time never gives your body a chance to recover; you have to be strategic about when and how you ramp up and ramp down. Life, and careers, can be approached the same way."
>
> —Anne-Marie Slaughter, *Unfinished Business*

Joining a Large Law Firm

When I came out of law school in 1986, women were dressing in clothes that attempted to look like men's suits, except with skirts rather than pants. And we wore those really silly-looking bowties in the same power yellow intended to look like men's ties. We even went to men's tailors to make these suits for us. Our goal at that time was to "fit in" and to look and act like a man. We saw very few women in the partner ranks of law firms, let alone in management of those firms. However, despite all obstacles, we were expected to take our place in the male-dominated legal profession and show that we deserved to be there in all respects. So, in the language of interval training, I started the uphill climb, determined to make it in San Francisco at Morrison & Foerster. Then I moved to Seattle in 1989 to join Davis Wright Tremaine when my husband took a job in Seattle.

Neither I nor my female classmates thought about what that climb meant in relation to other traditionally female expectations for family and household responsibilities. We plunged forward full steam ahead to work hard, bill long hours, and spend evenings on client development activities. In the interval training analogy, this was the long uphill climb to reach the next peak of the mountain. It didn't occur to me to do otherwise. And when I made partner at Davis Wright Tremaine in January 1993, 6 months after the birth of my first son, I thought I had it all and had reached the top of the ladder.

Reality was about to set in. After a 3-month maternity leave, I returned to a firm that had very few women raising young families, particularly as partners. We were a new phenomenon. Due to the larger number of female law school graduates starting careers in the mid-1980s, many law firms at the time were dealing with this issue in a way that had not occurred before. There were three women (two already-partners plus myself) who all gave birth within several weeks of each other in mid-1992. Davis Wright offered what seemed to be a great option—work on an hourly, nonequity partner basis, which I did for several years until after the birth of my second son. Taking this alternative path meant giving up the position as equity partner that I had worked hard to achieve. And even if I were to decide to go back on equity track after a year or two, the compensation model wasn't set up for women coming in and out of full-time work. In addition, I didn't have time in my life to bill hours, do the after-hours client development expected of partners, and still get home to be with my young children. The law firm model just didn't work for me. By the start of 1997, my legs on the metaphorical treadmill were giving out, and I couldn't sprint anymore. This was the start of Career Transition #1.

In-House Counsel

During Career Transition #1, I joined a satellite telecommunications company, Teledesic, where I was responsible for negotiating contracts with vendors that would design, develop, manufacture, and launch a global satellite system. This opportunity seemed to offer me the ability to do my job and then go home—in short, to level out the ride. I could maintain a challenging but steady job with mostly 9 a.m. to 6 p.m. days and some travel that I was able to coordinate with my husband's travel schedule.

And then the unexpected happened. I was diagnosed with multiple sclerosis. But I was lucky—it was identified early and I began an aggressive medicine regime that has stabilized its progression to this day. But that was a signal to slow down on my career journey again. My hours changed to 9 a.m. to 3 p.m., which gave me time to take care of myself more than before and enabled me to focus on my family. Within a few years, the dot-com bust happened, so Teledesic needed to downsize in response. In mid-2000, I was offered a package to work on an hourly basis for the company while it transitioned to another business model. At the time, these changes seemed to be the end of my career as I knew it, and I wondered if I had made the right decision to leave the law firm world. However, the reality is that this job gave me unusual exposure to global manufacturing companies and the opportunity to learn about the design, development, and commercialization of cutting-edge technology as part of a large-scale project. I would never have gotten this kind of in-house counsel perspective and business insight if I had stayed at a law firm. Also, moving to an hourly position at Teledesic set the stage for my next career transition.

Solo Practitioner

Career Transition #2 meant becoming a solo practitioner. I started doing work for Teledesic and then picked up projects with a couple of Seattle-area tech companies. Several attorneys from my former law firm had moved to in-house counsel roles and asked me to support them as an independent outside counsel. This period of my career took the interval training down yet another step in intensity. I had to figure it out project by project. However, this stage of my career was built on the technology transaction exposure from my in-house job and caused me to think about client development in ways that I had not done while I was with a law firm. I was responsible for finding and growing my own client relationships and managing my time to fit client commitments without the support of other attorneys. Clients were looking for experienced lawyers who gave them flexibility outside the standard law firm model and rate structure. This was an important lesson for later career development. There were several periods when I didn't take on any work, and during summer breaks, I had an extremely light workload, averaging 5 to 10 hours per week. I enjoyed serving on local nonprofit boards and spent more time with my young children. Over time, the work started to grow and I established several clients that brought me consistent engagements. One client relationship led to Career Transition #3 when I least expected it.

Founding My Own Law Firm

Career Transition #3 occurred in 2005 when my largest client, Microsoft, asked if I would hire a former full-time equivalent senior paralegal (whom I had worked with on several projects before she left Microsoft) through my firm. Well, I didn't exactly have a firm at that time; I was a sole proprietor with a malpractice policy. I moved forward (picking up some speed in the interval training analogy) and the Law Office of Amy Ragen, PLLC was born. Immediately, Microsoft saw the benefits of bringing back their valued paralegals and attorneys who, for various reasons, had left as full-time employees on-site at Microsoft, and I became the vehicle to do that. These professionals were themselves on their own interval training journeys without realizing it either.

Within a few years, I was running a law firm of about eight professionals (attorneys and paralegals). People left Microsoft and then joined me, and then left the firm to go back in-house when it made sense for them. I was known for hiring only top quality people and for offering them flexibility to work a lot of hours when that fit their lives at the time, or to cut back if they needed to make changes in their personal and family lives. I paid my employees on an hourly basis, so they could decide how hard or how little they wanted to work from time to time. Many of my team members were women who were raising young children or taking care of elderly family members. Others were looking for more work-life balance. And they worked from several different states around the country. This firm that was only supposed to be a temporary solution at a fork in my career ended up being the start of a new career as I headed back up the hill on my metaphorical treadmill with Career Transition #4.

Bringing on a Partner

In 2009, Kevin Swan joined me on the journey and Career Transition #4 began. He was also looking for a flexible career after leaving a large Seattle law firm. It is not only women that engage in interval training. Kevin enabled us to spread our workload and share the responsibilities of managing the firm at a time when my capacity was stretched. We renamed the firm Ragen Swan PLLC a year after Kevin joined and became a certified Women or Minority-Owned Business Enterprise, with me as the majority equity holder. The size of the firm fluctuated between 10 and 15 employees during this period. This was a time of great pride because Kevin and I were enabling our terrific professionals to maintain meaningful careers and do complex work for sophisticated clients in a way that also allowed them to balance life and career (i.e., to interval train themselves). It didn't mean that we worked less hard, but we had a sense of control over our commitments and could manage the peaks in a smoother way. I was honored as a Woman of Influence by the *Puget Sound Business Journal* in 2012.

The business model worked because it met the needs of our attorneys and paralegals. And the clients benefited because they could retain these experienced, dedicated, and highly productive professionals who could step right in and support their fluctuating needs. Our firm was entirely remote, long before remote work was thrust upon us by a pandemic. One of our valued paralegals spent an entire year traveling around the world living at Airbnb locations. We joked that the firm's motto should be "Join Ragen Swan and see the world." We had our firm meetings at a local Mexican restaurant and celebrated being able to reach this balance.

This stage of my career taught me a lot about growing and managing a team—in particular about creating trust and transparency with the people with whom I worked. Treating people well and helping them build meaningful and sustainable careers go a long way to creating loyalty that is irreplaceable.

By 2021, times were changing again. Ragen Swan PLLC had outgrown our business model and I had exceeded my personal bandwidth. Twenty-five years had passed since leaving a traditional law firm practice when I started climbing that first hill. My children had been launched and were starting their own careers. The firm's business had grown beyond expectations. I was billing hours comparable to those I billed when I made partner back in the early 1990s. And we were turning down clients because we couldn't find resources to do their work. Further, our remote working style had become the everyday practice after the onset of COVID-19. The business world had realized that physical office space wasn't necessary to practice law. This was particularly true for a transactional practice working with technology companies. We had always used the prevailing conferencing methods to work with our clients, whether dialing in to conference calls or using video calling with Microsoft Teams, and negotiating agreements with remote sharing tools. We needed to figure out how to adapt to our growth. This all culminated in Career Transition #5.

Joining Shook, Hardy & Bacon

For Career Transition #5, I did what I never thought I would do: I went back to the world of big firm law. In June 2021, Ragen Swan PLLC joined the law firm of Shook, Hardy & Bacon, and I became Chair of the newly formed Technology Transactions Practice Group. My career had come full circle. But times had changed in the intervening 25 years. Just as many other firms realized, Shook understood that a successful legal career didn't need to take place completely in a physical office. And part-time arrangements were no longer exceptions handed out only in unusual circumstances with significant loss of career opportunity and extended compensation impact. My entire team at Ragen Swan PLLC has joined Shook, many of them continuing with flexible schedules. Many law firms have adopted policies that recognize the need of attorneys and other professionals to make adjustments throughout their careers. Offering part-time work schedules enables firms to keep talent while still realizing profit. Considerable loss of efficiency and wasted training investment take place when valuable professionals leave. I have been rewarded by my team's extraordinary gratitude and loyalty over the years by my team for enabling long-term, flexible career development.

Final Thoughts

Careers don't need to be endless treadmill workouts going at full speed until we drop. I have benefited, and so has my family, from the opportunities to slow down and even jump off the treadmill from time to time and then jump back on at full speed. These intervals enable us to reenvision, or even reinvent, our careers with new energy.

I have also discovered that it is truly impossible to "have it all." There are trade-offs and compromises at each stage. Golda Meir once said: "At work, you think of your children you've left at home. At home, you think of the work you've left unfinished. Such a struggle is unleashed within yourself. Your heart is rent." However, looking back, there is gratification in knowing that both roads of work and family could be traveled, albeit at various speeds from time to time.

A career is an accumulation of experiences. Looking back, I find that Teledesic gave me the "technology bug" and an unusual opportunity to understand how to work with executives to strategize and negotiate sophisticated transactions. Starting my own firm taught me about law firm management, client development, partner collaboration, and employee satisfaction. These career transitions gave me experiences and perspectives that may not have been possible if I had stayed on a single course.

In short, interval training as an attorney is not only possible but leads to a long-term productive and satisfying career where each interval adds new experiences to the ones that came before.

Amy Ragen

Career
Partner and Chair of Technology Transactions Practice Group, Shook, Hardy & Bacon LLP

Education
- JD, University of Chicago Law School (1986)
- BA, *cum laude*, Economics and Political Science, Yale University (1983)
- HS, Choate Rosemary Hall (1979)

Best Advice
Obstacles in our personal and work life are inevitable. When possible, address them as challenges to be overcome that sometimes can even create unexpected opportunities for growth and discovery.

Personal
Amy Ragen is married and has two children (aged 28 and 29). She enjoys tennis and exercise in general, reading (particularly current events and historical fiction), and eating dark chocolate. She is active in the American Jewish Committee (AJC) as a member of the Executive Council and Board of Governors and serves as the Chair of Interreligious Affairs. Her role with AJC took Amy to Indonesia and Vienna in 2022, and already in 2023 to Israel, with a planned trip to Rome for interfaith consultations. Her grandfather was a lawyer, and all three of his sons (including Amy's father) were lawyers, but she is the only female lawyer in her family's three generations of lawyers.

For More Information
https://www.shb.com/professionals/r/ragen-amy
aragen@shb.com

Forging Your Own Way: Transitioning to Public Interest and In-House

By Christina Yang

I am the child of immigrants from Taiwan. My parents immigrated from the island nation in the late 1970s, and I was born in Southern California a few years later. My mom is fond of recounting how she decided to move to America because my uncle (who had arrived a couple years earlier) had proclaimed to her that American pizza was one of the most delicious things he had ever eaten. My parents built a life for themselves here, despite not speaking much English, and not bringing much money with them either. My dad eventually started his own small business selling welding supplies, and my mom helped him with accounting and packing shipments. She also held a series of other part-time jobs—at various times she worked in a hair salon, a coffee shop, various banks, and she provided childcare for other families. Growing up, there were no attorneys in my family or among our family friends and going to law school never crossed my mind.

As the first attorney in my family, I love working for Asian Americans Advancing Justice Southern California (AJSOCAL). I currently serve as the General Counsel and Pro Bono Director for AJSOCAL, which was founded almost 40 years ago. We are the country's largest nonprofit focused on serving Asian American/Pacific Islander (AAPI) communities. We focus on areas ranging from litigation to policy advocacy to direct legal services such as immigration and family law, and we have offices in downtown Los Angeles and Orange County. It's not common to find a nonprofit willing and able to invest in in-house counsel *and* a pro bono director, so I'd like to share with readers how I landed where I am today.

I have not always been attuned to the issues facing AAPI communities. I attended a magnet high school in Southern California with a very diverse student body, and I barely dwelled at all on my own identity as a woman of color or as a minority until I arrived in Philadelphia for college at the University of Pennsylvania. There, I was suddenly confronted with much less diversity, and at times I experienced being treated like an outsider simply because of my physical features or even just my last name. As a result, as an undergraduate, I became involved in AAPI student activism on campus. I connected with like-minded students through the Asian Pacific Student Coalition, and the group worked on issues such as advocating for more university investment in Asian American studies (which during my time there was available only as a minor).

It was also during college that I first began to consider being a lawyer. In my sophomore year I learned of AJSOCAL (then known as the Asian Pacific American Legal Center of Southern California) when the organization filed a class-action lawsuit challenging Abercrombie & Fitch's discriminatory hiring practices and English-only policies in the workplace. I was inspired by the bravery and strength of the multiracial, multicultural plaintiffs, who included Black, Latinx, and AAPI young people, led by the nonprofit's litigation director at the time, Julie Su (now U.S. Deputy Secretary of Labor). I wanted to go to law school and learn how to effectively litigate and work at a civil rights nonprofit like AJSOCAL, where many of the clients might come from backgrounds similar to my family's.

Upon arriving as a bright-eyed 1L at Berkeley Law, I immediately began plotting how I could work at AJSOCAL. Befriending a 3L whose girlfriend was a litigation staff attorney at AJSOCAL, I learned as much as I could about the organization before submitting my application to clerk there for the summer. I was so happy to spend my 1L summer as a law clerk with the impact litigation unit at AJSOCAL. A few years later, one silver lining of graduating from Berkeley Law during the recession in 2009 was that I had the opportunity to work with the same litigation team on a year-long deferral fellowship, generously funded by Mayer Brown LLP. I worked primarily on a consumer fraud case representing a large group of mostly monolingual Chinese parents who had been defrauded by an art school in the San Gabriel Valley, and I was given a huge amount of responsibility in working directly with these clients and earning their trust while putting the lawsuit together. Also, I had never used Mandarin in a professional setting before, and this year provided an amazing opportunity to hone my language skills.

After the deferral fellowship, I returned to Mayer Brown LLP and spent a few years there as a general litigation associate. In the small Los Angeles office, I was often the sole associate working on cases with just a supervising partner. I received great training there and built key foundational litigation skills, including drafting substantive motions, filing papers, taking and defending depositions, making oral argument, and of course conducting discovery. In addition, I was able to devote time to pro bono work, including representing a single mother of three girls in obtaining a favorable settlement regarding child and spousal support. However, I missed the nonprofit world, and wanted to broaden my experience to include transactional work in a nonfirm setting. So when a friend asked if she could send a recruiter my way to discuss the possibility of going in-house at AIDS Healthcare Foundation (AHF), a global HIV/AIDS nonprofit, I decided to throw my hat in the ring. Leaving the firm to go in-house relatively early in my career put me in a unique position. I remember well the conversations I had with colleagues back then. In particular, I recall one partner who congratulated me for leaving "before I got too used to the money." (Sidenote: Looking back, I see that leaving was certainly easier then. Now that my husband and I have a dog, two kids, and a mortgage, I can't say I don't miss that Big Law money!)

My time at AHF did allow me to build transactional skills through interesting projects such as reviewing MOUs and contracts supporting HIV/AIDS clinics and advocacy around the world, but I spent much more time on litigation than I had anticipated. It illuminated for me that I needed a break from litigating. While I could do the work well, I ultimately found it too stressful, and I felt drained by the constant conflict with opposing counsel. I did know that I enjoyed being in-house, even though AHF's budgetary constraints as a nonprofit meant that we handled as much as we could in-house rather than relying on outside counsel.

As I pondered my next move, I wasn't quite sure what that should be. I knew I didn't want to litigate anymore, but I did want to stay connected to legal work in some way and, in an ideal world, I wanted to work with the AAPI community. At the time, I was serving on the board of the Asian Pacific American Bar Association of Los Angeles County (APABA-LA) with someone who was leaving the pro bono director position at AJSOCAL because she missed practicing law. Though I didn't possess quite the number of years of experience they were looking for, she encouraged me to apply for her old job anyway. I took her advice, and also chatted up my interest to the AJSOCAL colleagues I had kept in touch with over the years. To make a long story short, I got the job, and that was over 8 years ago now.

The pro bono director role had just been established about a year before I was hired, so the first few years it was really fun to put on my creative thinking cap and build our pro bono programs from the ground up. I strengthened existing pro bono relationships and created new ones, especially when I established the Pro Bono Advisory Council (PBAC) in 2015, which consists of an impressive group of over 30 representatives, including attorneys from firms of all sizes and in-house counsel. Our PBAC members take on pro bono matters themselves and promote them in their offices and networks, and they help raise vital funds as well. I have successfully placed pro bono matters large and small with our firm supporters over the years, which has led to increased giving from these firms and has deepened their engagement with us through pro bono. I derive so much satisfaction in finding the right pro bono support for my colleagues (e.g., locating a volunteer who speaks a very specific Southeast Asian language dialect to interpret for a citizenship client). I always enjoy hearing that private-firm attorneys had a fulfilling experience doing pro bono with us, especially when they share their pride in being able to serve AAPI communities.

Four years ago, my work at AJSOCAL evolved in a huge and exciting way. The AJSOCAL management team invited me to take on the additional role of the organization's first-ever in-house legal counsel. As pro bono director, I was already securing pro bono firms as outside counsel for our organization on different matters (e.g., to advise on an employment law concern raised by our HR team) and I was also often serving as the point person on these matters, so it was a natural progression in many ways. In this role, which eventually resulted in a promotion to General Counsel, I mitigate risk for the organization and provide advice and counsel to our leadership and middle management teams, which I enjoy tremendously. And again, in this new role, I engage in the time-consuming yet rewarding building of systems and policies where none existed before (e.g., launching the organization's first-ever data security policy last year).

This is not to say that the role has been without significant challenges. The first couple of years were bumpy to say the least. Shortly after I became legal counsel, the AJSOCAL staff unionized, and I was thrust into learning labor law almost overnight (thankfully while leaning on our pro bono outside labor counsel!). I eventually guided our executive leadership team and Board through negotiating AJSOCAL's first collective bargaining agreement (CBA) during a period of over 18 months, and I have handled a myriad of other labor relations issues since then, including negotiating wage reopeners and CBA amendments.

As an in-house legal department of one, I could not possibly cover everything I do without the support of our pro bono firm partners who act as our outside counsel. I am very lucky that our strong existing pro bono relationships mean that I can tap into Big Law expertise on a pro bono basis, even though the work these firms do on General Counsel matters isn't in direct service to the AAPI community members our organization serves.

Finally, my third job (as I like to call it) is bystander intervention training. Last year, in response to the incredible spike in anti-Asian hate incidents, our executive leadership team decided that AJSOCAL should offer bystander intervention training as a resource to the community, and I was asked to lead this new program, including coordinating a team of 15 trainers representing various programs across our organization. We have trained over 7,000 individuals already since launching our program a little over a year ago, and we offer the virtual training in both English and five Asian languages. It has not only been well received by attendees, who walk away after just a one-hour training feeling equipped to intervene safely if needed, but it has also provided the chance for our staff trainers to collaborate and build relationships where their core programmatic duties might not otherwise bring them together.

Despite leaving the world of billables behind long ago, my job still requires me to work hard and sometimes long hours, which can be difficult with two young children at home. However, AJSOCAL has more women than men on staff and is filled with working parents, and our leadership team is incredibly supportive of flexible schedules—which has been invaluable, especially during the pandemic. Our CEO models taking time off that's *really time off*, and by that I mean she is generally off email almost all of the time she's out, even on longer vacations. I also must credit my husband, Jon, who has supported all of my career transitions, even those that have involved significant pay cuts. He leans in tremendously on the home front, including handling nearly all the cooking for our family, which enables me to lean in more at work.

What advice do I have for a woman seeking to transition into public interest or nonprofit work, or the in-house world?

First, what's served me well time and time again, and has helped me to be "in the right place at the right time" when an opportunity arises, is a strong network—the connections I've built through going to events and conferences, law school, APABA-LA leadership, other lawyer moms, and staying in touch with former colleagues. This same network has provided me invaluable mentorship and trusted support all along the way.

Second, develop transferable skills *and* think outside the box about what value can be brought to a role that's a big change. This might be a demonstrated commitment to pro bono work to make the case that someone is a good fit for a nonprofit, or highlighting work that showcases how legal issues can be framed through the lens of common sense and business judgment, which is often required in-house.

Third, don't be afraid to apply for a job even if you don't "check off every box." If I hadn't taken the risk to apply for the pro bono director role that I didn't quite qualify for, my professional life might look a lot different today. Finally, if you're not content with where you are, know that there is no obligation to stay—there is somewhere better to be. However, don't leave too hastily. Take some time to determine the top priorities to make the right transition when it comes along.

Christina Yang

Career

General Counsel and Pro Bono Director, Asian Americans Advancing Justice—Los Angeles

Education

- JD, University of California, Berkeley—School of Law (2009)
- BA, English, Communication, University of Pennsylvania (2003)

Best Advice

Don't be afraid to ask for help—people are almost always happy to lend support!

Personal

Christina is a past president of the Asian Pacific American Bar Association of Los Angeles County, and she chaired its Judicial Endorsements and Public Appointments Committee for many years. She is also a member of the Pro Bono Coordinating Committee for the California Commission on Access to Justice. Christina lives in Culver City, California, with her husband, two young children, and beagle mix (named Berkeley after her law school alma mater—Go Bears!). Her hobbies include supporting local eateries, brisk walks outdoors, entertainment-related podcasts, and napping.

For More Information

https://www.linkedin.com/in/christina-y-709a7412
cyang@ajsocal.org

Finding Success in Public Health and as In-House Government Counsel

By Heather Anderson-Fintak

In October 1997, during the fall semester of my senior year in college, my mother came to visit while I was studying abroad in Torino, Italy. It allowed us to get to know each other in a way that we had not done so in my adult life thus far. As Spanish was her first language and the Italian people are so welcoming, all she needed to know was *prego*[6] and just speak Spanish; it was close enough to Italian. After a week of traveling to Venice, Rome, Florence, and back to Torino, my mother sat me down to tell me her plan for my life. She told me that I would go to law school, represent those who had no one else to speak for them, and one day, be a congresswoman so that I could make a difference in others' lives.

I laughed. I told my mother that I had plans to obtain my Master's in Business Administration so that I could one day be a CEO of a multinational corporation. However, my mom, like others, saw something in me that I could not see myself. It is a unique experience to have someone believe in you so deeply.

Less than 2 years later, I found myself driving across the country from Nevada to Washington, DC, for law school. On the way, I listened to a variety of books on tape to keep me alert. One book was *The Street Lawyer* by John Grisham. I promised myself that I was only going to law school for power and money, and I would never be a legal aid attorney. I eventually arrived at American University Washington College of Law (WCL), which is known for international law, clinical programs, and a majority female student population. It is a wonderful environment for learning about the legal world and offers practical opportunities to utilize newly obtained legal skills.

As a student attorney in WCL's International Human Rights Clinic, my first client was an Angolan refugee who was seeking asylum after fleeing from Angola to the United States because he was in danger of being

---

6. The Italian word *prego* means many things to the Italian people. Usually translated as "you're welcome," it literally translates to "I pray." Therefore, it is also used to mean "no problem" or "you first." Said with enough passion, *prego* can mean almost anything and shows that one has manners.

arrested and killed by the Angolan government. The Angolan government suspected him of rebel activities, which were imputed to him because of his mother's rebel activity. In reality, he had little knowledge of his mother's rebel activities, and he had been raised in another part of Angola by his paternal grandmother. And as an adult, he lived a quiet life with his girlfriend and her son. He worked far away from his mother in the diamond mines and had limited contact with her.

The Angolan government officials had come to arrest him, and when they did not find him at home, they destroyed his house. While in hiding herself, his girlfriend was able to get word to him not to come home, as they knew the dire consequences of arrest. He eventually found his way to the United States with his passport and a U.S. visa, which his girlfriend purchased for his passport. However, because "purchased" visas are not valid, upon entering the United States, he was tagged for deportation. Without knowing about U.S. immigration law, he completed the first hurdle toward obtaining asylum when he told a customs official that if he was returned to Angola, the government would kill him.

My client was placed in detention in rural Virginia. At the beginning of the law school year, I told the clinic professors that I wanted a case involving a detained refugee. I wanted a hearing in front of an administrative law judge. I was assigned the case, in part, because I had a car and was willing to drive the hours into Virginia. My clinic partner and I visited our client five times in 3 months. Though a translator accompanied my non-Portuguese-speaking partner and me on our visits, my Portuguese comprehension eventually increased to such a level that I no longer needed the translator. My Portuguese paternal grandmother would have been so proud!

We prepared a 10-page affidavit and a 20-plus-page brief in support of our client's asylum claim. On the day of his hearing, I realized that he was not appearing in person but rather was appearing on a video screen from the rural Virginia jail, and he was wearing his orange jumpsuit. I was so mad, but it had not occurred to me to ask about his appearance in the courtroom. I started my 90-minute direct examination of my client. My back started to ache; my professor noticed, as I was slipping one shoe off behind the podium. I did the opening and direct. My partner examined the client's friend and did the closing. While we were waiting for the judge's decision, our professor, Beth Lyon, began preparing us for the fact that we had lost the case. The case, an imputed political opinion asylum claim, had never been won by the clinic. She talked to us about next steps. When the judge finally came back and told us that he was granting asylum, my client jumped up, and I noticed for the first time that he had been in shackles the entire 4 hours.

Three days later, the government put him on a bus to Washington, DC. I picked him up at Union Station, and he stayed in my extra bedroom. My Army boyfriend (now husband) thought I had lost my mind. But I had just saved his life. Of course, he would not steal or harm us. He called me his sister and told me that I had changed his life forever. Within a few days, he was staying in an apartment with other recent refugees and started his career path.

That year, I had the privilege of winning two asylum cases and became addicted to the prospect of changing people's lives. I broke my pre-law school road trip promise to myself and became a legal aid advocate shortly after graduation.

In August 2002, I interviewed for positions at the Baltimore City office and the Hughesville office of the Legal Aid Bureau (also known as Maryland Legal Aid). The southern Maryland office in Hughesville offered me a position first. The position was to provide general representation to the elderly and low-income community in Charles, St. Mary's, and Calvert counties. As I was not initially admitted to practice law in Maryland, my case load involved all of the elderly outreaches, state and federal benefits, and matters that did not require me to file or defend actions in court.

My 3 years at Maryland Legal Aid was an education for me. As a generalist, I had the opportunity to provide representation in a variety of poverty law issues. However, after having a baby and at my mother's insistence, I returned home to Nevada.

At first, I was excited for the new challenges that faced me at Nevada Legal Services. I was able to transfer my federal administrative law skills without skipping a beat, and learning Nevada law on certain issues did not slow me down. As the first younger woman attorney hired, there was a transition period of convincing the support staff to trust me. After a bumpy start, I found my place through my advocacy and willingness to mentor others.

After my hiring, many younger women attorneys were hired from other legal aid organizations in other states or fresh out of law school. It became a training ground, and I had the privilege of training new attorneys on either how to be a Nevada attorney or how to be an attorney at all. In a few short years, I became the senior attorney of the office. I enjoyed running the day-to-day operations and helping new attorneys develop into the best versions of themselves.

While I was passionate about the work, I soon felt I had hit the ceiling due to the low pay and the lack of upward mobility. When the office's pro bono coordinator position opened, I decided to take the lateral position in hopes that I could find my place again. I quickly found myself unmotivated. The best part of my days was spent helping pro bono attorneys with their cases or training private law firm attorneys in areas of the law in which they had never practiced. Unfortunately, most of my time as pro bono coordinator was spent event planning.

After one particularly tough day in May 2012, I spent Memorial Day weekend searching for a job. I applied for both the county public defenders' office and the Southern Nevada Health District. The public defenders' office called me first. I ended up having three interviews with that office. Our clientele were similar, but the defenders would have to teach me criminal law. I had one interview in August 2012, with Annette Bradley, General Counsel of the Health District. Annette and I clicked immediately. It was the most relaxing and interesting interview I had in a long time.

By the first week in September 2012, I had not heard from either governmental agency, but honestly, the time delay is pretty typical for local government recruitment. Then I got a call from Human Resources at the Health District. The woman calling asked me if I was still interested in the associate attorney position. I said yes, and we agreed on a start date of October 8, 2012.

Ten years out of law school, I started a new career path as in-house lawyer for the government in public health. I thought it would be an easy transition. It was not. Annette was the first woman attorney the Health District had hired; she was also the first African American attorney. Annette is still one of the most thoughtful, strategic, and skilled speakers and writers I have ever met. She was tough on me. However, that is her style. Annette had been fighting the uphill battle against the "good old boys club" a lot longer than I had. She taught me that we could never allow anything to leave the office unless it was perfection, because people are looking for fault with our work and will enjoy nothing more than to be proven right. Even though Annette demanded perfection, she was the first person to defend me if someone else tried to find fault.

After several years, I found my footing. I did all of the environmental health work, which included monthly illegal dumping prosecution, isolation and quarantine petitions, public and medical records management, staff education on Health Insurance Portability and Accountability Act (HIPAA) privacy and compliance, and more. I acted as counsel in Board meetings when Annette was not available and I helped a variety of staff with the regulation approval process.

While I appreciated all of the opportunities, in 2017 I started to think about my career path. In the fall, while I was meeting with Annette, I confessed that the Health District had been my 3- to 5-year plan, and it was now over 5 years. While I truly appreciated what she had done for me, I thought it was time for me to consider my options. I promised Annette that I did not have a current job offer and that I would give her as much notice as possible when I did. She looked at me and asked, "What if I retire?" I said, "Tell me more." Annette explained that she was closing in on retirement age, and she would like to train me and prepare me to take over. I agreed.

During 2018, Annette made a consistent effort to place me in front of Board members. She sought my input on hiring and retaining staff. She made opportunities for me to learn from her. By summer of 2019, while I had always been her right-hand woman, I was now intimately involved in the inner workings of the legal department and a variety of programmatic issues. In the winter of 2019, Annette happily announced to me that she was retiring, effective August 2020. She had a two-week island vacation planned and was ready to let go.

And then COVID-19 hit. Even those of us who were working in public health could not fully grasp what was before us. At a meeting on February 28, 2020, I stood in front of a room of 200 local government representatives and explained Nevada's isolation and quarantine law. As part of my explanation, I said (naively) that as the local health department, we would be in charge of a public health response to a communicable disease outbreak.

I spent the next few months being batted around by the press, other governmental officials, and the absolute exhaustion of our staff. By the end of May 2020, Annette came to me with the news I expected to hear—she would not retire on August 1 as planned. She could not, in good conscience, walk away from the Health District now. As a side note, her island trip was definitely off, as well.

We in the legal department commonly referred to our work at that point during the pandemic as drinking from a fire hose. Everything was an emergency, and all of the programs and outside agencies determined that their work was the most important; therefore, we were to drop everything we were working on to provide them service. And it only got worse as time wore on. For example, in 2019, we did not track when programs asked to have a contract expedited. In 2020, 30 percent of contracts were "expedited." In 2021, 69 percent of contracts were requested to be expedited. As Syndrome says, "If everyone is super, no one will be."[7]

In February 2021, Annette told me that the legal department and the Health District were in the place that she wanted us to be, and she would be putting in her retirement. She provided her resignation/retirement letter to our District Health Officer at the end of March with a June 1 retirement date. In the same conversation, she told the District Health Officer that I was ready to be General Counsel, and he agreed.

On June 2, 2021, I officially became General Counsel to the Southern Nevada Health District, one of the top 10 largest local health departments in the United States. The Health District serves 2.2 million residents, and, in a normal year, over 40 million visitors to Las Vegas. The legal department consists of a General Counsel, Associate General Counsel, contract administrator, compliance officer, paralegal, law clerk(s), and a legal secretary. Our organization has approximately 775 employees and—with grants—a budget of over $180 million. As Associate General Counsel, I considered myself "leadership adjacent." As General Counsel, I am part of the leadership team.

In 2012, I had decided I needed something different for myself; however, making a difference in my community was a central part of my employment considerations. I mentor law students and young lawyers not to be afraid of change, to ask for what they need, not to negotiate

---

7. *The Incredibles* (Pixar Animation Studios, 2004).

against themselves, and to find the right employment situation that's best for them and their family. I am lucky to have found public health, developed under the tutelage of Annette Bradley, and that Annette made me her succession plan.

My children, Aidan, Class of 2025 at University of Nevada, Reno, and Zoë, high school class of 2025, have always known a world where women can be lawyers, leaders, and difference makers.

Heather Anderson-Fintak

Career
General Counsel, Chief Compliance Officer, Risk Manager, Public Health Advocate, Southern Nevada Health District

Education
- MBA, Healthcare Management Concentration, University of Nevada, Las Vegas Lee Business School (2025, anticipated)
- JD, American University Washington College of Law (2002)
- BS, Business Administration, Management, University of Nevada, Las Vegas Lee Business School (1998)

Best Advice
Never negotiate against yourself. As women attorneys, we are taught to zealously advocate on behalf of clients, but we cannot forget ourselves. We need to zealously advocate for our compensation, our free time, our work duties, and more. There is only one of you. One of my favorite sayings is: "No" is a complete sentence.

Personal
Heather is on the Clark County Bar Association (CCBA) board of directors and is the prior Editor-in-Chief and still an editor of the *Communiqué*, the CCBA's monthly magazine. In her tenth year of volunteering with Girl Scouts, she loves the time with her daughter, helping the girls try new activities, and teaching them that being themselves is enough. She is looking for more opportunities in public health advocacy and was recently invited to speak about the importance of HIV data privacy, even against law enforcement's prosecutorial requests. Her two children are 15 and 19. In her free time, she loves to travel to the beach, read a good book, and chat endlessly with her husband, Matt. She has now returned to school so that she can be a better advocate for the health care side of public health.

For More Information
https://www.linkedin.com/in/heatherandersonfintak

Changing Career Paths: The Challenge to Have a Dream Career

By Mary Catherine Roper

This essay is for all of the happy, unhappy, ambitious, cautious, neglected, or respected women lawyers who are looking to (or must) disrupt their established careers. They may want to make a change because the job has grown, because the job hasn't grown, because the boss or co-workers are sexist, because they want more money or more family time, or because they have an opportunity that they cannot ignore. They may *have* to make a change for any of the same reasons.

No matter why a person is making this change, it will be scary and hard, and because each already has an established career, it will feel like (and may be) a much bigger risk.

The good news is that as established professionals, experienced lawyers also have or have access to, a much better set of tools and resources than they did when they were entry-level lawyers. That means that they have many more options to consider and much more control over where this change will take them in terms of the type of work they will do, their income, and their work-life balance.

And, let's face it, we are fortunate to have such choices. Most of our mothers did not have the opportunities that we have. Most people—and especially women—around the world today do not have the same freedom to pursue work that is rewarding on an intellectual, social, and material level. It would be a shame, in the face of all of that potential, to settle for work that makes us unhappy. Take this as a challenge to pursue not just "better" work, but the work that you really *want*.

How does one do that? It takes a team. It takes research. And it takes preparation. In my experience and that of the many women I have asked about this type of transition, the most important resource in any transition is their team.

The team should include mentors, trustworthy informants, and cheerleaders (who will double as shoulders to cry on when things get tough). The team might include one's partner (especially if shared expenses are an issue). The team should include people who will serve as references, formal and informal. The team should include people who know where you have been and people who have done things you have not done.

First thing, make a list of the team members and, for each, the role they play and the information they have that is needed. The team may need to expand if there is a need for a perspective that no one on the current team has. Find someone who has that knowledge or experience and ask them if they will help advise (one of the team members might know the right person). Lawyers love to give advice. I spoke with one woman who moved to a new city to follow her partner's work, a place where she knew no one. She dove into local bar association committees and other volunteer work to meet people and start expanding her network. She asked nearly everyone she met for an informational interview (a.k.a. "coffee"). In a matter of months, she had a rich and varied network and some of her new connections were connecting her with job openings. She kept building her team as she moved from "a job" to getting the work she wanted.

Next, use the team to help plan research. If this change is unfamiliar, you might not know all of the questions to ask of yourself and others. Ask everyone on your team, "If you were in my shoes, what would you want to do? What information would you need to pick a direction or prepare yourself to pursue this goal?" Write down all of the answers you get, whether or not you agree with them. Keep all of the notes together and periodically review them. The perspective might shift during the process.

Now it is time to learn as much as possible about the available options. Online resources like Glassdoor.com, Fishbowl, and even AbovetheLaw.com can provide valuable insight into workplaces and hard-to-find information like pay scales. Another terrific resource might be the career services office where you went to school—or the online resources posted by other law schools' career services offices.

But there is no substitute for a conversation with someone who has been there. When one of my friends decided to jump from Big Law to a plaintiffs' personal injury firm, the first thing she did was to ask her friends to introduce her to people who could tell her about the workflow and especially the business of personal injury law.

Ask people who are in the types of positions being considered—and, importantly, people who have left those positions—what they like and do not like about what they do. Ask about the challenges. Ask about the rewards. Ask about the office culture and the workload expectations. Ask them to describe their most and least favorite task and coworker. Ask about time off.

Always ask about the money (including retirement benefits). The money matters, whether looking to join a Big Law firm or a struggling nonprofit. The work may be rewarding, but the work is not "its own reward." Even if a person is independently wealthy or has a family member willing to subsidize the choice, each should be paid fairly for work. If possible, find out what the men in the organization are paid. They tend to make more than women, often because they ask for more. Beware of "shoestring" operations where everyone is paid poorly except the top executive. That lack of respect will manifest in other ways as well.

This is also the time to do some "research" on oneself. From my experience and that of other women I have spoken with, if someone has been undervalued at work, she may have forgotten just how awesome and marketable she is. Ask mentors and cheerleaders to help identify strengths and weaknesses. There may be things one prefers not to hear, but it is also likely that there is admiration for things that have been taken for granted.

Frankly, self-confidence may need work. Even when we know we are being undervalued, it is hard to feel proud of ourselves. And even though we know that our experience is valuable in the workplace, in most areas of our society women are viewed as "less" as we age. It is hard to keep that out of our professional self-image.

So put some real time and effort into reminders of accomplishments. And when your team and others tell you that you are praiseworthy, do not deflect that praise or explain it away. Say "Thank you." And write down what those people see (preferably in your draft cover letter!). The future boss or colleagues will see those things, too.

Now for the planning. Before applying for jobs, make a list of the attributes of the new job that are "must have," "would like to have," and "will not accept." What was enjoyable about the former job? What is never to be repeated? What is needed to grow? To feel secure? To do the best work? How do you want to interact with colleagues? At one of the law firms I worked in before law school, the support staff was terrified of the lawyers, and the atmosphere was oppressive. I vowed I would never work in a place like that again and, therefore, I asked questions about the relationship with support staff in every future job search.

Do not skimp on this process. Schedule time for the research, for the planning, and for checking in with team members. Ask the team to critique the cover letter and resume. Ask them to do mock interviews. If needed, get professional help with the resume. And buy a new suit—you and your future are worth it.

When you do find a new position, be sure you leave the last place on good terms. The law is a surprisingly small community, and a person is never more than a few degrees of separation from the people previously worked with. Give lots of notice, thank colleagues for the good times, and do not badmouth former colleagues or organizations—even, and perhaps especially, if you think they will be talking behind your back. Although it may feel good in the moment, there is never anything to be gained from leaving unnecessary bad feelings in your wake. In the law, your networks are your greatest asset. No good comes of burning bridges.

Whether looking for more of a challenge or more free time, a brand-new vista or the chance to develop your expertise more deeply, a person is more likely to get what is wanted by assembling a team, doing research, and planning the search.

The last thing needed is patience. Lean on team members to help keep spirits up if the search drags on. If there is the flexibility, pass up the offers that are "just okay." You have invested years of your life and untold hours to become a candidate who can shoot for the stars. Honor that work and those investments. The excitement of finding a job to grow and thrive and expand professional impact is well worth the time.

Mary Catherine Roper

Career
Of Counsel, Langer, Grogan & Diver, PC

Education
- JD, University of Pennsylvania Carey Law School (1993)
- UC College of the Law, San Francisco (formerly UC Hastings College of Law) (1L)
- BA, English, Bryn Mawr College (1987)

Best Advice
Always try for more—more for you, more for the clients, more for the public good. Don't accept that what is happening is what has to happen.

Personal
Mary Catherine Roper (she/her) litigates civil rights and consumer protection cases with Langer, Grogan & Diver, PC, in Philadelphia. Throughout her legal career, which includes 16 years with the ACLU of Pennsylvania, Mary Catherine has been known for creative strategies that achieve results, whether that is relief for individual clients or broader law reform. She has led successful collaborations with firms large and small, with public interest coalitions, and with government agencies. Mary Catherine has received many awards for her service to the public interest community in Philadelphia and beyond.

Before joining the ACLU in 2005, Mary Catherine was a partner at Drinker Biddle & Reath LLP (now Faegre Drinker Biddle & Reath LLP), where she had a diverse complex litigation practice with extensive experience in class actions, consumer protection, corporate governance, defamation, and commercial litigation. Prior to joining Drinker Biddle & Reath, Mary Catherine clerked for the Honorable Anita B. Brody of the United States District Court for the Eastern District of Pennsylvania and served a year with the Disabilities Law Project as the first recipient of the Philadelphia Bar Foundation Public Interest Fellowship.

Mary Catherine is committed to fostering the next generation of social justice warriors. She serves as adjunct faculty in the Trial

Advocacy Program of Temple University Beasley School of Law, teaching trial skills to law students and lawyers in the LLM Trial Advocacy Program. She also co-teaches a seminar on Remedies and Litigation Strategy at the University of Pennsylvania Carey Law School. She has mentored and advised scores of law students and young lawyers seeking to pursue public interest careers.

Mary Catherine grew up in Southern California but now considers herself a Philadelphian and a Phillies fan. She lives in West Philadelphia with her partner. Her hobbies include motorcycle riding, baking, glassblowing, mentoring, and providing First Amendment advice to activists.

For More Information

https://www.langergrogan.com/our-team/marycatherine-roper

Discussion Questions

1. Discuss whether knowing and being your true authentic self are prerequisites to being content with the practice of law. Does it, or would it, help you navigate or prevent obstacles?

2. How do you identify yourself—all of yourself? Would other people at work, or those who know you professionally, identify the same or similar facets about you? Discuss how these responses affect you and your practice.

3. How do you incorporate the things you identify about yourself into your work?

4. Do you feel like you have to hide or change certain parts of yourself in your career? How does that affect you?

5. If you don't feel you can be authentic in your work or career, what is holding you back? How can you be more true to yourself?

6. Based on reading this chapter, or the entire book so far and its references to finding a community, have you identified your community? If so, describe it. How do you engage with that community? If you have no community, consider who should be in your community and what steps you can take to find one.

7. What do you dream your career could look like? Describe what steps could be taken to reach your dream situation.

8. If you were not earning money for your work, what would you do with your time? Could you incorporate that into your current career?

9. What activities are you involved in outside of the law? If none, what activities would you like to become involved with?

10. How do you maintain perspective when you experience an obstacle?

11. What ideas can you take away from this chapter and incorporate in your life?

CHAPTER 6

Guideposts and Beacons: Getting More of Us on the Road

In attempts to eliminate or minimize obstacles and get more attorneys on the road to success, the essays in this chapter discuss the value of goal-setting, planning, and mentorships.

These essays will address planning in its traditional sense, as well as planning for our new reality where we will likely have many more years of practice with multiple career changes. The essays will also discuss planning for retirement and succession, something that takes years to cultivate.

When planning becomes difficult, the essays will show you that mentoring is the next guidepost that becomes instrumental. This collection contains essays explaining the mentor and mentee roles, what a mentor should do, and examples of how mentoring and role models shaped the lives of attorneys, and how, in turn, they pay it forward. For all readers anywhere—ranging from those starting in the practice of law to the highly seasoned attorney in a leadership position—take the time to reach out to mentor someone. Humbly reach out to those who need it most, not just the child of the well-connected superhero. And then, upon reaching a certain position with a platform, consider using the platform (as one writer does) to raise awareness about diversity and elimination of bias to get more women, and women of color, on the road to success. Finally, since women attorneys alone cannot fully elevate all women attorneys, the essays address male engagement in these efforts.

We hope the essays in this chapter inspire you to make plans, set goals, create mentor circles, and make wise use of platforms to minimize obstacles.

The Value of Effective Goal-Setting

By Patricia H. Thompson

These quotations raise intriguing questions: Is it a waste of time to set goals? Or, worse, do we delude ourselves in thinking we are able to plan our lives?

I do not need to debate these questions. I can testify that much is to be gained by thoughtfully setting goals, making short- and long-term plans to reach those goals, and then, intentionally, taking the steps necessary to achieve and, when wise to do so, revise our objectives. That is because challenges, obstacles, and opportunities will always arise, and, in response, we should set new or revise old goals to make the best of what comes our way.

>
>
> "We plan, God laughs."
> —Yiddish Proverb
>
> "If you don't know where you are going, every road will get you nowhere."
> —Henry Kissinger
>
> "Life is what happens while you're busy making other plans."
> —John Lennon, "Beautiful Boy"

For a lawyer graduate, getting hired by a law firm or company is just the beginning; there is much more to plan for. What kind of law to practice now? In 20 years? In 40 years? What to do to keep busy upon "retirement"? How to earn a reputation for excellence? From whom to seek advice at every stage of a professional life? Through it all, how best to accommodate inevitable, but unforeseen, change?

Planning simply never stops. For example, after 20 years of practice, the chair of a firm I had recently joined warned me that my chief area of specialty and primary source of income was too risky and narrow to last more than a few years longer. Rather than resent or ignore his blunt assessment, I started devising a plan to diversify my client base and substantive areas of practice. As a result, I was ready and secure when he was proven correct. This change of course was neither the first nor the last of many unexpected detours in my 46-year career.

My goal in this essay is to share some methods and benefits of effective goal-setting. While my stories may not resonate with every reader, the advice should prove true regardless of differing challenges.

What Do We Mean by "Setting Goals"?

Goal-setting is a process by which we envision some aspect of our future, whether short term (e.g., creating daily "to-do" lists) or over longer spans of time. The process may involve practical plans or personal dreams.

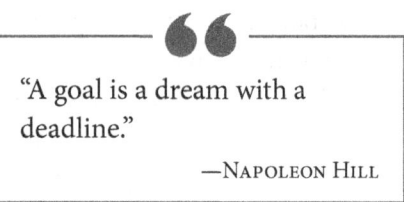

"A goal is a dream with a deadline."

—Napoleon Hill

For example, if we see ourselves as attorneys, then as part of that vision we need to give priority and organization to our desires concerning both the kind of attorney we want to be and the life we want to lead. Are we willing to take on the stress and personal demands of litigation? We must be honest about what type of work will make us happy and valued: divorce work? criminal? products liability or other personal injury? probate? commercial? With what kind and size of firm or company would we want to work, and where would we want to live? How would we be happiest spending the rest of our time and the treasure we earn? Overall, how would we want to be remembered, and what else would we want to accomplish at any one point of time? The best way to realize these life-defining dreams is to set goals to reach them.

Properly set goals should be realistic, ambitious, motivating, and measurable. Thus, goals should be attainable given our circumstances and our abilities. They should be specific so we can know where we are going and when we have arrived. They should inspire and add meaning to our lives because they are formed by our personal priorities and values.

The goal-setting process should be thoughtful, intentional, and reiterative. First, we make plans to formulate a strategy for reaching our goals. Then, as circumstances intervene, it is important that we continually reevaluate what to do and why, rather than merely reacting to events or letting others set our priorities. This reflective and mindful process teaches us about ourselves, others, reality, and what we can accomplish at any one time, which knowledge we then use to refine our plans or reset our goals.

I experienced a major resetting of my goals in my last year of college. I had long planned to teach high school English. As I was completing my student teaching assignment during the spring of my junior year, I realized that spending my life with high schoolers would drive me nuts. I started senior year with no idea about what to do next, when, on a whim, I attended a luncheon at the home of a female judge for a discussion of "women in politics." Prior to that luncheon, I knew few lawyers and never had any thought of practicing law. However, just being in the presence of this distinguished jurist inspired me to think that I, too, could be a lawyer. And so I set new goals, applied to law school, and transformed my life journey.

Why Set Goals?

Properly done, the setting, planning for, and endeavoring to accomplish goals can enrich our lives. The process is so important that even though some desires and dreams are never realized, we often benefit by the time spent pursuing them.

"The great secret about goals and visions is not the future they describe but the change in the present they engender."[1]

—DAVID ALLEN, *Making It All Work: Winning at the Game of Business and the Work of Life*

Improving Performance

Setting goals can motivate and enable us to be better versions of ourselves. Deciding in advance what we want to accomplish and planning how to reach that goal will result in better performance. This has proven true in big and little ways in my life. Each new area of my practice over the years, such as bank transactional work, mortgage foreclosures, regulator bank closings, surety and fidelity claims, life insurance and other types of first-party insurance coverage, construction defect litigation, employment defense, and several other types of commercial practice, arose from different opportunities. But my proficiency in each new legal specialty required a similar discipline as I set short-term and long-term goals to learn and earn credibility in the subject matter and enlist allies and teachers to better enable me to be the best lawyer I could be. And over time, learning all of these substantive disciplines, as well as litigating for 40 years, taught me what I needed to know. In this way, when I was ready to leave my firm, I could retire to become a full-time neutral with sharply honed ideas about how better to resolve disputes in many areas of law.

Facing and Adapting to Reality

Setting goals begins a learning process that requires us to address and reconcile issues and challenges we might not stop to consider otherwise. As part of the planning process, we need to continually analyze: what is important; what is possible; what are our skills and talents; what are the benefits to be achieved and the costs to be incurred; how do the needs, abilities, and contributions of other people factor into achieving these goals; what is needed and how can it be obtained; and what steps must be taken to reach the goals? This analysis also helps us face the truth about what we cannot do, for whatever reason.

Facing reality means that we should hold our plans loosely. They do not define our self-worth, and we are not always in control of what happens in our lives; that is the nature of unexpected obstacles. Our plans may need to be revised or abandoned.

For example, when I learned I was pregnant at the old age of 41, I recall tearfully calling my parents to tell them how upset I was because "This is not what I planned." With the wisdom of his 68 years, my father gently reminded me, "You are not the only one making plans." As it turned out, my son has been a blessing, and I have learned much from the new plans we made and remade as we learned how to raise him and then enjoyed his company as a young adult whose interests often were much different than ours.

Sixteen years after my son's birth, when my father and I happened to be enduring different kinds and severities of cancer treatment, we both were faced with the need to make new plans. This process turned out to be encouraging. Facing the future at such a time was an act of hope as we focused on what we could do rather than on what we could not change.

Defining Our Personal Priorities

According to marketing mavin Seth Godin, "Everyone has their own Mt. Everest they were put on this earth to climb."[1] I would suggest that Mr. Godin's wisdom is phrased too narrowly. We may be asked to climb a number of mountains over our lifetimes. Nevertheless, he is right to suggest that identifying our personal goals provides balance and centers us as we decide what mountains are important enough to be worthy of the time and effort necessary to climb them.

For example, I have always been impressed that one of my male law partners made it a goal every night to be home early enough for dinner with his children. Because this treasured time with family was more important to him than working uninterrupted at the office, he often had to resume work after dinner until late into the evening.

Another example of life-balancing that is closer to my heart was the choice my husband made to work from home and work less so he could raise our only child, which my professional obligations did not allow me to do. Personally providing all-day, everyday infant and childcare for his son was the priority by which he organized his days, notwithstanding that such work was not the goal he had envisioned for his middle age.

Not every father would have made the same choice as my husband, but I have learned that it is important that we define our own mountains to climb, based on *our* beliefs, values, and relative priorities. If we do not, others will be more than happy to tell us how to spend our time—perhaps helping them reach their goals.

Leading More Interesting Lives

The motivation that comes from setting and accomplishing personal goals can make our life journeys more interesting and satisfying. There is an intrinsic reward in the pursuit of goals, especially when we reach those goals in accordance with our own plans and standards. Problem solving can be quite satisfying, and setting goals can be a way to achieve a solution to a problem. Even the challenge of using time wisely to accomplish a simple task is a reward in itself.

---

1. Seth Godin, Linchpin: Are You Indispensable? (Portfolio, 2011).

Consequently, those of us who like to make lists to order our days find it encouraging to tick off each item we accomplish. Of greater moment are accomplishments that make our lives and those of others better, improve systems at work or in society, create harmony in our families or other communities, or foster financial security for those we love or those with whom we work. In any case, regardless of how impactful our goals may be, it gives us a sense of worth and meaning to accomplish them.

Getting More Done and Avoiding Distractions

Zig Ziglar quipped, "If you aim at nothing, you will hit it every time."[2] He is correct: planning simply gets more work done than failing to plan. A businessperson once told me, "If you want to get something done, give it to a busy woman to do." Regardless of gender, a busy person has no time to waste and usually knows how to plan the best use of the scant time available.

Wise planning involves a series of thoughtful choices to do what is necessary to reach our objectives. Once we have made such decisions, it becomes easier to pursue those plans while avoiding whatever will distract, delay, or disrupt our efforts.

Planning also gives us the discipline to stop trying to do everything or too much. Only a few things at any one time are important to the accomplishment of our goals. I am always reminding myself that I can only do one thing at a time. Finish this task first. I find when I do one thing at a time, I get more done.

Living Mindfully

As a benefit of getting more done, having goals helps us focus on what we are doing at any one time. Thus, we live by design, not default, and we become better stewards of the gift of the present. When we are mindful of the time we are given and how we are using it, we can better live in each moment, finding ways and time to enjoy each activity, event, person, or thing of wonder.

---

2. *See* Tom Ziglar, *If You Aim at Nothing*, ZIGLAR, https://www.ziglar.com/articles/if-you-aim-at-nothing-2 (last visited on Sept. 20, 2023).

Working with and Learning from Others

Much of what we want to accomplish cannot be done alone. Setting and accomplishing goals with others is not only necessary for success, but it also builds relationships, which in turn can make the pursuit of commonly held goals more effective and satisfying.

I have always known that to be successful, litigation requires well-planned teamwork in pursuit of well-defined goals. Indeed, when I was in private practice, that was one of my favorite things about being in trial: the choreographed and crucial roles each member of the litigation team played in the courtroom battle.

But my longest-lasting example of group planning occurred during my years in leadership with the American Bar Association (ABA). For decades, I had been active with a large, very active committee of the Tort, Trial, and Insurance Practice Section, and eventually I was asked to chair that committee. I spent almost 1,000 hours over a several-year span before, during, and after my tenure as chair: planning, overseeing, and participating in that committee's many activities. However, from the moment I was named "chair-elect presumptive," I did not stop asking for advice and assistance from those who had already chaired the committee, from ABA staff, and from other committee leadership. Not only did our committee "profit" from our collective wisdom and work, but I gained lifelong friends among my collaborators.

Indeed, it has proven to be true throughout my career that planning alongside others is the best way to reach goals, achieve recognition, and, in the process, engage in meaningful work.

Building Self-Confidence

Setting goals allows us to mark and celebrate our progress. When I retired from practicing law as an advocate and joined JAMS, I had to learn and develop an entirely new career as a neutral. I had to measure progress in becoming a competent arbitrator and mediator by defining interim steps toward those objectives and celebrating individual victories along the way, with each new arbitration or mediation, each CLE speech or webinar given, or each article published, all of which taught me something new. In turn, each milestone added to my sense of competency and fueled my confidence in tackling each new case.

How Should We Set Goals?

So how do we effectively set goals? Some of my advice is implicit in the discussion above, but I also offer the following.

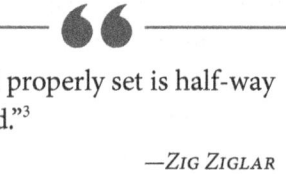

"A goal properly set is half-way reached."[3]

—Zig Ziglar

Seek Wisdom

1. If we want to achieve something new or reach a goal we have failed to reach in the past, we should admit our ignorance and our need to acquire the knowledge necessary to succeed at something new and challenging.
2. We should seek out the people who possess the information we need. Foster relationships with mentors and leaders who have already traveled the roads we need to navigate and colleagues from whom we can get feedback and who will be ready to help with unforeseen challenges when they arise.
3. We should seek out other resources, such as books written by experts in relevant fields, or wisdom literature, and revered books of philosophy, theology, and other sources of guidance for balanced, healthy, meaningful living.

Embrace Lessons Learned

1. We should learn from our successes. We should celebrate the power of even small wins and incorporate the actions and thinking that led to those victories into our toolbox of skills so we can repeat those successes by doing what works. As we make progress, we should be mindful of who deserves credit for our success, show appreciation to those who helped us, and consider how best to work together going forward.
2. We should learn from our failures, too. We should ask ourselves why we "failed" and what we might change, so we can do better in

---

3. *See* Tom Ziglar, *Attitudes, Goals, and Success*, Ziglar, https://www.ziglar.com/articles/attitude-goals-success (last visited Sept. 20, 2023).

the future. We should consider whether our goal was unrealistic. What were we unable to control or overcome? Did we overestimate our abilities or the difficulty of the task? Did we try to do too much? Did we say "yes," when we should have said "no" to tasks set for us by others that distracted us from our own? Did we get bogged down in the urgent or the trivial and so had no time or energy to address what was vital to our success? What were the obstacles and can we overcome them next time?
3. Be realistic and practical, even for the most ambitious, inspiring goals. As we progress, we always need to be open to whether there is good cause to revise our plans.

Make and Execute Your Plans to Reach Your Goals

1. Armed with wisdom based on the counsel and example of others and lessons learned from experience, we will have a better sense of where to go and how to get there. Then we should begin our planning with the end result in mind. That is, we should start by defining our goal, very specifically, so there can be no doubt what success will look like. Some advocate putting the goal in writing for future reference.
2. Then, we should plan, prepare, and perform thoughtfully:
   a. Break the goal down into "bite-sized" chunks, subgoals, steps, or mile-marker activities that can be accomplished within a set amount of time based on a defined set of activities, the doing of which gives us satisfaction or enjoyment.
   b. Write down or otherwise clearly articulate how we will be able to accomplish each step and what and who we will need to accomplish it.
   c. Arrange for the support of colleagues, friends, or family. They can encourage us and hold us accountable. This can provide crucial motivation and assistance.
   d. Believing we can do it, aim at the first subgoal and go full speed ahead.
   e. Celebrate each milestone we reach so it will be easier to stay on course.

Patricia H. Thompson

Career

Arbitrator and Mediator, JAMS

Education

- JD, Vanderbilt University Law School (1976)
- BA, *magna cum laude*, St. Olaf College (1973)

Best Advice

Having goals helps us focus. Thus, we live by design, not default, and we become better stewards of the gift of the present. When we are mindful of the time we are given and how we are using it, we can better live in each moment and enjoy each activity, event, person, or thing of wonder.

Personal

Patricia H. Thompson is a full-time arbitrator and mediator with JAMS Miami, concentrating in construction, surety, employment, financial, fidelity and related business insurance, and other complex commercial disputes domestically and internationally. She is regularly listed by The Best Lawyers in America, Chambers USA Guide to America's Leading Business Lawyers, The International Who's Who of Construction and Business Lawyers, and similar Florida publications ranking attorneys in her areas of practice concentration, such as the South Florida Legal Guide. She is a fellow of the Chartered Institute of Arbitrators and the American College of Construction Lawyers. Before joining JAMS in 2017, she enjoyed a successful career for 40 years as a trial and appellate lawyer and arbitrator in Florida, most recently with the law firm of Carlton Fields. She has long been active in the ABA, where she chaired the Fidelity and Surety Law Committee of the Tort Trial and Insurance Practice Section and co-chaired the Construction Litigation Committee of the Litigation Section. She is a frequent author and lecturer for both ABA sections, the Forum on Construction, and the Florida Bar Association.

For More Information

www.jamsadr.com
pthompson@jamsadr.com

The Gift and Challenge of Longevity: Preparing for Long Careers Marked by Changes

By Ida O. Abbott

Star Trek's Mr. Spock famously used the greeting "live long and prosper." As a lawyer, the odds are good for both. Whatever the age today, a person can expect to live longer than previous generations. The average life expectancy for American women today is 79, and those who are well educated and more likely to be affluent, have better odds to live even longer.

Longevity is both a gift and a challenge. Living longer does not mean more years of "old age"; those extra years will be scattered throughout one's life, not tacked on at the end. People will be able to do and enjoy more over many more years. But most likely, they will also have to work longer. And the career one plans so carefully today may be the first of several careers that take a person in various directions over a lifetime.

A person won't necessarily work continuously during all those years. It's likely people will take breaks from time to time to switch jobs, have children, explore the world, get a new degree, or do something else. Breaks might be by choice or forced; they might be temporary or permanent, and they will probably happen more than once. At some point, a person may decide to conclude a career and retire. But even stopping work completely at, say, age 75, may be with another 20 to 25 years of retirement ahead.

Looked at from this perspective, it's reasonable to plan for a long career marked by periodic changes and retirements. This new reality is one reason retirement is being completely redefined. Retirement today is not about becoming old, useless, and put out to pasture. It is a time when people can choose the things they want to do and do them—and say no to everything else. People who retire from a career today stay active, engaged, and vibrant, and they often begin encore careers, start new businesses, or otherwise continue to work in some fashion. There are no rules, timetables, or models regarding retirement; we're living in a time of widespread social and personal experimentation.

That's why career planning needs to include readiness for multiple changes and transitions over the years ahead. This will take a new kind of thinking. People will need abilities and mindsets beyond those prized in law practice to navigate the vicissitudes of life that lie ahead, whatever they may be.

My own career has lasted almost 50 years. It included several breaks, including a retirement and "unretirement," and I'm not done yet.

My Personal Story

I have been in the legal profession since 1975. For the first 20 of those years, I practiced law. My first job was at a small firm, where I had my first son in 1978. A year later, I moved to a large firm, where I had my second son in 1981. During that period there were no maternity leave or other "work–life" policies, so I made them up, and both firms supported me. After each birth, I took six-month leaves and came back part-time. In fact, my second firm hired me as a part-time associate. I always took vacations, occasionally for as long as 6 weeks. I became Special Counsel, which is like a nonequity partner today. I ran the firm's professional development and pro bono programs, which were among the finest in the country. Although I experienced discrimination and some harassment, all told, I had a happy and satisfying career as a practicing lawyer.

Yet in late 1995, I decided to retire. I was losing interest in my practice, unhappy with the direction of law practice in general, and I wanted to leave before I became completely disillusioned. I liked being a full-time mom for a while, but it didn't take long for me to realize I was not cut out to do it permanently. As I explored options for the next chapter in my life, I saw that law firms were growing and expanding but losing legal talent through attrition. This degree of lawyer turnover had never happened before, and firms needed help finding remedies. With my knowledge and experience in lawyers' professional development, I had the expertise to help them. But I hesitated starting my own business because I had never run a business before.

The challenge attracted me. The next 20 years of my practice, during which I consulted with the legal profession on talent development and management, were great, but I started to feel restless. Many of my clients and colleagues who held top leadership roles asked me for advice on what they might do next. Many were in their 50s and 60s and were not ready to stop working entirely but were looking for something new that would keep them engaged and vital. They wanted guidance but didn't know where to look for help. Once again, I spotted an unmet need.

I then narrowed my consulting practice to mentoring, sponsorship, and women's leadership development, which were my greatest interests, and I added a new service: advising individuals on nonfinancial aspects of retirement planning and advising law firms on processes that facilitate respectful retirements for senior partners. In a sense, this is a continuation of the work I have always done. It acknowledges that a legal career has a long arc that eventually gives way to retirement from practice and entry into the next stage of life.

My own career is moving ahead even as my 76th birthday approaches. My husband just retired, but I expect to continue working as long as people find my services helpful to them and keep calling me. Being a consultant, author, and speaker inspires me to stay relevant, and because I am my own boss, it allows me to keep working.

What Does This Mean for Others?

The legal industry has changed a great deal since I started my legal career. While I was in practice, most lawyers deemed the very term *legal industry* an affront because they viewed law as a profession, not a business. Today that seems almost quaint.

The changes in the legal industry are accelerating, and a legal career will need to withstand the uncertainties, risks, and challenges that accompany continuous and rapid upheaval. Lawyers in this position have made it through college and law school and have proven in many different ways that they are smart, capable, and hard-working. Those are fundamental qualities for any career in law. But for a long, successful, and fulfilling work life, other attributes will be just as essential.

Based on what I have learned through my own career, as well as from colleagues, clients, and women leaders I have known, here are some of the assets that will help lawyers thrive professionally and personally during the long future ahead of them.

- **Professional competencies.** These are the assets that will make a great lawyer with a successful career and a nice income. In addition to legal proficiency and integrity, they include the reputation held among clients, colleagues, and the legal community; the aptitude for business development and client management; the ability to function well within a team and organization; the facility for managing oneself and others; the ability to use legal technologies; and a knowledge of business, both one's own and those of one's clients. These are the fundamental competencies needed as a lawyer. They will also well serve those who move to a new field within or outside of law.

- **Professional connections.** Professional relationships and the social capital held with peers, co-workers, clients, mentors, and sponsors have much greater importance and value than one might realize. The formal professional networks one builds and is part of will be useful for promoting one's reputation and other professional competencies. To the extent networks are diverse and extensive, they will also give a broader picture of career possibilities open now and in the future, and they will provide connections with jobs, opportunities, business sources, influencers, and decision makers who can help clarify, improve, and achieve aspirations.
- **Resiliency assets.** These assets are the core of well-being and inner strength. They enable a person to face and bounce back from adversity. They include physical, mental, and emotional health; family relationships; personal friendships; social connections and activities; and habits that keep one fit, manage stress, and support the psyche. Law is a very tough and often isolating profession. Striving for professional success in law demands a great deal of time and energy, and women tend to set high expectations and to be very hard on themselves. Many lawyers sacrifice friendships, self-care, and other sources of resilience as they move up in their careers. Don't let that happen—and don't wait. Get out of the office and out of the house. Call a friend; use vacation time; schedule a quiet evening alone with a spouse; go for a swim; sign up for an art class; dig out that old guitar and strum a few tunes.

We will always be strapped for time and be pulled in too many directions. But resiliency assets are vital, especially for those who want to enjoy a long life. Remember, women's life expectancy may lengthen, but it's the average across a population, not a guarantee.

We need to take care of ourselves. Research shows that while lawyers generally suffer from alarmingly high rates of depression, suicide, and drug and alcohol abuse, women lawyers seem to be particularly vulnerable to these problems. In a profession that is inherently stressful and adversarial, especially during times of major change, assets that support well-being and resilience are more than just important; they can be lifelines.

- **Self-knowledge.** Workplace changes and life transitions are filled with ambiguities and uncertainties, and difficult decisions between competing alternatives will often be present. Being clear about values and priorities enables a person to know what is truly important, to set meaningful goals, and to make good choices. The more tuned in one is to feelings, health, goals, and needs, the faster the problems can be identified and remedied. The surer we are about who we are and what we want to achieve, the more likely we are to attain our goals and remain our authentic selves.
- **A positive mindset.** Successfully overcoming obstacles and navigating the ups and downs of a career require a positive mindset. Staying positive lessens the discomfort, instability, and risk that accompany change, and helps a person cope more effectively. Even if someone is highly risk-averse, a positive mindset helps to assess, manage, and reduce the risks we face. It propels us forward rather than letting us stay stuck. Components of a positive mindset include:
  - **Optimism.** Optimism makes a person more resistant to adversity and able to function more effectively. Optimism is not common among lawyers; pessimism is closer to the norm. But pessimism depletes energy and makes a person feel helpless. Optimism is not a naïve belief that all will be well. Rather, it helps a person to understand and appreciate both the positive and negative aspects of a situation; look for opportunities; and focus on solutions, not just threats. It helps a person accept the facts of adversity and counter them with constructive action.
  - **Self-confidence:** Self-doubt is common among lawyers, and many highly capable and ambitious women lose confidence as they experience unpleasant work experiences. When people

let external events cause them to fear failure or doubt their own abilities, they undermine their own desire to succeed. Instead, we need to focus on what we know we are capable of. We demonstrate our intelligence and accomplishments every day; we need to own them. Know and focus on strengths. We need to remind ourselves, and enlist friends and supporters to reinforce these strengths, any time we feel our confidence eroding. A mentor, therapist, or coach can also be a good source of support.

- **Curiosity and openness to new experiences.** Curiosity is the most underappreciated quality. To me, it is the key to a happy career and life. The main feature of curiosity is wondering about things and wanting to know more. It's driven by a desire for new and stimulating ideas and experiences. Intellectual curiosity can make someone a better, more effective lawyer. Being curious about people makes networking easier, and being curious about their needs makes a person a better rainmaker. But lawyers tend to get so wrapped up in becoming experts with answers that they overlook how much there is to learn about and experience beyond the matter at hand.

  Curiosity introduces people to new ideas, people, and possibilities; it makes us question why things are as they are and helps us come up with innovative solutions; it also keeps us more engaged and active. When people have many interests and are open to new learning and experiences, they can see things with a broader perspective, appreciate all that is good in their lives, recover more nimbly from setbacks and disappointments, and deal better generally with mutable circumstances.

- **Adaptability and flexibility:** Sometimes we choose to make a change, but changes may also be surprises or outside our control. We might opt for a different position, a new organization, a different career, or retirement. Or we might lose a client or a job, face a health problem, or be restricted by a pandemic. Whether planned or unexpected, the conclusion of the change process is a new status quo. For a successful outcome, we need to adapt.

Staying flexible rather than rigid is a key to adaptation. If we are wedded to a particular schedule or goal or way of doing things, resistance to change can be damaging when unplanned obstacles or deviations occur. Rigidity can prevent people from seeking something better when they're unhappy or in a rut and can make them miss favorable opportunities that appear unexpectedly. In contrast, accepting change as a common and frequent part of life, and being willing to go along with it, opens people to varied and creative possibilities. It makes it easier to change on one's own initiative, reduces risk and anxiety, and makes the process of adaptation smoother.

- **Self-reliance.** Kids often retort to reprimands by saying, "You're not the boss of me." But we are not kids; we're lawyers, and we aspire to be successful. So whatever obstacles we face, we remember that we are in charge of ourselves. We may work for a firm, company, or agency, but we are not beholden to our employer for our success. We must rely on ourselves to gather or create what we need to have the career we want. Whether that's a large client base, expertise in an esoteric high-demand field, or one's own law firm, develop a strategy, and go for it. We will be working very hard for a very long time, so it is important to make sure we enjoy what we do. If we don't, then we need to find something else.

Everything about the legal profession is being transformed, including the jobs, functions, and contributions of lawyers. That turmoil is creating opportunities for those who are willing to embrace, lead, and adapt to change. With the right skills and attitudes, we can navigate that turmoil, design the career we want, and flourish.

Ida O. Abbott

Career

Retirement Strategist and Coach, Speaker, Author, Expert in Mentoring, Sponsorship, Advancing Women, and Legal Talent Management

Education

- JD, UC College of the Law, San Francisco (formerly UC Hastings College of Law) (1975)
- MA, University of Miami (1971)
- AB, American Studies, Smith College (1969)

Best Advice

In the moment, all obstacles are frustrating. But with some perspective and reframing, most can be surmounted, sidestepped, or even ignored. Step back and look at the obstacle in a larger context of your overall goal. How big is this obstacle? What is your strategy for removing it? How much effort will it take? Is it worth the effort required? Is there a way around the obstacle? Is there a way to neutralize it—or even make it work to your advantage? If the obstacle can't be budged, how else might you achieve your goal? However you proceed, who can you enlist to help you?

Personal

Ida Abbott's career has provided wonderful adventures and opportunities to learn, serve, travel, and work with fascinating people around the world, and she has long been a leader in the legal profession. Ida lives in Oakland, California, with her husband of 53 years, and is within an hour's drive of her fabulous three-year-old grandson and his parents (Ida's son and his wife). Her other son lives in New York after 20 years as an expat; he does not live very close, but no passport is required to visit. Ida is an avid walker, reader, and baker, does crossword puzzles and Spelling Bee, and loves to study Yiddish language and culture.

For More Information

https://idaabbott.com/about-ida
https://www.linkedin.com/in/ida-abbott-9a0736
https://www.retirement-by-design.com
Ida@IdaAbbott.com

Considerations on Retirement and Succession Planning for Lawyers

By Eileen M. Letts

How does one decide how and when to retire and how to plan for it? I will have some thoughts about succession planning later in this essay, but let's start with retirement.

Some lawyers never retire, they "die with their boots on." I don't plan to be that lawyer. I want to have some time when I don't have to think about anything other than what I am going to have for breakfast. It is hard for lawyers to retire. When I look around at friends and family (nonlawyers), at least 70 percent of them have retired. Many individuals decide to retire when they hit 55, but this is not so easy for lawyers. I don't think I know any lawyers who have "retired" at that age. I think there are several reasons for that: many don't have pensions, no mandatory retirement age or 401(k) plans—and some don't have the means to retire. Because we don't have those "automatic" savings plans, retirement requires thought and planning. Let's face it, do we really want to have a second job or become a greeter at a big box store? So the discussion is, how do I plan for retirement? I have practiced law for over 40 years and am giving serious thought to retiring in the next few years.

Several years ago my partner and I had a small minority-owned litigation boutique law firm. We were happy and doing well. We had been approached numerous times to have conversations with other firms about merging. However, a merger never appealed to us for several reasons. For one, it was nice having my name on the door and being in charge of "my destiny." But, one day, our office manager received a call from a recruiter and she suggested we have a conversation with him. I am not sure to this day why she thought talking to him was a good idea because at that time we were still not giving any thought to merging our practice with another firm. However, it was intriguing to get a call from a firm in California that wanted to have a Chicago office. Shortly prior to the call, I had been giving some consideration to making some changes, as my partner was having some major health challenges and all the management, client development, and other matters related to the firm were falling on me. So the timing was not all bad, and it turned out to be a good time to have a conversation with another firm. (However, I had no idea what the "changes" were going to be.)

We had lengthy conversations with the firm and decided to become their Chicago office. This was not an easy decision, and the courtship lasted for over a year. I had many conversations with my partner and others about this very weighty decision. A very important part of the decision was: did we like each other, did we want to work together, and did we want to build something together?

At the time, I was almost 60 years old but had no intention of retiring. I liked what I was doing (mostly). During conversations with the other firm, it became clear that I would no longer have to worry about payroll, human resources, and other major management decisions. I was really getting tired of being responsible for the day-to-day management. I think that as one becomes more "seasoned" in the law, those responsibilities become more and more challenging. I had not given any thought to what I would be doing in 10 years, but this was the beginning of my thoughts about retirement and succession planning. I knew then that I would not continue practicing law for the next 20 years, but what was I going to do?

Since we had been a minority-owned firm for almost 25 years, in making the decision to merge we considered it very important to stay as a minority-owned firm. We wanted to make sure that other lawyers of color would continue along the path we had begun in running a minority-owned law firm. That the California firm was minority-owned was a critical piece of our decision to merge. As I think back on it now, I know that merging as we did was part of our succession plan.

However, the downside to merging can be that "we are no longer in charge, we no longer have our name on the door," which was important at one time in my career. Is it worth giving up the name to have other benefits? Will it work to let someone else manage instead? It is very important to give thought to all these questions before you go down the path of merging because, if it does not work out, the firm could be back to square one. Even worse, you could no longer have a firm and would no longer be in charge of that firm's destiny.

Skipping ahead to the current time, we have now been successfully merged with the California firm for over 5 years, and the merger has gone well. I must say that in looking at the whole situation, I think it prepared me to begin thinking about retirement and succession. In doing so, I still have many management responsibilities but none of the day-to-day minutia that is required when someone manages her "own" law firm. I am the Chief Administrative Partner, on the management committee, the finance committee, and head of the litigation department. That is plenty! What about succession planning and leaving the firm—what will it look like? I need to give more thought to who will handle my clients. This is a tough issue because clients can be very selective, and we are too when we have to decide who we want to work with them in the future. I have begun to think more seriously about who works with my clients and how to transition them to other lawyers. One of the challenges is wanting to make sure that a diverse team is working on my matters. As an African American female attorney, I am committed to and feel it is my responsibility to make sure that a woman, and hopefully a woman of color, can take over my clients and my matters. This is a goal I have, and one I want to accomplish.

My clients are generally used to my involvement in their matters, so it is my responsibility to make them comfortable with someone else. I have developed personal relationships with many of my clients. Clearly, there should be a strategy for developing future leaders at the firm, and I have been trying to put that strategy in place. I work with several younger junior associates in my practice area and I supervise their work. There are challenges to making sure they have client contact when working on projects, as it is not always easy to put clients in touch with junior associates. However, that is a necessity and requires certain outreach to clients to get their buy-in.

It is not always easy to let go. Introductions are key because I want my clients to be comfortable with the lawyers they work with. I have learned through the years that having a good relationship goes a long way in keeping clients. When I am working on a matter, I make sure the associate is on the emails, attends meetings, and sometimes handles a matter solo and just copies me. Making this procedure work requires conscious effort. I now work on it much more diligently than I did in the past, but to be honest it is not automatic. Our firm is big on "collaboration," one of the things I love about the firm. We encourage diverse teams on matters, which is what clients want, so that makes it easier to stay focused on planning for the future.

Some lawyers I know have been "forced" to retire because of their firm's mandatory retirement age. This sometimes puts lawyers who did not plan to retire in a difficult position, and they are unsure what they are going to do once retirement becomes a reality.

Others who have been planners have thought that when they reached the age of 65 or 70 that was going to be "it" for their practice of the law. Upon retirement, however, many of them decided to engage in side ventures like consulting on various subjects, such as diversity, equity, and inclusion training, recruitment, or human resources. A friend of mine who retired recently knew what she wanted to do postretirement: start her own legal consulting firm. She works with clients in providing advice on diversity matters and consults on employment issues. She made this decision while she was still a partner at her law firm. She knew that she wasn't ready to stop working, but she decided to do what she loved doing and to do it on her own terms. I know others who have left the practice and become authors. In short, a lot of options are available, but, at the end of the day, one has to sit down, weigh the pros and cons, and decide how to approach it.

I still do not know how I plan to make the change from practicing law full-time to not practicing and retirement. I do believe that everyone should have "a plan" upon retirement. I have seen many people decide they are going to stop working and think about their future for a year or so. I think that is a very bad idea. I have seen too many people who sit in a chair all day, watch television, do not exercise, and just lose touch. I do not plan to be one of those people. When I retire, I will have a plan.

In talking about retirement and succession planning for women, a comment on women lawyers of color is in order. After having worked on "Left Out and Left Behind," a study sponsored by the American Bar Association (ABA), I learned that many women of color who practice law are unhappy with their profession but don't leave it for a number of reasons, especially the money, because they are the sole or most substantial financial contributor to the family income, or because they are the first in their family to go to college or law school. Do we get to retire when we want to, and are we in a position to help others succeed? I wonder. I don't think that is always the case, and more attention should be given to help women lawyers of color succeed and be able to retire when they want to and have business they can pass onto others.

I have decided that I will probably "ease" out of the practice. I anticipate reducing my hours substantially for billable matters while staying involved with management. The pressure of billable hours and dealing with the personalities of lawyers, clients, and judges can be extremely exhausting. Also, one should make the decision to enjoy a few years of just doing something they want to do, which may not involve the practice of law.

My firm is very involved in diversity, equity, and inclusion (DEI) efforts and I play a major role in the firm's involvement with several DEI commitments. The decision will have to be made as to who is going to continue with those efforts and ensure that we continue to have a very diverse workforce, as we currently do. I plan to play a role in that decision as I begin to look around the room now. I have had many internal conversations and debates with myself about this succession. It is an important role to fill.

To be clear, retirement is not for everyone. However, if one does decide to retire, they need to make sure that several things are in place from their personal perspective. As cliché as it may sound, I think one has to decide what will make that person happy. I am going to look in the mirror and ask myself what I want to be when I grow up. However, I am also going to relax, enjoy my own company, the company of others, and life in general. If a person wants to continue practicing law until they are unable to because they "love the law," then that is what they should do. However, I think consideration must be given to bringing others along, encouraging them to "take your place," and making sure that positions of power are filled. I look forward to retiring and looking back on my life in the law and hopefully on some contributions I have made along the way—ones I have made to the practice of law, to my law firm, and to others individually.

Eileen M. Letts

Career
Partner, Zuber Lawler LLP

Education
- JD, Illinois Institute of Technology Chicago—Kent College of Law (1978)
- BA, Ohio State University (1975)

Best Advice
I believe that you should stay focused on what you want and figure out a way to get it. That is, would becoming a member of an organization that will help you overcome these challenges be worthwhile; are there people you should talk to and get advice from who may help you? See the goal you are trying to achieve and focus on that, not on the obstacles.

Personal
Eileen Letts lives with her husband in the suburbs of Chicago. She has two grown sons who are great human beings. She currently sits in the ABA House of Delegates as a representative from the Litigation Section. She frequently speaks on diversity, equity, and inclusion, and she co-chaired the *ABA Diversity and Inclusion 360 Commission* and co-authored *Left Out and Left Behind: The Hassles, Hurdles, and Heartaches of Achieving Long-Term Legal Careers for Women of Color* (ABA 2020). She belongs to several social and philanthropic organizations and sits on several boards. She has a friend who established a foundation for cancer survivors that focuses on food inequities and she works with her in supporting that organization. She belongs to a book club and she loves to travel and walk for exercise.

For More Information
https://zuberlawler.com/attorneys/eileen-m-letts
eletts@zuberlawler.com

Pursuing the Path for Progress Toward Diversity in the Legal Profession

By Hon. Bernice B. Donald

I began my education in Olive Branch, Mississippi, in 1957, in a two-room schoolhouse with no running water and with an outhouse for a toilet. Excited for school, I opened the cover to my tattered schoolbook and noticed that there was already a name written in big letters across the top. On the back of the front cover, other names were listed such that all the spaces denoting ownership were already filled. There was no space for my name, which signaled to me that I did not belong and that there was no space for me. I slowly lifted my head up and glanced around the classroom. Every one of my classmates' books had different names inside that were not theirs. I quickly realized that the books that we were using to learn from were used books discarded by the white schools. That was the first time that I fully understood the disparities in education, resources, and the consequences of others' perception of my value.

For 6 to 8 weeks every school year, the all-Black Union School closed so that Black children could work the fields. I watched my white counterparts ride the school bus past our homes every single day for a month or two as we harvested the crops. At a young age I desired equal access to education, and I carried that passion with me when I became one of the first Black students to integrate into the all-white Olive Branch High School in Olive Branch, Mississippi, at the beginning of my junior year.

I thought high school would be scary. In fact, I was terrified because I previously had no meaningful interactions with white people, and certainly not in the classroom. Before high school, the classroom was the place where I was the most curious and innovative, and where I felt validated that I would one day go on to achieve everything that I dreamed of. However, this experience was very different. There was no collaboration with my classmates. During one class I was relegated to sit on a row by myself. It was embarrassing and demoralizing, an experience that I will never forget. But I have no resentment; little did I know my high school experience would foster the resilience necessary to climb mountains unseen.

Despite the difficulties that I faced in high school, I graduated top of my class. Due to my high school's policies, the school never informed me that I had been awarded scholarships for college. So, unable to pay for college on my own, I did what I had to do. I enrolled in Memphis State University and applied for grants and loans, and later worked at South Central Bell Telephone Company to pay my way through school. I continued to work for the telephone company through law school and envisioned a future in their legal department.

Nearly a decade with the telephone company and I was turned down for a job in its legal department, whereupon I briefly opened my own law practice and then worked in nonprofit and public interest organizations, defending indigent and low-income clients at Memphis Area Legal Services. I won my first case as a "baby lawyer," fresh out of law school. Much as I had in college and law school, I worked nights and weekends to prepare the case, and I was rewarded with a victory. Shortly thereafter, my boss left the public interest organization to become the County Public Defender, and he recruited me to join the office as an Assistant Public Defender. As I worked to represent indigent people accused of crimes, I observed disparities in the criminal legal system and was moved to alter the arc of justice.

Three years after my law school graduation, I ran for my first judgeship. I was 30 years old at the time. The pressures were high because an African American woman had never held the position of judge in the state of Tennessee. During my campaign, I sought to place a campaign ad at a radio station. As I sat in the waiting room, one of the receptionists was heard to exclaim, "where is this Bernice Donald! If she isn't here in 10 minutes, we are leaving!" I stood up from my chair and said, "I am Bernice Donald. I am here, and I have been here." The receptionist stated, "you're Bernice Donald? You don't look like a judge." To which I responded, "what does a judge look like?" While I was taken aback, I did not take any offense to her comment. Her statement simply highlighted the issue that is ever prevalent even at this time in American history—the lack of diversity on the bench.

In 1982, I became the first African American female judge in the state of Tennessee. Six years later, I became the first African American female in the history of the United States to serve as a Bankruptcy Judge, serving in the Western District of Tennessee. In 1995, President Clinton nominated me to serve as the first African American female judge of the U.S. District Court for the Western District of Tennessee, a position that I held for 15 years. And in 2010, President Obama nominated me to serve in my present position, as the first African American female judge to serve on the U.S. Court of Appeals for the Sixth Circuit.

I knew that I had a tremendous responsibility as the first African American female to serve on these various courts. Early on in my career, however, I did not fully appreciate the impact that I would have on those who would follow me. Being the "first" can be a tremendous honor, and I have been honored to serve in my various capacities as "the first." But I am keenly aware that the opportunities of those who come after me may be enlarged or limited based on the caliber of my service. This awareness is what motivates me to excel.

Every room in which I have been invited to participate—whether that be to sit on a board, committee, panel, or study group—I am aware that my voice may represent the many. I carry with me a diverse set of life experiences that challenge the status quo. But the most rewarding part of my presence is that it gives breath to those persons who may not be able to make it into the room for their story to be told. Raising awareness of the value of diversity and perspective has been the focal point of my career.

When I was first elected to the General Sessions Criminal Court, the first defendant to ever appear before me was a young white male. He entered a courtroom where the entire courtroom staff and the judge were African American. There were two minute clerks who were Black; surrounding the courtroom were four Black Sheriff's deputies and a Black prosecutor. The defendant approached the bench with fear and trepidation and requested a continuance, which I granted. When the defendant returned 30 days later, he had hired a Black lawyer to represent him. The young man was likely concerned about his ability to receive justice in a courtroom without any diversity. I took immediate action to create a diverse courtroom.

Justice Sandra Day O'Connor often is credited with having said that "a wise old man and wise old woman will reach the same conclusion in deciding cases." This is often true. But it is just as true that life's perspectives and experiences influence the lens by which people view the world.

Everyone wants justice, no matter their color or background. Reducing bias in the decision-making process is so important to me that I travel the country discussing the implications of implicit bias in the courtroom. I have encouraged municipalities to implement implicit bias training for government workers. I have even co-authored a scholarship that provokes meaningful discussion around the issue.

Yet, one of the best parts of my tenure as a judge has been the opportunity to contribute to diversity on the international stage, that is, to participate in a sort of judicial cross-pollination. I have served as faculty for numerous international programs providing technical legal assistance and capacity building for lawyers and judges in such countries as Turkey, Brazil, Russia, Zimbabwe, Armenia, and numerous African countries. Many countries look to the U.S. system of justice as a model for their own. Their support affirms the strength of traditions Americans sometimes take for granted, such as an independent judiciary and self-governing bar. Still, our system is not perfect, and I do not assume it is the right one for every country or jurisdiction I visit. Instead, traveling and teaching allow me to critically examine our own system and consider what we can learn from other approaches. Traveling also deepens my appreciation for the opportunities that I have had while recognizing that there is still much to do.

My diverse set of experiences has also influenced my judicial philosophy and the way I approach cases. And I have to say that, above all else, my experiences have made me a pragmatist. I do my best, as does any jurist who adheres to their duty, to decide each case as fairly, narrowly, and expeditiously as possible, based on my understanding of the law and the facts relevant to that case. I also recognize that the legitimacy of the judiciary—and, indeed, that of any branch of government—depends on the perceived, as well as actual, fairness. I am constantly reminded that the people we serve must understand the judicial system not only as an ideal through which hypothetical wrongs may be righted, but also as a living, breathing organ of society that speaks to their everyday needs. To that end, I strive to always be accessible, clear, and consistent.

The future of the legal profession is driven by those lawyers who have the courage to reach and pull. Justice Ruth Bader Ginsburg once stated: "fight for the things that you care about, but do it in a way that will lead others to join you."[4] As the "first," I found myself reaching for answers to questions that many were not yet prepared to confront. I pulled back on assumptions buttressing others' confirmed ideas about who I was. While sometimes difficult, I knew that everything that I experienced would mean something one day and that maybe my hardships would make the road a little smoother for the next person.

So as I watch the first Black woman nominated to the Supreme Court, I feel so much gratitude. Dr. King once said: "the arc of the moral universe is long but it bends toward justice."[5] Just as I was able to walk through doors that were not open to my parents' generation, I trust that the generations after mine will be able to do the same. It is my fervent hope that, one day, the doors of opportunity will have been open to everyone long enough so that each person who walks through them will have seen someone like themselves go before.

---

4. Colleen Walsh, *Honoring Ruth Bader Ginsburg*, THE HARVARD GAZETTE, https://news.harvard.edu/gazette/story/2015/05/honoring-ruth-bader-ginsburg (last visited Sept. 20, 2023).

5. Dr. Martin Luther King Jr., "Remaining Awake Through a Great Revolution," (speech given at the National Cathedral, Mar. 31, 1968).

Hon. Bernice B. Donald

Career
Senior United States Circuit Judge, United States Court of Appeals for the Sixth Circuit, Retired

Education
- JD, University of Memphis School of Law (1979)
- BA, University of Memphis

Best Advice
Surround yourself with people who affirm your value, have confidence in yourself, go forward with boldness, be willing to work hard, define yourself, don't let others define you, and NEVER GIVE UP!

Personal
Against a lot of odds, Judge Bernice Donald became an elected judge at 30 years of age. People told her that it was not possible, but she surrounded herself with supportive family and people who believed in her success! And it worked! In law school, her employer changed her work schedule, making it impossible for her to attend her regular classes. Rather than quit, she developed a creative solution to attend other professors' classes and take her designated professors' classes. Once she presented the proposal, each bought in. Lesson: You never know until you try. Don't give up.

Judge Donald, a 40-year jurist, has served on four courts, two of which were presidential appointments. She is a national and international lecturer and has held numerous leadership positions, including: President, National Association of Women Judges Association; President, American Bar Foundation; Chair, National Conference of Special Court Judges; Chair, Criminal Justice Section, American Bar Association; Founder, 4-Life, A Youth Development organization; Director, Financial Literacy Project, Tort Trial and Insurance Section, American Bar Association; and Faculty, Race and the Law, Regent University and Arizona State University.

Judge Donald enjoys reading, travel, music, theater, and experiencing diverse cultures.

She is a chapter author in the ABA publication *Enhancing Justice: Reducing Bias* (ABA 2017) and is co-editor of the book *Extending Justice: Strategies to Increase Inclusion and Reduce Bias* (Carolina Academic Press 2023).

For More Information

Judge Donald is currently a neutral with Resolute Systems.

The Power of Women Leadership in the Legal Profession

By Ashley Coleman

I graduated law school in 2008 at the height of the great recession. I was thrilled to have found a job, albeit, not in the legal field I dreamt of, but I was happy to practice civil litigation, which was my goal. I remember during my on-campus interview with the firm that ultimately hired me, one of the named partners, an older white-haired male, asked me why I wanted to work for the firm. When I responded by saying that I wanted to be a litigator and was looking for litigation experience, he looked at me, smirked a little, and said: "You have to be tough to be a litigator. Can you be tough?" At the time, I felt he was suggesting that I could not be tough based on my appearance. I was taken off guard by this comment but laughed, a bit uncomfortably, and replied, "Don't let the blond hair fool you. I can be tough." After the interview, I was convinced that I was not going to get a call back, let alone a job at the firm. But thankfully, I got the clerkship and was selected to work for the main named partner of the firm. I was one of six clerks and the only female. There were no female partners at the time I joined, and there was very little diversity. I wasn't in a position at the time to do anything about that, and frankly, even if I could have, I wouldn't have done anything to jeopardize my position because I was so thrilled to have a job in a tough labor market.

I went on to work for the firm for several years, and though they were very good to me and I have no complaints about my time there, I experienced several comparable instances throughout my early career that highlighted the fact that I was a young female in a male world. Countless times I walked into a room to take a deposition only to be asked if I was the court reporter. I think most of my female classmates experienced similar occurrences early in their career. On one occasion, I had a male paralegal close the door to my office so he could "tell me how things worked around here," all because he did not like taking direction from a female. At the time I was in complete shock by his behavior, and I took it personally, as though I had done something wrong.

Perhaps the most disappointing instance was during my first-ever court appearance. I prepared for the appearance, and so I was ready to share everything I knew about the status of the case with the judge. The opposing attorney was not prepared, which became clear when he introduced himself to me and asked me about the case before the hearing started. I naively told him everything I knew. When the judge called for our appearance, the only words I said were my name and who I represented. After that, the court addressed all questions to my older, male counterpart, who simply parroted the summary I had shared with him. Later that day, when I arrived back at my firm, the partner who sent me told me he had been listening to the hearing and he apologized for what he viewed as either sexism or ageism, or both.

In looking back on the early days of my career, the one missing element in each of the scenarios described above was the presence of women at the top. My first law firm did not have a single female partner. That changed over the years, though I did not stick around long enough to watch it develop.

In my next few roles, I saw that having women at the top made a difference for an organization. A few years into my practice of law, a friend from law school told me that his firm was looking for employment lawyers. I had some employment experience, so I applied and got the job. The only real downside to this job was that it came with an hour-plus-long commute each way. There were several female partners at this firm, including two who were very influential for me. They, and the female associates whom I met there, taught me what it meant to be a successful, strong, (and well-dressed) attorney. The firm had a wonderful policy called "learning time," in which young attorneys were allowed to sit in on depositions and attend mediations and trials and still get credit toward their billable hours. I remember being in awe of the way these female attorneys and senior associates owned the room, and I developed my own idea of the type of strong attorney I wanted to be.

I want to be clear that I feel strongly that having women at the top of organizations is only part of the solution. It is also critically important, however, to have male leaders supporting women in the workforce. I have had the privilege of working for several male leaders who not only encouraged me but also saw my strengths and gave me opportunities to grow and excel.

One piece of advice that has served me well over the years is not to burn bridges. Whenever I left a job over the years, I made sure to leave gracefully, grateful for the experience I had gained and remembering the mentors and friends I gained. Some of those influential partners and friends are still my mentors and friends, and they are big firm partners and judges, and some lead in-house legal departments. One of those influential partners whom I met at my second law firm helped me launch my career as an in-house lawyer by introducing me to one of her clients and for that, I will be forever grateful. Looking back now, I realize what a strong woman at the top did to: (1) mentor me as an attorney, and then (2) introduce me to a career I loved. Now, I worked hard to develop a reputation for myself as a hard worker and a good lawyer, but without that mentoring and boost from her, I would not be where I am today.

Today I am very proud to be part of a company that is devoted to promoting diversity and encouraging women to follow their passions to succeed. Not only do I have a diverse team today made up of men and women, but also my company is made up of a diverse pool of talented individuals with some impressive female leaders. We have employee resource groups (ERGs) that focus on these topics. Our HUSSLE ERG, which stands for Humans United to Support the Ladies' Experience, is dedicated to bettering the female experience and building a workplace where women can thrive. Our UNIFIED ERG, which stands for United Network of Influencers Furthering Inclusion and Ethnic Diversity, brings awareness, knowledge, and understanding of workplace ethnic challenges and community issues, advancing an environment for personal and career growth free from discrimination and inequality, and provoking ways to provide access, seats at the table, and communication channels for multicultural voices to lead.

In both of the in-house legal teams on which I have served, there have been more women than men, and not just on the team, but in leadership roles as well. Just as important as having women in leadership roles is having men in leadership roles who promote diversity and encourage women to step into leadership roles.

In 2022, our legal department, which is only 3 years old, decided to let our outside law firms know that diversity is important to us. We asked each of our firms to fill out a diversity survey, letting us know not only about the makeup of their firms, but also providing information to us about the lawyers who work on our matters. The results were excellent—not just from the standpoint of learning more about the diversity policies of our firms, but also from the standpoint of our firms learning that diversity is important to us. Several firms reached out to me to thank us for having them engage in the exercise because it raised their awareness of the diversity (or lack thereof) in their firms. Others reached out to me to say they appreciated our commitment to diversity.

As a child, I never questioned that I could do whatever I put my mind to, probably because that was the rhetoric my parents framed for me. In school I never experienced any limitations because I was a woman, nor did I ever feel that I was treated differently because of my gender. That alone tells me that we have come a long way. I think of women who pioneered their way through law school when there were no women. Probably similar to many other women my age and in my profession, Ruth Bader Ginsburg was a huge role model for me.

Despite how far we have come in a relatively short period of time, there is still work to be done. My hope is that my own daughter will not have to undergo the experiences I had as a young lawyer, as innocuous as they were—whether in the legal field or any other field of her choosing. I truly believe that the only way to continue to improve conditions for young women is to keep talking about diversity and raising awareness.

I want to share three things to consider to promote diversity and female leadership in the profession:

1. Take the time to invest in activities that promote diversity. We all get busy in our careers and it's tough to take time away from your career to do extracurricular things that are outside of what is required and/or your family commitments. The only way to make change is to participate in it and encourage it. Whether it's creating a diversity committee or participating in one, or just mentoring a female new to the field, it's important to participate. There may be something unknown to be learned. There may be something to teach someone else. Taking the time can make a positive change in your organization.
2. No contribution is too small if it makes a difference for just one person. Sometimes it is overwhelming to think about how to contribute to diversity and promoting female leadership. I know

at times, especially as a young attorney, I wondered how I could possibly make a difference. The fact is, we often don't know the end result when we start out. We may have a plan or a goal in mind, but it doesn't always turn out exactly as expected. If someone had told me that I would end up working as an in-house lawyer for a company that I adore when I first started out, I'm not sure I would have believed it, even though that was definitely a goal. I remember thinking how I would love to work in-house for a cool company someday. Had I not had the support of a female mentor, I'm not sure I could have achieved that goal as quickly. I am always looking to pay it forward to other hardworking female lawyers.

3. Stick with it. There were times in my career, especially after my twins were born 7 weeks prematurely, that I really wanted nothing more than to quit my career to stay home with them. I'd be lying if I told you that, at the time, I was disappointed that this wasn't an option for me. Now I am thankful that I stuck with it, even if it wasn't by choice, because I have a career I love. Had I left early given the circumstances I was addressing at the time, I would not be where I am today.

Ashley Coleman

Career

Assistant General Counsel, Litigation & Employment, Chipotle Mexican Grill

Education

- JD, Chapman University Fowler School of Law (2008)
- BA, International Relations and Communications, University of Southern California (2004)

Best Advice

When the going gets tough, work hard, always do your best work, and never let someone else's opinion of you change what you know about your value.

Personal

Ashley Coleman currently serves as Assistant General Counsel, Litigation & Employment, at Chipotle Mexican Grill, Inc., where she oversees labor and employment compliance and litigation matters for over 100,000 employees. Since April 2019, Ashley has managed Chipotle's litigation, labor and employment compliance, governmental audits, agency charges, and claims management, among other duties. Prior to Chipotle, Ashley spent almost 4 years at Allied Universal Security Services serving on the legal team, overseeing wage and hour class action litigation and employment compliance. Before going in-house, she worked as a litigator, specializing in employment law. At Chapman University, she served as the Notes and Comments Editor on *Chapman's Law Review* and participated in Moot Court competitions. Before law school, she attended the University of Southern California, where she double-majored in International Relations and Communications. In her free time, she enjoys spending time with her husband and 8-year-old twins, running, paddle boarding, and traveling.

Mentoring and Supporting Each Other on the Road Ahead

By Hon. Ebony M. Scott

I must admit, I have not sought the definition of "resilient" in quite some time. I certainly use the word with some regularity. But as I prepared to write this essay, I quizzically turned to Merriam-Webster to search for the definition of a word that many have often used to describe me, almost as if to determine if I truly measured up to the definition. Here is what I found:

> **Definition of *resilient*:** characterized or marked by resilience: such as
> **a:** capable of withstanding shock without permanent deformation or rupture
> **b:** tending to recover from or adjust easily to misfortune or change.[6]

I stared at this definition for some time. Was I *that*? Am I capable of withstanding shock? Do I recover easily from misfortune or change? Most importantly, should *I* author an essay in a publication about resilience? After more time than I would like to confess, I concluded that I am indeed a resilient woman. My resilience has been shaped and solidified by my personal experiences, personality traits, and the support I received from my mentors. Indeed, I can honestly say that I have not traveled this road alone (no one does if we are being honest), and the support I received from my mentors has made the road less traveled more palpable for someone like me. So, who am I? Let's start from the top—then it will be apparent why mentoring and supporting each other on the road ahead is vital.

I was born in upstate New York to a teenage mother. In fact, I was in the audience when my mother graduated from high school. My earliest memories of my life undoubtedly included my mother working long hours at the local hospital and me somewhere reading or pretending to play "school" or "court" with my cousins, who all thought I was the biggest

---

6. *Resilient*, MERRIAM-WEBSTER.COM, https://www.merriam-webster.com/dictionary/resilient (last visited on Mar. 14, 2022).

nerd they ever saw. I did not care because all I ever really wanted to do was learn. I was an only child to my mother and I was never bothered by the fact that I was alone because I always had . . . books. Surely my middle school teacher noticed the quiet discipline I exhibited and placed upon myself. She pulled me aside one day and suggested that I apply to a program called Buffalo Prep (Prep). According to its website, Prep was founded in 1989 to help talented underrepresented students prepare for, obtain entrance into, and excel at demanding college preparatory high schools.[7] I interviewed for, and was accepted into, Prep in the fifth grade and spent a few summers and weekends "prepping" to attend a high-caliber and high-achieving college preparatory high school. Prep undoubtedly changed my life and placed opportunities at my fingertips that my family did not have the resources to provide. Looking back, I realize that the middle school teacher who recommended me to Prep was my first "trusted counselor or guide"[8]—indeed, my first mentor. It pains me that I cannot remember my teacher's name, but I can remember how she made me feel—hopeful, smart, and capable. While I did not know how to characterize the nudging and support that my teacher provided to me as a child, as I matured, I would recognize this behavior over and over again in various people in varying stages of my life and came to know that it was "mentoring."

Mentoring, to me, is helping someone actualize their dreams by providing them with tools for their toolbox. For me, those tools were access to an excellent education and gaining different perspectives by traveling outside of upstate New York and immersing myself in different cultures and traditions, but also staying true to who I am and the edicts that I lived by—namely, humility, faith, family, and education. For others, their toolbox may look different, but that is the beauty of the mentoring relationship. Everyone needs something a bit different to reach their goals, but we all need support along the way.

I have had many mentors since my very first one. More often than not my mentors have come from within the circle I am trying to penetrate,

---

7. *Getting to Know Prep*, BUFFALO PREP, https://buffaloprep.com/about (last visited on Mar. 14, 2022).
8. *Mentor*, MERRIAM-WEBSTER.COM, https://www.merriam-webster.com/dictionary/mentor (last visited on Mar. 14, 2022).

and the relationships have grown into that of a mentor and mentee. For example, I have a mentor from just about every area of law that I have practiced, and this is not by accident. Each time I began a new job, I would seek out people I had developed admiration for based on their work ethic, work style, and temperament. I watched how these people treated others, especially those who were not considered their professional equals. Remarkably, after some time, these individuals would invite me into their orbit, or I would extend an invitation to lunch or coffee, linger after a meeting to chat, or stop by an office to ask a question, and the mentoring relationship would develop. Now, I do not want to suggest that I have hundreds of mentors, as this is not the case. A mentoring relationship is a valuable relationship, and so time and space are needed to nurture these relationships for them to be enduring and meaningful. Having served as a mentee and mentor for over two decades now, what follows is my perspective on this coveted relationship.

The Role of a Mentor

We must not be self-serving, and the desire to mentor cannot be based on a desire to add the role of "mentor" to a resume. A mentor must be committed to meeting their mentees where they are and ultimately committed to the process. For example, I have served as a mentor to young people whose parents have reached out to tell me that their son or daughter would like to be a lawyer and who asked if I would be willing to chat with them. I have also served as a mentor in more structured settings, such as those created by College Bound[9] and the Abramson Scholarship Foundation.[10] No matter the setting, my goals have always been to enrich my mentee's life by supporting them in reaching their personal and professional goals, even when they are sidetracked. I recall one young lady I mentored who was very bright, but also very shy. I spent a considerable amount of time thinking about how to reach her in a way that she would respond. I wanted her to know that I was not just mentoring her

---

9. Visit the College Bound website at https://www.collegebound.org (last visited Mar. 14, 2022).
10. Visit the Abramson Foundation website at https://abramsonfoundation.org (last visited Mar. 14, 2022).

each week because I had to, but because I wanted to support her and was anxious to see her succeed. Well, she became pregnant while still in high school. She was scared to tell me because she thought I would be disappointed in her. So her mother told me. Admittedly, I was disappointed. However, what she did not know, and I soon revealed, was that my mother had me at 14 years of age, and while the road would be a bit harder, it was a road traveled by many, and success was still waiting for her on the other side. So our mentoring relationship changed. I attended her baby shower and met her extended family. But I always made sure to talk about her professional goals and support her without judgment. Because she wanted to be a lawyer, I began the mentoring relationship expecting her to shadow me at work, stop by my office for a tour, and attend meetings with my colleagues. But I had to be malleable and dispense with my rigidness. I had to meet her where she was, and I did. As mentors, no matter the relationship, we must be willing to go off script and find a meaningful way to support those we commit to mentor, especially during those times when we are challenged with the curveballs thrown our mentee's way.

Although I am recalling a mentoring relationship that I had with a teenager, the same tenets are true for those mentoring young lawyers or even judges. Life is extremely unpredictable. What will we do if our mentee is fired from a job, has a hard time finding a job, has a conflict with a partner at a firm, or is simply underperforming? Walk away? Stop reaching out because we are only comfortable when your mentee reports good news? No, we must support our mentee in a way that we are comfortable and that is appropriate for the relationship. Often, this means that we become still and simply listen. When it is time to speak, we should speak words of encouragement and power, and introduce solutions that may have worked in similar situations, or work with the mentee to brainstorm solutions together. This, of course, should all be done in confidence. Even if there is no solution to the issue(s) at hand, the mentee will forever remember the support that was provided along the way, and my experiences have taught me that they will be inclined to mentor others and will be equipped with the tools needed to continue to support their mentee in both good and bad times. When this cycle is created, it is very hard to break. I truly believe that mentoring is one of the greatest legacies that we can leave to the next generation of legal professionals and one of the simplest ways to ensure continuity and integrity within our profession.

The Role of a Mentee

A mentee must be an active and full participant in the mentoring relationship. In other words, a person who does not want to be mentored will have a hard time benefiting from the relationship. What do I mean? Well, one of my staunchest mentors is the Honorable Anna Blackburne-Rigsby, who currently serves as the Chief Judge of the District of Columbia Court of Appeals. I clerked for Chief Judge Blackburne-Rigsby during her first term on the appellate bench, and my desire to be mentored by her was as strong as my desire to deliver a perfect work product. Not only is she a brilliant jurist, but I saw how she pursued excellence in all that she did and how she treated everyone with dignity and respect. I admired her intellect and compassion and knew that she embodied the type of lawyer and judge I wanted to be. So I asked questions and showed a genuine desire for her mentorship, and I did not simply clock in and out as her judicial law clerk. Now, I must admit, the Chief is a natural-born mentor. I later learned that she viewed clerkships as mentoring relationships and looked forward to serving as a supervisor and mentor, so forming such a relationship was not uncommon in her chambers. However, this relationship, and others, flourished when I took an active role and exhibited a desire to be mentored as well as an appreciation for the mentoring relationship.

For me, mentoring has taken many forms, including pep talks, moots before a big case, interview preparation, wardrobe advice, a LOT of resume review, the celebration of victories, and the space to vent. My mentors have created a safe space for me to grow professionally and fail gracefully. These relationships have played such a significant role in my life that I have yet to turn down the opportunity to mentor someone who wishes to be mentored or simply wants to chat about the legal profession. It is especially important that we, women in the legal profession, recognize the unique position in which we find ourselves and commit to supporting each other and sharing our unique perspectives and stories with those on different legs of their journey. The victory of mentoring is truly actualized when we witness someone whom we have mentored conquer a goal or realize dreams. We understand that it is not all about us, but truly about how we can help someone else. The road ahead may be chilling, but to know that someone else traveled it, and is willing to walk alongside you, is life-altering. So, become a mentor and change the life of another, as well as your own. You will never regret it.

Hon. Ebony M. Scott

Career
Associate Judge, Superior Court of the District of Columbia

Education
- JD, American University Washington College of Law (2006)
- BA, Political Science, University of Rochester

Best Advice
One of my favorite quotes is the following from Nelson Mandela: "I never lose: either I win, or I learn." Accept obstacles and failures as an opportunity to learn, and later win!

Personal
Judge Ebony M. Scott has always been committed to public service. She previously served as an Abramson Scholarship Foundation mentor, played an active role on its mentoring committee, and remains involved in the extraordinary work of the Foundation. Judge Scott is also an Adjunct Professorial Lecturer at American University Washington College of Law and enjoys serving as both a lecturer and mentor to her students. Judge Scott resides in the District of Columbia with her husband, and they love to travel and explore all the great local attractions that make Washington, DC, so exhilarating!

For More Information
https://www.dccourts.gov/sites/default/files/2023-03/Associate_Judge_Ebony_Scott_DCSC_1.pdf

The Mentor's Toolkit: Action Steps to Help Mentees

By Kristen Reeves Jones

As a woman in law, there is so much to be optimistic about these days. We comprise a majority of law students and we've seen a steady increase in the number of women attaining equity partnership, state and federal judgeships, and more. In addition, more and more employers are making a public commitment to hiring more women, more people of color, more people with disabilities, and more veterans and military spouses. These employers are also offering flexible schedules and work environments, better support for parents, and targeted training and advancement opportunities in a concerted effort to retain and develop talented professionals. There is no time like the present to reach for your dreams—and to encourage others through mentoring to follow your lead.

>
> "A true measure of your worth includes all the benefits others have gained from your success."
> —Cullen Hightower

Many of the essays in this collection were written to inspire people to build the skills and mindset they need to succeed in the law. At times a career will follow a well-worn path traveled by decades of women attorneys. On occasion, a lawyer will be called upon to blaze the trail. Either way, we'll never travel this road alone. At every juncture in our career, we have the opportunity to seek and give support to the women around us. Let's make the most of those opportunities.

Below I describe why mentoring is important to me. I also provide a toolkit with action steps mentors can take to support their role.

We Need Mentors

By way of background, 6 months into my marriage to an active-duty Airman, I was absolutely convinced that I would never practice law again. It would be impossible to move every other year, take another bar exam, obtain a new license, secure a new job, and build any sort of professional momentum. I would have to choose between my career and my marriage. I chose my career.

I attended law school in Virginia at night while working as a court clerk and a paralegal. I built an impressive network of judges and attorneys, and I was handed a series of good jobs by people who knew and trusted me. After law school, I clerked for a local judge, and I expected to follow in her path. I would enjoy a successful career in a tight-knit community, surrounded by friends and colleagues who were invested in my success. Instead, I married a law school classmate, and we moved from Virginia to Wyoming—home is where the Air Force sends you. I had no contacts, no job, and no law license. It would take at least a year to become licensed and by then we'd be planning our next move.

I was a high achiever with very specific goals. At the time, I could only imagine one professional path, and reaching that first major obstacle meant the journey was over. I imagined my life had turned onto a sidetrack, which was taking me farther and farther from my goals. I had to get back on track. I gave my husband an ultimatum: if I couldn't find a job by Christmas, I would move back to Virginia. Miraculously, I was hired by the Wyoming Attorney General's office for a position that required a Juris Doctor (JD) but no license. When I became licensed, they graciously moved me into a "permanent" position with a federal focus so I could develop transferable skills. When it was time to move, they wished me luck and encouraged me to come back if I ever could. I found an employer who understood and supported my needs and genuinely cared about setting me up for success.

What truly saved my career, though, was meeting other military spouse attorneys who had overcome similar obstacles and found ways to persevere and even thrive within the profession. I began to understand that other paths were open to me, and I trusted that I would eventually discover the right fit. I also found ways to use my skills and be of service outside my 9-to-5. No matter my perceived professional failures, I had valuable skills to impart and (my own brand of) optimism to share. I joined the board of the Military Spouse JD Network, which allowed me to speak with and on behalf of hundreds of attorneys and law students facing the same barriers that almost derailed my career. Within 10 minutes of meeting another military spouse attorney, we shared our stories, our goals, our frustrations, and not a few tears.

This is the support we women owe each other on the road ahead. Each and every one of us can become the ally, the friend, and the mentor that another woman needs. We can change this profession, and we should accept no other outcome.

What Is Mentoring?

More than passing along skills and sharing templates (although these are also crucial), mentoring means making a personal commitment to developing another woman professionally. It means offering her unconditional support, consistent encouragement, and genuine care. To be a mentor is to help guide another woman's career over and around the obstacles that are all too familiar—and maybe change the entire landscape as you go.

Mentoring is also the way to develop a living legacy. This is the best sort of pyramid scheme whereby we multiply our own accomplishments by empowering others to have a similar impact. The goal of mentoring is not to train a group of competent followers, but to equip the next generation of inspired leaders. Through mentoring, we are the rising tide that lifts other boats.

The judge I clerked for was the first woman to wear pants to court in our county. She was one of the first women in the prosecutor's office and on the bench. She didn't have an easy time reaching her goals, and some of her dreams went unfulfilled. In spite of and because of the obstacles she faced, she was determined to make things easier for the women who followed in her footsteps. To amplify her personal achievements, she made a commitment to mentoring other women, encouraging them to become better lawyers and to don the robe. Her law clerks became her friends and could count on her support for life.

Let's Get Started

Good news. I've got a checklist. Whether teaching someone to knit or training a C-Suite replacement, the formula is the same: show them the ropes, then turn them loose.

I do. You watch. We talk.
I do. You help We talk.
You do. I help. We talk.
You do. I watch. We talk.
You do. Someone else watches.

But recall that mentoring is more than mere training.

Make a commitment. Start by making a commitment to developing the people around you. There may be a formal program through a firm or local bar, or it might be possible simply to identify a colleague you can take under your wing. Mentoring will require a serious outlay of time and energy, but the effort will certainly pay dividends. This is an investment for the future.

Get personal. Establish a personal relationship. Get to know the person's unique goals and challenges and explore what is held in common. Genuine care and trust will follow. These are the bedrock of any mentoring relationship and part of the joy reaped in the process.

Give help unconditionally. Without question there is a benefit in seeing others succeed and build a better profession, but there's no quid pro quo to mentoring. Go in ready to help mentees in whatever way they need—with no expectation of personal gain.

Identify clear goals. Most of us emerged from law school with only the vaguest sense of purpose and only an inkling of where we were headed in life. For me, reality struck time and again, and my goals shifted over the years. Start by helping a mentee identify and fine-tune her personal goals, whatever they may be. There's no need to aim for the stars just yet. Start with achievable, measurable, meaningful milestones which will put the mentee on the right path.

Equip others for success. Share the tools, resources, and tips that helped you succeed. Point out the CLEs, hornbooks, and conferences that will be most useful. When I was a young associate, a partner unceremoniously dropped a file on my desk: "Have you ever handled a partition?" Blank stare. "Call someone and figure it out."

That was the assignment. Naturally, I read the file and the statutes, but the way I learned to handle the case was by calling a mentor. My friend the judge referred me to one of *her* mentors, who gladly took my call, explained the process, and sent me his templates. I handled the case solo, and I won. (The partner knew I would. The sink-or-swim approach was his brand of mentoring.)

Take someone with you. Whenever you do anything worth sharing, take someone along. Take a young associate to a new client meeting so she can see how it is handled. Bring a colleague who is new to the practice area to the next trial or hearing. Invite a boss to the next bar meeting; maybe she's been looking for a way to become more involved. But don't just show them how it's done. Explain the why. Point out the pitfalls. Discuss potential setbacks and how they are managed. Then step back and let the mentee try it; watch and offer suggestions.

Check in. The mentee will soon take the wheel, but there will invariably be obstacles to her success. Monitor the mentee's progress by checking in regularly. This could be a monthly coffee date or videochat, but it has to be calendared. Carve out this time as critical to protecting your investment! Discuss the mentee's achievements and help her set new measurable goals. Review the obstacles she has encountered and be prepared to recalibrate the route as needed. Give honest and constructive feedback with unrelenting support and encouragement.

Celebrate their success. Keep up the momentum by celebrating every triumph. And remember, their success is your success! This is not a race or a competition. Best case scenario, mentoring means watching other women pass by as we cheer loudly from the next lane. The heights we reach will be all the more meaningful if our success propels others still higher.

Remember the big picture. When we make the commitment to mentor another woman, it is not necessarily with the intent to make her a managing partner or CEO or Supreme Court justice. We are helping her define *her* purpose and meet *her* goals. Regardless of her path, we're here to make her feel more confident, secure, and appreciated within a challenging profession. Some mentees will bring in big business for a firm, some will become bar leaders who train other leaders, and all will be fine attorneys improving the lives of their clients one by one. Whatever the result, our commitment to mentoring others will have a positive effect on the profession.

Down the Road

The beauty of mentorship is that it doesn't end when a mentee masters a particular skill or is promoted to a particular rank. The cycle continues with the mentee becoming a mentor, showing others what she has learned and inspiring them to reach their own goals. And always, always sharing those templates.

We haven't just trained another lawyer; we've created a leader. Our support, encouragement, and care will be magnified with each new generation. We've done our part to chip away at the obstacles that slowed us down to clear the path for others.

But What about Me?

A woman doesn't have to be on any particular path or have reached certain heights to be an effective mentor to another woman. Her personal struggles and triumphs are valuable lessons and inspiration to the woman following in her footsteps. *Find her and tell her your story.* Help her understand that this career is navigable (enjoyable even!) with the right equipment and the right support. Be that support.

Many years ago, a college essay prompt asked me how I would fit into the mosaic that was the student body. I answered with confidence: I may never be one of the brilliant, glittering glass pieces, but I will serve as the cement holding them all together.

Sure enough, I got my start in bar leadership as the treasurer. I made my mark by paying the bills and keeping the lights on. I worked behind the scenes to streamline processes, jettison redundant software, and develop a strategy to sustain our small organization. For my talents, I was honored with the Military Spouse JD Network's annual leadership award. As a bar president, I continue to search out and implement those incremental improvements to leave a stronger organization in my wake. I strive to mentor our members and support my board through quiet leadership.

Ten years into my legal career, I don't supervise anyone, and I don't have much seniority. I can't say I've achieved any dreams, but I continue to set and diligently pursue my goals. I've been licensed in four states and have gained broad experience across a number of practice areas. I have learned from my mistakes and grown through my struggles. I am an expert in resilience and silver linings. Against all odds, I have achieved success—and I am committed to encouraging others to do the same.

Take some time to recognize *your* strengths and make a plan to share them with others. A true measure of your success includes all the benefits others have gained.

Kristen Reeves Jones

Career

Supervising Attorney, Office of the Wyoming Attorney General, Criminal Appellate Section

Education
- JD, George Mason University (2010)
- BA, Government and Spanish Literature, Dartmouth College (2005)

Best Advice

Life is too short. Follow your passions.

Personal

Kristen Jones is a graduate of Dartmouth College and George Mason University Law School. As an Air Force spouse, she has lived and practiced law in four states and is now proud to call Wyoming her "forever home." Her broad professional experience includes a judicial clerkship, criminal defense, family law, civil litigation, administrative law, government contracting, and estate planning. As she notes, when you move every 2 years, you have no choice but to tackle every new challenge and learn everything you can! From 2013 to 2014, Kristen worked for the Wyoming Attorney General's Office representing the state's Medicaid program. In 2020, she was excited to return to the Wyoming Attorney General's Office and join the Criminal Division. Kristen recently served as the president of the Military Spouse JD Network, a bar association committed to supporting the professional development of military spouse legal professionals. She is also passionate about conservation and sustainability.

For More Information

Kristen.Jones1@wyo.gov

The Importance of Role Models
By Grace Speights

When considering what to write on this topic, I tried to think of the most important role model in my life, and it occurred to me that I could not pick just one. I have benefited from multiple role models and mentors; perhaps that's not unusual, although it might also mean that I was particularly fortunate.

My first thought was of a place, not a person, and my choice might seem counterintuitive since it would not fit the classic definition of a "nice" place, although it was certainly formative. It's where I grew up, a tough neighborhood in Philadelphia, one frequented by gangs who, with some frequency, settled their differences with gunfire. There, I learned some valuable lessons, such as where to go and when, whom to avoid, and how to stay out of trouble if avoidance was not an option. I also learned how to be brave, or at least not to show my fear when I felt afraid. I suppose this place also gave me a desire to seek peace and order that I found in books and school and, eventually, college and law school and, finally, the law.

But I would not have known how to navigate those streets or developed the capacity to seek a way forward without the influence of my mother, my first role model. She, more than anyone, demonstrated the value of hard work and how to be tough without being obnoxious, and she imparted to me the motivation to succeed beyond my immediate circumstances. She sometimes spent 14 hours a day at her job in a factory folding fiberglass draperies and then would come home itching from the fiberglass fragments embedded in her skin. Believe me, it gave me an important perspective whenever I began to feel sorry for myself, toiling over legal briefs into the early morning hours.

The grit and resilience I inherited from my mother, combined with my experiences on the streets of Philadelphia, also instilled within me some characteristics that would prove invaluable later in life. For instance, in a courtroom, a lawyer must learn to take over the room without being too domineering; she cannot be timid, but she certainly also needs to avoid the impression of demanding too much. It's a balancing act that I learned threading my way through those early years.

Mom's insistence on hard work also paid off when I became the first person in my family to graduate from high school and go to college, let alone law school. All along the way, I could hear her in my head urging me to work as hard as I could. It paid off with my getting good grades, thus positioning me to successfully seek scholarships, which was really the only way I could afford higher education.

At this point, it took an unexpected role model, a partner at a law firm in Philadelphia whom I met at a scholarship event, to steer me toward the University of Pennsylvania instead of the small state school I had planned to attend. This man, whom I had never before met, helped arrange an interview for me at Penn, which I ended up attending on a full scholarship. Because of this timely intervention, I received a degree from an Ivy League institution, thanks to someone far more familiar with the hierarchy of education and law firms than either my Mom or me. As a result, I made it through another great school, George Washington University (GWU), where I received my law degree.

During my second year at GWU, I applied to become a summer associate at Morgan, Lewis & Bockius, a firm I really did not know much about even though it was only about eight blocks or so from the neighborhood in which I grew up. Unbeknownst to me, it would become my professional home for my entire career. Here, I quickly learned the lesson that an overabundance of humility could prove detrimental, when, during my interview with Washington office partner Mike Kelly, he was astonished to learn how well I had done in school. His surprise stemmed from the simple fact that I had not included any of this information on my resume, which had led him to wonder if perhaps I had not posted great grades. When he found out the opposite was true, he spent the next 10 minutes telling me why I should make my success clear in my resume. "Suppose," he said, "I didn't ask you those things?"

I was maturing as a person and I was becoming a lawyer, but I still had much to learn, and all along the way I fortunately encountered people who were willing to teach. Upon graduation from GWU, I clerked for Chief Judge Aubrey E. Robinson Jr. of the U.S. District Court for the District of Columbia. This pioneering Black judge, a Renaissance man in every sense of the word, had ascended to the bench in 1966 at the age of 42 upon his appointment by President Lyndon B. Johnson. Judge Robinson eventually became the chief judge of the Washington, DC, court.

Daily, I enjoyed the privilege of watching him preside over a room filled with—mostly white—lawyers, commanding the respect of everyone present, even though he would subsequently decry the increasing lack of civility in the courtroom. Later, I would draft opinions back in his chambers under his careful direction. This amazing experience left me with just one conclusion: I wanted to become a litigator. I also owed Judge Robinson another debt of gratitude, this time for his efforts, including a lawsuit he had filed, that helped lead to the integration of the District of Columbia Bar Association and its library.

Upon the conclusion of my clerkship, it was back to Morgan Lewis, now fully armed with the knowledge that I needed to, at least a little bit, toot my own horn and at the same time try to fit in with a law firm and a legal industry overwhelmingly dominated by people who did not look like me at all. In fact, the firm had only one Black partner at the time, a man named Gerri Brawner, and a single Black associate, who started at the firm on the same day I did. Race, of course, was only part of the difference between me and the other lawyers at the firm; the cultural gap could be vast. Gerri was instrumental in confidentially advising me during the early part of my career.

The firm also assigned me an official mentor, Mark Dichter, the former head of our Labor and Employment practice, who took every opportunity to make sure that I found my way within the firm. He facilitated my transfer to the firm's Washington, DC, office, my involvement in such organizations as the ABA Labor and Employment Section, the American Employment Law Council, and the ABA's Equal Employment Opportunity Committee. All of these were incredibly important venues for building what nowadays would be known as my own personal "brand" as a labor and employment practitioner.

Others, including Bill Gardner, then head of the firm's litigation practice, also took a leading role in helping me develop a client base, which is critical to succeeding at a law firm and eventually making partner. He often stepped aside so that I would be the one in front of the clients. Finally, after I had spent about 5 years at the firm, he told me that since several of the clients had routinely begun to contact me directly instead of going through him, he was transferring full responsibility for these client relationships to me. This constituted a tremendous boost to my career; it was my first real book of business when I reached the partnership.

There were others. George Stohner, a partner in the Labor and Employment practice, essentially taught me everything I knew about class actions, particularly those relating to allegations of employment discrimination. This was fundamental to my career.

No one mentor or role model was more important, however, than Fran Milone, the former chairman of Morgan Lewis, who urged me—"prodded" is a better word—to become involved in firm leadership. He knew me well, and he knew that my youngest child had gone off to college, and so, in his words, I had "no excuses" but to devote more of my energies to Morgan Lewis, specifically to leadership roles within the firm. Fran appointed me to partner committees, giving me the kind of deliberate, focused attention we all need from time to time. It obviously worked. Over the years, I've held numerous leadership positions, including Managing Partner of the Washington, DC, office, and I am now head of the firm's Labor and Employment practice.

As the familiar saying goes, "It takes a village to raise a child." That was certainly true in my case. From each of these role models I extracted important lessons and gained life and career-changing opportunities. But of these "village" leaders, notably only three were Black and only one, my mom, was a woman. Does that mean having almost no Black women as role models is unimportant? The answer to that question is complicated, because I certainly wish there had been more women who shared my life experiences as role models, but they just did not exist. When Morgan Lewis elevated me to the partnership in 1991, I became the first Black female to achieve that level in the more than 100 years since the firm's founding. Under Fran and his successor, our current firm Chair, Jami McKeon, our firm has since made great strides, placing women, including women of color, in important leadership and client positions throughout Morgan Lewis. Of course, still more must be done, and our industry lags far behind in any measure of equity. According to a 2021 survey conducted by the National Association for Law Placement, people of color comprised slightly more than 8 percent of partners in 2020, and Blacks overall accounted for just more than 2 percent of partners. Black women? Less than 1 percent.

Those kinds of dismal figures suggest several things. One, that with the help of my many mentors and sponsors, I threaded an incredibly small needle in my path to partnership and leadership. Two, we need substantial change. To that last point, I would add that as individuals we need to put in the work to be ready when opportunities arise, and, once we achieve positions of leadership, we need to take the time to act as role models and mentors for others.

That is why I now spend much of my time working to improve the numbers of lawyers of color moving through the pipeline, while also reaching out to my peers. Race can really play a negative role in a person's career, even derail it entirely, and it can damage one's self-confidence, especially if it results in becoming excluded from teams or representations, even if no one is acting in an overtly racist manner. Being one of a few can be problematic.

So, as a firm leader and as a role model and mentor myself, I know that our commitment to diversity cannot end at the recruitment level. We must retain and promote good lawyers, regardless of external factors such as ethnicity, gender, or sexual orientation. We have an obligation to work with lawyers, especially those in underrepresented groups, to make sure they get in front of clients. That also means keeping other partners accountable for diversifying their teams and making sure they know that is an expectation. We must be intentional and deliberate, just as my role models were with me.

That demands we work across firm boundaries to raise our profile within the industry. I still have lots of role models, and many of them are members of the African American Managing Partners Network (AAMPN), an organization I have been involved with for more than 10 years, starting when there were about six of us, all within the DC area. Today, this group includes some of the outstanding legal minds in the United States, all of whom act as role models for one another. I hosted AAMPN's first nationwide meeting in 2012, and we now meet annually during the National Bar Association convention. At one of our most recent dinners, about 250 lawyers from all over the country attended. Of course, we discussed how to recruit and retain upcoming young talent.

We also share information about the industry and law firm management, and we offer mutual support, including serving as a referral source for diverse lawyers. That latter aspect, business development, is a critical factor in the success of all lawyers. That is especially true of Black and other lawyers of color who may, for whatever reason, feel left out of the networking opportunities and may be taken for granted by their white counterparts. Financial and business development success—and modeling that for younger lawyers—can also play an important role in thwarting the discouragement that can too often accompany a lawyer of color as they struggle to become noticed in the crowded halls of Big Law. It can keep a person from throwing in the towel and encourage them to fight a little harder, for another day, or another month, or another year.

These kinds of organizations play an extremely important part in helping to formulate the environment in which young lawyers of color and women lawyers can thrive by creating a space where they can meet many role models. That's why I am active in groups such as the Women in Law Empowerment Forum (WILEF), which is explicitly dedicated to fostering women in leadership roles at large firms. This is consistent with my philosophy that we need to be deliberate in creating opportunities for diverse lawyers at all stages of their career, from recruitment throughout their rise to leadership positions. WILEF's extraordinary board, of which I am a part, provides a forum for mentorship, idea-swapping, and—not to be overlooked—fun.

Within my firm, in addition to my other roles, I am a leader of what we call Mobilizing for Equality (MFE), which our Chair, Jami McKeon, formed in the wake of the horrific murder of George Floyd in 2020. We have ambitious plans for MFE—no less than transforming our society into one that is more racially just and economically equitable—implemented through 14 working groups devoted to education, voting rights, impact litigation, and access to education, among others. Forming this structure, which acts as an important organizing tool for much of our firm's pro bono activities, has caused us to look inward and focus on how we can better move lawyers of color into and through our firm. Gratifyingly, the response to MFE has been overwhelming from all sectors of our firm. It's a true rainbow coalition, and it proves that we have allies everywhere and many people, of all races and ethnicities, who look to us as role models.

I guess this all just underscores the fact that while we may never be exactly color-blind in looking for role models and mentors, we also cannot be picky. Help is often available, if we are willing to accept it. In return, we must be willing to do the work ourselves, and sometimes that is hard. But some of us got that memo early on.

Thanks, Mom.

Grace Speights

Career
Partner and Global Leader of the Labor and Employment Group, Morgan, Lewis & Bockius LLP

Education
- JD, The George Washington University Law School (1982), Order of the Coif
- BA, University of Pennsylvania (1979)

Best Advice
It takes grit and resiliency to overcome obstacles and challenges. Develop and practice those two qualities.

Personal
Grace Speights lives in Washington, DC. She spends her free time in Newport News, Virginia, where she and her husband have a second home on the James River. Grace and her husband are the proud parents of four adult children and two French bulldogs. She enjoys spending time with her family and dogs, and loves to travel. Grace is a lifer at Morgan Lewis, having been at the firm almost 40 years. She started as a summer associate and rose through the ranks of associate, partner, and senior partner. Currently, she also serves as the Chair of the Board of Trustees of the George Washington University.

For More Information
https://www.morganlewis.com/bios/gspeights

Mentoring and Supporting Each Other: Supportive Male Mentoring of Women Attorneys Yields Success

By R. William Ide III and Judy Perry Martinez

How well we mentor and how much we benefit from being mentored is dependent on a constant cycle of learning among those involved in mentoring relationships. It also is dependent on passing along the lessons we learn as mentors and mentees to the next generation to follow. In this essay, two past presidents of the American Bar Association (ABA) with experience in private practice, corporate law departments, and the organized bar share their thoughts about some of the lessons they have learned as both mentors and mentees over the decades.

Perspective from R. William Ide III

I began my life, like most men of my generation, living in a "man's world." My story is about how thoughtful women and men transformed that world for me. There were no women in my boys-only high school, boys-only college, only three women in my University of Virginia law school class of 1965, and none in the large Atlanta firm I joined straight out of law school. In fact, that was the policy or, at least, practice at most of the top law firms at the time: they would not hire women straight out of law school, ever, no matter how well the women did academically nor their other many talents, skills, integrity, or connections. This kept all the best clients with men. There was no "circle unbroken"—each top client was passed on from (white) male to (white) male. This is where I got my beginning and my earliest training that, rather quickly, was transformed through mentoring.

After 4 years at that firm, I left to start my own firm. We recruited women from the start. I would like to say it was because I realized the inherent injustice and unfairness of not doing so while I was at a prior Big Law firm. It was not. In our startup firm, Huie, Brown, and Ide, we worked on political projects, and our clients pushed us in the right direction by asking about the demographics of our firm, even in the early 1970s.

Government and government-funded clients, as representatives of our societies, have often led the way in bringing focus to law firms, both big and small, regarding whether they reflect the institutions they will serve. We knew in our hearts that inclusion was the right thing, but when we realized that the number of women lawyers we had mattered to our potential clients, it emboldened us to take actions showing it mattered to us.

As we began to recruit women, we saw that women were an untapped, unrealized resource with limitless potential. After a while, we began to view the hiring of women—particularly when other law firms were not consistently hiring women—as a competitive advantage, reaching out to their talent pool while many firms ignored them. While we saw this growth opportunity for the firm, at the time we did not appreciate the growth opportunity it gave to each of us individually to better understand the many implicit barriers women face in the workplace. They not only had to be brilliant; they also had to have high emotional intelligence. My male partners and I had no real awareness of our bias, but of course, it was there. These women had to use diplomacy to confront that mindset, without seeming to be what some white males would see as confrontational. They had to change those of us around them, without seeming too challenging, while still carrying their workload at an extremely high level of success. Fortunately for us, they were willing and able to do so.

In any pattern of discrimination, a number of legitimate responses are possible. We observed women getting on the inside to open the windows of opportunity for women. This was the mindset of the women in our small law firm: they chose to dig into the foundation of the firm and make it stronger by making themselves the basis of its strength.

When my male partners and I started out, we did not see these women's career paths beyond hiring them. We were not looking to them to be partners, but their work spoke for itself. We were certainly not looking at them to teach us anything. But that's what they did. We became their mentors by sharing our "how to" experiences, and they in turn became our mentors by expanding our visions of the strengths and benefits of diversity with "how to" guidance in achieving authentic diversity. They shaped, and are still shaping, my life to this day.

When I later focused much of my time on the organized bar—in the Atlanta and Georgia Bar Associations, the ABA, and the Association of

General Counsel—once again, I experienced growth as a mentor. Those experiences taught me the importance of mentoring even when one is not locked into a hierarchal structure, and they also showed me how mentoring and sponsorship can be effective among colleagues and peers. Once I plunged into the corporate world as Monsanto Senior Vice President and General Counsel, Monsanto's inclusive culture taught me that formal mentoring programs and sponsorship of women talent were essential to daily operational success as well as to long-term succession planning. In each of these settings, the young women lawyers supported and trained me to be a mentor by helping me understand that my years of prior experience and my accompanying network would not only benefit them but also better the firm's organizational missions. They opened my eyes to the means and methods of discrimination, both explicit and implicit, and taught me about the emotional intelligence needed for more effective collaboration, active listening, and "win/win" outcomes. My role as mentor and mentee began when we founded our small law firm and has continued throughout my time at the organized bar and throughout my corporate life. It bleeds into my current work, which is now launching a mentorship program for women of color in law.

But I'm jumping over decades of learning, failing, restarting, improving, and investing in mentoring and sponsorship relations, all of which gave birth to many lessons for mentors and sponsors that I and my co-author, Judy Perry Martinez, want to share through her journey.

Perspective by Judy Perry Martinez: Learning from Mentors

Like most women of my generation, I began my life in a "man's world." When I and a female classmate arrived at my New Orleans law firm straight out of Tulane Law School, there were 2 women lawyers in a firm of 18 attorneys. On my first day at the firm, one of my named senior partners took me to lunch at a downtown lunch club and when I walked ahead of him toward the main dining room, he politely told me I was not allowed to lunch in that area and steered me toward the grille. The year was 1982, and even though over 33 percent of my law school class were women and 20 percent of the law firm I was joining were women, it was readily apparent that there were miles to go. Looking back on that incident many years later, I sometimes wondered if I should have protested, stomped my feet, or simply walked out. In the moment, however, I chose not to do so—perhaps because I was scared, because I needed the job to pay off what then seemed like a lot of student debt, or simply because I did not know better. What I came to learn was that for that or any other mentoring relationship to work, as a mentee, I would have to learn to trust my mentor, and my mentor would have to grow to trust me.

I was one of the fortunate ones. I almost immediately found mentors among my named partners and other senior partners in the firm. I received one of the most invaluable pieces of advice from a mentor: always maintain a caseload that includes cases with each of the four named partners, for one day my designated (or perceived) cheerleader may not be in the room. I was a commercial litigator and that advice actually came from a tax partner who, true to his word, always weaved me into his client representations and helped stretch my known abilities and broaden my knowledge and skillset. He was, in fact, the same partner who had brought me to the luncheon at the discriminatory club on my first day at the firm. To this day, I still wonder whether he brought me to that club that day mindless that I would be offended by not being allowed in the main dining room, or whether he wanted to make a statement to his fellow club members that while they would not allow a young woman lawyer into the main dining room, much less as a member, he was choosing to eat with her in the grille. Reflecting back on that first day as a member of the New Orleans legal community almost 40 years ago, I like to think that may have been my first experience witnessing someone trying to change an institution from within, incrementally. When the lunch club later dropped its exclusionary rules and moved into our building in the late 1980s, I knew that women needed to reap the benefits of the business that was generated and negotiated at those lunch tables. I promptly joined and regularly dined there to make sure women would always be present and visible—in the main dining room.

Those early days taught me that mentors are not perfect and that often they too are navigating the system in which they find themselves. You may never know when they were unsuccessful in their earlier efforts to bring change, just as I will never know if my senior partner had tried to change the rules of who could sit in the main dining room before or after he chose to walk with me into the grille. But I do know that by working with me on cases and introducing me to his clients (and in some instances, handing over client matters to me when I was a young lawyer), he invested in his mentorship of me.

After 4 years at the firm, I was made nonequity partner, and 3 years later, equity partner. During those early years and most of the following years at the firm, I was the most senior woman. Thus, my mentors continued to be older, white males. They taught me invaluable lessons of mentoring.

The same was true for my many years in the organized bar at both the local, state, and national levels where most of my mentors were older males, although my service in the ABA afforded opportunities to develop friendships with and learn from the few more senior women who had made their way to top leadership positions and who generously shared their insights and knowledge.

Nine years after I joined the firm, as a young equity partner in 1991, I faced the daunting prospect of bed rest for the duration of my second difficult pregnancy. My first difficult pregnancy had landed me in the hospital for over a month, awaiting the birth of our first son. I advised my named senior partner and main mentor that he should cut my partnership draw as the bed rest I needed to assure a safe and healthy delivery of our second child could span 5 months, and I would not be able to work. There was a long, silent pause on the other end of the phone. I thought I might be let go or, at a minimum, be asked to leave the partnership. When I inquired what was wrong, my senior partner simply said he was just wondering if one of the guys had a heart attack whether he would urge the partnership to cut his pay while he was out. As it turns out, the firm supported me throughout those long 5 months and throughout my future maternity leaves (two more that followed) and my transition back to full-time practice.

After I became a member of the management committee, several years later, a young, single woman partner went to Central America to adopt her son, and she called me after 2 months to let me know that the adoption proceedings would take additional months and that she did not want to leave her baby. She suggested that we should cut her partnership draw.

She did not have to endure a pause from me as my mentor had made the right answer clear to me those many years ago when he had responded to my request: we would fully support her while she was out of the country awaiting the adoption of her infant son. She had left in June and made it home by Christmas Eve with the help of a U.S. senator who was a terrific adoption advocate.

I stayed at the firm 21 years before going in-house. Once again, I was fortunate to land thoughtful and engaged mentors in the aerospace, cybersecurity, and defense industry, an industry that in the early 2000s was not known for a significant presence of women in leadership positions. My mentors came from both within and outside the law department and included the C-Suite leaders and those in operations. They stretched me beyond what I thought I was capable of doing from the perspective of both business acumen and knowledge of the law. They selflessly served up opportunities for me to brief executives and the board and to manage large and complex case dockets. In addition, they embraced the next level or dimension of mentoring to sponsor me through challenging assignments and promotions.

When I finally had the opportunity—for really the first time in my professional life—to report to and be mentored by a woman colleague, I again learned from the best. She heaped responsibility and management roles on me within the law department and served up high-profile opportunities and promotions for me to take on at the corporate level. She supported my high-level engagement in the American Bar Association and encouraged others in the law department to take on active bar leadership positions. She made certain that I was well compensated and recognized for above and beyond efforts. I only hope that in some small way I invested in and helped others at my company as she and my earlier male mentors at the company did in me.

After 12 years in-house followed by a year out of town in school full-time as a fellow-in-residence as I studied advanced leadership, I had a decision to make about where I would land once I was back in New Orleans. I looked to only one firm—the one that had given me my start. It had done so much to support me, and it understood what gave me fulfillment over the decades—my service to the organized bar. As I returned to the firm, I could not help but notice the continued support the firm leaders lent to bar and community service work and pro bono. The new managing partner was someone who had become a dear friend: she was the very woman who had called me from Central America those many years ago. With her support and that of several of those senior, white, male partners who were still practicing and had mentored me so many decades ago, I embarked on a new journey and became privileged to serve as ABA president in 2019–2020. With the guidance and counsel of those long-standing mentors at the firm and at my company over the decades, and the more than several mentors I was fortunate to have in state and local bars and the ABA, I have been able to contribute to the work of the profession.

Ide and Perry Martinez: Our Joint Reflections on Mentoring

If there is any guiding light for us in being mentors today, whether to women or men, those reporting to us or our peers, it is to look to both the men and women who mentored us along the way, as well as to those whom we mentored, to appreciate all they contributed to those relationships as we made our way through a "man's world." They inspired us to try to emulate their contributions, big and small. They showed us what we did right and what we did wrong.

The legal profession has slowly made strides toward greater diversity, inclusion, and equity, but we still exist and operate in what significantly remain institutions built by men, for men. It is up to mentors and sponsors to break down barriers not only for women but for others from marginalized backgrounds and from those communities that for decades sadly were not welcomed into the profession. Only then will we see the full potential of lawyer contributions to society.

Mentoring is hard work. It requires candid conversations, commitment to the person who needs input and observations, and a willingness to step aside to give others an opportunity to shine, sometimes even when we think we can do a better job or through our better job we would be rewarded. It sometimes means defending a mentee when no one else will, and other times it means letting them know where they fell short and why we could not cheer for or sponsor them. It sometimes requires saying to a mentor or mentee that things are not working out. It also means acknowledging when we have let a mentee down or been distracted by other priorities. It means making the time to listen to their challenge of the day, even if it is their third one of the day. But most importantly, it means working as hard as we can to be a mentor who sees the value of the whole person who is the mentee and understands that sometimes they will disappoint us, just as we know we have on occasion disappointed our mentors or mentees over the years.

When mentees see us try our best as mentors, we gain their trust even when we fail. When they see that we don't need to achieve perfection before we try to mentor, they likely will be more willing to pursue their objective—a promotion, a first chair, or increased management responsibility—before they are perfect at it. When they see us work to be better at what we do, even when we fall short, they will understand that we will be there for them when they don't make the mark. And they will gain a sense that we are pulling for them to be the best that they can be. Every mentee has a right to expect that from their mentor. And then some.

R. William ("Bill") Ide III and Judy Perry Martinez

Career

Bill Ide III

Past President, American Bar Association (1994–1995); Of Counsel, Akerman LLP

Judy Perry Martinez

Past President, American Bar Association (2019–2020); Of Counsel, Simon, Peragine, Smith & Redfearn

Education

Bill Ide III

- MBA, Georgia State University
- JD, University of Virginia School of Law (1965), Order of the Coif, Virginia Law Review
- BA, *cum laude*, American History, Washington and Lee University (1958–1962)

Judy Perry Martinez

- Advanced Leadership Initiative Fellow, Harvard University (2015)
- JD, Tulane University (1982)
- BS, University of New Orleans (1979)

Best Advice

Bill Ide III: Follow the yellow brick road—it's the journey with others that counts.

Judy Perry Martinez: "To the world you may be one person, but to one person, you may be the world."—Dr. Seuss

Personal

Bill Ide III: Bill Ide III clerked for Judge Griffin Bell in Atlanta for the Fifth Circuit Court of Appeals in 1965 and observed firsthand the rule of law integrate the South's governing institutions. For 5 years in the 1970s he and his firm, Huie, Brown & Ide, served as outside counsel guiding the creation and construction of the Metropolitan Atlanta Rapid Transit Authority system. Upon his firm's merger, he served as vice-chair of Kutak Rock & Huie, a pioneer multicity firm in the early 1980s. He was

(Continued)

an investment banker and Southeast Director for E. F. Hutton's public finance department in the 1980s. He returned to the practice of law to serve as President of the American Bar Association (1994–1995). He then became general counsel to the Monsanto Company. Bill was Counselor to the United States Olympic Committee and served on the boards of Albemarle (NYSE) and Popeyes (NASDAQ). He was chair of the executive committee of the East West Institute, a global nongovernmental organization (NGO), and serves on the board of Clark Atlanta University. He was a co-founder of the Georgia Legal Services Program and chaired the ABA's Central European and Eurasian Law Initiative (CEELI) global rule of law program. He chairs the Conference Board's Environmental, Social, and Governance (ESG) Center Advisory Board. Bill and Gayle Ide's three children have produced 11 wonderful grandchildren.

Judy Perry Martinez: Judy Perry Martinez practiced as a commercial litigator at Simon, Peragine, Smith & Redfearn in New Orleans for 21 years, as a partner and member of the governing committee. Judy joined Northrop Grumman in 2003, where she served first as Assistant General Counsel for litigation and then as Vice President and Chief Compliance Officer. Judy also was appointed to the company's Diversity and Inclusion Leadership Council.

Judy retired from Northrop Grumman in 2015 to become a Fellow at the Advanced Leadership Initiative at Harvard, where she spent a year in residence. Following her time at Harvard, she returned to New Orleans and rejoined her former firm.

Judy served as chair of the ABA Standing Committee on the Federal Judiciary, which evaluates all prospective Article III nominees to the federal bench, and the ABA Presidential Commission on the Future of Legal Services, as the ABA's lead representative to the United Nations and as a member of the ABA Commission on Women in the Profession. She is a member of the American Law Institute and a Fellow of the American and Louisiana Bar Foundations. She currently serves as vice-president of the World Justice Project.

Judy and Rene have four amazing children, aged 27 to 32, who have awesome spouses/partners, and one precious granddaughter who lives one block away. Judy enjoys walking, helping law students and young lawyers think about their careers, and continuing the critical and impactful work of the ABA.

For More Information
https://www.spsr-law.com/attorneys/judy-perry-martinez

Male Leaders Hold Keys to Accelerated Advancement of Diversity, Equity, and Inclusion

By Teresa M. Beck

Women's bar organizations have been EVERYTHING to me. It's not just membership that provides value in these organizations, but more importantly, active belonging, building friendships and strategic alliances, and helping women lawyers build their personal board of directors. These are people we turn to when we have big decisions to make, who hold us accountable, and who provide unwavering support as well as confirmation when we feel we aren't being treated fairly. For me, Lawyers Club of San Diego, California Women Lawyers, the American Bar Association (especially the Woman Advocate Committee and the Women Rainmakers Committee), and the National Conference of Women's Bar Associations (NCWBA) have provided enormous encouragement and training, not to mention invaluable friendships and connections. Yet, there is only so much women lawyers can do on their own to advance women in the profession.

Women can, and have, started their own firms in great numbers. Organizations like the National Association of Minority and Women-Owned Law Firms have supported the movement to increase the number of minority- and women-owned firms, and this is important progress. Yet, women still lag behind men in law firms and in other important metrics. According to diversity champion Sheryl Axelrod of The Axelrod Firm, "If the glacially slow rate of positive change does not speed up, women will not make up even 30 percent of equity partners in major law firms until 2181. That is generations upon generations away. That notion is based on the rate of change to date, which factors in over a century of nonexistent, and near nonexistent, positive change."

The Power of Women's Bar Organizations and the Echo Chamber We Can Get Trapped In

In our women's groups, we discuss our experiences with other sympathetic women, our frustrations with the attitudes holding us back, and the impact of these frustrations on our lives. Only a few men have built relationships with our women's bar groups to the point where they are accepted members of our inner circles and privy to our shared experiences. As a consequence, our male supervisors, practice leaders, bosses, firm leaders, and so on, are rarely part of the discussions about what is going wrong in our work lives and are blissfully unaware of women's issues (and those of diverse men as well). Admittedly, one would have to bury one's head in the sand to be *completely* unaware of the lack of equal advancement in the profession, but understanding one's involvement in the systems that hold women back and the power of male leaders to effectuate exponential change takes *dedication* to these issues. Yet, without male leaders, the amount of progress we can make is limited. Ultimately, we can drive only limited change without integrating the movement with male leaders. This situation is the backdrop for why the NCWBA created GOOD Guys (GOOD = Guys Overcoming Obstacles to Diversity).

Not All Male Leaders Are GOOD Guys: A Personal Story

For much of my career, key male leaders were NOT mentors and sponsors for me. Unfortunately, the most critical male leaders were often sexist and unable to view women as equals, particularly a strong-willed, ambitious woman like me. I did not experience diversity, equity, inclusion, or belonging. Quite the opposite. I received advice from male leaders that would actually hinder advancement; for example, "Just focus on your work and doing a great job for clients, and don't worry about developing business." Such advice would be great if I always wanted to work for others, but I aspired to lead. Another male leader once told me that my compensation was appropriately less relative to that of a younger male partner because the younger male partner had great *potential*. Meanwhile, my actual track record for developing business was *proven*, and I had a sizable book of business, not just a *potential* book of business. Another male leader called me the "B" word (also including the "F" word) when I expressed concerns of bias from younger women attorneys in a work setting. Sadly, the behavior of these male leaders, likely both consciously and unconsciously, often tainted my relationships with other women attorneys, which was in some ways more painful than anything else.

But thankfully, not all male leaders I encountered were negative. An important one, the risk manager for a client, was hugely supportive, and he boldly chose ME(!) early in my career to litigate client cases at a time when championing a woman litigator was not popular. This type of support from male leaders outside of my workplace was priceless. But the lack of mentorship and sponsorship from key male leaders *in* the workplace often put me in the unenviable position of having to figure out how to succeed on my own—a seemingly impossible task. Thankfully, I developed a personal board of directors of women and a few men outside of work with whom I could commiserate and plan, and thanks to those people (and my personal persistence), my career advanced in ways I could never have predicted or even imagined. Given that experience, though, I (and other women with similar experiences) could be justified in questioning the efficacy of engaging with male leaders to advance diversity, equity, inclusion, and belonging (DEIB) for all women. In fact, given my experience, I'm probably one of the most unlikely people to advocate for the importance of male leaders. This is the story of how my thinking changed, and why, in fact, male leaders are critical to achieving accelerated advances.

The Need to Trigger Change

As a board member of the NCWBA, for many years I have participated in annual leadership conferences in which women leaders across the United States and Canada convene to address the obstacles facing all women attorneys (which are far worse for women of color) and male attorneys of color. In the 2010s, we conferred frequently about the need to do something different and drastic to trigger change, as the status of women in the legal profession had remained stagnant for quite some time. The National Association of Women Lawyers' (NAWL) *2021 Survey on Promotion and Retention* refers to "the slowed or stalled progress of women in large firms over the last 15 years" and concludes that "[t]he short version of the data story over the last decade is that not a lot has changed."[11] NAWL data have shown a modest, incremental increase in the representation of women as

---

11. *National Association of Women Lawyers (NAWL) Survey on the Promotion and Retention of Women in Law Firms*, NAT'L ASS'N OF WOMEN LAWYERS (2021), https://www.nawl.org/p/cm/ld/fid=2019 (last visited Sept. 21, 2023).

nonequity and equity partners. However, their numbers among law firm partners continue to reflect significant attrition relative to their representation among law school graduates and law firm associates.

The study also addressed compensation: "Over the last 15 years, NAWL data has captured the persistence of gender gaps in compensation *at all stages* of an attorney's career in the firm. *Even at the entry level*, women are paid less than men, and these gaps often grow as women and men advance to partnership, with the largest gaps occurring between equity partners."[12] NAWL identified a double standard with enormous impact on women in the profession: "The focus on flawless performance for women and potential separate from performance for men can lead women to experience greater barriers to advancement in law firms and beyond."[13] I experienced this double standard personally and blatantly—if I had not been involved in women's bar groups, I might easily have concluded the problem was *me*. We expect the experience of women in large firms is an indicator of the experience of women across the profession, and frankly the workforce in general.

With this history on our minds, women leaders of the NCWBA set out to create a movement to change the dynamics of the profession that hinder the advancement of women and men of color. One of the biggest realizations in these discussions was the understanding that women's bar associations often exist in an echo chamber. We appreciate our women's bar associations because in these groups, women lawyers find mentors, sponsors, training, and sometimes more importantly, friendships which carry us through difficult times. Yet when we discuss issues within the profession facing women and men of color, we are often preaching to the choir. Change, it seems, needs to come from elsewhere since we are aware of the obstacles and of what needs to change. Yet discussing these issues among ourselves will do little to trigger change. How can we get out of the echo chamber?

The talented and wise members of the NCWBA realized that the group with the power to dramatically change the systems holding back women attorneys is male leadership—that the group missing from the conversation is male leadership; that the demographic missing from

---

12. *Id.* (Emphasis added).
13. *Id.*

planning and strategy to resolve the inequities that plague the profession is male leadership; and that those missing from active efforts to change the status quo are male leaders. For these reasons, the NCWBA decided to create a program that would engage male leaders in DEIB efforts.

Another Personal Story

Around the same time, I traveled to Chicago to meet with a client—a large national builder with corporate offices in the city. I was meeting with the company's Vice President of Risk Management. At the same time, I was still working with male leadership in my career that caused daily strife, so I was not prepared at all to meet a gentleman who would change my opinion of male leadership. And while I knew there were male clients who supported me, I was not expecting leadership on gender issues from male leaders, since I had not experienced much of that in my career (the male client who chose me to litigate his company's cases notwithstanding).

The risk manager for this particular client in Chicago started a conversation about women in the construction field. He described how the company's women engineers and scientists face challenges working with male laborers who don't always respect female co-workers. He also described his position that the women deserved respect like any other worker, and he explained that he would tell male laborers that they could work elsewhere if they failed to treat women co-workers properly. This was the first time I had heard a male leader describe a commitment to equity for women, and I never forgot it. It was at that moment that I realized that if this one guy in Chicago who worked for a construction company was standing up for equality, then likely there were others. We just didn't hear their stories very often.

Around the same time, I learned of a male attorney in Mobile, Alabama, Michael Upchurch, who was then the bar president of the Mobile Bar Association. We didn't know each other, but he inspired me! Mr. Upchurch had attended a women's bar event and learned that women attorneys in the city had a lot of unresolved issues (which women lawyers know all too well!), and he invited male leaders of local law firms and women bar leaders to a private event to have a conversation about the issues. This was a bold and powerful move at the time; it created an environment where courageous conversations could be had to improve the work experience of women attorneys. This additional example of a man's advocating for diversity, equity, inclusion, and belonging, and using his power and position to do so, was giving me ideas about how these issues could escape the echo chamber.

Studying GOOD Guys

The NCWBA[14] examined studies about how to engage male leaders and from that developed what is now known as GOOD Guys. We learned from various studies that men hear the message of DEIB best from other men. We also learned that women are considered to have ulterior motives for their efforts in this area, but men are often considered heroes for theirs. Additionally, we learned that male leaders are particularly interested in information about the bottom line. Studies that show the positive impact increased DEIB has on the bottom line are especially appealing to male leaders. Based on what we learned, NCWBA built GOOD Guys.[15]

The GOOD Guys Movement

NCWBA decided to create a program that would attract male leaders, using the voices of other male leaders, to become more engaged in issues about DEIB. While women's groups have lots of programming for their women members, GOOD Guys is decidedly different, as the goal is to fill the room with male leaders and to leave male leaders engaged and empowered to join efforts to increase representation of women and diverse males at all levels of their organizations.

The GOOD Guys Movement began in 2015 with an inaugural program in San Diego, California. A notable contribution around that time

---

14. Board member Misty Blair, IP Counsel at Kaneka Americas Holding, Inc., who has co-chaired NCWBA's GOOD Guys Committee with me for many years has been a key force behind collecting information and making a toolkit available on NCWBA's website: https://ncwba.org/programs/good-guys-toolkit/.

15. *GOOD Guys: Guys Overcoming Obstacles to Diversity*, NCWBA, https://ncwba.org/wp-content/uploads/2017/07/04-GOOD-Guys-ResourceList.pdf (last visited Sept. 21, 2023) (*see Engaging Men in the Efforts*, p. 2).

came from the National Diversity Council: it designed a logo in which the "Y" in GOOD Guys is a tie. Not long after that, Lenny Comma, then CEO of Jack in the Box, spent an hour with me discussing ideas for the GOOD Guys programming, as part of our effort to obtain input from male leaders. Among his many contributions was his suggestion that the tie in GOOD Guys be pink, and that incredible branding has stuck! As GOOD Guys programming has developed, many variations of programs have been produced by bar organizations, diversity organizations, various nonprofits, and even insurance companies. A typical program begins with a presentation about the financial and organizational value of DEIB. A key part of the program is the discussion with panelists, who typically are mostly (though not always) male leaders. NCWBA believes that a GOOD Guys program is the one time a "Man-el" (all male panel) is acceptable because these male leaders are discussing their DEIB efforts and encouraging other male leaders to join these efforts. The male leaders are asked a series of prepared questions that are key to the programming, including:

- Do you have a personal story about why you care about diversity, equity, inclusion, and belonging?
- Why do you think other male leaders need to also care about diversity, equity, inclusion, and belonging?
- What is working in your workplace to increase DEIB, and conversely, what isn't working?
- What stops male leaders from getting more involved with DEIB?
- What specific concrete steps can male leaders take to make a change right now?

A typical program is as rewarding for the women who attend as the men because the GOOD Guys panelists provide hope that some male leaders truly understand the issues and are actively using their voice, power, and prestige to champion DEIB issues. At most programs, attendees receive the Monday Morning To-Do List for GOOD Guys, which walks GOOD Guys through an assessment of how diverse their workplace is and identifies ways GOOD Guys can start making a difference on Monday morning.[16]

---

16. Find the GOOD Guys Monday Morning To-Do List at https://www.americanbar.org/groups/young_lawyers/projects/no-limits/good-guys/checklist/.

Finding GOOD Guys

As of 2022, GOOD Guys programs have taken place all over the country, and even in the UK[17] (in early 2020 just before COVID-19 lockdowns!). In every city where a program is planned, one of the first questions asked is "Who are the GOOD Guys in this city?" and a key part of every program is featuring GOOD Guys panelists who are tried and tested advocates for equality. There have been times when we were certain it would be relatively easy to locate GOOD Guys (like, for example, in New York City or Los Angeles) and we learned the GOOD Guys were harder to find than we thought. And there have been other places where we thought it might be more challenging, like Kansas, where GOOD Guys abounded. Much of this has to do with our connections, but it can be telling when leadership of women's bar associations tells us they cannot readily point to known GOOD Guys in their city. We want to change this dynamic by finding the GOOD Guys and showcasing them.

Hearing from GOOD Guys

Over the years, we have learned a lot from GOOD Guys panelists. Many of them seem to have wives, sisters, and daughters who have faced challenges in the workplace, and they have been inspired to get involved to change the workplace for their families. One of GOOD Guys' most staunch supporters and champions is Steven Velkei, a trial attorney and founder of Velkei Law (formerly chair of Diversity for Denton's). Velkei says, "GOOD Guys is a bridge for men like myself who want to learn how to better collaborate with and support women in the workplace. The Good Guys program has been transformative for me in my dealings with women colleagues and I am deeply grateful for the opportunity." And Jerome Caldwell, a regular GOOD Guys panelist, who is currently Director of Legal Operations and Social Equity at Pleasantrees, notes that "[b]eing recognized as a 'GOOD Guy' is a lofty title in my view, especially in an era where it is often (and rightly) illuminated that men need to step up and do more. Nonetheless, for several years, I have the honor of

---

17. Many thanks to the Institute for Inclusion in the Legal Profession for making the UK events happen!

supporting this initiative with the clear understanding that whatever we are doing as men, we have to do more. Men must be not only allies, but also advocates and leaders in the charge toward a reality of equity and inclusion for all, regardless of sex or gender—and the work of GOOD Guys is a perfect and effective vehicle to move that needle meaningfully."

The American Bar Association's (ABA's) Commission on the Status of Women in the Profession has been an incredible partner in advancing GOOD Guys programming, along with the Commission's own study on how we can better engage male leaders as allies, with its *Men in the Mix* report.[18] Judge Peter M. Reyes Jr., who is a judge for the Minnesota Court of Appeals and a key figure with the Commission, says that "[g]iven the significant under-representation of women in the legal profession at all levels, it is imperative for male leaders to step forward and proactively coach, champion, and advocate for women. Achieving equity for women benefits the legal profession and society and should be a top priority." WOW! See what I mean about how inspirational these GOOD Guys are?

What's Holding GOOD Guys Back?

A few years after GOOD Guys began, the ABA's Commission on the Status of Women in the Profession conducted a series of focus groups across the country to find out directly from men and women attorneys about the challenges and potential solutions to underrepresentation of women in the profession. One of the major takeaways from the ABA's study, *Men in the Mix*,[19] is that male leaders often don't know what to do to advance DEIB and don't know when they're invited and when they're not invited to programming about gender and race. Many are sensitive enough to know they don't want to show up at an event that isn't meant for them. This is one of the key benefits of GOOD Guys, as GOOD Guys is precisely *for* male leaders—*all* male leaders are *always* invited—and they are clearly the target audience.

---

18. *See Men in the Mix: How to Engage Men on Issues Related to Gender in the Legal Profession*, AM. BAR ASS'N (2021), https://www.americanbar.org/content/dam/aba/administrative/women/men-in-mix-report_feb2.pdf (last visited Sept. 21, 2023).
19. *Id.*

We also heard from GOOD Guys that they are afraid of saying the wrong things, and this is another benefit of GOOD Guys events. GOOD Guys programs are designed to be places where male leaders can get answers without fear of judgment or risk of embarrassment.

The Future of GOOD Guys

The GOOD Guys Movement continues to spread across the country, and also revisits locations where GOOD Guys programs have already occurred, to reach even more male leaders. Sheryl Axelrod sums up the power of GOOD Guys as follows:

> Men currently hold roughly 77 percent of the equity in major law firms, according to a Glass Ceiling Report by Law360. GOOD Guys programs harness this untapped resource. The more GOOD Guys get involved in championing gender equity—in championing women for equity partnership and leadership roles in their law firms, in-house, in government, on corporate boards, in leadership roles in the educational, nonprofit, governmental, and wider public interest sectors—the quicker women will hold increasing percentages of the equity in law firms and the quicker the profession will benefit from the diversity contributed by women, the equity experienced by women, the inclusion of women at every level, and the sense of belonging this environment will create.

Circling Back to the Personal

My personal story is one of persistence and grit. Sadly, not everyone is able to compartmentalize (nor should they have to) in order to focus on just the work and not the challenges. The legal profession sheds talented women at an alarming rate.[20] Happily, my challenges took me on a path that led me to a firm headed by a female CEO, Heather Rosing,

---

20. Lee Rawles, *Why Are Women Lawyers Leaving the Profession Mid-Career? ABA Initiative Takes Up Issue*, ABA J. (Nov. 15, 2017, 7:00 AM), https://www.abajournal.com/news/article/why_are_women_lawyers_leaving_the_profession_mid_career_aba_initiative_hope (last visited Sept. 21, 2023).

and a female COO, Susan Nahama (among other fantastic leaders, men and women), who are legends you will hear about as the firm, Klinedinst PC, continues to grow and innovate, and to increase and improve diversity, equity, inclusion, and belonging (if you haven't heard of the firm already!). I now co-chair DEIB for Klinedinst PC, with tremendous support from the firm—a complete transformation of my career. So to those in the trenches, hang in there, and come to your local women's bar group's events, ABA bar groups, and NCWBA events for support. We are here for you. And encourage your bar group to hold GOOD Guys programs so we can continue to reach more and more GOOD Guys. The program is not "one and done"; we need to continue our outreach regularly.

In closing, here's to all the GOOD Guys, those who have participated in the past, and those who will participate in the future—corporate GOOD Guys, judicial GOOD Guys, and law firm leaders, including many who are not lawyers. May we know GOOD Guys, work with GOOD Guys, encourage and showcase GOOD Guys, transform ordinary guys into GOOD Guys—and may we all benefit from the transformative power of GOOD Guys, acting together with women's bar organizations to trigger and instigate meaningful and momentous change. Now, there is much work to do. Let's get to it!

Teresa M. Beck

Career

Managing Shareholder of Arizona and Nevada and Co-chair of Diversity, Equity, Inclusion, and Belonging, Klinedinst PC; President, National Conference of Women's Bar Associations; Advocate of NCWBA's GOOD Guys Movement (GOOD=Guys Overcoming Obstacles to Diversity); Co-chair, Book Sub-Committee Woman's Advocate Committee of the Section of Litigation, American Bar Association; Board Member, California ChangeLawyers, a community foundation that funds the next generation of lawyers, judges, and activists, founded in 1989 by the State Bar of California as California Bar Foundation. In 2015, California Bar Foundation became an independent organization and in 2018, changed its name to California ChangeLawyers. Through the organization's history, its mission has never changed: build a better justice system for all Californians.

Education

- JD, *magna cum laude*, University of San Diego School of Law
- BS, Political Science, San Diego State University

Best Advice

Love always wins, even where litigation is involved! The world is complicated, but ultimately, we all want to be seen and heard. We can approach our problems, even in our jobs—even with opposing counsel(!)—with love and compassion.

Personal

Teresa M. Beck has been married to her soul mate, Stephen Beck, for many, many years. They have three children, all grown: Ryan, a journalist, musician, and artist; Madison, a lawyer for Volunteer Lawyers of San Diego; and Evan, who is pursuing a master's degree in Math at NYU. Teresa, a longtime Episcopalian, is Vice-Chancellor for the Episcopal Diocese of San Diego and a believer and advocate for all of the goodness that DEIB has to offer in the workplace and in the world. DEIB is one of the ways that love wins. Teresa is also a believer in gratitude and is grateful to her parents, progressive Midwesterners who relocated to California because of the Navy, for instilling in her a belief that she could do anything. Her parents did not know of the obstacles ahead, but their confidence and support, and that of her entire family, has always been instrumental.

For More Information

https://klinedinstlaw.com/profiles/attorney/teresa-beck
https://www.linkedin.com/in/teresa-beck-a34a646

Discussion Questions

1. How often should attorneys set goals? And how often should goals be revised?

2. Consider what goals you would like to set and list two small, specific professional or personal goals that you would like to achieve in 1 month, another two to achieve in 6 months, and another two in 1 year; then identify the steps to achieve them.

3. Of the list of assets in the essay titled "The Gift and Challenge of Longevity," consider if you are missing any of the asset categories. How could you acquire one or two of those you are lacking?

4. Do you intend to retire from the practice of law at some point?

    a. If no, why not? Have you considered making space for someone else to flourish in your shoes?

    b. If so: At what age do you anticipate retiring, and what do you envision you will do after you retire? If you have a book of business, who will handle it upon your retirement? If you have a career or leadership position in which you can name your replacement, who would you like to fill it upon retirement? Have you groomed and told your successors about this? Are they women or men?

5. What would you like your legacy to be as mentor and role model? Would you be interested in being a mentor after you retire?

6. Discuss your experiences with mentor/mentee relationships. Do they meet up with the experiences of the writers of the essays in this chapter?

7. All other things being equal, should a prospective mentor choose a mentee based on the mentee's need or the potential upsides of the mentoring process? Explain the reason for your response.

8. Do you make evaluations of people's abilities based on their gender or physical appearance? Why?

9. Do you believe you have been treated differently than male attorneys? If so, why? How was the issue resolved, if it has been?

10. Statistics show the legal profession lacks diversity. What do you think is the reason for this lack of diversity? How do you promote and encourage diversity in the legal profession? Discuss your personal experience with diversity initiatives.

11. Were you familiar with the GOOD Guys (Guys Overcoming Obstacles to Diversity) Program before reading about it in this chapter? Would you like to become more familiar with this or host one of these events? If so, learn more at https://ncwba.org/programs/good-guys-toolkit.